Roman Society

A Social, Economic, and Cultural History

Second Edition

Henry C. Boren
University of North Carolina
at Chapel Hill

D. C. HEATH AND COMPANY   Lexington, Massachusetts   Toronto

Address editorial correspondence to:
D. C. Heath
125 Spring Street
Lexington, MA 02173

Cover design: Dustin Graphics

Cover photograph: Roman funerary relief of Gratidius Libanus and his wife, Gratilda. First century B.C. (*The Granger Collection*)

Published simultaneously in Canada.

Printed in the United States of America.

International Standard Book Number: 0–669–17801–2

Library of Congress Catalog Number: 91–65858

10 9

For Gail and Andrew

Preface to the Second Edition

In a sense, scholars change history constantly as they pursue their research interests and publish their findings; any sort of survey must, as far as is feasible, reflect this scholarship. In recent years those who investigate ancient Rome have given much attention to social matters. This revision therefore includes, along with other added sections, new material on the Roman family, the roles of women and slaves in society, the patronage system, and social aspects of the military. There is a new section on the origins and development of money, especially coinage, in the period of the Republic, to complement the corresponding discussion of coinage in the early Empire.

The political-chronological framework has been somewhat reduced, but the basic treatment of subject matter is chronological as it was before. In fact, a chronology has been added, similar to the one in the companion volume to this text, *Greek Society* by Frank J. Frost.

My special thanks are due to users of our first edition who took the trouble to make suggestions for this revision, and in particular to the formal reviewers, whose comments were especially helpful: Nathan Rosenstein, Ohio State University; and Allen M. Ward, University of Connecticut.

I also wish to thank the staff of D. C. Heath, who worked with me to produce the best possible text: Senior Acquisitions Editor for History, James Miller; Production Editor, Anne Starr; and Photo Editor, Mary Lang.

H. C. B.

Preface to the First Edition

The author of this volume believes that in a case like Rome, a state where almost all formal and informal institutional life was thoroughly politicized, it would be almost impossible to deal successfully with social structures or even social life over the several centuries involved without providing a political backdrop for the setting. For that reason, enough political history has been included to inform the social, economic, and cultural discussions and to give them chronological structure. Topical discussions therefore recur in various periods: there are, for example, treatments of society in early Rome, in the middle Republic during a period of rapid change, in the late Republic, in the early Empire, the high Empire, and (briefly) in the later Empire. An attempt is made to bring these together into a kind of whole, even though they are separated; this results in some overlap, but it is thought to be both unavoidable and useful, serving as it does to emphasize important and continuing aspects of development. Other topics on economics and cultural matters are dealt with in similar fashion.

The author hopes that no reader finds the title misleading, and that the parts add up to a coherent whole.

Special thanks are due to Professors Thomas W. Africa, Erich S. Gruen, and Mason Hammond, who read the manuscript. Their suggestions have been invaluable and have enabled the writer to improve the work and to escape some errors. The author is of course responsible for any errors, distortions of fact, or misinterpretations that remain. Thanks are due also to the members of the fine staff of the publisher, who have done much to make the final product a more readable and attractive book.

Contents

Index   333

Maps

Introduction

The Roman experience makes up a most important segment of the human story. Not only did the Roman Empire encompass much of the civilized world and endure for centuries but, more important, Roman institutions and legal structures, closely imitated by numerous successor states, have survived all the way down to modern times. So, too, has Rome's cultural influence. Even now, a millennium and a half after the Empire's demise, surviving elements may still be discerned.

Many thoughtful persons find profound meaning in Roman history and culture. Politicians and newspaper columnists frequently refer to Rome and her history, often to pontificate on the decline and fall of that great empire and to make doleful predictions of what her dissolution may portend for our own future if our government continues on its present course. In recent years, moreover, scholars not trained as historians—including sociologists, chemists, and psychologists—have also turned their attention to Rome's decline, advancing new theories or refining older ones to explain it. These pundits obviously believe that ancient Rome was important—*is* important. Though some of them do not really understand Roman history and misuse the evidence to bolster their own rationalizations, such attention serves to point up the continuing significance of the study of Rome.

Although the decline and fall have attracted the most comment, at least in the two centuries since Edward Gibbon published the first volume of his monumental work in 1776, the *idea* of Rome as a great, unifying world entity has probably been more significant over the longer period. It was this vision that inspired the ostensibly Christian version, the Holy Roman Empire, and that in our own time continues to encourage statesmen to establish broad, unifying international organizations in their quest of a *pax orbis* in imitation of the *pax Romana.*

The history of Rome is therefore more than just a summary of the past. It is a living idea with an evolution and importance apart from the events. That is, what people think about the history of Rome is important—to some, more important than the truth itself. Perhaps it is not too much to hope that those who read this account of Roman history and society will gain a clearer perception than they had before. Like every other history book, this one aims to approach the truth as closely as possible in the light of often scanty and abstruse evidence. It tries to inform the reader about political events and structures, since politics was a vital matter in Rome, but it stresses Roman society and the Roman economy as well.

The saga of Rome will undoubtedly continue to be used as an exemplar by many persons, whether teachers, politicians, newspaper analysts, or civic club speakers. Nothing is wrong with that; it is quite right, in fact, that each individual's picture of Rome take on some symbolic validity that goes beyond the facts. The author sincerely hopes that every reader will find here something thought-provoking, compellingly vital beyond the material set forth, and spanning past and present.

Chronology

Date	Historical Developments	Cultural and Intellectual Landmarks
ca. 1800–800 B.C.	Bronze and early Iron Ages. The coming of the Etruscans.	Terremare culture appears in northern Italy. Later and farther south, the Apennine and Villanovan cultures develop.
753–509 B.C. (Traditional dates)	Village of Rome founded on the Palatine. The Period of the Kings. Etruscan expansion to north and south, bringing domination of Rome during the reign of the last three kings. Greek immigration into southern Italy.	Extensive Etruscan and some Greek cultural influence in central Italy, including Latium and Rome.
509–265 B.C.	Founding of the Roman Republic. Gallic sack of Rome, 390 B.C. Gradual expansion of Rome against Etruscans, Gauls, Samnites, and into southern areas. The Pyrrhic war. Roman domination through an alliance structure of all Italy south of the Po Valley by 265 B.C.	Patrician aristocracy dominates early. The Struggle of the Orders produces a balance of power between influential plebeians and the broadened aristocracy (*nobilitas*) drawn from both orders. Rural economy and social structures.
264–238 B.C.	First Punic war, leading to acquisition of the first provinces: Sicily and Sardinia–Corsica.	Accelerated Greek influence from south Italy, especially in art, architecture, and language.
238–219 B.C.	A Gallic raid from the Po Valley leads to expansion into that region; to the east, penetration across the Adriatic into Epirus; to the west, alliance with Massilia.	Beginnings of the Roman theater and Roman literature.
218–202 B.C.	Second Punic or Hannibalic war. Acquisition of two Spanish provinces. First Macedonian war.	Introduction of new religions, with new and more complex religious festivals. Women gain more freedom during wartime. Roman soldiers exposed to Greek/Hellenistic culture and luxury. Comic theater and tragic theater flourish.
171–148 B.C.	Third and fourth Macedonian wars. Macedonia becomes a province. Corinthian war; third Punic war. Carthage becomes the province of Africa. Illyria and Cisalpine Gaul become provinces.	Latin prose literature. Greek philosophers in Rome. Scipionic circle. Influx of slaves used both in agriculture and in households. Rome grows into a large city.
133–122 B.C.	The Gracchi. Attempts at reform produce a century of recurring internal dissension and civil wars. Pergamum becomes the province of Asia.	A new subclass, the urban proletariat (urban plebs), and a distinct Equestrian Order develop. Beginnings of higher (rhetorical) education.

Date	Historical Developments	Cultural and Intellectual Landmarks
111–88 B.C.	Jugurthan, Celtic, and Italian wars. Latins and Italians become citizens.	Extensive literary output of satire, tragedy, historical works, and memoirs.
88–63 B.C.	Mithridatic war, civil wars. Sulla's dictatorship results in political repression. Bithynia becomes a province. Spartacus' slave rebellion. Pompey ends the third Mithridatic war. Syria becomes a province.	Demographic changes in the city of Rome, as slaves multiply; other foreigners come for political reasons or for business and trade. Corresponding changes in religion and culture.
63–44 B.C.	Cicero and the conspiracy of Catiline. First triumvirate. Caesar's conquest of Gaul. Civil wars of Caesar and Pompey. Caesar as dictator is assassinated.	Literature flowers in the writings of Lucretius, Catullus, Cicero, Caesar, and Sallust. Caesar builds a forum, a temple, and a library. Calendar reform. Colonization in provinces.
43–30 B.C.	Renewed civil war. Second triumvirate. Octavian is victorious over Antony and Cleopatra at Actium. Egypt becomes a province.	
27 B.C.–A.D. 14	The Principate. Octavian/Augustus "restores" the Republic. Roman power expands within Spain, into Germany, along the Danube, and results in several new provinces.	The city is refurbished; marble is used in many public buildings. Roman culture expands with emigration and colonization of the western provinces. Golden Age of Latin literature: Livy, Vergil, Horace, Ovid.
14–68	The reigns of the later Julio-Claudians: Tiberius (14–37), Caligula (37–41), Claudius (41–54), and Nero (54–68). Conquest of Britain and Mauretania. The end of hopes to reestablish the Republic.	An expanded aristocracy adapts to the imperial pattern. Early Silver Age literature: Seneca, Lucan, Petronius, Pliny the Elder. Christians appear in Rome and are charged with arson in the great fire of 64.
69	The "Year of the Four Emperors."	
69–96	The reigns of the Flavian emperors, who were former Italians: Vespasian, Titus, and Domitian.	Continued Silver age literature: Persius, Quintilian, Tacitus, Martial.
96–192	The reigns of the "good" emperors: Nerva, Trajan, Hadrian, Antoninus Pius, and Marcus Aurelius. Commodus becomes emperor. Civil conflict.	Late Silver age literature: Pliny the Younger, Juvenal, Suetonius; the Greek biographer Plutarch. The Classical period of Roman law begins.
193–235	The military monarchy of the Severi: Septimius, Caracalla, and Alexander. The Julias (Domna, Maesa, and Mamaea) assume important political roles.	The Classical period of Roman law continues. Focus of the political aristocracy shifts from the senate to the army. Great jurists serve as praetorian prefects.

Date	Historical Developments	Cultural and Intellectual Landmarks
235–284	A period of disorder characterized by civil wars, plague, invasions, inflation. Military leaders including Decius and Aurelian vie for power. A new wall is built around Rome.	A breakdown of the economy with depreciation of the coinage. Low levels of prestige and power for senators; they are no longer eligible for military command. Local aristocracies also decline while the depredations of undisciplined armies put stress on all social classes. Intermittent persecutions of Christians.
284–305	Beginning of the Age of Absolutism. Diocletian restores order, both internally and on the frontiers. The tetrarchy develops.	Diocletian begins to regiment society at all levels. The price edict and reform of the tax structure lead to some stabilization of the economy.
306–337	Constantine gains power in the west, then over the whole empire; issues edict of toleration. Constantinople is founded as an eastern capital.	The Empire begins to change toward a Christian state. Massive churches are built in Rome, Constantinople, and Jerusalem. The Empire intervenes in church affairs. The Council of Nicaea formulates the Nicene creed.
337–395	A series of moderately successful, primarily Christian emperors. Julian is an exception; Gratian and Theodosius (the last to rule the entire empire) are the most aggressively Christian.	Publicly-supported pagan institutions gradually end as society is Christianized. The gladiatorial games (but not horse racing) are abolished. Some repression of the old Roman religion. Christianity is made the official religion of the empire. The Church is organized more formally, with attention to education and doctrine.
395–451	The empire is divided with weaker emperors in the west. Goths and others invade the empire. Alaric and the Visigoths take Rome in 410. Atilla and the Huns are turned away from Gaul, then Italy.	Although most tribes are by now Arian Christians, society in the north and west is barbarized.
455	Rome is more thoroughly sacked by Gaiseric and the Vandals, who invade by sea from their position in north Africa.	Pockets of classical culture persist in the west, but large areas adopt a hybrid culture that has little appreciation for the art and literature of the past.
476–500	The last "Roman" emperor is displaced by a German, Odoacer. Major succeeding kingdoms include the Saxons in Britain, the Franks and Burgundians in Gaul, the Visigoths in Spain, the Vandals in north Africa, and the Ostrogoths in northern Italy.	The Eastern Roman Empire continues until 1453.

Roman Society

1 Beginnings

Elements of Destiny

The Land

IF SOME WISE prophet of, say, the mid-seventh century B.C. had been asked to predict what city or state of the Mediterranean was destined to rule the whole area, only a touch of the divine could have induced him to pick Rome. The prophet would surely have looked to the east, for the western Mediterranean in many ways lagged behind the more civilized and richer east. Perhaps he would have suggested Saïs in grain-rich Egypt as a candidate for such domination, where a resurgent dynasty (the Saïte) was vigorously attempting to reestablish an Egyptian empire that might rival that of seven or eight centuries past. He might have named one of the flourishing cities of the Phoenician coast, or of the western coast of Asia Minor. Several Greek cities then were pressing outward with great vitality and, like the Phoenician states, colonizing widely, to the west as well as to the Black Sea area: the prophet might have identified the strongest of these, perhaps Corinth, as predestined to power.

Even if our imaginary prophet had confined his prognostications to the states of the western Mediterranean, he would have been unlikely to point to Rome. Carthage in North Africa, Greek Massilia in the south of France, Gades in southern Spain, one of a dozen Greek cities in Sicily or southern Italy, the Etruscan states in Italy to the northwest of Rome: all these showed more promise than Rome, which in the seventh century B.C. was not much more than a village on the Tiber even if it was, as tradition has it, a "kingdom."

In retrospect, geography often looms large. Yet Italy seems not very impressive geographically, even by ancient standards. Only in contrast to Greece does the long, boot-shaped peninsula seem well endowed. Much of the land is too mountainous for cultivation. Yet a Greek historian of the first century B.C., Dionysius Halicarnassus, citing the balance of agricultural, mining, and timber resources, saw Italy as an ideal country.

A spine of mountains, the Apennines, connects with the Alps in the northwest, then angles across the upper peninsula, cutting it off from the broad valley of the Po in the north, ranges the length of the country, down to the toe of the boot, and even, with a dip at the straits of Messina, continues into Sicily. Volcanic Etna in eastern Sicily, though separately formed, connects with the range and, at more than 10,000 feet, is its highest elevation. Mount Corno, northeast of Rome, rises to more than 9,550 feet. Much of Italy along the flanks of the hills and in the valleys is cultivable. The richest areas agriculturally are the Po valley (which was not important to Rome before the middle Republic); Campania, to the south of Rome; and the regions of Apulia and Calabria, on the east side of the peninsula along the Adriatic down toward the boot-heel.[1] Etruria and Latium (wherein Rome was situated) on the western side were fairly productive also, as was the region eventually called Umbria, across the peninsula to the northeast. Samnium, the rugged region to the east and south of Rome back from the coasts, and Bruttium, in the toe of the peninsula, were too mountainous to be very rich agriculturally. Sicily, though it seems poor today, was surprisingly productive throughout antiquity, especially in grain.

In the raw materials important to ancient technology Italy was rich, though not as rich as Spain. There was some copper as well as some—inadequate—supplies of tin, silver, and gold; and iron abounded. Etruria especially, but other areas also, had abundant forests; offshore, the little island of Elba contained the richest deposits of iron ore. Rome

---
[1] Calabria, in modern Italy, is now the toe of the Italian "boot."

faced west from a centralized location in the Mediterranean, beside a river, far enough from the sea to discourage pirates. The Tiber, happily, was navigable as far as the city, though only for comparatively small ships; timber, farm products, and the like could float down from the north in rafts or shallow draft boats. But the Romans could not easily develop a sea trade. The Tiber Isle at Rome was the lowest point at which the stream could conveniently be forded or bridged, and because of this and other features of the land, natural routes converged on the site, or, as the later proverb had it, all roads led to Rome. But Rome was

not the only transport hub in Italy, or even in western Italy. Capua in Campania to the south of Rome, its soil much richer than that around Rome, was also a focus for important roads. So was Naples farther on south; the latter city also was blessed with an excellent harbor, something Rome never had despite the expenditure of vast sums to improve it during the early Empire. The Etruscan city Caere (modern Cerveteri), forty miles north of Rome, was strategically placed as well. Routes, land, and resources made it a prosperous city before Rome rose to importance.

As the soil of Latium was far poorer than that of the Po valley or of Campania or Calabria, so Roman mineral and other resources also were unspectacular. Caere and several other Etruscan cities to the north had better access to iron, copper, precious metals, and timber. Their technological abilities long ranked high above those of the relatively backward Romans.

The geography of Italy, as compared with that of Greece, offered an important advantage: the mountains did not compartmentalize the country so completely as in Greece. Moreover, if one state could manage to gain control of the whole peninsula it would have (by Mediterranean standards) a vast and fairly homogeneous population, with adequate agricultural and other resources at hand.

The People

Once Rome became great, generations of Roman children learned that the determination, persistence, discipline, and endurance of her people made possible the stiff climb to dominance. There was something to this cultural ethos: certainly the small farmers who manned the cohorts and maniples of infantry for the Roman legions persisted doggedly even in dire adversity. Moreover, the upper classes who staffed the officer corps demonstrated remarkable ability as generals and field officers, though of course a few were egregious failures. Yet it is doubtful that Roman soldiers were any more doughty than the men of the other Latin tribes, and certainly some of the related Italian peoples—the Samnites, for example—were man for man the equals of the Romans for centuries. Probably most of the Greeks also were as courageous and competent, though both they and the Etruscans showed some tendency to grow sophisticated and sometimes effete. The simple Roman peasants made admirable soldiers, but their prowess was by no means unique in Italy.

The social institutions of the Romans also differed little from those of the Latins and Italians and in some respects resembled those of the Etruscans. The highest social class, the patricians, dominated not only society but also the army, the priesthoods, and the higher political offices. They were the largest landholders, for as among their Italian counterparts, all classes in Rome were rural. In the three-class society, all other free citizens were called plebeians; beneath the plebeians were the slaves, probably not a numerous group in the early age. We shall look more closely at Roman social classes later in the chapter. Here we wish only to note that they were similar to those of other societies in Italy.

The later Romans prided themselves on their religious devotion, which too they thought an important reason for their rise to power. In religion as in society and politics, however, Roman practices resembled those of the other Latins and Italians, whose racial and linguistic backgrounds were very similar. All worshiped a great sky god, as did other peoples of Indo-European origin, who by then had scattered over the world from Italy to the Indian subcontinent in Asia. The Romans called this god Jupiter. They venerated a typical war god, Mars. In various locales, crossroads, rivers, fountains, streams, woods, they worshiped other deities often referred to as *numina*. They did not anthropomorphize the *numen*, but in animistic fashion thought of it only as a spirit or force or power. In any case, few modern historians would think religious devotion a satisfactory explanation for the rise of Rome.

The Romans attributed their ascent to greatness in part to their willingness to learn and to borrow from others. There seems to be an element of truth here, though it is impossible to be sure whether the degree of tolerance of alien ways was in any way exceptional. Probably most of the Latins and Italians, the Romans' kin, were equally quick to learn from their more advanced neighbors, the Etruscans to the north and the Greeks to the south. Certainly the Romans were profoundly influenced by both. Yet it is possible that the later Roman scholars were right: from the beginning Rome had a mixed population; perhaps Romans did adopt and adapt new ways more readily than did other peoples. Rome also received foreigners much more readily than most states in antiquity. The law giving citizenship to emancipated slaves, traditionally ascribed to the sixth king, Servius Tullius, but retained throughout Rome's history, illustrates this trait. In fact, for centuries the Romans generously (by comparison, at least) granted citizenship to the peoples they had earlier conquered.

As we shall see, Rome's ultimate success relates more to political organization than to any geographical or economic determination. The Romans learned, if reluctantly, to treat the conquered fairly, a lesson perhaps first learned through accommodation in domestic disorders. Of course the city's central location in Italy and the peninsula's resources helped make her hegemony possible once Rome had gained a strong political position.

If Rome did not have particularly plentiful resources, if her men, customs, and institutions resembled those of her contemporaries, then obviously we must seek elsewhere an explanation for that first surge of accomplishment that raised the village on the Tiber above its neighbors and set it on the path to power. The credit for this achievement surely belongs to the Etruscans. It was they who made Rome one of the most important cities in western Italy. But before giving our attention to the Etruscans and their influence, let us note briefly the rise of civilization itself in Italy.

Italy Before Rome

Archaeology constantly renews ancient history, so that often it is, in a sense, not ancient at all, but contemporary. We now know much more about ancient Italy than did the Romans of Caesar's day. We have learned of a paleolithic Italy in which Neanderthal and later Cro-Magnon people lived. Through aerial photography we can actually see the outline remains of hundreds of neolithic villages. We know what sorts of houses people lived in: round or oval, dug partly into the ground, the house's frame supported by poles sunk even deeper and closed in with wattle and daub, the smoke from the center hearth escaping from an opening in the thatched roof. Tourists today can see, at a site that was an attraction in the days of Rome's greatness, the holes made by framing poles in excavations on the Palatine Hill, the so-called House of Romulus.

We have learned that the Bronze Age (beginning about 1800 B.C.) brought more complex cultures. The Terremare people in the north of Italy produced not only bronze tools but also a distinctive pottery of high quality, houses of considerable size, both round and oblong, and evidence of at least a modicum of town planning. Farther south in central Italy the Apennine culture of the same period, named after the mountains that range down the peninsula, was distinguished by its polished black pottery. The Apennine people buried their dead, whereas the Terremarans practiced cremation. Linguistically and ethnically, however, the two culture groups may have been closely related.

The Iron Age began in Italy around 900 B.C., a little later than in the eastern Mediterranean. Here too archaeologists distinguish various culture groups. Most important is the Villanovan culture, with its northern and southern variations: the northern group extending into the Po valley, the southern reaching down to the Tiber and into Latium. Villanovan culture thus blanketed ancient Etruria, the homeland of the Etruscans. Even though this culture developed in the Iron Age, the finest metal objects found in local tombs are of bronze—swords, helmets, and the like. The Villanovans sometimes put the ashes of their dead in biconical urns covered with bronze helmets, and sometimes in little pottery urns modeled on the homes in which they lived.

Etruscan Civilization: Origins and Development

The land of the Etruscans was Etruria (modern-day Tuscany), but whether the Etruscans were an indigenous people who there developed a high culture under the influence of the Greeks and others, or whether they came in from the east, perhaps Asia Minor, is as vexing a question now as it was in antiquity. The Greek historian Herodotus, writing in the fifth century B.C., asserted that the Tyrrhenoi (as the Greeks called the Etruscans) came from Asia Minor, and most other ancient scholars accepted this judgment. In the first century B.C. Dionysius of Halicarnassus, after careful research based on the information available to him, decided they were an indigenous people. Some scholars today still find this view tenable. Against Herodotus' claim, Dionysius objected that the language of the Etruscans bore no resemblance to any in Asia Minor. However, Dionysius failed to note what is just as significant, the fact that, although most peoples of central Italy spoke related languages, that of the Etruscans was altogether different. Moreover, some eight centuries intervened between Etruscan beginnings in Italy and Dionysius' time. Modern scholars have discovered traces of a language somewhat similar to that of the Etruscans and approximately contemporary with it on islands of the Aegean just off Asia Minor. Finally, Etruscan religious practices—the practice of hepatoscopy (examining the livers of sacrificed animals for the purpose of divination), for example—and certain Oriental features of their art, along with information derived from archaeology, also support the Herodotean view.

The language question is frustrating. We have a considerable number of short inscriptions, and even some gold plates found in 1964 on a temple site at Pyrgi, a few miles northwest of Rome, with a bilingual text, Punic and Etruscan. Unfortunately, the Punic seems not to be an exact translation of the Etruscan. Much progress has been made, but what ought to tell us most about the Etruscans has revealed little. In any case, the question of origins is not very important to the real history of either the Etruscans or the Romans. Etruscan culture, along with Etruscan power, developed to its height from a base in Etruria, and nowhere else.

Wherever the Etruscans came from, they established themselves firmly in the area northwest of Rome named after them. Possibly they constituted only an upper class; the lower classes of the population may have been indigenous. Such was the pattern in the areas to which Etruscan power gradually extended itself: into rich Campania south of Rome, then into Latium and Rome itself, and finally into the fertile and productive Po valley to the north. In Etruria they may for a time have been organized into a monarchy under the *lucumon,* "king," of a single city. But soon they set up a loose league of twelve cities, each under a *lucumon,* bound together by ties perhaps more religious than political.

Their chief was a kind of chairman of the board of the twelve *lucumones* at their annual meeting, a religious celebration at a town called Volsinii (modern Bolseno or possibly Orvieto). Other such loose federations may have been set up in Campania and the Po valley. In no area did the Etruscans ever form a politically strong and well-organized union. The Etruscan city-states did not always stand together, a weakness that contributed to their ultimate political failure and subjugation to Rome.

The Etruscans developed a great metals industry, a fleet, and a strong export trade. Their imports seem to have been primarily luxury goods, as remains of large quantities of the finest Greek pottery illustrate. Eventually the Etruscans came into conflict with Greek immigrants in the western Mediterranean. We hear of a naval battle with Greeks near Corsica about 535 B.C. Greek fleets from Sicily and south Italy eventually defeated the Etruscans in 474 B.C. and contributed to their decline. The Etruscans generally cooperated with the Carthaginians against the Greeks, as may be inferred from such evidence as the gold plates found at Pyrgi. But the relationship did not last.

Most of the Etruscan city-states evolved into aristocratic republics during the sixth and fifth centuries B.C. This development may have weakened their federation—and provided a model for Rome after she gained her independence. But perhaps the greatest calamity for the Etruscans was the Celtic invasion of their northern holdings in the Po valley, a little before 400 B.C. Already weakened by trade losses, the naval defeats at the hands of the Greeks, and the rebellion of the Latins, with Rome as a chief antagonist if not leader of the Latins, Etruscan power went into swift decline. During the fourth and third centuries Rome conquered even the cities of the Etruscan homeland.

Earliest Rome

Just as scholars today know more about Bronze Age Italy than the Romans did, so also we know more about Rome in its earliest years than did the Romans of Cicero's time. Armed with new information, researchers earlier in this century proposed to strike down the literary traditions of early Rome as complete fabrication. Yet for all the archaeological information and ingenious comparative studies in linguistics, religion, and the like, modern scholars have had to learn humility. Heinrich Schliemann's discovery a century ago that there really was a Troy; Sir Arthur Evans's later demonstration that there was some factual basis to Greek myths bearing on ancient Crete; a score of revelations that on occasion the Hebrew writers of the Bible were right and modern critics misled by their scholarship; such episodes have taught historians to be more respectful, not only of the historians of antiquity, but even of the myths and legends of the ancients. Indeed, some have now become too credulous.

For our early history of Rome—that is, the literary history—we are dependent on Latin and Greek authors who lived centuries after the events they chronicle. Naturally, some of their information was bound to be defective; but once again, we have learned to discriminate carefully. The most important of these ancient historians for earliest Rome were Livy, a Roman who lived until A.D. 17, and Dionysius, a Greek from Halicarnassus who lived and composed his work in Rome about the same time (beginning about 30 B.C.). Livy perhaps started earlier and continued longer than Dionysius, but apparently their works were composed in isolation from each other. Both Livy's 142 volumes (that is, rolls) *Ab Urbe Condita (From the Founding of the City)* and Dionysius' *Romaike Archaiologia (Roman Antiquities)* in 20 volumes depended on accounts that were probably no more than a century or two old. Only about a third of Livy survives, and about half of Dionysius, including, however, in both instances, the earlier books.

Some of the information available to the two historians was older than the compilations (based on annual records) they mainly relied on, but not much solid historical fact before about the fourth century B.C. was known to these authors. For the earlier period they used the motley collection of folktale, legend, and family eulogy that passed for history. The scholarship they brought to their task was primarily limited to choosing the most believable of two or three unlikely stories, or revising them on the basis of anachronism; sometimes they simply passed on the tales as they were received, with some indication of where skepticism was in order. Both deserve some apology for the savage criticism modern scholars have given them. We must be grateful that they passed on to us even information they considered untrustworthy. Some of their evidence helps us fill in the context of our archaeological data.

One discovery archaeology has made is that the Aeneas story, once thought to have been invented in the third or second century B.C., actually goes back to a time coeval with early Rome. Both Greek and Etruscan art of the sixth and fifth centuries B.C. employ the motif of Aeneas bearing his father, Anchises. The tale, told by Livy but best enshrined in Vergil's *Aeneid*, linked the founding of Rome with the destruction of Troy. Aeneas, the son of Venus, driven by fate, arrived at length in Latium and married into a royal family. Romulus and Remus were his descendants through their mother, Rhea Silvia; their father was the god Mars. Romulus was, of course, the reputed founder of Rome and its first king. Varro, a scholar of the first century B.C., computing closely on the basis of tradition, set the date at 753 B.C. According to the received stories, six other kings followed, ruling until the last was driven out in 509 B.C. and the Republic was established. Archaeologists have found remains of human habitation on the Palatine Hill that antedate the eighth century B.C., but their work seems to confirm that approximate period for the founding of a true village on the site.

As the early kings are presented to us, it is apparent that they are types—even archetypes—rather than real figures. Romulus was the conqueror who gave form to the state and its early institutions; his successor was Numa Pompilius (a Sabine; the Romans saw themselves as assimilators from the beginning), the great religious and secular law-giver. Tullus Hostilius was another great conqueror; Ancus Marcius greatly resembled his grandfather, Numa. The specific works attributed to each—in fact, the very existence of these kings—may still be doubted, given the present state of our information. As for the last three kings of Rome, the evidence is a bit more substantial.

Etruscan Kings Raise Rome to Regional Importance

Though the Roman sources avoid saying it outright, it is clear that the last three kings of Rome were Etruscans. Tarquinius Priscus was the first of these, Servius Tullius the second, and Tarquinius Superbus the last. The name Tarquin itself is Etruscan; the Romans also called Priscus

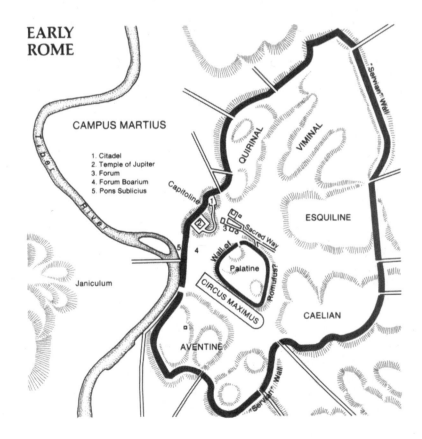

EARLY ROME

CAMPUS MARTIUS

1. Citadel
2. Temple of Jupiter
3. Forum
4. Forum Boarium
5. Pons Sublicius

QUIRINAL

VIMINAL

Servian Wall

Capitoline

Sacred Way

ESQUILINE

Tiber River

Wall of

Palatine

Romulus

Janiculum

CIRCUS MAXIMUS

CAELIAN

AVENTINE

Servian Wall

lucumo (a variant of Etruscan *lucumon*, "chief"), although they thought he or his family had emigrated to Etruria from Corinth. Archaeology again helps fill in the picture: at about the time corresponding with the traditional period of the Etruscan kings (616–509 B.C.), or more likely a little later, there was a surge of Etruscan influence in Rome.

Only in this period did Rome become a real city, with pebble-paved streets radiating from the Forum. There were, in fact, two fora; the Forum Boarium—whose name (*bos* = "ox," "cow") indicates the importance of cattle in early Rome—belongs to this same early date. It is significant that the street connecting these two fora was called *Vicus Tuscus*—the Etruscan Street. Under the Etruscan rulers Rome acquired important public buildings. The attention given to Rome undoubtedly stemmed from the city's position as a natural transportation hub in the Etruscan trading area. The route from Etruria to Etruscan holdings in Campania passed through Rome, for example. It is notable that when, under the last Etruscan king, Tarquinius Superbus, the temple of Jupiter on the Capitoline Hill was completed, it was the largest temple in all Italy. Rome had arrived.

When did Rome first become dominant over the other Latin peoples? The Romans of Livy's time thought their city had dominated the Latins by the second century after Rome's founding. Probably the Etruscan kings used Rome as a center from which to penetrate into other areas of Latium, making Rome a sort of regional capital. Thus, from the date of the expulsion of the kings Rome was, as the literary tradition indicates, already a most important but not necessarily the dominant Latin city.

The Etruscan Influence

The influence of the Etruscans on Rome was enormous, second only to that of the Greeks. Indeed, much of the early Greek influence was transmitted to Rome by the Etruscans, whose culture had been powerfully affected by Greece. This influence shows clearly in art: vase painting and frescoes developed along Greek models, particularly apparent in the treatment of draped fabrics.

Etruscan art had its effect on Rome, but much more significant was Etruscan influence on religion and politics. The Etruscans gave Rome new gods—Juno (Etruscan Uni) and Minerva (Menerva), for example—and many religious practices, including the rites for the taking of auspices and the Oriental practice of reading livers or scanning the sky for omens. Such lore required real specialization with long apprenticeship, and for centuries Romans used Etruscan experts in hepatoscopy.

Also in the area of religion, the Etruscans taught the Romans to make cult statues of their gods; they drew up plans for the earliest important Roman temples, with three rooms for a triad of deities, elaborately

Etruscan tomb painting from Tarquinia. Obviously some Etruscans hoped for a joyous afterlife (*Alinari/Art Resource, New York*)

decorated cornices, terracotta antefixes (decorations at the eaves of roofs), and other typical details. The temple of Jupiter (and Juno and Minerva) on the Capitol, reputedly dedicated in 509 B.C. after the expulsion of the last king, was built by Rome's Etruscan rulers and naturally was Etruscan in style. Etruscan-style antefixes have been excavated in several other locations, attesting to the breadth of the influence.

In the realm of political administration, the functions of some higher officials in the Roman Republic seem to have been based on Etruscan models, as were some of their insignia. The lictors who preceded Roman officials, their number, and the *fasces* (the bundle of rods enclosing a double ax) they carried as symbols of the magistrate's power were, it appears, all Etruscan. The Senate was probably patterned on an Etruscan prototype. The army was organized into a phalanx in a manner first used in the area by the Etruscans. The Romans also borrowed gladiatorial combat and some aspects of festival and funeral games from these northern neighbors.

Social and Economic Influence of the Etruscans

The most significant influence of the Etruscans on Rome is the most difficult to demonstrate because it lies in a shadowy sphere where cause and effect are largely hidden: social and economic organization and methodology. In early Rome the social order was pervasively important, as one would expect, since those who dominate a society usually dominate the state and the army as well. The patron-client system in Rome, discussed below, was probably derived from the Etruscans. The Romans later extended the system into foreign affairs during the period of

expansion beyond Italy, with Roman leaders acting as patrons to provinces and even to autonomous monarchies.

Etruscan social organization, like that of the other peoples of central
Italy, emphasized *gens*, "family" or "clan." Etruscan women seem to
have enjoyed a social position more nearly equal to that of men than was
customary in the eastern Mediterranean. Artworks show them participating in banquets, for example, and Etruscan sarcophagi often portray
husbands and wives in ways that imply at least near-parity in marriage.
Some Greek writers had uncomplimentary things to say about feminine
morals among the Etruscans, but such criticism may only reflect the
relatively high status of women. Their social status may not have been
unique to the Etruscans in Italy, but in any case the Romans too allotted
to women higher status than did the Greeks and other Mediterranean
cultures.

Etruscan economic influence on Rome was quite profound, even
though the Romans themselves—at least the aristocrats—tended not to
get directly involved in trade or commerce, choosing instead to invest
primarily in land. Yet Roman plebeians and clients of aristocrats, along
with citizens of states dominated by Rome (especially Greeks but also
the Etruscans themselves, as well as other Italians), engaged in small-
scale but intensive economic production and trade. Roman armies in
the period of expansion demanded large quantities of materiel: lumber,
copper, iron, food supplies. The Etruscans doubtless instructed the
Romans in metallurgy or did the work themselves. Without the iron
industry and iron weapons from Etruria, along with some of Italy's best
shipbuilding timber, Rome would never have become a Mediterranean
power. It may well be that the great slag piles at Etruscan Populonia,
marking the locations of ancient iron smelters, symbolize better than the
temple of Jupiter Optimus Maximus the most significant contribution of
the Etruscans to the rise of Rome to greatness.

Rome and Greece

It has been mentioned that much Greek influence came to Rome indirectly by way of the Etruscans, who even while fighting Greeks in the
west maintained close connections with the Greek states in the east. The
Etruscan city of Caere, we know, maintained a treasury at Delphi, as
Athens and other Greek city-states did. But Greeks inhabited Italy also;
they were so numerous in the south that the Romans called the area
Great Greece (Magna Graecia). The Greeks also exerted important direct
influence on earliest Rome, as Roman historians and poets emphasized
in the Aeneas story. We can see this influence, for example, in the fact
that the Romans and Latins used an alphabet somewhat different from

that adopted by the Etruscans, surely learned straight from Greeks who visited the area, probably for trade.

Greek influence is seen in the early Republic as well, even before the Romans had completely put off the mantle of Etruscan cultural domination. The cult of Ceres at Rome, for instance, established quite early, retained Greek rites and a Greek priestess. The major temple to Ceres, built at a time when Etruscan styles dominated in Rome, is thought to have been designed in the Greek style. The altar of Hercules was constructed about the same time in the Forum Boarium, and the rites solemnized there were also basically Greek. Interesting parallels exist too between Roman and Greek practices in military organization, legislation, and landholding. Another wave of Greek influence came with the Roman conquest of southern Italy in the third century B.C. Still another and continuing surge of influence came with the conquest of Greece itself a century later.

Ultimately the Romans turned primarily to Greek models in art and architecture, completely dropping outmoded Etruscan ways. In religion they identified their gods with those of the Greeks and adopted the Greek myths as their own. When at last they were sophisticated enough to want a philosophic undergirding to their lives and their state organization, they turned again, quite naturally, to the Greeks. It was first said by Horace, the Roman poet of the first century B.C., and often since, that the sophisticated Greeks conquered their barbarian conquerors. The comparison holds an element of exaggeration on both sides, yet it remains in a broad sense true.

The Roman Family

The primary social structure in any society is that oldest of all human institutions, the family. However, only when the extended family serves as an economic as well as a social unit (as in a rural setting with landed families) can the family dominate the entire social system as it did in Rome. We know most about the workings of upper-class families in Rome, but lower-class families probably followed the same patterns.

It is curious that the Latin language had no term that meant exactly "family" or "nuclear family" in ordinary English usage. The word *gens*, as we have noted, designated a clan or tribe. By contrast, the word *familia* referred to the household, including slaves. The extended family was headed by the *paterfamilias*, the oldest male member. The *pater* and *mater* were, of course, the parents. Perhaps the shorter life spans of that time meant that the *paterfamilias* was usually the biological father of those under his *manus*, ("hand," i.e., control).

The *paterfamilias*, acting with the advice of a family council, had complete power over family members, even to the right to execute those who disobeyed. This feature of Roman social organization is enormously significant—not that large numbers of persons were so put to death, but its existence shows how pervasive family control was. Only a few actual instances of such family-ordered executions are known, each involving a father's killing his son for some lapse that the Roman people in general would have thought worthy of death. One such example—which may be no more than legend—is that of the hero of the founding of the Republic, Lucius Junius Brutus, who while consul executed his own son for engaging the enemy contrary to orders when left in command of the army.

Social Organization and the State

Probably most Americans today, if asked about the organization of our society, would first think of that order imposed by the state through the Constitution and through law—federal, state, and local. But family and class; voluntary groups, religious and social; and even personal friendships also shape the organization of our society. We often fail to recognize the extent to which these latter groupings define, order, and give clarity to our relationships with each other. Our government does not attempt to impose a class structure (unless in connection with the tax code!), but much more than any government in antiquity, it does—not altogether successfully—try to dispense equal justice, to prevent exploitation of individuals and groups, and to provide opportunities for education and careers. When persons in our society feel the need of help they may indeed look first to family and friends, but deprived groups tend to look first to government.

In earliest Rome the government did little through law to establish personal relationships and prevent exploitation. Our information on social structures in early Rome must be inferred from later practices, and it is thus uncertain at best. As in many primitive societies, Roman social organization was rooted in the family, the *gens* or clan, and the tribe. Many problems, such as those involving property disputes, were settled within the family or *gens*. Even crimes might be dealt with by the family, and to some extent this practice continued even after Rome had developed a complex governmental system. Adultery, for example—a serious offense because it made parentage of offspring uncertain—was punished within the family for centuries. The role of government was simply to recognize the right of an offended husband to exact retribution—even, in some instances, by killing his wife. Later, both spouses were probably able to divorce an adulterer.

Other structures that probably existed before Rome became a state helped to order Roman society. As in most societies, in Rome there was a horizontal ordering of society through a class structure, and also a vertical social structure that we term the *patron-client system*, which involved relationships between persons of different status or social class. These components of the social system gave stability—sometimes approaching rigidity—to the Roman people. This social system also was reflected in the governmental structure of the Roman Republic. We must, therefore, give more attention to these two elements of that system.

Social Classes: Horizontal Structures

During the monarchy and for a time in the period of the Republic, the Roman aristocracy was made up entirely of patricians. Patrician families were limited in number, and a Roman could become a patrician only by birth; the patriciate was therefore a closed order. The word *patricius* is related to the word *pater*, suggesting that the early patrician families were those whose leaders (i.e., the *paterfamilias*) comprised the royal council that eventually developed into the formally constituted Senate.

Roman citizens who were not patricians were plebeians. The plebeian class was, however, a diverse group from an early period, including both well-to-do and poor families. As Rome expanded, both in the monarchy and in the Republic, and other states were incorporated into Roman dominions, all new citizens became plebeians regardless of their prior status. Thus some who had been aristocrats in their own cities became plebeians when Rome conquered and absorbed their cities. As we shall see, a distinct group of upper-level plebeians emerged during the Republic, the equestrians, so called because they were wealthy enough to meet the property requirements for service in the cavalry. Finally, at the bottom of the social order were slaves, who were not citizens. More will be said of them in following chapters.

Within the nobility, the patricians stood together as a group in their relationships to the lower classes. This pattern was especially notable in politics. From the shadowy early period, patricians had monopolized the higher offices, the senatorial seats, and the priesthoods (which were political as well as religious in nature)—and any matter that threatened their status met with formidable solidarity. The power of the patricians tended to limit and weaken the monarchical authority of the kings, and conversely, any increase in power of the kings tended to weaken that of the aristocrats. The patrician conspiracy to overthrow the monarchy may have been largely sparked by the effort of the Etruscan kings to weaken the nobles' position by appointing plebeians to offices formerly held only by patricians, by bringing plebeians into the army in large numbers, and by granting them higher political status through a popular assembly.

With the foundation of the Republic, the patricians initially managed as they had during the monarchy to monopolize all higher offices.

However, the Senate was now made up of persons who had been elected to the highest offices, and as plebeians began to gain important offices (during the Struggle of the Orders, discussed in Chapter 2), they too entered the Senate. Members of the expanded Senate, made up of both patricians and plebeians, were henceforth addressed as *patres conscripti*. In this changed situation, families of patricians banded together to attempt to control elections. They long maintained their predominant power, not only through cooperation within their own class—through horizontal relationships—but also through vertical relationships, in which individuals and families formed connections with those of lower status.

Vertical Relationships

The primary vertical arrangement that evolved, the patron-client system, involved voluntary relationships and thus was subject to change. It defined a special, reciprocal relationship between persons of different social status or class. In this early period, patrons and clients took oaths to each other, oaths that had a religious component. Although the relationship was a voluntary one, the connection was not easily laid aside.

Perhaps, in the shadowy period when this system originated, all patrons were patricians and all plebeians were the clients of some patron. The historical evidence that we have from a later age, however, indicates that the system was more complicated; some—perhaps most—plebeians were not anyone's clients, and some plebeians were themselves patrons of other, lower-status plebeians.

Patrons looked out for the interests of their clients in various ways. Their help was invaluable when clients were involved in court cases, but they might also aid clients who were in economic straits, recommend them for appointment to positions in the military or elsewhere, and so on. In return, patrons got the prestige that went with having an entourage of clients. In the monarchical period, clients possibly served under their patrons in the army. During the Republic, clients supported their patrons in elections. Gift giving seems always to have been a feature of the system. In the monarchy and the early Republic it may chiefly have involved clients giving presents to their patrons. This is indicated by the fact that in the late third century B.C. the government curbed the practice. Much later, when most patrons and their clients lived in Rome, small gifts were given by patrons to their clients.

Patron-client relationships could become hereditary, making them almost familial rather than individual. Although a breach of loyalty in such a long-term and religiously sanctioned relationship was a serious matter, the system was never closely controlled by the state, and the relationships could be somewhat fluid.

Both the class structure and the patron-client system were nongovernmental institutions that greatly affected political practices and the political order as a whole. The cynical might view these structures as the means used by the aristocracy to maintain its social and economic power. The same could be said of the structure of the government itself, and the law as well. But such institutions, if they are not completely inflexible, can promote harmony between members of society and help to integrate them.

Religion in Family and State

Religion entered intimately into Roman family life. In typical Indo-European fashion the Romans venerated their ancestors, offering small portions of food at the hearth daily and carefully seeing to other special ceremonies. Upper-class families kept death masks of deceased family leaders. In the later Republic and in the Empire it was mostly a matter of prestige to have these wax images—eventually, finely sculptured stone busts—on display; earlier, however, the practice was part of a living religious tradition. The gods closest to individuals were the guardians of family, house, and land. Vesta, goddess of the hearth, received regular homage. Roman families never neglected the Lares and Penates, gods of boundaries and of storehouses. On marrying, a woman would leave her family and come under the control of her husband's *paterfamilias*; when she was first brought to her new household she would be carried through the door so as not to offend Janus, the god of the threshold, or the other family deities. A host of other gods were important to rural families, from Ceres, the goddess of grain, to the numerous *numina* already mentioned, of crossroads, streams, springs, hills, and so on.

The patricians, who exercised strict control over religion in their families, also controlled the state religion. Patricians filled the colleges of augurs, priests (*pontifices* and *flamines*), and vestal virgins. One of their number was the *pontifex maximus*, who supervised the colleges and their work. Since the priests were usually also members of the king's advisory council (the body that later became the Senate), the Senate came to decide most important questions regarding religious ceremonies and festivals as well as rule on special sacrifices to propitiate the gods in times of crisis. Because the pontiffs were custodians of the law, which was deemed sacred in Rome as in other primitive societies, they also controlled the courts in the early centuries of the city's history.

Many of the structures of family religion paralleled those of the state. As with the family, there were state cults to Janus, Vesta, Ceres, and the Lares and Penates. Although the chief gods were probably Jupiter and Mars, people throughout Italy worshiped Hercules, the man-become-god. In the Forum Boarium in Rome the altar to Hercules was called the *ara maxima*, as if it was the most important of altars; a temple was later built behind it. The cults of Juno, Minerva, and Ceres were almost as important. In both family and state a host of other deities were worshiped.

Living in a country where the roles of religion and government have been carefully separated, Americans sometimes have difficulty conceiving the degree to which religion and the state were integrated in antiquity—and certainly in Rome. The pontifex maximus and other priests, scions of important patrician families, were usually influential politicians. No important action was taken, no assembly held, until religious omens were observed and interpreted. All festivals had a religious aspect, which was often dominant. The calendar was organized into days on which legal and public business could be transacted (*dies fasti*) and days on which such official business was prohibited for religious reasons (*dies nefasti*). Even on *fas*, "lawful" days, according to the dictates of religion, omens such as thunder and lightning could cause an assembly to be dissolved immediately.

Restrictive religious rules circumscribed elective assemblies too. The results of elections could be voided, for example, if the presiding official remembered that he had omitted some religious rite. And awareness of the observances and obligations of religion permeated the Roman legions. When inducted into service, soldiers took a solemn religious oath. No army fought or even moved until favorable omens occurred, and generals who violated the rules and lost might be prosecuted. In every aspect of their lives, Romans sought and usually followed the expert religious advice of specialists, and they felt collectively threatened by any failure of state officials to adhere meticulously to established religious tradition.

Small Farmers and Shepherds of Early Rome

Though large cities did exist in antiquity (Rome eventually became one), ancient society was predominantly rural. Like other ancient peoples, most Romans depended on the land for their livelihood, usually farming small plots of only a few acres. A single family could not till more than ten or fifteen acres. Most Roman peasant families lived in huts, sometimes sunk partly into the ground for warmth in winter. The household focused on the hearth, its fire rarely allowed to go out; smoke found its way through vents in the roof. Here all the cooking and baking was done, over—or in—the hot coals and ashes. When the fire did go out, it meant a trip to the neighbors' for a hot coal, and if one failed to set aside leavened dough for bread making, another such trip had to be made.

Small farmers engaged in "subsistence farming"—that is to say, they raised most everything they needed and purchased very little. On their small acreages they would have a few animals: if they were doing well, a yoke of oxen and perhaps a cow or some goats, along with a dog and a few pigs and chickens, which mostly foraged for themselves. Animals were chiefly valued not for meat, which formed only a small part of the Roman diet, but for their labor as well as for products like wool, milk (as often from goats as from cows), cheese, and eggs.

Smallholders did not usually own the best land; indeed, some peasants were shepherds and owned no land at all, making use of commonly held pastures. Some practiced "transhumance," driving their animals into the high pastures in summer and back down in winter. These seminomadic shepherd families made do with even more primitive housing than did the small farmers. Rural Romans knew how to make use not only of land and pasture but also of forests, where they found wood for fires, for tools, and for building materials, and where they gathered acorns to feed their pigs (eating the acorns themselves in bad years) and nuts to supplement their diet. They made extensive use of wild plants also, both for food and for medicinal purposes.

An eight-day period called a *nundinae* helped to pace the lives of rural citizens.[2] Each eighth day was a market day, when farmers would trade their produce with their neighbors for whatever they needed. In such a barter exchange, a few eggs might be traded for some turnips or a couple of pecks of grain for some wool; in many backward areas, coinage probably never played a large role, even in the high period of Roman history. Rough valuations were established through custom: one ox was worth ten sheep, for example. At larger markets or fairs (*mercatus* or *conventus*), occasionally staged for itinerant traders at the nearest town or perhaps at an important crossroads, farmers might purchase tools (or the metals with which to make them), oil, and salt. If they lived within a couple of days' travel from the sea they would probably not buy salt, instead making a trip to the seashore in the summer, where they would dip seawater into shallow rock formations and wait for it to evaporate, leaving salt deposits to be collected. Salt, of course, was of value not only to make food more tasty, but also to preserve foods, especially meat.

Each Roman farmer would have had a vegetable and spice garden, the preparation of which was probably the earliest task of the farm year. Hardy vegetables were planted first, others later. Spring field crops followed. The harvest of the winter grains came in early summer. In late summer came the harvest of the spring-planted crops, then if there were vines the grape harvest, and still later fruits and olives. Fall plowing and planting ended the busiest part of the agricultural year. A variety of

---

[2] The seven-day week gradually supplanted the *nundinae* during the early Empire.

vegetables, spices, and grains was grown, the choice constrained by the quality of the soil; farmers necessarily planted whatever did best on the land available, which often meant growing barley or millet rather than the more desirable wheat, for example.

The work was unrelenting, and all members of Roman farm families were expected to help however they could. This difficult life produced a folk able to endure hardship, who formed the backbone of the army if not the state.

2 The Early Republic, 509–287 B.C.

Independence Brings Problems

Generations of Roman youngsters learned to revere the men who expelled the Etruscan kings. Lucius Junius Brutus and the others had saved the people from tyranny, and the Romans venerated their leaders as much as Americans have praised the fathers of the American Revolution. In truth, however, the leaders in the expulsion of the Tarquins made up a small group of conservative aristocrats, and the "revolution" was not so much a blow for general freedom as it was a conservative reaction against kings who had favored the lower classes in order to weaken the entrenched aristocracy.

Historians have inferred from the literature that the expulsion of the kings was mostly an aristocratic reaction. They have also compared what happened in Rome with events in neighboring states. All over Italy, it appears, aristocracies took over the powers of kings, even in the Etruscan cities themselves. Reforms attributed to Servius Tullius by the ancient writers illustrate this trend, which had been established much earlier in Greece. This king is said to have reorganized the army on a centuriate pattern (by groups of one hundred, according to type of armament) and established an assembly of all Roman citizens on the same basis. Those citizens who had the most property served in the higher levels of both the army and the Centuriate assembly, and those with less property at lower levels; the poorest did not serve in the army at all and voted last in the assembly.

The army reorganization has usually been accepted by modern scholars, but the corresponding political reorganization has often been placed later, in the Republic. An army of 192 centuries could not have existed in this period, as the sources state. However, if, as seems likely, Servius enlarged the army—especially the heavy infantry—by his reform (this too was being done all over Italy), he would most likely also have given added privileges to the new infantrymen, perhaps full voting rights. The larger army was a military necessity, but the new organization no doubt aided the tax assessor as well. The larger citizen body, or at least a larger group of full citizens, held military and political rank on a timocratic basis (according to wealth). Servius attempted by this new arrangement to broaden popular support for the monarchy, to defend his position against the attacks of the aristocracy, and to increase the military power of the growing city. Perhaps it worked, but only for a short time until Tarquin the Proud, successor to Servius and the last of the kings, was expelled.

The Tarquins' attempt to regain control over Rome failed. Another king, however (Porsenna, of Etruscan Clusium), mounted a powerful attack on the city from the north, across the Tiber. Among the tales repeated over the centuries to Roman children—and into the present century even in Great Britain and America[1]—is that of a Roman named Horatius, who single-handedly held off the Etruscan army while his fellow citizens cut down the wooden bridge over the Tiber and so saved Rome. Traces of a different tradition indicate that Porsenna actually did retake Rome (probably for himself, not in behalf of the Tarquins) and forced the city into a dependent alliance for a time. Certainly it was a difficult period. Around the middle of the fifth century (traditional dating) other nearby peoples, especially the Volsci and the Aequi, also attacked Rome; they were said to have been repelled one time by a sort of minuteman army raised by the appointed dictator, Cincinnatus, another of the legendary heroes of the early history of Rome.

The cutting of ties with the Etruscans brought economic depression to Rome, for much of her economy depended on Etruscan trade. This economic depression is well attested by archaeology. Imports of fine

---

[1] Horatius Cocles is the hero of Macaulay's *Lays of Ancient Rome*.

Greek pottery ceased. The remarkable growth of the city slowed; building activity after about the middle of the fifth century B.C. almost stopped. Things did not pick up again for several decades, and even then only on a limited scale. Economic stringency surely exacerbated internal tensions.

The Romans had external problems other than the attacks by the Etruscans, Volsci, and Aequi. They were often at odds with their nearest kinsmen, the other Latin peoples, who had doubtless cooperated with Rome in the struggle against the Etruscans but did not want Roman dominance to replace that of the Etruscans. That eventually happened, but not for a century or so.

The Struggle of the Orders

The aristocrats of the infant Republic seized the offices of the state in a stranglehold. The resulting social tensions, compounded by economic problems after about 475 B.C., led to an extended period of recurring dissension that was later termed the Struggle of the Orders. By Roman chronology, the struggle took place from 494 to 287 B.C., but this lengthy conflict was discontinuous and not as well defined as these dates imply. Indeed, some historians have plausibly argued that the struggle lasted through the entire period of the Republic.

As we have seen, the later Romans to some degree misunderstood the Struggle of the Orders, but modern scholars have contributed their share of misunderstandings. Often, historians have viewed the struggle as an uprising of the lower-class plebeians against the upper-class patricians. The conflict was not that simple, however. The leaders of the struggle were plebeians, true, but they came from important families. In the later stages of the struggle they were frequently aristocratic heads of states that had been absorbed by Rome—local aristocrats who, on attaining Roman citizenship, found themselves lumped in with that polymorphous group at Rome called plebeians. The "urban plebs" did designate the lower class in the city in the last years of the Republic, but during most of the republican period the plebeians included both upper- and lower-class individuals. The patricians comprised only some fifty or so clans (gentes) at the beginning of the Republic. By the middle and late Republic, only about fifteen of these old clans remained important, whereas the number of plebeians had increased enormously. Patricians thus constituted only a minority of all Romans in the early Republic, and by the middle Republic they were a minority even of the aristocracy or nobility (nobilitas), which by that time included all families whose members had filled the highest offices.

The lower classes supported plebeian leaders and benefited from some of the concessions gained in the Struggle of the Orders. The chief winners, however, were the upper-class plebeians, for after the struggle ended these persons stood politically equal with the patricians, though perhaps not quite at their level socially.

Initiating the Struggle

The protests that began the Struggle of the Orders, according to traditional accounts, occurred in 494 B.C. A heavy military burden and its accompanying taxation (the *tributum*, a direct tax on Roman citizens, was always levied strictly for military purposes) precipitated the crisis. The fledgling state had to defend itself against attempts by the Etruscans to regain control, and there were troubles also with other near neighbors. Because of the economic decline, the tax burden likely hurt as much as the long military service. Some plebeian leadership came from a center on the Aventine Hill. The keepers of the temple of Ceres on the Aventine, called aediles, made the temple the focus of a sort of cult for plebeians, keeping the archives of plebeian actions at the temple and probably themselves assuming leadership of plebeian causes. During the Struggle of the Orders, the office of aedile became an official one, ranking just below that of praetor, another new official with judicial powers. The focus of discontent on the Aventine may have come from traders, members of the small community that lived there, though they seem to have been mostly Greek; at any rate, these merchants must have been affected by the economic decline that came with the expulsion of the Etruscans. The Roman peasants were also in straits, however. The area was heavily populated and farms were small. Freedom from the Etruscans probably meant a shrunken market for farm produce. Our admittedly undependable evidence indicates that several times in the first century of the Republic, bad weather and famine struck the state, which had to import grain to relieve shortages. Peasants sometimes had to borrow to survive, and the accounts mention their complaints about the burden of interest rates. We hear too of recurring demands for distribution of publicly owned land among poor citizens.

Plebeian Officials and the Plebeian Assembly

In 471 B.C. the plebeians came together in unofficial assembly and elected magistrates from among their ranks, the "tribunes of the plebs." The people swore to consecrate to Jupiter anyone who laid violent hands on these tribunes, thus conferring *sacro-sanctitas* on them. Though the patricians resisted acknowledging the new plebeian officials, they eventually accepted the fait accompli. The two tribunes— whose number soon increased to ten—had mostly negative powers. They could prevent the regular magistrates from carrying out punishments of plebeians. Eventually they gained the right of *intercessio* ("veto"), the power to halt the operations of the assemblies and even of the Senate. They called together the Plebeian Assembly, the *concilium plebis*, for elections of their successors and of aediles; *plebescita*, proposals passed by this assembly, were at first only resolutions of the assembly, but during the Struggle of the Orders, these measures attained official status as law.

The patricians did not give up these rights and powers willingly. The plebeians applied pressure by a sort of strike, refusing to report for the army draft in time of military emergency. Once or twice they "seceded" by leaving the city and assembling nearby. (Tradition has it that such withdrawals occurred five times, but the accounts are repetitious.)

The Centuriate Assembly, or *comitia centuriata*, whose organization paralleled that of the army, elected higher officials, such as consuls. The centuries voted as units, with those made up of richer citizens always voting first. The assembly that elected the tribunes of the plebs and the plebeian aediles was organized on a tribal basis, modeled on the Assembly of the Tribes (*comitia tributa*), which seems to have been established earlier. While the Tribal Assembly comprised all ranks of citizens, plebeians, and patricians, however, the Plebeian Assembly excluded the patricians, and it was presided over by the plebeian tribunes rather than the consuls. When the governing oligarchy accepted the election of tribunes of the plebs, it in effect validated the Plebeian Assembly as an official body of the state. The Tribal Assembly was at first, it seems, made up of sixteen tribes (corresponding to residential districts); by 241 B.C. there were thirty-five, four urban and thirty-one rural. No new tribes were added after that date. As Rome acquired new lands within Italy, she merged them with the city-state, the *ager Romanus*, adding them to existing tribal areas in crazy-quilt fashion; blocks of territory assigned to a single tribe were sometimes completely disconnected.

Written Law

In the middle of the fifth century (traditional date 451–450 B.C.), the patricians acceded to yet another demand of the plebeians. The body of the law—previously unwritten and known only by the patrician priests—was codified by a special board of ten men (*decemviri*) and publicly displayed on twelve wooden tablets. The XII Tables, which laid the groundwork of what was to become one of Rome's most treasured contributions to the world, heralded a millennium of development in the law. The bulk of the laws dealt with the sorts of issues important to a rural people: possession and sale of property, the control of roads and pathways, debt, theft and other crimes, trial procedures, family relationships, and inheritance. Though a written law was an important gain for the lower classes, its administration still lay in the hands of the priests, who continued to be selected from the patrician class until the end of the fourth century. Still, for centuries justice could be obtained only with the help of an influential patron.

Only fragments of the text of the XII Tables survive. Enough remains, however, to illustrate the constitutional nature of some of the laws. The decemvirs did much to order the developing political structure of the Republic. For example, the XII Tables first embodied the notion of popular sovereignty, the constitutional principle that the last enactment of an assembly of citizens was the law. By implication, neither orders of the magistrates nor decrees of the Senate could overturn the assembly's acts. No assembly could pass laws without the prior approval of the Senate, however, and the edicts of the magistrates also came to be an important source of new law. When toward the end of the Struggle of the Orders the Senate's check over the assemblies was removed, the concept of popular sovereignty became in theory an unrestrained principle; though potentially a very important factor in the constitution of the state, it was little applied in practice before the Gracchi (133–122 B.C.).

Lengthy but suspect stories tell that the decemvirs, led by Appius Claudius, aimed to tyrannize over the Romans by seizing permanent power, only to be overthrown by a virtual revolution caused in part by reaction to Claudius' outrageous attempt to enslave as his own the fair and virginal daughter of a respected Roman citizen. The truth behind the story may only be that the decemvirs were reluctant to lay down their power.

Plebeian Eligibility for Higher Magistracies

Plebeian agitation for the right to hold the consulate led to the establishment of substitute chief officers, the "military tribunes with consular powers." In most years between 444 and 367 B.C. these officials—usually five to seven of them—replaced the consuls. The Roman historians thought that establishing these new offices prevented the plebeians from actually holding the office of consul. Perhaps, however, Rome simply needed a larger number of magistrates.

An important series of laws passed in 367 B.C. on the initiative of the radical tribunes of the plebs C. Licinius Stolo and L. Sextius not only required that one of the two consuls be a plebeian (or possibly allowed that one could be a plebeian), but also added the new offices of praetor and curule aedile.[2] Like the consuls, the praetors held *imperium*—the right to command troops—but their primary duties were judicial, while the aediles administered activities of the fora or markets and attended to important religious festivals. The Roman "constitution," it should be

---

[2] The curule offices—the consulship, praetorship, and curule aedilate—were so called for the curule chair in which these officials sat when transacting business. Until the Struggle of the Orders these offices were restricted to patricians.

noted, consisted of law and tradition, and changing the constitution or making an exception to a law—even a basic one—was consequently only a matter of passing a resolution. Exceptions were made most often to laws governing elections; thus there were years later in the century when both consuls were still patricians. The successful struggle of the plebeians for the right to hold office culminated in 300 B.C., when the Lex Ogulnia opened the priestly colleges to plebeians, making them eligible for all major offices.

The assemblies also gained a measure of independence from the Senate around this time. Although the source evidence is difficult to interpret, it appears that the Publilian Law of 339 B.C. gave the *comitia centuriata* the right to pass laws without prior Senate approval; the Hortensian Law in 287 B.C. gave the *concilium plebis* the same right. (In the sources there is some confusion between the *comitia tributa* and the *concilium plebis*.) The Hortensian Law marked the last reform of the Struggle of the Orders.

Q. Publilius Philo and A. Claudius Caecus

The plebeian Quintus Publilius Philo figured prominently in the later years of the Struggle of the Orders. Elected to the consulship for 339 B.C., he pushed through the Publilian Law, which first allowed the centuriate assembly to act independently of the Senate; two years later he became the first plebeian to hold the new office of praetor. Philo seems also to have opened the office of censor to plebeians, serving in that post himself in 332. He was consul three additional times.

Despite his social background, the patrician Appius Claudius Caecus likewise helped to enhance the plebeian role in government. As censor in 312 B.C. he extended the voting rights of landless citizens, and he appointed to the Senate not only plebeians but also even sons of freedmen. Both Philo and Claudius probably supported the expansion of Roman power within Italy, and both may have backed a law of 311 that provided for the election of many of the military tribunes—field-grade officers who had previously been appointed by commanders. A former member of Claudius' staff, perhaps with his support, published for the first time the legal forms needed to take action in the courts, which before had been known only to the patrician priests who controlled court procedures.

Claudius was notable also for his oratory and writing; as censor he constructed the first aqueduct at Rome, the Aqua Appia, and the Via Appia, the first in the great network of paved roads that centered on Rome. The Via Appia ran south to Capua (later to Beneventum, and still later to Brundisium on the heel of the peninsula). Constructed during the Second Samnite War, in which Claudius and probably Philo as well were active, its original purpose was probably chiefly military. As an old man Claudius, by then blind, gave a rousing oration before the Senate in which he opposed accepting the terms of peace offered by King Pyrrhus, who had twice defeated the Romans, in 280 and 279 B.C.

Economic Problems and the Later Phases of the Struggle of the Orders

Although they are less well documented than the political upheavals of the period, acute economic problems chronically plagued Rome during the Struggle of the Orders, and their effects were similarly long-lasting. The scanty evidence indicates continued problems, reporting agitation by the poor for land, need for legislation to supplement a provision of the XII Tables against maltreatment of debtors, and the enactment of laws to reduce or even eliminate interest rates in the latter half of the fourth century B.C. The Licinian-Sextian Laws of 367 included a notable measure on the ager publicus ("public land"). We know little about this measure; certainly our ancient sources, misrepresenting some of its details, have confused it with later measures. The law required that the public or state-owned land be regularly leased, and it set an upper limit on the amount of such land a single citizen could hold. Presumably more citizens now found it possible to acquire or lease public land.

The Struggle of the Orders benefited all Romans in one way or another. New laws permitted appeal from the death sentences handed down by magistrates and restricted the sale of debtors into slavery to satisfy debts. The office of the tribune of the plebs opened an umbrella of protection, although most tribunes throughout Roman history came from the ranks of upper-class plebeians and so had an upper-class outlook. Well-to-do plebeians benefited from their new eligibility to high office and to the priesthoods. Over the centuries, the New Men (novi homines)—that is, the first of their families to reach the upper magistracies—almost invariably came from the upper-class ranks just below the patricians.

The Expanded Nobility

Access to the higher offices brought with it the assimilation of upper-class plebeians in an enlarged governing oligarchy; this in turn meant entrance into the nobility, since the nobility was very politicized and consisted of those families that had had at least one member attain a high office. The nobilitas automatically included the patricians, the older aristocrats, but gradually expanded with the addition of newer plebeian families, until by the middle Republic, plebeian aristocrats and nobles outnumbered the patricians. In the later Republic, the definition of nobility became further refined: besides the politically active patrician and older noble plebeian families, it embraced only those additional plebeian families that had one member to serve as consul.

The Developed Constitution

Officials

The constitutional machinery of a state ordinarily reflects the realities of social, economic, and military structures; when it does not, some sort of overturn almost inevitably occurs. The structure of government in the early Republic, with its monopoly of office by the patricians, was from the beginning somewhat out of phase with the actual socioeconomic structure. After the Struggle of the Orders, however, a nobility that included the more powerful plebeians and a system that guaranteed some political privileges for all plebeians produced a more harmoniously attuned system. Every Roman, through some combination of high social status, wealth, patronage, or sheer ability, might rise to hold office; no citizen was arbitrarily excluded from opportunity. The enlarged *nobilitas* monopolized the highest offices and priesthoods, however, becoming almost a closed body. Nobles also naturally dominated the Senate, making day-to-day decisions, and in time of war they led the army as well. Yet it remained possible for new men who rose in extra-governmental circles to rise within the government also.

The two consuls, annually elected by the Centuriate Assembly, remained the chief executives and the top generals of the state. After 367 B.C. a growing percentage of the consuls were plebeians. A consul presided over the Senate and put questions to it for consideration (and ordinarily took the advice it gave); one of the consuls normally presided over the Centuriate and Tribal assemblies also, and so could influence the major elections and the enactment of laws.

By the middle of the third century B.C. there were two praetors. One of the two was designated *praetor urbanus*, presiding over judicial proceedings involving Romans. The other, called the *praetor peregrinus*, handled cases involving foreigners. Praetors could also command armies and, in the absence of a consul, preside over the Senate or either of the assemblies of all citizens. Praetors, like consuls, were chosen in annual elections by the Centuriate Assembly. Also by the third century, both praetors and consuls sometimes served beyond the year for which they were elected; that is, their terms of office were prorogued. Their official titles in such cases were proconsul and propraetor.

The Centuriate Assembly also elected two censors, but only approximately every five years. The censors held office either until they completed their work or for a maximum of eighteen months. Their major duties were to take the census and assess property. Thus they not only determined levels of taxation and classification for army service, but also the placement of each individual in the voting centuries and tribes. They appointed men to vacancies in the ranks of the Senate and the cavalry and could remove them for cause. These powers of the censors were important socially as well as politically, especially since they involved the regulation of morals. Some censors penalized persons who neglected their property as well as men who remained unmarried. Among the censors' more important functions by the middle Republic were letting contracts for public works and leasing public lands.

The quaestors, whose numbers increased to ten in the middle Republic, took charge of the treasury and served as financial staff members for consuls, and later for praetors, proconsuls, and propraetors who governed provinces or held other important commands. They were elected annually in the Tribal Assembly. Curule and plebeian aediles were also elected in the Tribal Assembly, the former under the presidency of a consul, the latter under the presidency of a tribune of the plebs. The aediles kept order in the Forum; supervised mercantile activity there, with judicial powers; and also superintended the major state religious festivals. The aedilate was not part of the regular order of magistracies,[3] but a popular aedile often went on to higher office and so ambitious men usually sought the post.

The tribunes of the plebs had broad, mostly negative powers that differed little from those gained during the early Republic, but the positive side of their power had been accentuated by the Struggle of the Orders. After the adoption of the Hortensian Law the Plebeian Assembly, under the presidency of a tribune, could pass laws without prior approval of the Senate. Thus tribunes could now propose bills, conduct public debates, and get bills enacted into law.

The Assemblies

An assembly important only in a vestigial sense in the historic period, the Curiate Assembly still granted *imperium* to consuls and praetors, but on a purely formal basis. It occasionally filled other functions— registering adoptions involving patricians, for example. But only thirty lictors, the attendants of the curule magistrates, met as delegates of the moribund assembly to transact its affairs.

The Centuriate Assembly elected consuls, praetors, and censors, as we have seen. It could pass laws, though the Tribal Assembly more often enacted legislation, and it served as an appellate body in cases involving death sentences. The Tribal Assembly elected aediles, quaestors, and other minor officials such as the military tribunes and the decemvirs, who participated in the judicial processes and superintended religious affairs. No formal debating of measures voted on in any Roman assembly took place, though members did hold preliminary informal meetings to discuss proposals.

---

[3] The *cursus honorum*—the sequential holding of the offices of quaestor, praetor, and consul—was legally fixed only in the second century B.C., but the tradition of the regular *cursus* was established earlier.

Members of the Tribal Assembly who were not patricians composed the Plebeian Assembly. This body elected the ten tribunes of the plebs, one of whom presided over the assembly. Voting procedures in the Centuriate and Tribal assemblies differed fundamentally. Roman citizens were ranked in the 193 centuries according to wealth, in the manner of the earlier organization of the army, using military terminology. The top 18 centuries were cavalry, the rest mostly infantry. The first census class contained 80 centuries, the second through fourth 20 centuries each, the fifth 30. The Centuriate Assembly included four centuries of engineers and other artisans and buglers, and finally, a single century of men whose property holdings were so small as to make them ineligible for army service. Each century voted as a unit. Voting always started at the top of the centuriate ranks and proceeded downward until a majority was reached. Thus the votes of the wealthiest citizens counted heavily, while the votes of the poorest citizens counted for almost nothing. In the Tribal Assembly, by contrast, men were placed according to where they resided or held property. Voting was by tribe rather than by century, and the procedure was somewhat more democratic, with lots being drawn to determine which tribe would vote first. The vote of the first tribe or the first century in the assemblies strongly influenced the outcome.

Though the Tribal Assembly represented the interests of the less wealthy or privileged Roman citizens better than did the Centuriate Assembly, it was not genuinely democratic. The thirty-one rural tribes were more sparsely populated than the four city ones, and attendance of rural members in the city at the time of the convening of the assembly was even sparser. Since voting was by tribe, not by numbers, the votes of rural landholders were heavily weighted. Even if they lived in the city they could be registered in an area where they owned land. Moreover, the influence of patron over client, wealthy man over poor, was great, particularly since voting was open rather than secret. The aristocratic oligarchy of patricians and upper-class plebeians dominated the assemblies and thus, most of the time, the offices, the laws, and the courts.

The Senate

The Senate remained a powerful body even after it lost control over which legislative proposals would be submitted to the assemblies. Circumstances during Rome's expansion even enhanced its power. Most patricians or plebeians who reached the quaestorship acquired a Senate seat in the next census. Membership was for life, though the censors could remove members. Consequently the Senate included all major officials as well as those who had previously held high office—in short, almost all the politically important and experienced men in the state. Ordinarily, several ex-consuls (consulars) would be in attendance. The advice of the Senate, offered by decree (*senatus consultum*) in response to a question posed by the presiding officer, was not to be lightly disregarded. The membership of about three hundred was manageable, and it could meet frequently as necessary. Its great influence (*auctoritas*) far surpassed its formal legal powers. As Rome expanded and fought numerous wars, the Senate came to control the assignment of magistrates, the chief expenditures of the state (and thus the treasury), the provinces (as they were acquired), foreign affairs, and many other state concerns. Both major policy decisions and myriad decisions of detail were settled in the debates of this body.

The Roman system of government was hardly unified by the changes brought about through the Struggle of the Orders; indeed, the struggle continued, but now within the system. For perhaps two centuries or more, on the one hand, tribunes of the plebs could not be senators, though eventually they gained that right, and even the right to convoke the Senate. For a similar lengthy period, on the other hand, sons of living fathers who had held curule offices (consulship, praetorship, some aedileships) were ineligible to serve in plebeian offices. Apparently aiming to keep even upper-level plebeians from the tribunate, this law too was finally allowed to lapse. But it was Rome's successful expansion, with its benefits for all social classes, that did most to relieve internal tensions.

Social and Cultural Change in the Early Republic

Armies tend to reflect the society that produces them; if somehow they do not, they inject an element of instability into the system. As we have seen, the later kings of the Roman monarchy had enlarged the army in accord with contemporary practice elsewhere, and the king's new army, its soldiers given full citizenship, was perceived as a threat by the Roman aristocracy, who expelled the monarch and attempted to assert full control within the oligarchical Republic they established. The Struggle of the Orders was in part the effort of plebeians (many of whom served in the army) to gain political privileges matching their military status. This outline is not, of course, the full story of what happened, but it does point up an often overlooked aspect of the Struggle of the Orders. The principle that the organization and composition of an army must somehow correspond to social and political realities helps illuminate later changes, especially in the last century of the Republic.

Like the corresponding Centuriate Assembly, the army was organized according to the wealth of the citizens. All able-bodied free men between about eighteen and forty-five were required to serve for periods that varied with the military situation. (The term of service was eventually limited, in theory, to sixteen years.) Upper-class citizens generally served in the cavalry or heavy infantry, and their ranks furnished the army's officers as well. The commanders were the elected officials of state. Any person who wished to run for election to one of the higher offices had first to serve ten years in the army. Lower-class persons served in the infantry: heavy infantry if they met the property qualifications, one of the lighter infantry classes if they didn't. Free citizens whose property holdings fell below a certain minimum could not serve in the army on a regular basis, though they might be called up, usually for support services it seems, in emergencies. The restructuring brought about by the Struggle of the Orders harmonized the social and political order with the expanded military organization.

The state religion was just that—a part of the state, as it was a part of society and of military decision-making and military routine as well. Controlled in the monarchy and early Republic by the patricians, after the Struggle of the Orders religious positions, like political offices, came to be shared with upper-class plebeian nobles. The assemblies occasionally enacted laws governing religious matters, but it was the Senate, the priestly colleges, and the elected officials who built and maintained temples, arranged religious festivals and sacrifices (some performed daily), performed rites of expiation when the gods had shown their displeasure, and took omens before important actions such as moving an army or committing it to battle, as well as before more routine undertakings such as convoking an assembly. Unless the gods approved, nothing good could come of human decision and action.

Under the supervision of the pontifex maximus, the most important priestly colleges included the pontiffs, the augurs, the flamens, and the vestals. Other groups such as the decemvirs also carried out some religious functions, especially the care of the Sibylline oracles, which conveyed the will of the gods in times of crisis. Most colleges were eventually filled by a form of election, and membership was for life. None of the members (with the qualified exception of the vestal virgins) were professional; rather, citizens from politically active families filled these posts.

The pontifex maximus controlled the religious calendar and in the early period had much influence over the law. The augurs took the auspices before important events to ascertain the approval of the gods. Posts in the college of augurs, which required extensive study of the lore, conferred great dignity and public exposure and so were much sought after. The flamens were priests to various state gods; chief among them were the Flamen Dialis (to Jupiter) and the flamens of Mars and Quirinus. The six vestal virgins kept the temple and the sacred fire of the goddess Vesta. The fact that the same persons who dominated society, held the top offices, and commanded the army controlled religion as well attests the importance of religion in the Roman state.

Early Expansion and Consolidation in Central Italy

The problem of overpopulation and the economic doldrums that plagued the early Republic did more than cause internal tensions; they also shaped the new state's external relations. The ancients expected to profit from war. Everyone understood that the victors got the spoils, and no one thought it unreasonable. Moreover, waging war was accepted policy. Ancient societies eagerly went to battle if there was any likelihood of victory, and they assumed that the strong would rule the weak. Athenian orators in the fifth century B.C. (as reported by the historian Thucydides) and Aristotle a century later stated this principle clearly, and few persons in antiquity would have quibbled with it.

If Romans had to fight the Etruscans to retain their political freedom, they also expected a reward of Etruscan territory if they won. And when Romans contested with the Latins for supremacy and won, they naturally took spoils and land. In this early period, and even later, when Rome had expanded far and wide, enough Romans profited—at the expense of others, of course—to bring about an easing of internal tensions because of increased prosperity.

We need not comb through the semifictional accounts that survive of Rome's numerous struggles in the early Republic, which brought victories—and sometimes losses—over the Etruscans, the Aequi, the Volsci, and other nearby peoples. The pattern Rome followed after achieving her victories, however, deserves attention.

When Romans and Latins won joint victories and land was available from the conquered, the Latins usually set up separate, independent or quasi-independent states settled by their own citizens. Rome seems to have joined in some Latin foundations that were intended as protectors of the frontiers. However, Rome usually settled her citizens *viritim,* "individually," on the new land, incorporating it in the Roman territory (*ager Romanus*). As a consequence Rome soon outstripped the neighboring Latin states in size of territory and in population, one important reason why Rome rose to dominate central Italy by the end of the fourth century B.C. Rome did later adopt the practice of establishing both citizen and allied colonies, however.

A crucial victory for Rome was the first successful offensive against the Etruscans. The latter had been weakened by the defections in Latium, by losses at sea to Sicilian Greeks, and in the Po region, by an incursion of Celts (whom the Romans called Gauls). Disunity among the Etruscan states contributed to the general malaise. Rome besieged and took Veii (traditional date, 406–396 B.C.), located on a valuable site north of Rome across the Tiber. The long and difficult siege was something new for the Roman army, which was unaccustomed to year-round fighting. Then, it was said, the troops were paid for the first time. Peasants might fight in midsummer without damage to their own affairs, but they needed time off from fall to spring for plowing, planting, and harvesting. Veii provided some fine land for distribution to Roman citizens.

The Gauls Burn Rome

The next great event was disaster, not success. The Gauls moved into central Italy, probably against the Etruscans. Rome refused a Gallic alliance, whereupon the Gauls attacked and utterly defeated the main Roman army at the Allia River in 390 or 387 B.C. Thereafter the city, except for the citadel on the Capitol, fell to the enemy. Eventually the Romans bought off the invaders. In the following year, under the famous dictator M. Furius Camillus, the Romans avenged themselves on the Gauls and the threat receded. Rome was rebuilt, though there were those who wanted to move the city to the more defensible site of Veii. The city would not again be sacked by alien troops for almost eight hundred years.

Reorganization of the Army

Camillus is thought to have reorganized the Roman military, restructuring the previous crude phalanx in a precisely organized army aligned for battle. In front came the skirmishers, young, light-armed *velites*. Next, in the first main battle line, were the *hastati*, "spearmen." The second main battle line was made up of prime warriors, the *principes*. The third line, a kind of last-ditch defensive force, was made up of the *triarii*, who were older veterans. Within a few decades the standard legion consisted of about 4,000 men, drawn up in maniples of 120 each. In battle, the light-armed troopers threw their missiles and retired back through the ranks. The mainline heavy infantrymen advanced, threw javelins to further harass the enemy, and then closed in to fight it out with the sword, unlike the Greek phalanx, for example, which depended on the thrusting spear in close fighting. In addition, the Roman arrangement was more flexible and open than the Greek and could be employed on rough terrain. The Roman cavalry played a subordinate role; it was used on the march, on reconnaissance, and for protection of the flanks more than for combat. Alexander the Great (356–323 B.C.) made his heavy cavalry the shock units that carried his assaults, and the successor states of the Hellenistic world imitated him. The Romans, however, continued to depend primarily on infantry. With this army they made themselves the dominant Mediterranean power.

3 From City-State to Domination of Italy, 360–264 B.C.

DURING A PERIOD of about two centuries, Rome broke out from her consolidated base of power in west central Italy to make the Mediterranean into Mare Nostrum ("Our Sea"). We may distinguish three major thrusts in this period of expansion: first, the swift rise to supremacy in Italy; second, victories over Carthage in the contest that decided the control of the western Mediterranean; and finally, a vigorous expansion into the Hellenistic east at the expense of the great successor states of Alexander. This chapter deals with the first phase.

Expansion into Empire: Demographic, Geographic, and Economic Factors

If there was a single most important factor in the seldom paralleled imperial success of Rome, it lay in the Roman people themselves, Rome's most dependable asset. A kind of rugged cohesiveness characterized Roman society, an ability to hang together in critical situations. (The plebeians and the patricians did indeed come into conflict, but ground for compromise was always found.) The reasons for this not entirely explicable cohesiveness have been indicated earlier. Roman society was not too diverse, distinctions between rich and poor not yet great. The society was integrated ethnically, linguistically, religiously. The stresses independence had brought had not seriously disturbed this basic stability.

Individual Romans were inured to hardship by agricultural toil and were trained to obey, yet they felt themselves involved as participants in the main political processes of the state. Roman soldiers were usually well disciplined, courageous, and persistent in the face of obstacles. Of course they were not always victorious, but they did maintain the military virtues at a consistently high level.

Numbers were important. The Latins, the Samnites, and other Italians, equally tough, equally disciplined, certainly matched the Romans, man for man. But there were usually more Romans. In each phase of the outward struggle, the size of Rome's manpower made a difference. Rome had an advantage over the Latins because land policies made the city-state larger and more populous than any combination of the Latins. Later, in the critical struggles against the Samnites, the Romans had the Latins on their side. Similarly, in the crucial struggle against the Carthaginians, most of the Latin and Italian peoples were Roman allies. The later penetration into the eastern Mediterranean was backed by an enormous reserve of manpower.

Geography influenced the struggle in Italy. From her central location, Rome often had the advantage of quick communications as well as of relatively easy movement of troops and supplies against even massive mélanges of foes—Etruscans, Samnites, and Gauls—spread out along the perimeter of the theater of operations. One cannot say quite the same thing for the importance of topography in the second and third phases of expansion (considered in the next chapter). The fact that Rome faced west doubtless affected the order of events. The challenge to Carthage naturally preceded any advance into the Hellenistic states. But Carthage's location was also central, close to the strategic straits at the waist of the Mediterranean; Rome had no real advantage there. Later, in eastern campaigns, topography played no central role. Only the extent of Italy with its comparatively large population gave Rome an edge.

Economically Rome had no advantage over her opponents in the first phase of expansion. Indeed, since the state was somewhat overpopulated until the mid–fourth century B.C. at least, it may well have been poorer than some rivals—for example, the Etruscans. Even after Rome had dominated all Latium and Roman influence reached southward into rich Campania, her people could hardly be described as affluent. But Rome then needed no large and expensive navy; foot soldiers were paid little and provided most of their own equipment.

In antiquity, however, as in modern times, money could be the sinews of war. Fortunately for Rome, with expansion came increased economic potential. The conquest of Etruria brought iron mining and smelting operations Rome needed. Even so, Rome faced severe economic problems in the first and second wars with Carthage during the second phase of expansion. The conquest of Sicily brought for the first time, however, an annual tribute from a conquered area (collected in grain). The occupation of much of Spain during the Hannibalic War was most important of all, ensuring an almost inexhaustible supply of both precious and nonprecious metals for centuries, along with additional tribute. By 200 B.C., Rome's economic resources matched the city's territorial gains.

Was it through a policy of deliberate imperialism that the Roman Republic pieced together an empire? This general question is much disputed. Some historians have thought that Rome developed a master plan for domination of the world in the early Republic and faithfully followed it thereafter. Other historians have argued that Rome was not really imperialistic at all and that mostly fortuitous, unplanned circumstances combined to bring about her expansion. Two things are certain: the Romans were conditioned to war, and they took advantage of opportunities. They sometimes rationalized offensive operations as really defensive—as nations have done ever since.

In antiquity, as today, imperialism took more than one form. It is notable that Rome hesitated to acquire provinces in the Hellenistic east even after intervening there in four major wars during the late third and early second centuries. But Rome nevertheless did penetrate the area politically through her system of friendships and alliances, with rewards and punishments for friendly and unfriendly behavior.

Challenges Within Italy: Samnites and Latins

In the mid–fourth century B.C. the Samnite League was perhaps the most extensive and powerful alliance in Italy. Its territory, in the hilly region to the east and south of Rome, did not abut the territory dominated by Rome in the early period, and no competition developed between Rome and Samnium until after about 350 B.C. In fact, the Romans and the Samnites were allied against the Gauls about that time. The Romans' conquest of the Volscians to the south, however, brought them to the Samnite frontiers. Actual conflict came in competition over the rich soil of Campania, which was occupied by another group of Samnites, a plains people called the Oscans, who were not allied with their hill-dwelling cousins.

In the second half of the fourth century the Samnite League launched a drive to gain control of certain iron-bearing hills near Campania. The local inhabitants enlisted the aid of the Campanians; the Samnites thrust into Campania itself and besieged its principal city, Capua. The reputation of the Campanian prosperity for being enervating was perhaps justified as the Samnites proved themselves indeed more vigorous than their Campanian relatives.

The Oscans in Campania turned to Rome for help. The Roman historian Livy, in an account that seems quite unbelievable, says that the Roman Senate at first refused aid because of Rome's alliance with the Samnite League, but that when the Oscans offered to surrender themselves and their territory to Rome, the Romans then decided to accept the Campanians as subjects. More likely, however, Rome simply wanted Campania—or didn't want the Samnites to have it—and repudiated the Samnite alliance for one with the Oscans.

However it developed, the First Samnite War (343–342 B.C.) followed; we know little about it, except that Rome remained in control of Campania with or without the blessing of her Oscan allies. The terms of peace must have been favorable for Rome.

The Latin Revolt (340–338 B.C.)

Surprisingly, the Samnites allied with Rome only a couple of years after the first war, when the Latin states in the Latin League decided to rid themselves of Roman dominance. The Latins must have been dismayed at the growth of Roman power. From the low point in 390 or 387 B.C., when the Gauls had sacked Rome, the Romans bounced back to defeat the Gauls the following year, under Camillus, as they did again in 360 and 349 with the help of allies. They rebuilt their city, surrounding it

A portion of Rome's earliest real wall, preserved near the main railway terminal of the modern city. Though often called the Servian wall, it probably was constructed after the Gallic sack of Rome in the fourth century B.C.

with a sturdy wall, remains of which may still be seen. Clearly, in the mid–fourth century Rome was a resilient, burgeoning state. And the Romans now controlled fertile Campania.

For the Latins, the last chance to avoid Roman domination had come. They probably hoped that the social and political tensions that had erupted in the Struggle of the Orders would weaken the Roman response (the Publilian Law, it will be recalled, was passed in 339 B.C.). But it was too late. With the help of the Samnites, the Romans defeated the Latins and now at last could impose whatever settlement they chose.

The Settlement of 338 B.C.: A Pattern for the Organization of Italy

Whether by chance, necessity, or wise policy, Rome laid the foundation for all her future success in the political arrangements of 338 B.C. for Latium, Campania, and a couple of states that lay in the corridor between Rome and Campania.

Historians quite properly emphasize those events that lead to significant change. But quite improperly, their emphasis all too often makes it appear that historical process embodies a kind of inevitability. Along with Livy and the great poet Vergil, we often think Rome was fated to become the Eternal City, the mistress of the ancient Mediterranean world. But Rome's rise was not inevitable: on several occasions from the fourth to the first centuries B.C., the Roman state might easily have collapsed if the solid core of allied strength in Latium and central Italy had not held firm. The reason it held firm was Rome's decision in 338 not to attempt to rule the vanquished Latins and Italians as subject peoples.

The defeated Latins and disgruntled Campanians saw little that was generous in the settlement. For them the arrangements formalized a lost liberty. But by comparison with the treatment that had been meted out not so long past by Athens or Sparta to their allies, the Roman pattern was liberal indeed. The people of some of the Latin states and some upper-level Campanians became Roman citizens; the people of some cities became citizens, but without the right to vote in Rome; and the rest, each state with its own treaty, became allies of Rome. The allies were not taxed by Rome and had autonomy at home—that is, the right to elect their own officials and run their own governments. They were, however, required to furnish soldiers for the Roman army, under a Roman commander, on call. Furthermore, they could not make an alliance with any other state, not even with each other. Rome thus controlled foreign policy for all.

The treaties varied, but most allies had the right to trade at Rome and to intermarry with Romans. Some Latins had the right to move to Roman territory and become Roman citizens. All the Latin states gradually gained full citizenship in later years, and so too did the Campanian and other Italian states that became Roman allies.

The grants of citizenship were not sham. Lists of high elective officials in Rome (the *fasti*) include Latin names soon after 338. Former Latins even began to attain the consulship. The men so honored must have come from the most powerful social classes in their own states before assimilation into the ranks of the Roman aristocrats—those who attained high office, that is. Such nobles would, however, have remained plebeians in Rome; they could not become patricians.

Later Samnite Wars

The second and third Samnite wars grew out of the first. In an effort to secure communications to Capua, Rome placed colonies along the Samnite frontiers. Fregellae, founded in 328 B.C. to control the Liris River valley, may have been placed on Samnite land. The Romans sought allies to the south and southeast of Samnium, while the Samnites developed relations with Naples in south Campania and negotiated alliances to the north with the Gauls and some of the Etruscans. Both sides

Heavily-armed Samnite warrior (modern representation). Note the bronze bosses on the leathern breastplate. (*Alinari/Art Resource, New York*)

prepared for a long struggle; the prize, we can now see in retrospect, would be the control of all Italy.

The first years of the second war (ca. 326–304 B.C.) saw only limited skirmishing and raiding. In 321, however, the Romans attempted a major penetration of Samnium, with disastrous results. At Caudine Forks a double consular army of perhaps sixteen thousand men was trapped and forced to surrender. For about five years the Romans conducted no military operations of any importance. But then the war resumed and the outcome was a definite victory for Rome. The Liris valley, the communication corridor between Latium and Campania, was now securely Roman. In the third war (298–290 B.C.) the Samnites finally achieved the coalition they had long worked for as both Etruscans and Gauls joined in the struggle. In 296 a Samnite general, Gellius Egnatius, managed to effect a junction with Etruscan forces. The following year a Gallic force arrived, and the moment of decision with it. Unfortunately for the Samnites and their allies, the Etruscans were not present at the critical battle at Sentinum in 295. The fighting was desperate. One Roman consul, P. Decius Mus, was said to have devoted himself—and the enemy—to the infernal gods through appropriate rites; then he deliberately plunged into the enemy ranks in self-sacrifice. The Romans won, though losses were heavy on both sides. Hard fighting still remained, but Sentinum was the turning point.

In the peace, Samnium lost more of her best lands, retaining mostly the relatively unproductive mountainous regions. Furthermore, the Samnites were now forced to become allies of Rome in the typical pattern that left them autonomous at home, though in some ways subordinate. They did not have all the privileges that Latins held, nor did any receive the citizenship. Samnite troops had to fight with Roman armies for Roman objectives. The Samnites would again rebel against Rome, as we shall see, in the first century B.C.

Wars with Tarentum and Pyrrhus

An extension of power also extends responsibilities and multiplies problems. The relationship Rome had cultivated during the Samnite wars with the Lucanians, who lived to the south of the Samnites, brought friction with the Greek states of southern Italy. Moreover, the military colonies that Rome had established, especially those in Apulia, had commercial potential, and the major Greek city in southern Italy, Tarentum, felt itself threatened economically. Tarentum decided on war. The casus belli was the penetration into the Gulf of Taranto of a small Roman naval squadron chasing pirates. Entry into the gulf violated an old treaty with Tarentum. The Tarentines smashed the Roman fleet and refused any attempt to negotiate differences. They then brought in King Pyrrhus of Epirus (across the Adriatic) with his army to conduct the inevitable land war. At sea the Tarentines would be unchallenged.

Pyrrhus, a second cousin of Alexander the Great, arrived with about twenty-five thousand troops plus elephants and in set battles twice defeated the main Roman army, at Heraclea (280 B.C.) and at Asculum a year later. Both the Macedonian superiority in cavalry and the use of elephants—the first the frightened Romans had ever seen—made the difference. The Romans claimed that Pyrrhus had won a "Pyrrhic" victory, based on a reported comment that should he win another such battle he would certainly be ruined. Pyrrhus did not follow up with an attack on Rome itself. A weakened Rome now faced revolts of her Samnite and Lucanian allies.

Pyrrhus moved on into Sicily to aid the Greeks in Syracuse against the Carthaginians, who at this point became allies of Rome. Again Pyrrhus was initially successful. Pyrrhus' whole remarkable career, as Plutarch's life of the king makes clear, seems to have consisted of bold enterprises, quick victories, but then, perhaps through boredom, failure to follow through to a successful conclusion.

The Romans meanwhile retrieved many of their losses, and when the Greeks in Italy entreated Pyrrhus to return, the result was yet another hard-fought battle at Beneventum in 275 B.C. Neither side won a clear victory, but the Romans this time were left in possession of the battle-field. Pyrrhus then withdrew to Greece, chiefly to pursue his fortunes in a contest for Macedonia. Possibly Tarentum could no longer afford his expensive services. Moreover, many Greeks in Sicily and Italy feared that Pyrrhus' ambitions in the area were personal and imperial.

Within a few years Rome had defeated Tarentum and integrated all the Greek city-states of southern Italy into her alliance system. The Greek cities furnished manned ships for Rome's small navy rather than men for her army, but otherwise the settlement followed the pattern established for the Latins and Italians. Some Lucanian states, and the Samnites also, suffered the confiscation of part of their territories as they were forced back into Roman alliance.

Meanwhile in these same years (280–265 B.C.), Rome was in frequent conflict with the Etruscans to the northwest and the Gauls to the north and northeast, successfully reducing all organized opposition. As in the south, portions of the best lands of these old enemies went to Rome, and the most productive parts of Etruria, Umbria, and Picenum were opened to Roman occupation. Forced alliances were established in these areas also.

Colonization and Settlement as a Means of Control

Following another earlier pattern, Rome secured her position by establishing citizen and Latin colonies on the most strategic sites, especially along the coasts. To name only a few, Cosa in Etruria was established in 273 B.C., Paestum south of Naples in the same year; Rhegium, at the toe of the peninsula opposite Sicily, though not a colony, was carefully controlled after 270 B.C. On the eastern coast Brundisium, established in 244 B.C., would become the chief port of embarkation for Greece and Asia Minor, displacing and eventually bringing about the decline of Tarentum and other Greek ports. Other colonies included several in Apulia established during the Samnite Wars (notably Luceria and Venusia) and, farther to the north, Asculum in Picenum. The citizen colonies were small, almost always on the coast, and designed for strategic military security. The Latin ones were larger. Populated by Latins and by Romans who gave up their citizenship to enter an allied state, they helped to "Romanize" the peninsula, to support Roman interests, and to prevent defections.

The lands confiscated from conquered states or from rebellious allies by this time amounted to perhaps a tenth of all Italy south of the Po valley. Some of this land was of course colonized; some leased, mostly to rich Romans; and some assigned in small lots to lower-class citizens. One strip of state-owned land stretched eastward from Rome and effectively cut the peninsula in two, no doubt deliberately so as to prevent rebellion. The Romans were nothing if not systematic.

In 264 B.C., then, Rome was firmly in control of all Italy south of the Po valley. There was now land enough to benefit all classes of citizens. Manpower resources were enormous by ancient standards. Mineral resources, despite the acquisition of Etruscan metal-working areas, were still minimal, however. Actual monetary wealth, too, was not great, for Rome's allies did not pay tribute to Rome, but because of her wealth in land, forests, and men, Rome now ranked as one of the great Mediterranean powers. She would soon strive for supremacy over the others.

The Limitations of Roman Political Structure

Though Rome had become a great power, dominant throughout Italy except for the Po valley and the Alpine approaches in the north, the government was still that of an oligarchical city-state, a fact that molded Roman perspectives.

The chief Roman citizens lived in or near the city of Rome itself; citizens who moved to nonmilitary colonies in territories not contiguous with the *ager Romanus* ("Roman land") had to give up Roman citizenship and accept Latin rights only. No conception of dual citizenship, Roman and local, as yet existed.

City-state society and government were hardly suitable to controlling so large a territory, which was soon to grow into a vast empire. Yet by extending citizenship to the top elected officials of allied states and eventually to whole city-state populations, Rome fashioned a governmental system that resembled an association of oligarchies. Not merely political but also social ties held the system together. When local nobles became citizens they sometimes moved to Rome, and they—or their children—became involved in Roman government by election to office.

Rome thus adapted, to a degree, to the growth of the state. And Romans later used the same system in organizing an empire that spanned the Mediterranean. They tried to fashion a union of oligarchies, but because the subject provincial peoples were hardly allies, like the Latins and the Italians, they met with limited success. The end result was that the Roman Republic gave way to a more authoritarian state. But that is a look into the future.

4 Rome Dominates the Mediterranean, 264–133 B.C.

ONCE ROME CONTROLLED all Italy it became a great power—but only one of several others in the Mediterranean. One by one Rome eliminated the others, and in little more than a century determined the course of history throughout the area. Rome's competitors fought strongly and well; the goddess Fortuna would seem to have favored Rome in some of the confrontations. Yet the Romans with their Latin and Italian allies generally maintained an indomitable resolve; Roman commanders led with a confidence that bordered on arrogance; and Italy's reserves of manpower made up for occasional, inevitable disasters.

Carthage: The Great Power of the Western Mediterranean

Our literary sources for the history of Carthage are either hostile or indirect. For the early period we rely on Greek writers; our knowledge of the Punic Wars between Carthage and Rome comes almost entirely from

Roman sources. We have some background information from Phoenicia, some bits of evidence derived from coins and inscriptions, and some inferences based on the archaeological examination of ruins on the site of the ancient city and its dependencies.

Located near the modern city of Tunis, in North Africa, Carthage was founded, according to our Greek sources, as a colony of Tyre in Phoenicia about 816 B.C., half a century before the traditional founding of Rome. Archaeology has turned up nothing at the site quite so early, but the date may be not far wrong. The Phoenicians established numerous and varied colonies; Carthage was one of the sort that was both a trading station and a permanent settlement for numerous colonists, who developed the land for agricultural production. Carthage retained ties with her founding city, but when Tyre and the other Phoenician city-states weakened under the attacks of Babylon and finally fell to Alexander the Great (332 B.C.), Carthage took up the role of leader of the Phoenician-occupied areas in the western Mediterranean.

Long before the Romans, the Carthaginians developed plantation-like farms worked by slaves. Smaller farms about the city were mostly worked by natives. Agricultural yields made the city virtually self-sufficient in grains, vines, olives, and fruit. Whatever other produce Carthage needed could usually be obtained from nearby Sicily.

Trade, however, was the major consideration of the founders of Carthage. On the site were two harbors, one completely within the city defenses and partly artificial. The city's location at the narrowest part of the Mediterranean, about a third of the way between Spain and the Phoenician coasts in the east, likewise favored an active trade. For this trade the Carthaginians needed precious metals; gold and silver were also needed to pay the mercenaries on whom Carthage depended for her imperial strength. These precious metals came mostly from Spain. Tin used in making bronze may have been brought all the way from Cornwall in southwest England. The early Phoenician traders, and their descendants, the Carthaginians, after them, coasted not only the Mediterranean but also the Atlantic both north and south of the Pillars of Hercules (as the ancients called the promontories at the eastern opening of the Strait of Gibraltar) in their search for items of trade.

By the fourth century B.C., Carthage not only boasted a flourishing trade and held a strong political and economic position in its home territory, but she also controlled directly or indirectly long stretches of the coastal regions in the west. All of the seaboard of North Africa from Cyrenaica to the Strait of Gibraltar was within Carthage's sphere of influence if not under her actual domination. So also was southern Spain, western Sicily, and other island areas. Like Rome, Carthage remained a city-state but headed something of an empire.

Carthage's government, also like Rome's, was an aristocratic oligarchy. In Carthage, however, no struggle of the orders had redistributed

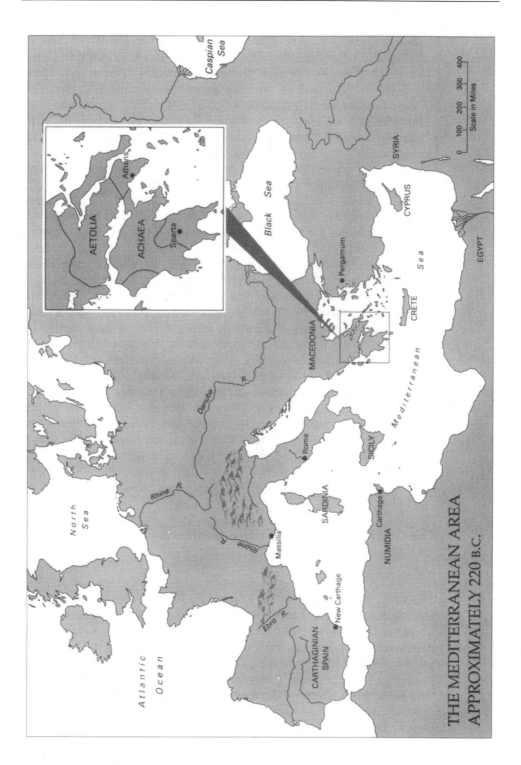

THE MEDITERRANEAN AREA
APPROXIMATELY 220 B.C.

social rank and power as it had to some extent in Rome. All citizens voted, but the Carthaginians had been very chary of extending their citizenship. Their Senate was even larger than that of Rome, but the real power lay in the Hundred, an inner group of senators given extensive judicial powers, and in another group, the Thirty, a sort of executive committee of the Senate; both of these were dominated by a restricted oligarchy. Two elected officials, the sufets, held posts comparable to the Roman consulships. Generals and admirals, however, were not elected; scions of the great aristocratic families usually held these positions. Military leaders could be called to account before the Hundred.

One consequence of the policy of keeping the body of full citizens small was that Carthage could not, like Rome, depend on a citizen draft to meet her needs for military manpower. So far as military quality is concerned, this matter was probably not important, contrary to what students have so often been told. Polybius, the Greek writer of the second century B.C. whose history provides us with the most dependable account of some years of the Punic Wars, was quite certain that mercenary troops were better than citizen levies. Yet in the end, military disaster meant economic difficulties, which in turn made it impossible to continue to pay a large force of mercenaries. As one would expect in a trading state, Carthage's military establishment gave priority to a rather expensive navy. So long as Carthage had the funds to build and man fleets and to hire mercenaries, she would be a strong power.

Native Carthaginians did not, however, aim to avoid military service completely by hiring mercenaries. Carthaginians furnished the officer corps for both land and sea forces, and a moderate-sized army unit of Carthaginians both defended the city and provided a reserve for use elsewhere in crises.

The Great Powers of the Eastern Mediterranean

Macedonia

Students usually remember Macedonia, the kingdom in northern Greece, from the days of Philip II (reigned 359–336 B.C.), who with a clever and effective combination of diplomacy and force succeeded in dominating all Greece in the fourth century B.C., despite the best efforts of Athens' thundering orator, Demosthenes. Even more vivid is the memory of Philip's son, Alexander the Great (336–323 B.C.), who not only dominated Greece and conquered the great Persian Empire but also initiated a new era of history, the Hellenistic age. In this new epoch, Greeks and Greek language and culture spread over the entire Near East; native influence, notably in religion, combined with the influx of Greek learning and ways to produce a distinctive, hybridized culture. Alexander's premature death in 323 brought an untimely end to his empire, but various Greek dynasties continued to rule large chunks of the territory he had won, and the penetration of Greek culture continued.

Throughout the Hellenistic age, Macedonia, along with the other great powers, was sought after and fought over by the successors of Alexander. The Greek Pyrrhus of Epirus, who fought the Romans in the third century B.C., was one of those who contended for the throne of Macedon. Two major federated leagues that formed in Greece during this period, the Achaean League in the northern Peloponnesus and the Aetolian League just north of the Gulf of Corinth, naturally tended to contest with Macedonia for dominance of their areas. Athens and Sparta were still important but were overshadowed by the great monarchies of the age.

In earlier days the army of Macedon had played both a military and a political role, somewhat similar to that of the Roman army. The army voted on important matters and named or deposed the kings, at least in theory. Now, however, the Antigonids, ruling Macedonia since early in the third century, made the succession hereditary. After Philip II and Alexander, the army came to include non-Macedonian, mercenary elements, as did the armies of the other Hellenistic monarchies. The king's power tended to become more arbitrary, though Macedonian traditions resisted this trend. Cities that had once enjoyed considerable autonomy found themselves more and more subject to the king. Lands outside the core area of the older state were controlled by the monarch. Yet compared with other rulers of the age, the Macedonian kings remained more popular national monarchs since, after all, they ruled over their own; the other Greek dynasts used their mercenary Greek armies to dominate non-Greek natives. The Macedonian kings also put less stress on claims to divine ancestry and, unlike other Hellenistic rulers, did not demand to be worshiped as gods.

Macedonia was self-sufficient in most agricultural commodities and in timber. Early conquests had brought control of important gold and silver mines in the northern Aegean region and in Thrace. The currency minted from these precious metals helped to pay soldiers and to maintain a strong navy, both necessary to the balance-of-power politics that sometimes brought precarious peace or more often endemic war to the Hellenistic east. The native manpower and also the quality of nearby Thracian mercenaries made it easier for Macedonia to obtain good troops than for Syria or Egypt, whose kings did not use natives at all but recruited troops from the Greek areas.

Syria

Of the great Hellenistic monarchies, that of Syria varied most radically during the age in both size and diversity of population. Under the founder of the Seleucid dynasty, Seleucus I (king after 305 B.C.), or under a powerful monarch such as Antiochus III, the Great, (223–187 B.C.), the polyglot kingdom included most of the former Persian Empire; under less able kings and in more troublous times, the kingdom shrank to little more than geographical Syria. The name Syria is used because Antiochus I established his capital there, at a city named after himself, Antioch, which became one of the great metropolitan centers of the Hellenistic world. Sardis in Asia Minor and Seleucia near Babylon were important regional capitals of the kingdom during much of the age.

The Seleucid monarchs strove long and hard to unify their diverse empire. The early kings established an extraordinary number of Greek colonies all over their dominion. Efforts were made, too, through emphasis on the divinity of the king, to provide a symbol of unity through religion. Rather late in the Hellenistic age, in the reign of Antiochus IV, attempts to impose this ruler cult on the sternly monotheistic Jews backfired in 167 B.C. A rebellion, which was never completely put down by the Seleucids, created a precariously independent Jewish state.

This lack of real unity, of any widespread loyalty to the regime, was the Achilles' heel of the Seleucid Empire. Yet the empire possessed notable strengths: a vast supply of manpower, even if mostly unusable for military purposes; extensive trade in and along the fringes of the empire; and abundant if scattered resources in metals, timber, and the like.

Egypt

The southern neighbor and chief enemy of Syria was the third of the great Hellenistic powers, Ptolemaic Egypt. Egypt and Syria fought six major wars during the age, mostly over lands running from Sinai north along the Palestinian coast—the approaches to Egypt—a territory fought over for millennia.

Egypt was the most unified of the Hellenistic monarchies, primarily because of geography. The Nile gives to all the country an economic and social similarity, and Egypt's protective geographical isolation tends to produce a sameness in the population itself. The richest agricultural area of the Mediterranean, some of the Black Land (the ancient meaning of the word for Egypt), produces, with irrigation, two and even three excellent crops a year. But Egypt is poor in metals and timber, and even in certain agricultural products.

Beginning with Ptolemy I (king after 305 B.C.), the kings of Egypt (the Ptolemies) held most of the land, following a pattern that had existed in Egypt since the beginning of the Old Kingdom nearly three thousand years earlier. They tightly controlled the economy, regulating exports and imports in the interests of the state and the Greco-Macedonian ruling class. The major exports were grain and papyrus; the major imports included lumber, olive oil, and wine. The capital and chief port,

Alexandria, became the greatest city of the entire Mediterranean world in this period. The system worked rather well from every point of view except that of the natives until the mid–second century B.C., when very low grain prices—presumably caused by a universal overabundance of crops, with consequent low income from exports—dealt the economy of Ptolemaic Egypt blows from which it never fully recovered. Prices rose sharply in the decade of the 120s B.C., but only because a series of bad harvests reduced agricultural production. Native unrest was rampant, as was rivalry between members of the ruling family for the throne; moreover, the kings of Syria and Macedonia in collusion began to seize Ptolemaic holdings in southern Asia Minor.

Hellenistic Culture

Although the great Hellenistic monarchies (except for that of Macedonia) were ruled by foreigners who imposed on the natives not only a military-political but also a cultural system, a surprising amount of influence went in the other direction as well. This influence is most easily discerned in religion. The age was one of syncretism, of identification between gods of different regions and different names, of an emphasis on universalism and on likenesses rather than differences. As an illustration, the Greeks identified and equated their Aphrodite with various goddesses of the Near East—the Egyptian Isis, for example. Isis the omnipresent, almost omniscient deity, however, was in conception, representation, and cult more Egyptian than Greek. Her worship and that of several other eastern gods eventually spread to Greece, then to Rome, and thereafter over all the western Mediterranean.

Despite the continual fighting that characterized the age, relatively uniform mercantile practices, interchangeable coinage systems, and a body of commercial law, much the same everywhere, developed and allowed trade to flourish. Roman law, so often praised as Rome's most notable contribution to Western civilization, owed much to these Hellenistic legal systems.

Rome was to absorb each of the great powers of the Mediterranean, Carthage, Macedonia, Syria, and Egypt, after defeating them in crucial contests-at-arms. Against Carthage the Romans fought three wars; against Macedonia, four; against Syria only one but with further interference at times that might well have brought war had the Seleucid rulers felt able. With Egypt, Rome quite early established a policy of friendship, apparently on the initiative of the Ptolemies. This relationship continued until the last of the Ptolemies, Cleopatra, made the mistake of casting her lot with Antony, a Roman who turned out to be a loser. Throughout all the wars, power and influence, as well as territory, accrued to Rome; somehow she always emerged the victor.

The Wars with Carthage (264–146 B.C.)

The long and bitter struggle between Rome and Carthage for supremacy in the western Mediterranean was not inevitable. Carthage was a city of merchants whose power lay chiefly in her navy; Rome had few merchants and almost no navy. Furthermore, Carthage and Rome had been allied at various times, most recently in their common enmity against Pyrrhus. They made their first treaty when the Romans expelled the Tarquins, and they renewed it—perhaps twice—during the fourth century B.C. The early pacts called on Carthage to stay out of Italy, and on Rome to recognize the Carthaginian trade monopoly in a wide expanse of the Mediterranean, which created no sacrifice for the Romans at the time. Yet if the Romans were not traders, the Greek allies they acquired in southern Italy were, and as sole ally, patron, and protector, Rome must eventually make the interests of her Greek allies her own. Roman leaders no doubt wanted Carthaginian Spain.

War came with an unplanned confrontation at the most sensitive spot geographically: the Strait of Messina. The city of Messina, in eastern Sicily just across from Italy, sought aid from Carthage and then from Rome against King Hiero of Syracuse. Both states sent aid, and this incident led to the First Punic War, as the Romans called it, lasting from 264 until 242 B.C. The Romans felt they could not permit the Carthaginians to control the straits, and neither side would back down.

The war made exceptional demands on both sides. The Carthaginians had to hire larger mercenary forces than they were accustomed to, chiefly for use in Sicily, but eventually to fight off a Roman army under the consul M. Atilius Regulus, which landed in North Africa in 256. The Romans for their part discovered they could not overcome the Carthaginians without a fleet, or rather a succession of fleets, which they lost one by one to defeat, to inept seamanship, and to storms. It was a titanic struggle, with losses for the Romans and their allies of probably a quarter of a million men. Both sides spent heavily in the war at sea. But it was the Carthaginians who first weakened in this match of wills after losing a fleet off Sicily in 242. By the subsequent peace treaty the Romans gained Sicily, plus a considerable indemnity. Three years later, in 238, the Romans professed to feel threatened by a Carthaginian buildup on Sardinia, which was part of a barbarous struggle between Carthage and her own rebellious mercenary troops. The Romans threatened renewed war, then demanded and obtained Sardinia and Corsica along with still more indemnity. War usually breeds war; certainly this imposed and unjust seizure sowed dragon's teeth for a second struggle.

The Second Punic War (218–202 B.C.) must be treated at greater length. In this conflict Rome confronted Hannibal, one of history's most competent and indomitable military commanders. At the same time, the alliance structure that was the basis of Rome's power bore the most severe stress. In surviving this critical test Rome took a giant stride toward supremacy in the Mediterranean world.

Carthage rebounded quickly from defeat in the first war, mainly because of the work of Hamilcar Barca in Spain. Functioning almost as an independent ruler in his own domain, Hamilcar expanded Carthage's control along the southern and eastern coastlands of the Iberian peninsula. He developed the Spanish gold and silver mines, making new finds that greatly increased output. After his death he was succeeded by his son-in-law Hasdrubal and later by his son, Hannibal, then in his mid-twenties. Hannibal recruited and trained a very large army in preparation for a war of revenge against Rome. In the time of Hasdrubal the Romans, alarmed, had attempted to curb Punic expansion in Spain by an agreement, accepted by Hasdrubal, to establish spheres of influence. Neither Hannibal nor the Romans kept the agreement.

An incident in 219–218 sparked the long conflict. This was Hannibal's siege of Saguntum, a Roman ally that was located in the Carthaginian area of influence. The resultant war came inconveniently early for the Romans. They had faced another Gallic threat in Italy from the north a few years before and had decided to pacify and occupy much of Cisalpine Gaul (the Po valley); this action was still in progress. They had besides intervened in Illyria across the Adriatic to suppress piracy, which threatened the trade of their Greek allies in southern Italy, and those operations too were not concluded when Saguntum was attacked. Therefore Rome sent no help to Saguntum, and at length it fell. In 218, Roman ambassadors to Carthage obtained no satisfaction, and Rome declared war.

The Romans planned to take the conflict to the city of Carthage by sending one army across to Africa and to immobilize Hannibal by sending another to Spain. Hannibal seized the initiative, however—obviously he was more nearly ready than the Romans—and marched across southern Gaul (France), crossed the Alps, and descended on Italy. The march was made difficult more by the opposition of Alpine tribesmen than by the autumn snowfalls in the Alps. He defeated the Romans in a major battle at the Trebia River, a branch of the Po, in November (218), then spent the winter recruiting for his depleted army among the Gauls not yet driven out of the Po region by the Romans. In the spring of 217 he marched south, met another Roman army on the shore of Lake Trasimene, and again won a great victory. In both battles he depended on ambush to give him the edge. The Romans had already lost about forty thousand men.

The Romans now named Quintus Fabius Maximus dictator.[1] Fabius raised an army and dogged Hannibal's trail without fighting a major battle, while Rome took emergency measures. The following year, 216, however, the Romans felt strong enough to fight, and at Cannae, in Apulia, suffered their greatest defeat: in a single day they lost perhaps sixty thousand men to a smaller force under Hannibal. Hannibal's famous tactic was to let his center fall back, holding firm on the flanks; the Romans crammed men into the middle, where they seemed to be breaking through. Meanwhile the superior Carthaginian cavalry defeated that of Rome, and attacked the Romans in the rear. The Romans, now surrounded and packed together so tight that most of them could not fight at all, were slaughtered. Disaster followed disaster: some Roman allies in Italy defected; Syracuse in Sicily left the alliance with Rome and made common cause with Carthage; King Philip V of Macedonia also joined Carthage in the struggle against Rome. Syracuse was soon taken by Rome and the Italian allies were eventually punished. By 205 B.C. a separate peace was made with Macedonia.

After Cannae, Rome returned to the tactics of Fabius: for years one or more armies, always superior to that of Hannibal in total size, stayed close to the Carthaginians, but large engagements were avoided. From beginning to end, Hannibal's strategy was to destroy Rome by breaking up her alliance system. Roman tactics aimed to prevent defection of her allies. Italian allies of Rome could not declare for Hannibal without danger of immediate retaliation from a Roman army. The most interesting action of the Hannibalic War is military, and it is here that Hannibal's genius shines; but the more important battles were for the allegiance of the Latin and Italian peoples, for without these allies Rome would have sunk to the level of a minor power. Rome won this most crucial contest not just by Fabius' strategy during the war, but by having forged a relatively enlightened and unoppressive system of alliances a century earlier. The allies that defected after Cannae were mostly Greeks and Lucanians, the most recent members of the Roman alliance system. Of the older Latin and Italian allies only one state, Capua, went over to the Carthaginians. Hannibal marked time in frustration. He could not be beaten, but he could not win.

Meanwhile, under Publius Cornelius Scipio, the Romans conquered Spain. Carthage made a major effort to reinforce Hannibal in 207, but the Romans annihilated this army, led by Hannibal's brother, before it could join Hannibal's forces. Eventually Scipio, elected consul for 205, took

---

[1] For upper-class Romans, the first name was the *praenomen*, the given name; the second, the *nomen*, or *gens* name; the third, the *cognomen*, or family name. Additional *cognomina* were assumed or popularly awarded at times. Thus Fabius was called Cunctator, "the Delayer," because of his tactics against Hannibal. Victorious generals later took such cognomens as Africanus, Asiaticus, and Macedonicus.

an army into Africa, ravaged the country, and won over some of Carthage's allies. Carthage, in desperation, recalled Hannibal during a truce. He had been in Italy more than fourteen years. Hannibal got together a major army, only to be defeated at Zama in 202 by Scipio, who added a surname and was thereafter called Africanus.

Carthage paid an indemnity of 10,000 talents,[2] again on the installment plan, agreed to limit its navy, and agreed not to wage war without Rome's approval. Rome kept Spain, from which the Carthaginians had been completely expelled by 206. In this war, as in the First Punic War, Rome lost heavily in manpower; moreover, the depredations of Hannibal heavily damaged some of the rural areas of Italy—hurting people more than land, as we shall see. Yet Italy was still populous enough, and Spain brought Rome both tribute and income from the mines. Frequent wars with the natives certainly reduced the net gain, but the volume of precious metals coming into Rome was significant. So were the installments of the Carthaginian indemnity. Rome emerged stronger than ever, and now a contender for dominance of the entire Mediterranean world.

Carthage once more managed a quick economic recovery and as before offered to pay off far in advance the indemnity owed to Rome. But the state was no real threat anymore, and the Third Punic War (149–146 B.C.), from any point of view, seems to have been unnecessary. On the Roman side it largely resulted from fear, a legacy of the first two wars. For the Carthaginians it was a kind of irrational lashing out under the restrictions imposed by the peace of 201. The Romans seized on a pretext: the Carthaginians' efforts to defend themselves from Masinissa, the king of nearby Numidia, technically violated the terms of peace. When a Roman army landed in Africa, the Carthaginians surrendered to Rome in 149 on promise of their safety. But the Roman commander demanded that the Carthaginians evacuate their city, which was to be destroyed. The Carthaginians had already surrendered their weapons, but they now shut the city gates and, amazingly, managed to hold off the Romans during three years of siege. All in vain at last: the city was taken and utterly destroyed by the younger Scipio Africanus, grandson by adoption of the elder Scipio.[3]

Carthaginian territory became the Roman province called Africa, approximately modern Tunisia. It produced for Rome a tribute in grain, oil, and wine that in a few decades grew surprisingly large. Eventually

---

[2] A talent was 6,000 Roman denarii or Athenian drachmas. See page 71 for the value of the denarius.

[3] His full name was Publius Cornelius Scipio Aemilianus; the second surname indicated that he was adopted from a family of the gens Aemilia. He was the son of Lucius Aemilius Paullus, the victor over the Macedonian king Perseus at Pydna (see page 62). Since, like his adoptive grandfather, he defeated Carthage, he too took the additional surname Africanus.

much of the land was settled by Romans. Yet the Carthaginian population was not exterminated and the Phoenician influence remained strong in the area for centuries, as archaeological excavations clearly show.

Rome Penetrates the Hellenistic East

Both the reasons for Roman intervention in the eastern Mediterranean and the methods by which this was accomplished are difficult to work out in detail, despite much scholarly investigation. In any time and place, strong powers are drawn as by magnets into weaker areas. States that feel threatened by their neighbors will seek help wherever they can find it. Allies of strong powers must be protected. Moreover, some Romans at all levels of society had much to gain by war and were clearly imperialists. Other Romans felt a sense of kinship with the Greeks on an intellectual level, which led them to wish to help the older city-states against Macedonia, for example. In considerable degree the Roman penetration was gradual, one step leading to another, and not at all the consequence of any long-range policy. It was only partially a matter of military action; it involved also diplomacy and the actions of powerful individual figures in Rome as well as of Roman commanders in the field, who always had much latitude of action and helped to formulate policy. It seems clear that traders and merchants did not strongly influence important decisions in this period.

The First and Second Macedonian Wars (215–205 and 199–196 B.C.)

Friction between Rome and Macedonia first developed as the consequence of the Roman movement across the Adriatic to suppress piracy, shortly before the Hannibalic War. Offended minor potentates naturally looked to Macedonia for redress against Rome, and young king Philip V of Macedonia (221–179 B.C.) intervened. Later, as we have seen, he also joined in alliance with Hannibal against Rome after Cannae. This conflict is known as the First Macedonian War (215–205). Rome countered by making an alliance with the Aetolian League, an enemy of Macedonia, and despite the manpower demands of the fight against Carthage (Rome had as many as twenty-seven legions under arms in those years) found it possible to send a few troops to Greece to keep Philip off balance. The separate peace was drawn up before Rome carried the war against Hannibal to Africa.

The Second Macedonian War (199–196) was brought on by Romans who resented the first war, and by Rome's Greek allies who demanded that Rome do more for them. The Centuriate assembly at first refused to declare war against Philip, but later, persuaded that war was inevitable and that the only question was whether it would be fought in Greece and Macedonia or in Italy after Philip invaded as Hannibal had, the people voted as requested. The war went slowly until a young consul named Titus Quinctius Flamininus in 197 and 196 made allies not only of the Aetolian League but also of the Achaean and won a decisive, hard-fought battle over Philip's phalanx[4] in 196 at Cynoscephalae.

The Romans now saw the need to establish a general policy toward the whole Balkan area. Flamininus, a philhellene, persuaded the Senate to back him in what was at first thought by most Greeks and Romans to be an enlightened, even noble policy. Rome, it was announced at the Isthmian games near Corinth, would not retain control of any Greek city: no Roman garrisons would replace those of Macedonia. All Greek states were to be free. The crowd at the stadium dissolved into such raptures of enthusiasm that the games did not continue. As for Macedonia itself, Rome took only 1,000 talents in indemnity, a small sum indeed, and deprived that kingdom of only small bits of Greek territory that had been conquered in recent years. These lands were mostly freed, though the Aetolian League got some. Altogether it seemed that once again the Romans had come up with the sort of brilliant policy of enlightened self-interest that had worked so well in Italy. But there were flaws: the Aetolians were furious not to have fared better at the expense of the Macedonians. And since the Romans did not forge an alliance system as they had in Italy, they had no way of enforcing their policy. It was inevitable that Rome would be drawn again and again into Greek affairs.

The Syrian War (192–189 B.C.)

A war waged by Rome against Antiochus III of Syria intervened between the second and third Macedonian wars. The king was called into Greece by the disenchanted Aetolians, who made an obviously anti-Roman alliance with him. Antiochus had ambitions in Europe, for he laid claim to territories in Thrace once held by Syria. He probably thought that Philip of Macedonia, now recovering from his defeat, might join in the alliance against Rome. Antiochus had already given grave offense to the Romans by receiving the exile Hannibal and admitting him to councils of state.

The war was precipitated when Antiochus crossed the Aegean with a small army in 192 and spent the winter in Greece. Neither he nor the Aetolians had made adequate preparations; each seemed to expect the

---

[4] The phalanx was a dense formation of heavily armored infantry fighting with long, thrusting spears. The Roman infantry, in a more extended order, threw javelins and then closed to fight with swords. The weakness of the phalanx was that it required a level terrain so that troops could keep ranks.

other to make the major effort. Philip stayed aloof. Rome sent an army across to Greece and defeated the combined but inadequate Syrian and Greek force at Thermopylae in 191. The following year the Romans, led by Lucius Cornelius Scipio (soon to be Asiaticus), brother of Scipio Africanus, invaded Asia Minor. They had the substantial help of King Eumenes of Pergamum, who feared the power and ambitions of Antiochus. In a battle at Magnesia in midwinter 189 against the full military power of Syria, the Romans and their allies were victorious.

Rome still wanted no territory east of Italy. Lands in Asia Minor were indeed taken away from Antiochus, but they were handed over to Rome's chief allies in the area, Eumenes and the Rhodians, who had furnished naval support in the war. The Romans took only spoils and money—but plenty of that: Antiochus agreed to pay 15,000 talents in indemnity, 3,000 down and the rest by installment. Meanwhile, Roman soldiers garnered a rich return, not merely in spoils from the battlefield but also in "gifts" to the generals from the various cities of Asia Minor the armies visited, persuading the local inhabitants to submit to the changed order of things. Antiochus was killed after a year or so as he was attempting to collect money for the indemnity by despoiling a temple treasury.

The Third and Fourth Macedonian Wars (171–167 and 149–148 B.C.)

When Philip V of Macedonia died in 179 B.C. he was succeeded by his son Perseus. The succession pleased the Romans none too well. They had favored a younger son, Demetrius, who had made friends with influential Roman aristocrats while living as a hostage in Rome. But Demetrius had been executed by his father; it was said that Perseus convinced him that the younger son was disloyal.

Perseus' policy was like that of his father: to husband his economic resources, remain strong militarily, cultivate pro-Macedonian factions throughout Greece, but engage in no large and dangerous ventures. This policy, however, frightened some Greeks, who felt that the carefully groomed army of Macedonia would be used against them one day. The Romans listened to complaints against Perseus. Charges made in Rome by King Eumenes of Pergamum seemed proved when a gang of toughs, said to be agents of Perseus, set upon the king and nearly killed him as he was going up to Delphi on his way home. At any rate, Rome forced an unwanted and unnecessary war on Perseus. The king made little use of his well-filled treasury and inadequate use of his army, yet the Romans defeated him only in 168 after electing a veteran consul, Lucius Aemilius Paullus, and giving him the command. The battle, at Pydna in Macedonia, was another test of the relative effectiveness of the rigid Macedonian phalanx against the more open and flexible Roman legion.

As before, it was demonstrated that, while the phalanx was perhaps invincible on smooth terrain, the legion would prevail in a fight on uneven ground.

Again the Romans chose not to annex Macedonia but the kingdom was broken up into four small, separate republics, which were forbidden to have even commercial relations with each other. Perseus was led along the streets of Rome, a halter around his neck, in Paullus' triumphal procession. Imprisoned, he soon died or was killed. Small states in Epirus, which had cooperated with Perseus, were punished by widespread destruction and (it was said) the sale of 150,000 persons into slavery. Aemilius Paullus turned into the treasury a huge sum from the spoils of Macedonia and Epirus; the sources mention 5,000 to 12,500 talents—the latter figure enough to hire almost a quarter-million laborers for a year. Rome refused to permit any powerful state to exist in the Greek area, but did not accept the responsibility of leadership there. Rome did collect tribute not only from Macedonia but also from Illyria (which had also supported Perseus); the amount was small, but the Romans gave almost nothing in return.

The final Macedonian conflict came chiefly because the Romans in 167 B.C. had chopped up an area that had long been unified, not only politically but socially and economically as well. When, therefore, a man named Andriscus claimed to be the son of Perseus and attempted to overthrow the republics, he gained considerable popular support. In 148 a Roman army put down the revolt. It was led by Q. Caecilius Metellus, who of course was thereafter known as Macedonicus. Now, at last, half a century after Rome's first invasion of the area, Macedonia was formally organized as Rome's first province in the east. The governor of Macedonia was charged with overseeing Illyria also.

Rome had intervened substantially in Greek affairs in various ways since the Second Macedonian War. The Aetolian League was virtually dismantled after the Syrian War. Following the war with Perseus the Romans tried to eliminate the pro-Macedonian elements in various Greek cities, especially in the Achaean League, and took numerous hostages (among them the future historian Polybius), who were released only in 151 B.C. Actions of Roman commanders in the Peloponnese tended to weaken the Achaean League. Its leaders, goaded beyond endurance by a resentment that was as much psychological as substantial, mistreated some Roman envoys in an irrational outburst. Frantically, the league prepared for the inevitable war and just as inevitable defeat. L. Mummius conducted the major operations for Rome in 146 around Corinth, which was besieged and destroyed as an object lesson. (It will be recalled that Carthage was destroyed in the same year.) Corinth would not be rebuilt until the time of Caesar.

It seemed a long time since the Greeks had wildly cheered Flamininus' announcement that all Greece was free. Now Greece became a dependency of Rome under the oversight of the governor of Macedonia. Augustus would later make Greece into a province, called Achaea. Most upper-class Greeks were treated well by Roman officials, and sons of Roman nobles came to Athens to be educated. In the time of the Empire, many Greeks acquired citizenship, and a few even held high office at Rome.

Penetration of Asia Minor

Rome frequently intervened diplomatically in Asia after the Syrian War. After the war with Perseus, Eumenes of Pergamum was threatened with loss of land because of suspected sympathy for Perseus in the late stages of the war. Rhodes, which had committed the unforgivable sin of attempting to mediate between Rome and Macedonia in the war, did lose all the Carian property (southwest Asia Minor) obtained through Rome from Syria. Moreover, Rome made Delos a free port, and its competition undermined the economic basis of the Rhodian state. In 167 B.C., Roman envoys had a celebrated confrontation with Antiochus IV of Syria. Antiochus had invaded Egypt, and Ptolemy VI had called in the Romans. An embassy of Roman nobles, on the beach near Alexandria in Egypt, forced the king through mere threat to take himself and his army out of Egypt. Syria declined into insignificance in the following decades, until its absorption by Rome in 63 B.C.

Pergamum became Rome's first province in Asia when Attalus III died in 133 B.C. after willing his kingdom to Rome. The natives put up a fight to invalidate the will, but Roman arms ensured receipt of the legacy. About the turn of the century, in action against piracy in the east, Rome acquired still another province, Cilicia, along the south shore of Asia Minor (102–101 B.C.). By now the kings of Bithynia in the north and of Cappadocia in central Asia Minor were "friends and allies"—client states of Rome, which now dominated virtually the whole peninsula. These and other states in the area eventually became provinces as well.

Numbered among the provinces by about 133 B.C. were Sicily, Sardinia-Corsica, Hither Spain, Farther Spain, Africa, Macedonia, Asia, Cisalpine Gaul (probably), and Illyricum. Rome was unchallenged and supreme.

5 Changing Times, 264–133 B.C.

THE PERIOD of rapid expansion beyond Italy brought trenchant changes in Roman society and the economy. Rome's ruling classes experienced a heady growth in power and prestige. For them, along with a small but important rising group of businessmen and bankers, the expanded dominions meant expanded economic opportunity. Even the lower classes, if Fortuna smiled, might prosper, but long military service and debt crushed many lives. And the very prosperity that gilded the age for the fortunate only accentuated the poverty of the unfortunate. The gap between rich and poor gradually widened and finally became intolerable. In time, the whole social structure underwent a significant alteration, at length corrupting politics and bringing revolution to the state.

Along with these changes came a flood of cultural innovations that threatened to overwhelm the old Roman mores. Broader experience and opportunity brought greater sophistication. Romans began to produce a literature that would become noteworthy. They began to examine imported philosophical concepts and to experiment with new religions. New standards of luxury for the favored classes gave rise to changing morals. To many minds the *mos maiorum* or ancestral tradition seemed to be dangerously eroding.

The young naturally embraced the changes in life-style more rapidly than their elders. Just as in any period of rapid change, a generation gap was often apparent that was most painful to conservatives, of whom there were always many at Rome. This chapter will delve into some aspects of this change, so bewildering or threatening to some Romans, so eagerly embraced by others.

Changes in the Economy

In antiquity, most wealth came from the land. The economy of Italy was based on the soil, and whatever else happened that fact did not change. Ownership of land was coveted and respected. Wealth was conceived in rural terms, even though many men made their money through banking, trade, mining, or manufacturing. Despite the changes associated with a developing urban culture, the ruling classes of Rome preserved their characteristic rural outlook.

One of the most basic causes of rapid change in state and society was the artificial stimulation of the economy—especially of the city of Rome itself but to a degree of all Italy—through income from wars and the provinces. Each victory in war brought spoils both to individuals and the state, followed by payments of sizable indemnities over a period of years or by permanent tribute. The income must not be overstated: Spain, for example, although it paid some tribute and produced income from the important silver mines, must have been unprofitable at times because of widespread rebellion. Still, by ancient standards vast sums came into Italy and made many Romans affluent. The city itself sprawled with new growth. The state erected temples, basilicas, and aqueducts. Houses and apartments and other private structures such as warehouses spread outward along the Tiber and the spurs of the hills of the city. Other Italian cities grew as well, if on a lesser scale.

The governing classes of Rome, restricted by custom and sometimes by law from certain types of trade and business activity, left engaging in wholesale and retail trade and commerce to others, or participated indirectly through relatives and trusted freedmen or slaves. Money lending too was looked down on, though some rich nobles were indirectly involved in banking. The less restricted Italians and especially the Greeks continued to develop a sea trade. Italians and even some lower-class Romans got into wholesale and retail business, particularly in Rome, the largest city and the best market on the peninsula. The publicans, Roman citizens who bid on state contracts of all sorts, benefited most from state expenditure. They supplied the armies, built ships for the navy, and contracted with the censors to build roads, bridges, and other public structures. By the late second century B.C. the richest publicans were those who bought at public auction the contracts for collecting tribute in the provinces and the customs duties at major ports. The wealth of many entrepreneurs soon approached that of the richest nobles.

The Development of Coinage

Valuable metals such as gold, silver, copper, and bronze were used in the exchange of goods long before Rome was founded, earliest in the eastern Mediterranean and the regions of the Near East. For centuries the metals were weighed out, though sometimes they were carried in convenient small pieces or rings. Only in the seventh century B.C. were real coins invented, apparently in western Asia Minor. A coin may be defined as a portable piece of precious or valuable metal used in exchange for goods and services and stamped or marked by a responsible government, which warrants the piece as to its weight and fineness or purity of the metal. Coins naturally facilitated trade and the accumulation of wealth. They were first used not in everyday trade (where barter long continued to be the rule), but in paying mercenary soldiers, engaging in foreign trade, and collecting taxes. These activities stimulated the development of a money economy.

In the high period of Greece, after about 500 B.C., all the major Greek states coined money. Of course the most important trading and colonizing states produced the most widely circulated coins: Athens and Corinth, for example. The Greek states in southern Italy and Sicily also coined money from an early period, as did the Etruscan states a bit later. Doubtless the first coins the Romans saw were those of nearby Etruscan and Greek states.

Because of the rural nature of their society, the Romans lagged in producing their own coinage. They long depended on bronze, at first weighed in raw form, and later in the form of cast bars of several pounds' weight. The first round coins of uniform weight, also of bronze, were too heavy for easy portability. These coins, called *asses*, each weighed one Roman pound (*libra*, about 325 grams) of twelve *unciae* or ounces. They first appeared around 300 B.C. or slightly later, during or immediately after the last of the Samnite Wars. The later bronze *as* became successively lighter until it was standardized at one-half ounce in 91 B.C.

It was probably during the Pyrrhic War, around 275 B.C., that the first silver was coined for Rome, in southern Italy, by a Greek mint or mints. These coins are called *didrachms* because they weighed about as much as two Attic (Athenian) drachmas, almost eight grams. A few years later, probably in 269, similar coins were minted at Rome with the legend

ROMA. The first of these had the head of Hercules on the obverse (head) of the coin and, fittingly, a wolf and twins on the reverse.

By now all Roman coins were struck, not cast. Dies were prepared first; one—the obverse—was placed in an anvil and the other—the reverse—in a punch; blanks of metal of proper size and weight (approximately; the ancients could not be so precise as we are today) were heated and placed with tongs by a workman one by one on the anvil die; another workman held the punch die in place while a third hit the punch with a sledgehammer. The compacted metal lasted well, but the dies are often seen off-center.

The development of coinage at Rome and her victories in major wars are inextricably linked. During the First Punic War, the Romans lightened the bronze, and a few years afterward minted new but lighter silver pieces, called quadrigati because the reverse featured Jupiter in a quadrigatus or four-horse chariot; the god Janus was on the obverse. The Hannibalic War brought further and more drastic changes. The war had hardly begun before the bronze again was lightened and the silver coins debased. The emergency caused the Romans to issue gold coins, minted from precious bullion accumulated in their temple treasuries. In the whole period of the Republic, gold coins were issued only in emergencies.

Perhaps because of the complaints of soldiers, whose pay in bronze coins was worth less than before, Rome now (about 213 B.C. or a little later) devised a whole new and specifically Roman coinage structure. The standard silver coin was the denarius, worth ten bronze asses, which now were officially pegged at two ounces apiece, though they often weighed less. Smaller silver coins included the victoriatus, worth three-fourths a denarius or seven and a half asses; the quinarius, worth half a denarius or five asses; and the sestertius, one-fourth the denarius or two and a half asses. As before there were fractional bronze coins also, including the semis (half an as), the triens (one-third), and the quadrans (one-fourth). The triens was marked with four dots and the quadrans with three to indicate the (hypothetical) number of ounces of value. The ratio of the number of asses to the denarius was changed in the mid–second century B.C. so that this silver coin was now worth sixteen bronze asses; the quinarius, eight; and the sestertius, four. The sestertius had, in fact, not been struck for some decades; but about this time—possibly earlier in commercial use—it became the unit of reckoning or money of account, replacing the as.

The legal weight of the denarius was 1/72 of a Roman pound, more than four grams. The coin was about the size of one of our nickels. Soon, possibly even before the end of the Hannibalic War, it was lightened by one-sixth. After that the coin remained unchanged until the time of Nero, about 265 years later. The purity of the metal was maintained at a high standard, and gradually, as the Roman empire grew, the denarius became the most familiar coin throughout the Mediterranean world, though Roman currency never quite displaced local coinages, especially in the eastern cities.

The Roman mint was placed in the temple of Juno Moneta (hence our word money), and coinage was issued by a board of three, the *monetales*, minor officials who might aspire to a higher career. In the later Republic, so many coins were issued and so much opportunity existed for placing scenes on the coins to aggrandize one's family (or get name recognition, as we would say, with the voters) that the scions of aristocratic families also sometimes served on the board.

For the historian, Roman coinage is more important than other, earlier coinages. The Roman moneyers began to put their names on the coins in the second century and then mythical or legendary scenes glorifying their families. Eventually coin designs included references to current events. Not until Julius Caesar did any Roman put his own bust on the coins. The emperors of course continued the practice. Because the coins are more precisely datable than most Greek ones, they are more valuable as historical evidence. They can be studied for their artwork, especially portraiture, for architecture, for religion, for tracing trade routes, and for many other purposes. So complex have such studies become that Roman numismatics is a separate field of research.

Investment in Large Farms

The nobles, who accumulated capital during the period of rapid expansion and in later decades primarily from lucrative positions in government—particularly as governors of provinces—maintained their prestige chiefly by investing in land. Rich Romans might obtain land in several ways. They could buy from those unfortunates who were ruined by long absences during military service (not all soldiers brought back enough spoils to pay off mortgages). Then, too, unscrupulous aristocrats could find ways to force small holders off desirable acreages. But many small holders were willing enough to sell; they could go to Rome or some other city to find work or establish themselves in small shops that would provide an easier way of making a living. Mostly, however, the land available for capitalistic development was *ager publicus*, "public domain," land that Rome had confiscated from defeated states while conquering Italy. During and after the Hannibalic War, additional large chunks of land had been seized from states that went over to Hannibal and added to the publicly owned land of Rome.

Ownership of land was prestigious, but the owners of large estates also wanted profit. This usually meant emphasizing cash crops. Such farms were organized in two different ways. A growing number were operated by slave labor. Slaves must have been available at relatively low prices at times, as, for example, when Aemilius Paullus sold the

150,000 Epirotes in 167 B.C. Such slave-manned plantations were called *latifundia* ("broad acres") in a later period. In contrast to the small subsistence farms (see pages 19–21), these farms grew the most profitable crops possible. The *latifundia* were usually stock farms or orchards of olives and vines. The second method of working large holdings, less highly organized, requiring less care and supervision but probably yielding less profit, was to lease to tenants. Many a poor farmer who lost his own tiny acreage continued the only life he knew on rented soil.

The Small Farmer

The general prosperity in Italy did not trickle down much to the small farmers. A brisk market did indeed exist for animals, wine, olive oil, and other prized gastronomic items. But the needs were met primarily by the slave plantations or by import. In any period bulky farm products could not profitably be shipped much more than thirty or forty miles except by sea. Most farmers lived relatively isolated lives before the advent of modern transportation. There was, it should be remembered, no relief from the backbreaking labor that characterized farm work until the arrival of labor-saving machinery in modern times.

In consequence of the development of the *latifundia*, the difficult life, and the alternatives available, the number of small farmers declined. Yet Rome never lacked a considerable percentage of them, for one way or another their numbers were continually renewed. The number of tenant farmers seems to have increased, for army recruiting patterns indicate plenty of able-bodied men in rural areas who did not own land but who qualified for the military draft through ownership of personal property.

Colonization and individual (*viritim*) distributions of public land helped keep up the numbers of small farmers. The motivation was military more than political, and economic least of all, but the effects were nonetheless economically beneficial in many ways. In the early second century B.C. most colonists went to the Po valley, where the land was incomparably better than in other areas of Italy. Army veterans especially were likely to be permitted to settle in these new colonies. By the end of the Republic, veterans of emergency armies almost routinely were given land even when it was necessary to confiscate it from unlucky opponents in civil wars. Despite these policies, the gradual decline in the numbers of family-owned subsistence farm operations probably continued.

Migration to the Cities

For those farmers who were willing to leave the soil and strike out in new directions the rewards were often greater. The growing cities—

Rome in particular—provided opportunity. Carpenters, masons, brick makers, metalworkers, leather workers, potters, fullers, and many other skilled and semiskilled workers were needed. Work was readily obtainable that could put more silver in a man's pocket in a month than he might see in a year on the farm. Yet real wages were low: an unskilled worker probably earned about half a denarius a day at the time of the Hannibalic War, rising to probably one denarius a day by the end of the second century B.C.[1] Used for barest necessities only, this wage would support a small family.

Slaves tended to displace free workers in the city as on the land. It was a growing practice to buy and train slaves for various tasks. By the end of the second century B.C. freemen had a more difficult time finding work for this reason and because of a general economic decline; unemployment at times plagued the city plebs. The situation at any given time depended on the level of building and other economic activity in the city, the number of men coming in from the farms looking for work, and the number of slaves being put to the tasks freemen were once given. We cannot determine with precision these and other factors affecting the economy, but we know that together they brought about an urban crisis, as we shall see.

Some lower-class Romans came to the city with a bit of capital, which may have come from the sale of their farms or from spoils and bonuses derived from military service. Many of these men went into business for themselves and rose on the economic scale. In Rome they founded hundreds of small shops. Both wholesale and retail establishments were needed for local products such as food and for more expensive imported items. A man who sold fish or hammered out pots and pans might prosper, much as the man who built a warehouse along the Tiber waterfront. In terms of creature comforts and varied activities, city dwellers might live lives vastly preferable to those of their country relatives. The latter worked much harder to wrest a living from their tiny acreages, and for their pains were drafted into the army, often to such duty as the unprofitable, long-drawn-out guerrilla wars in Spain.

A few entrepreneurs became rich. These were the men who got into commerce or the private building industry or they were publicans who bid on contracts for tax collection, army supply, or constructing roads or public buildings. Increasingly they used large gangs of free and slave labor. These rich men, though never a large group, eventually gained some political influence.

---

[1] At the time of this writing, the amount of silver in a denarius is worth about seventy cents. In Roman times, however, it had much greater purchasing power; in normal crop years, for example, a denarius would buy about a bushel of wheat, enough for thirty large loaves of bread.

Most lower-class Romans in the city were day laborers. Their existence was likely to be precarious. Their work was on a day-to-day basis and completely insecure. The very prosperity that enticed them to the city effectively masked the misery that would befall them when money no longer flowed so freely. They were hardly aware that the city was becoming far too dependent on imported food supplies. Any shortage, inevitably accompanied by hoarding and speculation, would mean high prices that hit hardest at the poor.

The Changing Social Structure

The Nobles

Some of the changes in the social classes have already been implied. It is not possible to disentangle completely for separate analysis the various strands—social, economic, political, military, intellectual—that to-

Street scene, Pompeii: bakery shop. (*Alinari/Art Resource, New York*)

gether make up the fabric of an age. It is not even desirable to attempt to examine these different facets of life in complete isolation. Our discussions, then, must necessarily overlap somewhat.

For the upper classes in Rome the middle Republic must have been an exhilarating time. As the ruling oligarchy of the Mediterranean, they could feel with some assurance that they were the most important people in the world. Their sons took their education very seriously, knowing that they in their turn would help to determine the course of things in the Mediterranean cosmos.

Wealth came to these important Romans, as we have seen, along with prestige and power. Whether governors in the provinces, officials at home, or commanders in the field, Roman aristocrats had astonishingly unrestricted authority. For a period of time within their areas of command they ruled almost as kings. It was flattery, but not simply that, when an obsequious seeker of favor called the Senate an assembly of kings. The senators found it disgusting but heady when King Prusias II of Bithynia, whose policies had offended the Romans, prostrated himself at the door of the Senate and hailed the senators as Savior Gods (Polybius 30.18).

It is well to keep in mind what a diverse group the nobility of Rome was. A small number of patrician families formed the core. Most nobles, however, by now were of plebeian families, prominent because some of their members had held the highest offices in the state. Just below the nobles were other senatorial families. Scions of these families usually attained at least the lowest rung of the cursus honorum (the fixed sequence of officeholding: quaestorship, praetorship, and consulship), and they thus became eligible for appointment to the Senate. Though not all were, strictly speaking, of the nobility, all senatorial families were yet quite prestigious. On occasion a member of such a family might rise high enough to ennoble the family. A man who was the first of his family to achieve this was called a New Man (novus homo; sometimes he was so called when he merely sought high office).

The nobility was not vastly enlarged because of the growth of Rome and of the opportunities to serve. The numbers of praetors and quaestors increased as the Empire grew, but the number of consuls remained at only two. The number of New Men in the last two centuries of the Republic was not large. In fact, the great wealth and prestige that accrued to the nobles in the middle Republic and thereafter apparently motivated them to guard their privileges ever more jealously.

Change Threatens the Political Power of the Nobles

Though conservative in many ways, the Roman nobility nevertheless embraced with enthusiasm certain economic and social changes that ultimately were to destroy the Republic they dominated. This dichotomy may be illustrated in the life and work of Cato the Censor (234–149 B.C.).

Although he was a New Man—that is, a plebeian, no member of whose family had held high office in Rome—M. Porcius Cato was one of the most influential men of his age. The best Roman orator of his day (his rough-and-ready speeches were still read two centuries later), he tried with all his might to keep Rome on a conservative track. He opposed much that was new—especially the increasing luxury of life-styles, eroding morals, and effete sophistication he saw around him. But in the oldest prose work in Latin still extant, his *De Agricultura* (*On Agriculture*), Cato in effect advocated the investment of capital in the new slave-operated plantation-like farms. He explained how to buy land and told what machinery and how many slaves were needed in raising different types of money-making crops. He seemed unaware that the growth of such farming operations would effectively undermine the foundations of the kind of traditional state he upheld.

The Roman aristocrats, then, owned much land and many slaves. But slaves did not vote. The declining number of small farmers meant also a decrease in the number of clients who supported the careers of their patrons, usually important Roman nobles, with their votes. Many of the upper classes, moreover, moved into the city, leaving the supervision of their estates to slave or freedman supervisors. Most did not gain much influence over the city plebs, though some of their number ultimately became demagogic or popular politicians who appealed to and used the urban elements.

The Roman "Republic" was really an oligarchy, for the nobles pretty well controlled the state and especially the election machinery. What seemed most important was that their sons, like themselves, should attain the highest offices. Sometime around 241 B.C.—certainly before 218—a reform made in the most important elective body, the Centuriate Assembly, gave added weight to the tribal structure over the centuries. At first glance the reform appears democratic since the centuries were ranked according to wealth and the tribes were not, and likely to reduce the power of the richer elements in the assembly. But the number of persons from the rural tribes in Rome on election day was small, and the effect of the reform actually enabled men with control of even small numbers of votes from the rural areas to exercise greater domination of the plutocratic assembly than before. The urban plebs, restricted to only four of the thirty-five tribes, was for many years unimportant.

The nobles also developed elaborate means of putting together coalitions for the elections. In the middle Republic such coalitions were formed through cooperation among families, which tended to persist. In the later Republic politicians collected obligations in any possible way—by doing favors and expecting favors in return, for example—all with a view to payoff only two or three times in one's life: at election to each of the major offices. Cicero exercised his oratorical ability to obligate men to himself, as did Caesar and many others; patronage was widely used, as in all states in all ages, and men whose protégés received appointments as officers in the army or on a governor's staff were obligated to support their benefactors. It was not that the Romans never supported candidates on principle or because of their programs, but the realities of political organization usually put such considerations in second or third place. In fact, our evidence indicates that it was rare for a program of any sort to play a part in a given election.

Toward the end of the Republic the political organizers began to appeal not just to the important bigwigs who could indeed still influence the vote strongly, but to the lower classes whose support grew more and more important. The urban plebeians never, perhaps, determined an important election by themselves, but by the end of the Republic they could greatly influence the passage of laws in the Tribal or the Plebeian Assembly, which had great political implications. Indeed Cicero suggests (in his speech *For Sestius* 109) that those in charge of assemblies sometimes transferred voters from the city plebs to the rural tribes in order to produce a quorum or influence the outcome of a particular vote.

The Equestrian Class

As a distinct group the *equester ordo*, "equestrian order," as it was termed in the later Republic, only gradually took shape. The *equites* were originally the cavalry in the army; in the Centuriate Assembly they were assigned to the top class. In the assembly, these eighteen centuries included men retired from the cavalry who no longer "held a public horse." In the earliest age the only men rich enough to be placed in this group were the nobles, but as time went on some plebeians whose property put them into the first census class of course voted with the first class in the assembly, and some served in the cavalry, but they did not necessarily aspire to a political career as sons of nobles usually did.

The rise of a middle group of men like these, who were rich but neither noble nor particularly political, is an important phenomenon of the middle Republic. These were the men described earlier in the chapter, who often owned land but also built ships, contracted roads and buildings, and engaged in trade, banking, moneylending, and tax collecting. By the last century of the Republic, the most important equestrians were those publicans who bid on the largest government contracts of various sorts, as for the collection of certain taxes.

The significant role of the publicans even as early as the end of the third century is illustrated in a story from Livy (25.3.9–11) of the activity of one of their number in 213 B.C., during the Second Punic War. Those men who owned ships and used them to supply the armies were naturally fearful of loss. The state therefore in effect agreed to insure each owner against loss either from enemy activity or storm. One unscrupulous publican, Marcus Postumius, bought up old ships, filled them with junk, sank them out at sea, then claimed to have had valuable cargo aboard, and so collected an inflated value from the state. The scandal was brought before the Senate, but nothing was done for a time. The historian says that the Senate did not want to antagonize the publicans as a class. Presumably they were indispensable in the war effort. Yet the man was prosecuted the following year, and Livy may have been mistaken on the reasons for the delay.

Strictly speaking, nobles in the census were equestrians, but as a group the equestrian order excluded the nobles. The order was legally defined only in the last century of the Republic by a series of laws, such as the one carried by Gaius Gracchus, tribune of the plebs in 123 and 122 B.C., which forbade senatorial families from serving on the juries of the permanent courts. It was in this way that the nonsenatorial equestrian families gradually came to constitute a distinct order or class. Most of these equestrians shared the interests of the senatorial families, though the issue of the degree of political influence to be permitted to the nonsenatorial equestrian through the control of the courts was long a touchy one. These equestrians for the most part did not want to displace the nobles, but they did want influence in matters important to them.

So far we have discussed only equestrians who were businessmen, bankers, and the like. There was another quite important component of this group: men from families rich enough to be included in the first class of the census, but landholders and not businessmen. In fact, most equestrians must have belonged to such families. Many of them were politically important in their local municipalities. The family of Cicero typifies this group well. His father was a noted man in his own town, Arpinum, about seventy miles east of Rome. He had connections with the top political figures in the capital, and doubtless as a politically minded rural citizen of importance delivered a good many votes to his Roman friends on election day. Yet neither he nor any of his family held office in Rome until Cicero himself, who was thus a New Man.

These country gentry, to use a British term, perhaps acquiesced in the order of things; they had some status at Rome plus local prestige. A few of them held offices in Rome, the less important ones, elective and appointive. Many of these equestrians must have wished that it was easier to break into the closed circle of oligarchs who controlled the state. Our sources say little about them, and modern historians have too often ignored them. Many have mistakenly concluded that the middle class (to use a term subject to misinterpretation) at Rome consisted only of businessmen, publicans, and the like. But it is certain that the rural equestrians were quite numerous and that they helped to stabilize the state. In the Empire they would become more important than ever before.

The Lower Classes

The old mainstay of the state was the class of small farmers. Although they continued to decline throughout the Republic despite the extensive colonization and individual land distribution programs, they remained important in numbers. They served as another stabilizing component of society despite their hard life on the farms and the burden of the military draft. Ordinarily they were important politically only as clients of the great. The (probably) increasing number of tenant farmers shared the position and fate of the small holders except that the economic position of tenants was perhaps worse.

Worst of all in the countryside was the condition of farm laborers. Possibly there were fewer than before, since opportunity for better things in the city beckoned. However, we read in Cato's *De Agricultura* of gangs of men—free laborers under contract to some single agent, it appears—who moved about the countryside during the various harvest periods to help out during these busy days. It would have been uneconomical for slaveholders to purchase and house enough slaves for such seasonal activities as picking and pressing olives. These gangs of laborers, the migrant workers of antiquity, must often have lived in rather miserable circumstances as compared even to those of the tenant farmers, who at least had their own houses and gardens. Thus the farm laborers' lot was often inferior to that of slaves.

Growing in influence on Rome's future was that important segment of the lower class, the urban plebs. This increasingly large group of wage laborers did well enough when Rome bustled and times were prosperous, even with their slum housing and poor diet. The excitement of the city with its games, theater, races, religious festivals, and the like, compensated in part for the inadequacies of house and table. Most of these plebeians did not wish to leave the city for hard work on the farms. They wanted a better life in the city. They could get it only by demanding more of the state. Once they learned this lesson they tended to give their support—usually expressed negatively, through the threat of violence—to whatever leaders promised them most.

The Army in the Early to Middle Republic: Social Aspects

Throughout history, the military establishment of a state normally reflects its society. That is, the social class that dominates the government (including its priesthoods) usually controls the army as well, and the classes below are assigned roles in the state and the military that correspond to their social and economic status. Such a society may not achieve what we in the modern world call social justice, but it is likely to be stable. Indeed, any large deviation—any technical change, for example, that brings into the army many who belong to the lower socioeconomic strata of a state—may bring an increase in the influence of these previously unimportant persons and thus tend to destabilize the state. Or if a military draft places an unfair burden on one particular group—usually of the lower class—the ensuing reaction may even more acutely destabilize society and the state.

An example of the consequence of a technical change was mentioned earlier. Changes in arms and tactics increased the need for infantry, which in turn brought about the expulsion of the last of Rome's kings. The king (or his predecessor) had awarded full citizenship to the new soldiers, strengthening his position at the expense of that of the patricians, who rebelled and established the Republic. Prior to that time, the army probably consisted primarily of upper-class cavalry.

The new Republic still needed those infantry soldiers, however, and they could not be excluded from participation in the assemblies. So limits were set: only those citizens who held property could serve in the army, in an order determined by the value of their holdings. As we have seen, this order of things carried over to the important Assembly of the Centuries, where the citizens were also ranked by census class, so that the higher the social and economic status of an individual, the more important his vote.

By the end of the Struggle of the Orders, around the beginning of the third century B.C., a nice balance had been achieved. Patrician and plebeian nobles held the highest political and religious offices, dominated the assemblies, and commanded the armies. Freemen who possessed some property served in the army as infantry soldiers and lower-level officers, according to their census class, and their votes were correspondingly important in the assemblies. (It must not be thought that only the rich served: the property qualification in the historical period was never very high.) Those least important in society, who had no property at all, did not serve in the army except in extreme emergencies. They could vote, at least theoretically, but their votes accounted for little; no patron supported them as clients, and they usually did not bother to attend the assemblies.

So important was the army to the ruling classes that a ten-year period of service was a requirement for holding the higher offices in Rome. Such service aimed to fill two functions: it gave young nobles time to mature, and since the top Roman officers were the army commanders, it also gave them a degree of military expertise that would help them in political office.

Long periods of war, especially the Punic Wars and those in the eastern Mediterranean, demanded large numbers of infantry soldiers and long periods of service—as much as sixteen years. Moreover, once Rome began to acquire provinces, men were needed for what amounted to standing armies. Romans were frequently away from their homes for several years. This burden weighed especially heavily on small farmers, who needed to be home at work on their land. Unless a wife and children could keep the farm going in the absence of the father, disaster might soon follow. Roman soldiers were paid, but not well, though in successful campaigns they might benefit from spoils and distributions on discharge.

More men were needed when the number of small farmers eligible for military service was falling. To meet the need, property requirements for military service were lowered during and after the Second Punic War, so that by the late second century B.C. the property qualification was only a fraction of what it had been a century earlier, taking into account the inflation that came with the influx of money. Even then it was difficult at times to fill the draft quotas. The urban plebeians were numerous, and some of them must have had enough property to qualify for army service. But Roman generals tended to feel that they were soft, not hardy like the rural population, and would not make good soldiers; it appears that few if any were drafted.

The military draft thus began to bear heavily on a single category of the lower class, the small, subsistence farmers as well as tenant farmers, who were burdened in relation both to their numbers and to their ability to endure the economic hardships that often accompanied army service, especially in such areas as Spain, which produced little in the way of spoils. The army became a potential source of instability because it no longer corresponded well to the social structure; those who had little property and no political power bore a disproportionate responsibility for military service. The balance that characterized the middle Republic shifted.

The trend continued. In the later Republic, as we shall see, the military demands of the growing empire produced changes in the army that further skewed its structure so that it no longer reflected society at large, resulting in political instability and finally civil wars and the end of the Republic.

Women in the Second Century B.C.

One notable area of change in Roman society affected the role of women. Roman matrons from the earliest times possessed greater personal freedom than those of Greece or the Near East. As in ancient Sparta, some women, chiefly widows, were wealthy, as our sources for the time of the Hannibalic War indicate. Yet upper-class women were expected to be under the control (*manus*) of some man: father, husband, or guardian.

By current standards women married at an early age. Custom and law allowed for three types of marriage. *Confarreatio*, apparently only for patricians, was a quite formal affair that put the bride immediately under the *manus* of her husband. It is interesting that the chief priests or flamens of Jupiter, Mars, and Quirinus were chosen from the patrician sons of such marriages. *Coemptio*—a legal term not confined to marriage—also delivered the wife into the control of her husband or guardian. A third sort of arrangement called *usus*, which was perhaps similar to our practice of common-law marriage, did not put the wife under her husband's control unless she lived with him for a full year. To retain this status, such a wife would live away from her spouse at least three days each year. Though women married in this way did not depend on their husbands financially, they were still under the nominal control of their fathers (technically, the *paterfamilias*) or guardians. In effect, however, this institution often made them financially independent persons.

Brides came to their husbands with dowries, and husbands usually had the use of it. If the couple divorced (which was rare until the middle Republic and not common until still later), the wife (or her father) got the dowry back; a part might be retained for children to inherit, and if adultery was involved, another fraction was retained by the husband. In early Rome, a double standard applied in cases of adultery. Husbands could kill their wives—and the wives' male partners, if caught in the house—for adultery, but wives could not prosecute their husbands for the offense. Of course, if another husband were involved, he could prosecute. Actual executions for adultery seem to have been rare. In the middle Republic and after, divorce was the usual consequence of adultery, but we know of husbands who did not even divorce wives who were adultresses.

Roman women did not have the legal right to participate in government; they did not vote and could not hold office. Yet many women had considerable influence—more in the time of the Empire than the Republic, but there were notable women then, too. Cornelia, for example (women were called by their *gens* names), the daughter of the elder Scipio Africanus, mother-in-law of the younger Scipio, wife of an important statesman, and mother of the Gracchi (see Chapter 6), was a respected and influential person. She brought up her children herself after her husband died, and she maintained a sort of intellectual salon in her home. Incidentally, she also turned down a marriage proposal from the king of Egypt.

An episodic struggle for further liberation began in the second century B.C., soon after the Second Punic War. During the war a law, the Oppian Law was passed, which restricted women in several ways: they could not possess more than half an ounce of gold, they could not wear varicolored dresses (especially purple and gold), and they could not ride about the city in carriages alone. Probably the hardships and economic stresses accompanying that difficult conflict explain why the law was passed. In 195, several years after the war had ended, two tribunes proposed to repeal the law. Cato and other conservatives strenuously opposed the repeal. Women of course favored it. They flocked to the Forum, lobbied vigorously, and even virtually picketed the Senate. Cato, forcing his way to the Senate through a throng of women, called their protest a sedition; but the pressure tactics succeeded, and the restrictions were eliminated.

In 169 the Voconian Law restricted the rights of women in matters of inheritance, limiting the amounts they could receive. The law is itself evidence that women had been inheriting substantial amounts. Most of what we know about how this law worked is that women found numerous ingenious ways of getting around it. Our sources of the next century or so tell us of several women who were themselves full heirs and able to pass on their property through wills to whatever heirs they chose.

Roman women thus grew increasingly free of stifling controls, social and legal. Probably the new affluence made it possible for upper-class women to move about more freely and to control their own affairs. Household slaves, though requiring supervision, eliminated domestic duties for such women. What of lower-class women? We do not know. But probably many of them became freer as well.

Religious Innovation

In most times and places religion has been important, especially as a unifying (or divisive) factor within states. At Rome, religion changed as the city's dominions expanded in the middle and late Republic. The reasons were various: not only did Roman citizens come into contact with new concepts and new cults, but they also soon discovered that the traders and immigrants, even the slaves, who swelled the population of the emerging world capital brought new religions and beliefs along with them.

In the period when Hannibal's astounding victories terrorized Rome, anxious citizens naturally sought new ways of propitiating the gods. Women were said to have swept temple pavements with their hair. New gods and strange practices were introduced. Though Rome was relatively tolerant of religious innovation, the magistrates could be quite intolerant when they felt the security of the state was at stake. About 210 B.C. a praetor, on instructions from the Senate, forbade some of the more outlandish observances and called for books to be brought in, apparently for burning.

Official changes occurred as well, but in a more traditional way. New games were established for Apollo (the *Ludi Apollinares*) and other games were set up or lengthened. The decemvirs on request examined

the Sibylline Books and interpreted a passage to mean that success in
the war would follow if Cybele, the Magna Mater ("Great Mother"), were
brought from Pessinus in Asia Minor to Rome. Messengers were sent,
and in 204 B.C. a meteorite symbolizing this goddess was received in
Rome by representatives of two of the aristocratic families, Claudia
Quinta, a vestal virgin, and Scipio Nasica, named by the Senate as a
delegate of the young men. In a few years a temple to Cybele was
completed within the sacred boundaries of the city, on the Palatine Hill,
where its remains still indicate the site. However, repelled by the gyra-
tions and mouthings of her emasculated priests in their noisy processions, the Senate forbade any Roman citizen to serve as a priest to
Cybele.

The famous investigation of the Bacchanalian cult displayed some
Romans' fear of religious change. Cato was probably a leader in this
inquisition and suppression. The affair broke out in 186 B.C. Romans
were seized with panic on hearing that Bacchanalian rites were being
held in and near Rome and elsewhere in Italy, and that young Romans
were being initiated into the cult. Roman officials believed that not only
was it shot through with immorality, but it even constituted a serious
conspiracy against the state. The celebrants were doubtless mostly from

Denarii of the first century B.C., perhaps issued in connection with the great
festival in April to the goddess Cybele, shown left with her turreted crown,
and right, in her chariot drawn by lions. At Rome, the goddess was
especially associated with the nobility.

states that had supported Hannibal in the recent war, a circumstance that may have affected the Romans' attitudes. The consul, Spurius Postumius Albinus, received certain information that he reported to the Senate. According to Livy (39.19) the consul said that "nothing is more deceptive in appearance than a false religion" and reminded the senators of past book burnings and suppression of exotic rites. The Senate responded with a decree (which survives in an inscription found in southern Italy, the oldest lengthy Latin one extant) severely restricting the rites, though not banning them entirely. The decree, probably the first one that was so sweeping, led to an investigation throughout all Italy, and eventually Sardinia and Sicily as well. Thousands were reported executed, presumably for conspiracy. The whole affair remains a bit mysterious and can only be ascribed to hysteria. At about the same time, there was a "conspiracy" of shepherds along with suspicions of widespread poisonings of husbands by wives. In any event, the importation of strange religions was inhibited for a time. Not until the first century B.C. did the flood tide of religious change rise.

Moral Decline

All the ancient writers agree that Roman morals deteriorated in the last two centuries of the pre-Christian era. They attribute the decline to foreign influence and to the influx of wealth, disagreeing only as to the time when it began to accelerate noticeably. Livy puts the onset of Roman moral decay in the period of the war against Antiochus of Syria and immediately following. Polybius places it in the period after the war against Perseus of Macedonia. Sallust thought the real decay came with the destruction of that salutary enemy, Carthage. Perhaps some sources exaggerate the deterioration, but change there certainly was.

It was Cato who led the attack on declining morals and its cause, the new luxury. As censor in 184 B.C. (when the investigations into the Bacchanalian affair were still going on), Cato assessed luxurious items at ten times their real value, especially young slaves purchased at high prices, presumably for their sex appeal. He dropped the brother of the great Scipio from the roll of the cavalry (the Scipios were political opponents) and expelled from the Senate the brother of Flamininus, the victor at Cynoscephalae, for a reported moral lapse.

Cato was not alone in his concern; several of the censors in the first half of the second century B.C. were as severe as he in their strictures on bad morals. As late as 125 B.C. the censors were still trying to stem the tide of growing luxury. In that year one of the augurs was reprimanded for renting a house for 1,500 denarii annually—about enough to hire five laborers for a year.

Cato and the Philosophers

Cato blamed much of the lowered moral tone of society on Greek influence. The importation of Greek literature, he said, would ruin the nation. As for Greek philosophers, he felt they taught an amoral skepticism that would erode Roman virtue. An interesting incident of 181 B.C. illustrates his view. The praetor urbanus, Q. Petilius, a political ally of Cato, reported to the Senate that a clerk of his had dug up on the Janiculum (a hill just across the Tiber from the city) a tomb containing two stone chests. One had once contained the body of Numa Pompilius, traditionally the second of the kings of Rome; the other held linen books preserved in wax, in excellent condition, on teachings of the Pythagorean philosophy. The praetor declared that the books were subversive of religion and recommended that they be burned. A senatorial decree so ordered and Petilius consigned the books to the flames in the Forum, curiously as a kind of offering to the gods, the fire being brought by religious attendants called *victimarii*.

The whole story must have been trumped up. Even the Romans—at least in a slightly later period—knew that Numa had died long before the time of Pythagoras. This public holocaust in solemn sacrifice appears to have been a stern warning to Romans who were espousing Pythagorean views—for example, the poet and playwright Q. Ennius (239–169 B.C.), one of whose extant poems expresses Pythagorean ideas such as that of the transmigration of souls. A more personal political twist might also have been involved. Cato had originally brought Ennius, who was from south Italy, to Rome. In 184, in Cato's censorship, Ennius had been made a Roman citizen, but in more recent years he had left Cato to become a client of the Scipios, Cato's political enemies.

Cato and other conservatives continued the attack on Greek philosophy. In 173 some Epicureans were banished from Rome. In 161 all philosophers and rhetoricians were similarly banished by decree of the Senate. (Such decrees were never enforced for long.) In 155–154 three eminent Greek philosophers, including Carneades, leader of the Academy, visited Rome on an embassy. Carneades gave two well-attended lectures on justice. The first was of the sort that might warm the cockles of a conservative's heart. Justice was that which was in accord with old-established law and custom—the Roman *mos maiorum*. But in the second lecture this skeptic demonstrated why it was that everything he had previously argued so persuasively could not possibly be right. Cato was horrified at this frivolity. He saw to it that the three philosophers completed their business and were hustled out of town.

Cato was not simply an ignorant country bumpkin. He knew Greek, and even—with misgivings, to be sure—sent his son off to study at Athens. His fears of foreign influence were based on moral principle rather than ignorance.

The Younger Scipio and the Philhellenes

Some Romans were capable of admiring the great Greek teachers and writers for their intellectual achievements without picking up the penchant of other Greeks for luxury and sensual gratification. Of these our best example is P. Cornelius Scipio Aemilianus, who was, as we have seen, the son of L. Aemilius Paullus, victor of Pydna, and was adopted by the son of the elder Scipio. The younger Scipio's home became an intellectual center at Rome, partly, no doubt, because Paullus had brought back Perseus' library, which must have been the best in the city. Some writers have uncritically assigned every contemporary Roman intellectual to the Scipionic circle. Certainly several Greek and Roman intellectuals met there at times.

The group included Polybius, who was brought back from Greece as a hostage in 167 B.C. and who taught Aemilianus and became his firm friend. The extant text of Polybius' history, our best source of information on the period from the Second Punic War to his own time, was highly complimentary to the Romans. He much admired Rome's constitution, which he saw as a mixed one, with elements of monarchy, aristocracy, and democracy. He also warned that constitutions change, even stable ones like the Romans'. They could expect, he suggested, that the democratic element would demand more than its share of power, leading to instability and decline.

Another Greek who stayed in Aemilianus' house for several years was Panaetius of Rhodes, a Stoic philosopher. Panaetius popularized Stoicism among the Roman upper classes, emphasizing the pragmatic aspects of the philosophy, which fit in well with what the Romans already believed: the value of service to the state, personal virtue, and endurance in the face of misfortune. Beliefs in the fatherhood of God, the brotherhood of man, and in particular the rather elaborate cosmogony put forward by some Stoic teachers were less important to the Romans. From this time on, there were always a few prominent Romans who espoused the Stoic philosophy.

Roman members of the Scipionic circle were the younger Scipio's friend Laelius, who became a Stoic; Terence, a playwright, who along with Plautus popularized the Greek style of comedy; and Lucilius, the first important Roman satirist. Obviously Scipio Aemilianus did not see eye-to-eye with Cato as to the dangers of Greek influence. Yet he believed as strongly as did Cato in maintaining the old virtues, and in fact, Cato approved of the much younger Aemilianus.

The Roman Theater

It is rather surprising that we do not hear of a vigorous attack by Cato on the developing theater. The Romans used as models for their drama the

Greek plays of their own and an earlier day. The Greek "new comedy" was often filled with dissolute characters portrayed in compromising situations. But Roman playwrights were cautious, making sure that all immoral characters and suggestive plotters were Greek rather than Roman. No Roman matron could possibly be presented as an unfaithful wife or high-class prostitute, as some of the women in these plays were.

The first Roman production of a play took place before Cato's time, in 240. It was written by Livius Andronicus, who had been brought to Rome as a captive from Tarentum about 272. Rome had seen earlier stage productions, perhaps imported from Etruria, but not true plays with plot and theme. Andronicus' plays were presented as part of one of the great games, the Ludi Romani. There was thus a religious connection (as in earlier Greek drama), which tended to endure: the plays were normally parts of religious festivals. Andronicus not only adapted Greek plays for the Roman stage, but he also wrote poetry long and short and, on at least one occasion, a hymn, sung through the streets of Rome as part of a religious exercise. None of his works survive. A notable successor was Gnaeus Naevius, who was a few years younger; he was Roman or at least Italian, possibly from Campania. Though he too wrote on themes of Greek legend, we are told that he satirized important Roman politicians by name and was exiled for his pains. He wrote an epic poem, too, a historical chronicle in verse of the First Punic War, the *Bellum Poenicum*. Ennius was the next important playwright. Like Naevius, Ennius also wrote poetic history. His *Annales*, composed in Greek hexameters, more polished than Naevius' rough rhythms, was completed in the 170s B.C., late in his life, and apparently encompassed all of Roman history.

Plautus

The only Latin comedies to survive are those of Plautus (ca. 254–184 B.C.) and Terence (ca. 190–159 B.C.). By their time—after the Hannibalic War—plays were routinely presented at several of the major state festivals: the *Ludi Megalenses* (to the goddess Cybele) in April, the *Ludi Apollinares* in July, the *Ludi Romani* in September, and the *Ludi Plebeii* in November. The number of days devoted to theater in these festivals gradually increased. No permanent theater was built until the time of Pompey the Great, however, in 55 B.C. The Romans made do with temporary wooden structures built for each occasion; there were no seats even until late in the second century. In 154 B.C. one of the censors started construction of a stone theater, but he was forbidden to complete it. Perhaps the objections were rooted in religious scruple.

Most surviving Roman plays are comedies—which tells us something of the later Roman taste. Twenty of these are by Plautus. Based on models of the Greek New Comedy, they are boisterous, fun-filled, sometimes crude or obscene. They had to be fast-paced to appeal to Romans who had, perhaps, just been to the chariot races. It is not surprising that Plautus' plays seem to have had simpler plots and broader humor than those of his Greek predecessors. His plays take place primarily in Greece: the loose women, impudent slaves, and fumbling masters could neither with propriety nor accuracy be depicted as Roman.

Perhaps as a concession to the Roman *gravitas*, Plautus produced a couple of serious comedies. In the prologue to *Captivi* (*The Captives*), the playwright had the actor say,

> This play is not composed in the hackneyed style . . . nor are there in it any ribald lines unfit for utterance: here is neither the perjured procurer nor the artful courtesan, nor yet the braggart captain.[2]

And in the final lines at the close,

> Spectators, this play is founded on chaste manners. No wenching is there in this, and no intriguing, no exposure of a child, no cheating out of money; and no young man in love here makes his mistress free without his father's knowledge. The poets find but few comedies of this kind [*that is, in the Greek sources*], *where good men might become better.*

One wonders how the Roman audience received the play; *gravitas* notwithstanding, Roman audiences enjoyed the bawdier plays.

The sexual double standard is clear in the plays. In the *Menaechmi* (*The Twin Brothers*), an Old Man tells his daughter, a Wife:

> How often have I told you to be compliant to your husband? Don't be watching what he does, where he goes, or what he's about.

The Wife replies:

> But he's in love with a courtesan here close by.

The Old Man counsels the blind eye, and says:

> Do you want your husband to be your servant? You might as well . . . bid him sit among the female servants and card wool. . . . Since he keeps you provided for and well clothed, . . . 'tis better, madam, to entertain kindly feelings.

Actually, in this instance the affair is that of the unknown twin rather than of the husband, but that fact was hardly intended to modify the view expressed.

It is often difficult to tell whether any particular passage significant for social mores applied to Romans as it did to the Greeks for whom the

---

[2] All translations from Plautus are those of Henry T. Riley, in *The Bohn Classical Library* (London, 1852), with modifications.

plays were first written. One passage in the *Aulularia* (*The Concealed Treasure*) on marriage between a rich and a poor family probably reflects Roman as much as Greek social reality. The poor man, Euclio, says:

> Megadorus, you are a wealthy man of rank; I am the poorest of the poor; now, if I should give my daughter in marriage to you, it suggests to my mind that you are the ox, and that I am the ass; when I'm yoked to you, and not able to bear the burden equally, I, the ass, must lie down in the mire; you, the ox, would regard me no more than if I had never been born; and I should both find you unjust, and my own class would laugh at me.

A skit in the *Epidicus* (*The Fortunate Discovery*), satirizing women's new clothing styles, may have applied in Rome as in Greece; at least we know that there had been criticism in Rome during the Second Punic War of the dresses women were wearing. Epidicus says:

> Many women go through the streets decked out with farms upon them. . . . [W]hat new names every year these women are finding for their clothing—the thin tunic, the thick tunic, fulled linen cloth, chemises, bordered shifts, the marigold- or saffron-colored dress, the under-petticoat or else the light vermilion dress, the hood, the royal or the foreign robe, the wave pattern or the feather pattern, the wax- or the apple-tint.

We do not have the original plays in Greek to compare with the Latin versions. But certain lines were definitely added for Roman audiences. At the end of the first act of the *Cistellaria* (*The Casket*), presented during the Hannibalic War, a character says,

> Farewell, and conquer by inborn valor, as you have done before; defend your allies, both ancient ones and new; increase resources by your righteous laws; destroy your foes; laud and laurels gather; that, conquered by you, the Poeni [*Carthaginians*] may suffer the penalty.

Praise in some plays for the old ways may well represent concessions to the gravity of the Romans (or, at least, the ruling class) also. In the *Trinummus* (*Three Pieces of Money*), an older character advises his son not to hold any converse with profligate men, either in the streets or in the Forum.

> I know this age, what its manners are. The bad man wishes the good man to be bad, that he may be like himself. The wicked, the rapacious, the covetous, and the envious disorder and confound the morals of the age. Live after my fashion, according to the ancient manners.

Later in the play, another character bemoans the new situation ethics:

> Nowadays, men pay no attention to what is proper, only to what is agreeable. Ambition now is sanctioned by usage, and is free from the

laws. The public manners now have got the laws in their power; to them they are more submissive than are parents to their children!

Cato might have said that himself.

Terence

Terence wrote six plays, all extant. Composed two to three decades later than those of Plautus, they show a greater sophistication. The language is more polished, the plots and action less crude. A serious theme could govern a whole play: in the *Adelphi* (*The Brothers*), Terence depicted two sons of a farmer brought up one by the father and the other by his brother. The farmer and his brother employed vastly different methods. The farmer brought up his son strictly, while the brother, in an urban environment, brought up the other son permissively. The latter turned out to be a fine fellow, while the son brought up under a strict regimen turned out a scoundrel. Micio, the city parent, presents the theme in the prologue:

> My system, my theory, is this: he who does his duty under the lash of punishment has no dread except in the thought of detection; if he thinks he won't be found out, back he goes to his natural bent. When you link a son to you by kindness, there is sincerity in all his acts, he sets himself to make a return, and will be the same behind your back as to your face.[3]

Here perhaps one may see the influence of the Greek friends of the younger Scipio. The other plays of Terence were much less relevant to anything Roman, and the historian finds little in them to shed light on contemporary Roman society.

Terence had his difficulties with his audiences. His plays had not the wide appeal of those of Plautus. In the introduction to *Hecyra* (*The Mother-in-Law*), we learn that at the first presentation a simultaneous performance of a rope dancer and rumors of a gladiatorial contest elsewhere caused most of his audience to leave, so that the performance was disrupted. Terence was criticized on a higher level because of the way he combined plots and borrowed characters from the Greek originals.

Tragedies were also presented at the great games, about as many as comedies, but none are extant from the period of the Republic. Pacuvius (ca. 220–130 B.C.) was probably the best of the tragedians; Cicero thought so. The orator also admired his successor, Accius (ca. 170–86 B.C.), who lived long enough for Cicero to have had conversations

---

[3] Terence *Adelphi*. Translation of John Sargeaunt, Loeb Classical Library (New York: 1925).

with him. Cicero's interest illustrates what is probably true—that Roman intellectuals had a greater interest in tragedy than lower-class plebeians.

Lucilius

The Scipionic circle included Rome's first great satirist, G. Lucilius (ca. 180–103 B.C.). Satire was a genre of literature in which the Romans showed some inventiveness and independence from Greek sources. The fragments we have of Lucilius's work, around thirteen hundred lines, show that he was a political partisan of the Scipionians and that he wrote with sharp, incisive, and cutting wit. His influence extended throughout Roman literary history: Horace and Martial, for example, were influenced by him.

A Developing System of Law

The growth of Rome, the broadening experience of her magistrates, and increasing involvement with ever more diverse peoples brought a need for an expanded and more flexible law system. Change does not come easy: the first writing down of the law, in the XII Tables, had come only with struggle. Even after that the priests jealously guarded the operation of the courts. Actions had to be phrased precisely, and only they knew the wording. The very knowledge of the days on which court could be held was kept secret until late in the fourth century.

Accretions to the general body of law came in several ways: by action of the assembly, which passed *leges*; by action of magistrates, who had considerable powers both to issue edicts within their spheres and to determine what was the law; by Senate decree, which often had the force of law; and by interpretation, not only by magistrates, but also by men learned in the law, called jurisconsults. The son of Cato the Censor was one such jurisconsult; another was the consul of 133 B.C., P. Mucius Scaevola, the earliest jurist whose opinions were quoted in the Digest of the famed Justinian Code of 534 A.D.

The praetor was in general charge of the court system. About 242 B.C. the second praetorship was established; there were now a *praetor urbanus*, who tried cases of the *ius civile*, which technically applied only to Roman citizens; and the *praetor peregrinus*, who dealt with cases involving foreigners. The latter official could function with considerable latitude, and many innovations arose as the praetors dealt with men accustomed to the legal systems of Greece and the Hellenistic east. The Romans had a term for law based on widely used principles—*ius gentium*, the law of nations. By the first century B.C. and under Stoic influence there was talk, too, of the *ius naturalis*, natural law.

A most important procedural change was the substitution of a new formulary system for the old system of rigidly phrased actions. This change probably came gradually, but about the middle of the second century B.C. it was specifically legalized by a law, the Lex Aebutia. After this time the praetors conducted preliminary hearings and then sent to the judges they appointed a summary of the case and the points to be decided, stated as a formula. This system was simpler. The formulas were drawn up on principles of the law, to be sure, but the praetor could revise them or draw up new ones to fit the specific cases.

Provincial governors, like the praetors in Rome, drew up edicts, usually based in considerable part on local law. Large numbers of Roman magistrates thus gained experience in the laws of other peoples and in turn influenced legal development in Rome. Roman willingness to learn from others and to adapt foreign ways to the needs of empire was indeed, as the Romans themselves said, part of the Roman genius.

Changes in the Political System

It is sometimes suggested that the failure of the Roman oligarchy to adapt to the governance of an empire was the major reason for the decline and collapse into civil war of the Roman Republic. There is a large element of truth in this. But the degree to which Roman political institutions changed to meet the new situation is often understated or misstated.

The Roman propensity to give great power to magistrates was at once the blessing and the curse of the government under the Republic. Men of ability had the authority they needed to solve the problems they encountered. Unfortunately, there was also latitude for shady dealings. By law, the Lex Calpurnia of 149 B.C., a permanent court was set up that made it possible for provincials (if they could get a prominent Roman to take their case as their patron) to sue for recovery of money or property extorted from their citizens. But the jurors were drawn from a panel of senators, who were disinclined to ruin the career and family of an accused fellow senator, and the procedure did little to check an increasing number of rapacious or unjust governors.

The number of governors of course grew with the increasing number of provinces. The number of praetors was increased by two after each of the first two Punic Wars so that there would be enough praetors, propraetors, and proconsuls for the governorships. By the mid–second century four of the six praetors did not serve in Rome at all but went directly to provinces as governors. The other two normally went off to govern provinces as propraetors after their year in Rome. Consuls, too, governed provinces either in the years of their consulate or afterward as proconsuls. The number of quaestors was increased to allow one for each governor and two to serve in the city.

Much political procedure in Rome was conducted on a personal basis. In that fashion, the government of Rome was to some degree responsive to the needs of Latins, Italians, and provincials. Important Romans were patrons of cities, provinces, and even allied kingdoms in a kind of extension of the old patron-client system into provincial government and diplomacy. The patron at Rome looked out for his clients' interests in the Senate. To be sure the system had its disadvantages; it was haphazard, and there were no checks. But on the whole it worked. Patrons were consulted on important matters in which they were interested, and the needs of Rome's provincial and allied cities were brought to the attention of the Roman oligarchy, which was thus less isolated and more responsive than is often believed.

Obviously the government of the Republic did not change enough. The trouble lay primarily in the grasping and self-centered actions of too many Romans of all ranks, from nobles to urban plebs, who began to struggle for the spoils of empire. At the last, even civil war was not thought too great a sacrifice in the struggle for what men considered their fair share. Foremost among the avaricious politicians who must bear primary responsibility for the drift into civil conflict were many members of the closed and narrow oligarchy who jealously guarded their circle against intruders. Not enough competent New Men from the lower ranks of senatorial families were permitted to join that close circle. Not enough attention was paid to the welfare of the Roman lower classes, from the small farmers on whose shoulders lay the increasingly crushing burden of military service to the urban plebs who were citizens of the state that ruled the world and yet had little to show for it. Even less attention was given to the plight of certain provincials. Throughout the civil war they could only yield to whichever general was in control of the local situation, wait for peace, and hope for a better tomorrow.

6 From the Gracchi to the "First Triumvirate," 133–60 B.C.

THE CHANGES OCCURRING in the middle Republic put numerous pressures on the Roman state and society. The worst strain originated from the unwieldy business of governing the many millions of persons living in the Roman provinces, from Spain to Macedonia. During the last century of the Republic, Rome's dominions would enlarge even more, to extend across Gaul in the west and Asia Minor and Syria in the east. Despite enormous difficulties the Roman oligarchy, in a sort of informal and personal way, was more responsive to the needs of provincials than is sometimes believed. Yet their responses were inadequate, primarily because the oligarchs so jealously guarded their monopoly of office, power, prestige, and wealth that it became their chief preoccupation. Only a few gave much attention to the needs of empire, while most looked to their own advantage with single-minded zeal.

Since the political struggle within the oligarchy determined the course of events not only for Rome and Italy but for the provinces as well, the historian's attention both in antiquity and in modern times has been drawn to a rather narrow focus on that struggle, mostly in Rome itself. Our discussion here emphasizes social and economic aspects of the struggle.

Long-Range Rural Problems and Short-Term Urban Crisis

The most unhealthy segment of Roman society, as we have seen, was the class of small farmers. This class also formed the backbone of the state; the problem was, then, most serious. The dwindling numbers of small holders and their declining prosperity (at least in relative terms) meant trouble. Since only men of at least some property were eligible for service in the army, this rural group—which was still large—suffered under unreasonable demands for army service. Progressive lowering of the property requirement and even drafting quite young men did not solve the problem. The *latifundia*, slave-operated plantations, which in part replaced the small farms, did not provide men for the army, nor did they produce the staple foods needed for the populace; other crops were more profitable. Rome and possibly even other Italian cities became dependent on grain supplies brought in from outside, partly because of the transportation system. Bulky items could not be transported far by land and compete with similar products brought in by cheaper sea transport, even from a long distance.

Though the most basic problems related to rural affairs and the army, it was a temporary urban crisis that sparked action by a young Roman politician, Tiberius Sempronius Gracchus, tribune of the plebs in 133 B.C. The crisis, with economic recession and soaring food prices, had several causes, one of which was a long-continued influx of persons into Rome, many of them small farmers or sons of small farmers. Some came in freely, happy to work for wages rather than to grub at the resisting soil. Others drifted in because there seemed nothing better to do. All did well enough by ancient standards until recession descended on the city of Rome and perhaps to a lesser degree elsewhere in Italy.

This urban economic downturn resulted largely from a sudden drop in government spending in and around the city of Rome. The money Rome had received by way of indemnity, tribute, and spoils from the wars ending in 146 B.C. was freely spent by Roman leaders. One project, for instance, the new Marcian Aqueduct, built over a four-year period, 144–140, cost 180 million sesterces (4 sestertii = 1 denarius, about a day's wage for an unskilled laborer). The two existing aqueducts were repaired at the same time. Numerous other projects were carried through. Obviously the burgeoning city demanded expanded supplies and services. But after about 140 things changed. Extraordinary expenditures ceased. No profitable wars produced great spoils. Most campaigns were like that of Scipio Aemilianus, against Numantia in Spain between 135 and 132. Scipio called on allied states outside Italy to help with troops, since the Senate was reluctant to place any more burdens on Romans. And when the war ended successfully, his soldiers got only a few denarii as a bonus at the triumph. Indemnity from Carthage and Macedonia and Syria no longer filled the treasury either. The direct tax on citizens, which had always been a war tax, was permanently ended for Romans in Italy after L. Aemilius Paullus defeated Perseus in 167 B.C. The lowered state income went only for routine expenditures; roads, bridges, temples and other public buildings, and a host of other items could wait. In Rome there was unemployment with much distress.

For the city, the most serious immediate problem was a shortage of grain—and thus bread for the lower-class diet. The Roman shortage reflected in part a general shortage in the Mediterranean; Egypt, for example, had a series of bad crop years, and prices went up enormously. The situation was exacerbated by piracy. But most portentous for Rome itself was a slave war in Sicily (135–132 B.C.), the source of perhaps half the city's grain. The rebellion, led by an interesting character named Eunus, who called himself King Antiochus and was something of a magician, caused widespread disruption of normal agriculture in that island province. Lower-class Romans, many already without an income, could not pay the inflated prices; some must have been quite literally starving.

Tiberius Gracchus' Efforts to Solve Rome's Problems

As tribune of the plebs in 133 B.C., Tiberius Sempronius Gracchus, a son of Cornelia, daughter of the elder Scipio, initiated a struggle that was to continue fitfully for a century. A faction led by his father-in-law, Appius Claudius, supported him. Tiberius was chiefly actuated by a desire to correct rural problems, which affected Rome's all-important army. In the decline of the small-farmer class he saw the destruction of the mos maiorum, the old order. Doubtless he was also influenced by a setback his career suffered when, as quaestor in Spain in 137, he had become involved in a scandalous military disaster. Finally, Tiberius had an adviser of Italian Greek stock named Blossius, from Cumae, who was both a Stoic and a democrat. Blossius may have encouraged the thirty-year-old tribune in some of his more radical moves.

Tiberius proposed a law, the Lex Agraria, which, involving the state-owned land (ager publicus) only, did not touch privately owned property and was itself not at all radical. By this law the amount of public land that could be leased by any one person was limited; the excess was to be recovered. This land, along with other public land not formally leased to any citizen, was to be made available for leasehold distribution in small farm-sized allotments to landless citizens. At one sweep Tiberius would reduce the number of slave-manned *latifundia*, increase the draft pool of small landholders (the property requirement was so low that actual land ownership was not necessary), and decrease the dependence of the city of Rome on outside grain. He surely hoped to get some Romans out of the city and onto small farms, though when the land commission set up by the law began to operate, the commissioners probably found it more practical and realistic to give the lots to men who were already tenant farmers in rural areas. The land distribution program, which lasted several years, had very limited success.

Tiberius' greatest influence was on the oligarchy itself. When his rivals attempted to stop him by the veto of an opposing tribune, he conducted an unprecedented recall election and declared the man deposed, defending his action with an argument based on democratic principle. When his opponents persuaded the Senate to withhold money from the agrarian commission, he again turned to unprecedented means. News arrived that Attalus III of Pergamum in Asia Minor had just died, after willing his kingdom to the Roman people. Tiberius called an assembly and by law arranged that the Pergamene treasury be used for the commission's purposes. While he was about it, he also got a provision that the new province (Asia, the Romans called it) would be organized not by the Senate, as was customary, but by the assembly, with himself as agent of course. When Tiberius announced he was a candidate for reelection, his enemies, frightened by dark rumor about his ultimate intentions, killed him. It was the first such political assassination in the Romans' memory. His recent legislation was either voided or circumvented, except for the land law, which remained in effect.

Thus Tiberius Gracchus, while working toward conservative, time-honored goals, used radical means. The manner of his use of the office of tribune, outside the control of magistrates and Senate, amounted to a declaration of war on the oligarchical system. Some of his opponents feared he wanted to make himself a Greek-style tyrant. Other men had gained support for themselves through personal popularity, as he did; other tribunes had defied the system; but Tiberius did so with imaginative and daring innovation and with a considerable degree of success. He became the archetype of a new breed later called *Populares*. Like him they were scions of old families, mostly aristocrats, always upper class. None of them were either men of low class or true democrats, but rather, men who rose to high positions through use of Tiberius' methods. The traditional political leaders, opponents of the Populares, soon began to call themselves *Optimates* or *boni*, "the best," who rose to power through the customary ladder of offices (though they might serve as tribunes of the plebs) and through the Senate rather than through appeals to the people by means of popular laws and programs. The Populares and the Optimates were not political parties in the modern sense, with chosen leaders and programs. Attitudes and means separated the two amorphous factions.

The Senate permitted the agrarian commission set up by Tiberius' land reform law to continue its operations after Tiberius' murder, with Tiberius' brother Gaius serving as a member, as he had from the commission's inception, along with Appius Claudius. Licinius Crassus, Gaius' father-in-law, was appointed to replace Tiberius. The commission distributed land to at most a few thousand persons, but the urban problems eased with the end of the slave war in Sicily in 132 B.C., when the grain supply presumably returned to normal. General economic conditions, however, remained poor.

Gaius Gracchus: A Shift in Emphasis

Ten years younger than his brother, Gaius Sempronius Gracchus was identified with Tiberius' program from the beginning. Only with hesitation, however, and under popular pressure did Gaius resume his brother's program. He did so, as tribune of the plebs in 123 and 122, more deliberately than Tiberius, fully aware of the implications of his actions. He used no such unprecedented means as Tiberius' recall election or his challenge to senatorial authority over money and the provinces. Yet he too helped to form the mold of the Popularis.

Gaius shifted his attention to the lower-class city plebs. His most important early measure was a grain law by which he tried to ensure an adequate grain supply at reasonable prices. He set an artificial price— below the still inflated market price—for state-owned grain, but stores were inadequate and it became necessary to purchase other grain at high cost to sell at the low price. The treasury suffered, and Gaius tried to find new sources of funds. Most notably, perhaps in his second year, he passed a law to change the tax collection system in the new province of Asia. Publicans—later, companies of publicans—bid for the task of collecting the taxes; naturally they had to allow for expenses and for a profit. This tax-farming system was probably an improvement over existing practice (no government bureaucracy yet existed), but it was subject to abuse; the publicans came to be cordially hated by provincials everywhere the system was introduced.

In a small way, perhaps, Gaius continued Tiberius' land distribution. He also gave attention to the hard-pressed soldiers, obtaining new fringe benefits for them and forbidding the conscription of underage youths. A colonization program—the largest one planned for the site of Carthage—provided sizable allotments of land for citizens somewhat above the poverty level. Probably he hoped the beneficiaries would transport poor citizens and set them up as tenants. He attempted to detach the middle-class equestrians from the oligarchs who were his opponents, as they had been Tiberius', by giving the equestrians control of the juries for the Extortion Court, in which provincials attempted to recover damages from unscrupulous governors—who were, of course, members of the oligarchy. Senators had previously staffed this court. By now, possibly other permanent courts had been established and jurors for these were also involved.

In his second year as tribune, Gaius, following the lead of a colleague, M. Fulvius Flaccus, proposed citizenship for Latins and Latin rights for Italians. The two tribunes were opposed not only by conservatives but by some of the more liberal senators, including the consul G. Fannius and another tribune of the plebs, M. Livius Drusus. Their counterprogram and skillful attacks on the citizenship bill, especially effective while Gaius was out of the city establishing the colony at Carthage, led to Gaius' defeat in his bid for reelection.

Early the next year (121), Gaius and Flaccus tried as private citizens to keep their laws from being scuttled by their opponents. A minor official was killed in a scuffle by one of Gaius' men. In the ensuing disorder, the Senate seems to have declared Gaius and Flaccus outlaws. They took refuge, with armed men, in a temple on the Aventine, from which they soon were routed and killed without trial in a fate like that of Tiberius Gracchus and his followers more than a decade earlier. The consul who launched the armed attack, Lucius Opimius, did not dare use Roman troops against the popular Gaius but rather used foreign mercenaries, Cretan archers, who just happened to be in the city.

The Enduring Influence of the Gracchi on State and Society

After the Gracchi, almost every major question of the day—welfare legislation, of course, but also any agitated issue—tended to precipitate partisan squabbling between the Populares and the Optimates. One hotly debated issue was the legitimacy and specific uses of the Final Decree of the Senate (senatus consultum ultimum), first used by Opimius when he took armed action against Gaius and Flaccus and employed several times in the last century of the Republic.

The economic problems the Gracchi tried to solve eased somewhat after the two brothers were gone. They would recur, however, and the acute social ills of the ever-growing metropolis would intensify over the years. Efforts to help the urban poor invariably became entangled in politics, and mitigation of their lot—still without a real solution of the underlying problems—came only with the Empire. The Gracchan programs neither improved the condition of the small farmers notably nor substantially increased their numbers. As we shall see, the serious shortage of army recruits was overcome by drastically changing the army itself. Colonization programs beginning in the later Republic and continuing on into the Empire helped to maintain the small-farmer class as the backbone of the army, the state, and society. But the old order of things could never be completely restored.

In several ways the Gracchi had diminished the status of the noble oligarchs. In particular, they had challenged their bastions of power: senatorial control over finance and the provinces, for example. They had also struck at the patron-client system by which the nobles bolstered their social position and political power. The nobles' dependence on slaves to till the soil on the *latifundia* had already weakened the patronage system, since slaves did not vote. But now, in a massive way, the Gracchi had shown how popular politicians not in sympathy with the oligarchs could, through popular legislation such as land distribution and grain subsidies in the city, obtain large numbers of loyal clients, in effect using public land and money to make themselves powerful.

The nobles nevertheless managed to retain control of elections until near the end of the Republic. Probably the consuls who supervised the elections rigorously excluded from the Centuriate Assembly those who were not strictly eligible to vote. But in the assemblies that usually passed laws, the Tribal Assembly and the similarly composed Plebeian Assembly, the restrictions counted for less. In the Plebeian Assembly, moreover, popular tribunes of the plebs during the late Republic sometimes temporarily shifted citizens registered in city tribes to rural tribes (which normally had far fewer voters) in order to pass specific legislation. Not all tribunes of the plebs were in sympathy with the Populares—in fact, relatively few were, so far as we can tell (remember that many plebeians were nobles, and thus many tribunes were also). But Popular tribunes were quite powerful after the Gracchi, and in this connection too, things would never be the same.

Gaius Marius and the Military

Army Reform

Gaius Marius, a New Man who was the best general of his day, led the Romans in two major wars near the end of the second century B.C. Because of the problems with army recruitment, Marius for the first time enlisted many lower-rank plebeians into the army, proletarians who lacked the minimum property qualification for army service. He probably did so without specific authorization; Roman generals often acted with considerable latitude in various ways. But the result was permanent: all future armies tended to be manned largely from the same group, and these new soldiers gradually gained importance in a society that hitherto had found little place for them. Not all proletarians wanted to join the army, and the draft was still used. Military service could be hard and in certain wars brought little profit. Nevertheless, many soldiers fared much better than in civilian life, improving their economic and social status and even, in the later Republic, indirectly wielding some political influence in support of their generals.

These troops, previously clients of no one, now tended to become the clients of their generals—if these saw that they did well in the army and on discharge—and showed more loyalty to them than to a state dominated by noble oligarchs. The solemn military oath taken by Roman soldiers was to their commanding officers, not the state. Army command could further political careers not only through profit and prestige but through the votes of veterans.

Marius did not foresee these results; he simply needed men. Even in recruiting lower-class plebeians into the military, he and his successors continued to pass over the city poor; the best soldiers were still thought to be those inured to the hard labor of the countryside. Such men hoped for allotments of land on discharge that would provide a higher standard of living for them.

These soldiers, proletarians who had previously had no stake in society as it was structured, whose votes in the Centuriate Assembly (if these citizens bothered to attend) meant so little that they were usually not even counted, who had never been clients protected by a patron, who had benefited little from the growing empire, were likely to follow popular generals wherever they led.

During the period when these proletarian armies were being recruited, many of the Roman upper classes were distancing themselves from the military and no longer served. The higher military offices were still held by nobles, however—those who were elected as consuls or praetors, or who were appointed by those officials. However, a number of these elected officials were popular politicians, some of whom to achieve their ambitions would use their armies in political ways—ultimately even leading them into civil wars, Romans fighting Romans, which would have been inconceivable in the broadly constituted armies of the early or middle Republic.

Armies are important in any age: to them belongs, in the last analysis, the control of the state. The changes in the army initiated by Marius, along with other changes in the same period—the rise of Popular politicians not committed to the principles of oligarchy, and an upper class now in part distanced from the army—created the unstable conditions that led to the end of the Republic.

The Jugurthan War (111–105 B.C.)

Since the days of Masinissa, who had helped the elder Scipio defeat Hannibal at Zama, the kingdom of Numidia just to the west of the

Roman province of Africa had been an ally and friend of the Roman people, with members of the Scipio family as patrons at Rome. Jugurtha was a grandson of Masinissa and one of three sons of King Micipsa (148–118 B.C.). When Micipsa died his kingdom was divided up among his three sons, who soon were fighting over the pieces. Jugurtha defeated and killed his rivals. In the process, however, he offended some Romans and killed some Italian traders, allies of Rome from of old.

The question of what to do about Jugurtha became a partisan one for two reasons. First, those senators who investigated charges against Jugurtha and let him off easy were accused of having accepted bribes, as were those Optimate leaders who then conducted a "war" against Jugurtha and granted him an easy peace. Second, the Roman general, Gaius Marius, who finally defeated Jugurtha in the difficult guerrilla war that eventuated, was something of a Popularis.

Since Marius was a New Man, none of his ancestors had previously reached the consulate. He ran for that office in defiance of his patron and predecessor in command in Africa, one of the Metelli, who though of plebeian origin were dominant members of the aristocracy for several decades. Marius also found himself in conflict with other prominent Optimates. Yet it is necessary to say that he was "something" of a Popularis because he was his own man, no strict adherent of any partisan views, and because he was chiefly a military man and not much the politician of any stripe.

In Numidia, Marius completed the campaign that Metellus had under way and came home a popular hero, with Jugurtha as his captive. He was just in time to save Rome from another peril, one of the long series of Gallic—Celtic—invasions.

The Celtic Invasion (109–101 B.C.)

The Celts invaded Italy about once a century, though only two or three of the invasions seem important enough to get into the textbooks. A force consisting of several tribes, chiefly the Cimbri and the Teutoni, moved toward Italy as early as 113 B.C. and defeated a Roman army in the passes of the Alps northeast of Italy. But then they migrated on westward instead of coming over into Cisalpine Gaul (the Po valley). In 109 another Roman army met them in Transalpine Gaul (eastern France), and again the Northmen won without following up their victory. The story was repeated once more in 107.

In 106 the consul Q. Servilius Caepio, who was distinctly an Optimate (for example, he attempted to restore the permanent court juries to the Senate), won a victory over some allies of the Gauls and captured some treasure. But then the treasure disappeared on its way to Rome.

The following year, at Arausio in southeastern France, Caepio, now proconsul, by his failure to cooperate with the consul Cn. Mallius Maximus, a New Man, contributed to a horrible debacle in which Rome lost a reported eighty thousand dead. Again only the Celts' decision to turn away saved Italy. The Celts then entered Spain, where they suffered heavy losses. To the Populares and the lower classes, Caepio embodied all that was worst about the aristocracy: greed, incompetence, arrogance. Thus another war became a factional question. A Popular tribune eventually prosecuted Caepio, and he was condemned to exile; all his property was confiscated. The charge of this war also went to Marius, who served as consul for a second time in 104. Marius held his third, fourth, fifth, and sixth consulships in successive years until the crisis was over in 100. The major battles in which Marius annihilated the Northmen came in 102 at Aquae Sextiae, in southeastern France, and in 101 at Vercellae, in Northern Italy.

Marius' most significant political action was not his standing for an unprecedented string of consulships; rather, as we have already seen, it was his recruitment of propertyless citizens for his legions, a step probably taken out of necessity, without political intent.

Marius' former patron Metellus and the other Optimates saw in this upstart a threat to their ascendancy in the state similar to that of the Gracchi. Marius' alliance with the Popular tribune of the plebs, L. Appuleius Saturninus, reinforced this view. As tribune in 103 and again in 100, Saturninus helped Marius obtain land for his discharged veterans, in return for the general's support. The demagogic Saturninus cleverly procured the exile of Metellus; he also sold state grain for a tiny fraction of the price charged under the law of Gaius Gracchus (there was a grain shortage because of another slave war in Sicily in 103-101). He did not hesitate to use violence to influence elections, which led to his downfall.

Saturninus was a candidate for reelection in the campaign for 100, and a friend named Gnaeus Servilius Glaucia stood for the consulate. Glaucia seemed to be running third in the contest for the two posts when one of his opponents was murdered. Both he and Saturninus were implicated. The Senate passed the Final Decree, calling on the consul to take action against Saturninus, Glaucia, and their followers. Ironically, that consul was Marius. He nevertheless took the pair along with some others into custody, probably intending only to hold them for trial. But men who were probably agents of the Optimates climbed up on the roof of the Senate building, where the prisoners were being held, dropped roof tiles through the rafters, and killed them. Marius' political position deteriorated afterward. Neither the city plebs, who gave the Populares their chief support, nor the Optimates accepted him any longer, and he went into political eclipse for some years.

The Italian Allies: Struggle for Equality

The Italian War (91–88 B.C.)

One unexpected effect of the work of the Populares beginning with Tiberius Gracchus was to arouse Rome's Latin and Italian allies to bitter resentment because of their inferior status as compared to that of Roman citizens. They had helped Rome acquire territories far from Italy, but they had gained almost nothing themselves. Even lower-class Romans had gotten land and low-priced grain through laws of the Gracchi and Saturninus. Some of the land distributed by the Gracchan laws was held by Italians, even though it had been legally confiscated by Rome at the end of the Second Punic War decades earlier. Romans had not needed it until the time of the Gracchi, so much of the land had remained in possession of its former Italian owners; often it had even changed hands in good faith. The arrival of Roman surveyors to stake out the land naturally stirred great resentment. In addition, no Roman citizen had paid direct taxes since 167; Rome paid her soldiers and met other expenses from tribute and other income from the provinces. Meanwhile, Italians still had to tax themselves to pay their soldiers who fought for Rome.

The change in status of the Italians' relationship with Rome also fostered bitterness. The treaties between Rome and her Italian allies had originally been agreements between ostensibly equal states. Rome's rise in power—with the indispensable help of her allies—had upset that balance. Rome had become the hub of the Mediterranean world; Roman officials controlled vast territories, flaunting their prestige and power. The Italian peoples remained in the background, though of course some Italian soldiers and traders managed to benefit from the successful wars, and some procured Roman citizenship. Most Italians, however, considered themselves more as subjects than allies of Rome.

The Populares were willing, long before the conservative Optimates, to give deserved citizenship to the Latins and Italians. Fulvius Flaccus as consul in 125 B.C. (and with Gaius Gracchus as tribunes together in 122) tried to pass a citizenship law. But the Optimates opposed such measures, fearing that they might lose control of the elections. Whoever carried a law to give citizenship to hundreds of thousands of Latins and Italians, in effect becoming their patron, would acquire enormous power.

In the past, individual Latins and Italians had been able to attain citizenship in several ways. For example, Latins whose ancestors had once been citizens—expatriates who had emigrated to autonomous colonial communities—could simply move to Roman territory and register in the next census. However, the right of Latins and Italians to acquire Roman citizenship had been drastically restricted during the second century, chiefly because the Italian states themselves requested restriction, complaining of depopulation and the exigencies of the military draft. Early in the first century it appears, lenient Roman censors allowed large numbers of Italians and Latins to come to Rome and enroll themselves as citizens. But in 95 the consuls, by decree of the Senate, set up a court (quaestio) that expelled from the rolls all such questionable citizens. Indignant Italians began to form a conspiracy against Rome.

The Efforts of M. Livius Drusus, Jr., Tribune of the Plebs (91 B.C.)

The next major effort to obtain citizenship for Rome's allies was the work of one of the Optimates who aimed to weaken lower-class support for popular leaders. The tribune M. Livius Drusus was the son of the man of the same name who had been an opponent of Gaius Gracchus. The father had nevertheless proposed important benefits for Italians, and he had important Italian connections. The younger Drusus retained these relationships; he was guest-friend to one of the most important leaders in the Italian conspiracy, Pompaedius Silo. The Italians seem to have decided to give the Romans one last chance; they waited to see whether Drusus' citizenship bill would pass.

Drusus put forward a series of measures. He wished to bring more equestrians into the Senate, to restore the courts to the control of this

Three denarii of the late Republic. *Top:* a boar, symbol of Hercules, on a coin perhaps issued for the Plebeian Games; *left:* this type, showing soldiers taking the military oath, was used by the Italians to memorialize their conspiratorial oath in 91–90 B.C.; *right:* the goddess Victory in a two-horse chariot, pictured on a coin of an ancestor of the emperor Tiberius.

expanded Senate, to distribute grain to the city poor at low prices, and to found colonies. A majority of the Senate backed him initially, even in the scheme to enlarge the Senate body by the inclusion of three hundred equestrians. But when Drusus went on to propose citizenship for Italians and Latins, many of his backers turned on him, suspicious of his motives and fearful that the new citizens would be his clients. Drusus was assassinated, and the laws he had already passed were voided. The murder was quickly followed by a revolt of the Italians in 91, beginning what is sometimes called the Social War, from the Latin word *socius*, "ally."

The Italians now set up their own state, Italia, complete with magistrates and army. In some Italian towns Roman citizens were slaughtered. Hastily recruited Roman armies more often than not lost to the similarly trained Italians in the early months of the war. Rome now passed laws that would have prevented the war if enacted earlier. The Latins had not joined the conspiracy, nor had all Italians. The laws enfranchised these people, who then no longer had any reason to join the revolt. Next, a law was passed to permit even those fighting against Rome to become citizens provided they lay down their arms. By 88 the Romans had beaten down the last recalcitrants, but eventually gave them citizenship also.

The assimilation of the new voters brought out partisan politics in Rome. The Optimates feared the masses of new voters and tried to relegate the Italians to new tribes that would always vote last. The Populares, on the other hand, courted the new citizens, advocating complete equality for them. After a period complicated by foreign and civil wars, the drive for equality at last succeeded.

The new voters were not acutely interested in the Roman elections, and the Optimates need not have worried that they might lose control of the elections. The new citizens did not register with the censors in large numbers, though it is possible that they were impeded in some way. Italian soldiers served now in the legions and no longer in separate units, and the Italians, like the older Roman citizens, no longer had to pay the war tax to support the troops. Only in the time of Caesar did the allies who became citizens after the Italian War come to be integrated into the political and social life of the capital. Such men only then began to serve as magistrates of some importance. Following Caesar's footsteps, Augustus also made use of the former Italians—or of their sons and grandsons, for by his time the Italians had been citizens for more than half a century.

The Mithridatic War (88–82 B.C.)

The First Mithridatic War revealed the essential failure of Roman imperial governance in the eastern Mediterranean, and it provided the spark that finally brought civil war in Rome. Mithridates VI (120–63 B.C.) was king of Pontus on the south shore of the Black Sea. Two buffer states, Bithynia and Cappadocia, separated his territory from Roman Asia and Cilicia, on the western and southern coasts of Asia Minor (Cilicia had become a province after a campaign against pirates based there, about 101). The kings of Bithynia and Cappadocia looked to Rome for protection against Mithridates, and Rome had recently forced him to evacuate parts of those kingdoms that he had occupied. The Italian War seemed to provide Mithridates a golden opportunity to even the score. He invaded Bithynia and Cappadocia and overran the inadequately defended Roman provinces as well. Everywhere in the Roman provinces he was hailed as a liberator. Roman officials were captured and disgraced. On the signal of the king, eighty thousand Romans, it was said, were killed in a single day. That number is almost certainly inflated, and most victims were probably former Italians. But the native feeling against Rome became painfully apparent. The Greeks too saw the Romans as oppressors. Athens went over to Mithridates; her port, the Piraeus, became his chief naval base in the Aegean.

The news of Mithridates' inroads partially explains the Romans' willingness to end the Italian War through compromise. The Senate assigned one of the consuls of 88, L. Cornelius Sulla, to the war against Mithridates. As governor of Cilicia, Sulla had already dealt with Mithridates. Earlier he had served with Marius, not altogether amicably, in the Jugurthan War. He had demonstrated his military capacity, and as an Optimate he was a logical choice for the Senate to make.

But one of the tribunes of the plebs had other ideas. This was P. Sulpicius Rufus, a young orator of the day who had supported the younger Drusus in 91. As tribune Sulpicius led the attempt to give the new Italian voters justice by equally distributing them among all the existing voting tribes. The Optimates who had obstructed Drusus now forcefully opposed him. Sulpicius struck a bargain with Marius, proposing to give him the command against Mithridates by law. No situation better illustrates the dichotomy in the Roman constitution. The Senate had the legal right to name commanders, usually one of the consuls, to take charge of a war. But any of the assemblies also had the legal right to name such a commander by law. Technically a law passed by an assembly would have superseded a senatorial decree, for it was an established principle that the people in assembly were sovereign. Sulpicius' supporters, however, resorted to violence. In a melee, the son of one of the consuls—who was also the son-in-law of the other consul, Sulla—was killed. Now it could be argued that the law was carried by violence and thus invalid; there was no clear constitutional right or wrong in the matter.

Sulla decided to settle the issue by military action. He went to his soldiers, told them his story, and led them on Rome, the first time a Roman general had ever invaded the city. He convoked the Senate, or at least those senators who supported him, and got several of his opponents declared outlaws, including Sulpicius, Gaius Marius, and Marius' son of the same name. Sacrosanct tribune or not, Sulpicius was killed, along with some others; the two Marii fled for their lives to Africa. Sulla then led his army to the east to confront Mithridates.

Continued Civil Conflict

Sulla and his army were not long away from Rome before civil violence again broke out. One of the new consuls, L. Cornelius Cinna, on taking office in 87 B.C., attempted to rescind some of the legislation that Sulla had passed through threat of violence. Cinna, a patrician, was a moderate, but the right-wing Optimates had a way of making Popular radicals out of aristocratic moderates. They drove Cinna out of the city and declared him deposed. He raised troops, recalled Marius from his African exile, and with him marched on Rome in Sullan fashion at the end of the year and occupied the city. They surpassed Sulla in their vengeful slaughter of opponents. Marius, now old and embittered, was probably chiefly responsible for this grisly episode. The two were consuls for the year 86; Marius, designated to raise an army and replace Sulla in his command, died on January 13, in his seventh consulship, before he could organize the expedition.

Cinna gave the Italians equal voting rights and attacked economic problems. The Italian War, the civil conflict, and the demands of the Mithridatic War caused much economic distress, and not just for the lower classes, rural and urban, who indeed suffered. Civil war was always disastrous for upper-class debtors, for war, especially civil war, invariably brought a collapse of property values. Since property was often used to secure loans, debtors could not meet their obligations when loans fell due or were called in. The effect was cumulative, and sometimes there was a financial panic. In 86 the consuls therefore passed legislation permitting debtors to pay off their obligations at 25 percent of face value. The figure probably reflects the extent to which property values had fallen, so it is not likely that creditors suffered much. The mortgaged land would soon recover its value. In these years the economic situation in Rome was complicated by the appearance of a great deal of bad money, presumably forged. Means were developed to detect the forgeries, but only a period of stability could restore economic well-being.

Cinna held repeated consulships. He and his colleagues tried negotiating with Sulla, and they sent a new commander with an army to replace him. But neither tactic worked, and they could only prepare for the inevitable resumption of civil war.

Sulla meanwhile methodically attacked Mithridates' bases of power, first besieging Athens and the Piraeus before attempting to cross the Aegean with his army. For Mithridates, it was imperative to defeat Sulla in Greece. He therefore sent armies through northern Greece to relieve Athens. They did not arrive in time, however, and Sulla, though outnumbered, defeated the two armies in major battles before the end of 86. At this point the army sent by Cinna arrived, under the command of L. Valerius Flaccus. Flaccus and Sulla seem to have come to no accommodation, yet the armies cooperated loosely, both attacking Mithridates. Flaccus got across the Aegean first, but in Asia Minor his legate, Gaius Flavius Fimbria, killed him and took over his army. Sulla waited for a naval victory and then invaded Asia Minor also.

At the end of 85 Sulla gave Mithridates a negotiated peace based on the prewar territorial arrangement, including provisions that Mithridates give up some ships and pay an indemnity. Sulla then confronted Fimbria and his army; but Fimbria's troops went over to Sulla, and Fimbria committed suicide. Sulla collected a huge sum of money from provinces in Asia Minor, claiming five years' back taxes at once from the unfortunate natives, and arranged various settlements before he was ready to return to Italy for a third round of the civil war.

This denarius of Gaius Marius (not *the* Gaius Marius), serrated on the edges to indicate purity, may have been issued in connection with a colonization program. *Left:* Ceres, goddess of grain; *right:* a peasant plowing, perhaps marking out the sacred boundary of the colony. The coin dates to the period of Sulla's dictatorship.

The Sullan Settlement

Sulla returned early in 83 B.C., not as a triumphant general but as a vengeful invader. Popular leaders in Rome, including the son of Marius, made preparations to fight. Cinna had been killed the previous year. Sulla, who had the aid of many Romans, including the young Marcus Licinius Crassus and Gnaeus Pompeius Strabo, called Pompey, won most of the battles. He attempted to neutralize the former Italians, who were mostly in support of the other side, by guaranteeing Optimate acceptance of their new voting status. Yet thousands of Samnites fought on against him, notably at the battle outside the Colline gate at Rome (82 B.C.). After this hard-fought victory Sulla killed or captured most of his enemies. Among the captives were about six thousand Samnites, whom he summarily slaughtered.

Sulla convened the Senate and had himself named Dictator for the Reconstitution of the Republic, a new sort of dictatorship that was not limited to six months' duration, as in the past. While he was reconstituting the state he was also getting rid of his foes. He put up proscription lists—"enemies of the state" who were to be killed on sight and their estates confiscated. Over a period of time Sulla added names to the lists, and nervous men among the upper classes could not be sure that the omission of their names from one list meant they were secure. It has been estimated that Sulla killed about ten thousand persons, including the Samnites mentioned earlier.

Eliminating the dual nature of the constitution was Sulla's prime political objective. He therefore struck down the power of the tribunes of the plebs to call assemblies and to pass laws independent of the Senate. Bills had to be approved by the Senate, and then went to the Centuriate Assembly. Those who held the tribunate could not go on to higher office. The Senate was enlarged by the addition of three hundred men from the equestrian class, no doubt mostly chosen from the rural aristocracy. The permanent courts were again to be staffed by this body. The number of praetors was raised to eight and the number of quaestors to twenty. The latter now were automatically enrolled in the Senate. Sulla also passed a Lex Annalis that, like earlier laws of its type, set the ages at which one might legally hold the higher offices and forbade repeated consulships. The law did allow a man to hold an office a second time, but only after a lapse of ten years.

Sulla held the dictatorship from 82 to 79, and was consul as well in 80. In 79, after he had held elections for the following year, Sulla relinquished the dictatorship and retired, to die about a year later. M. Aemilius Lepidus, whom Sulla had mistrusted, allowing him only with misgivings to stand for the consulship, did indeed attempt to weaken the Sullan arrangements. When he demanded to be permitted to run for a second consulate, contrary to the law, he precipitated a brief civil war and was defeated. But the winners, close-minded and narrow core oligarchs, could not for long maintain the reactionary constitutional settlement of Sulla, and some of its key provisions were soon scuttled. There was, for example, continual agitation for the restoration of the powers of the tribunes of the plebs, whose full powers were reinstated in 70 B.C. This last action was the work of the consuls of that year, who, ironically, had supported Sulla in his military coup of the late 80s: Crassus and Pompey. Why did the Sullan oligarchs allow the election of two men who had given notice of their intention to restore tribunal powers? They had little choice: both candidates had armies near Rome. But we must look at some of the events that led to this point.

Spartacus and the Slave Revolt

The 70s were bad years in Rome. The events at the end of the previous decade, civil war, proscriptions, and confiscations with economic dislocation, were compounded by new wars: in Spain Q. Sertorius, a Marian, still held out, with consummate skill; in Italy itself the gladiator Spartacus led a slave revolt; and in Asia Minor Mithridates tried yet again to overthrow Roman power in the east. After others failed to pacify Spain, Pompey took an army there and eventually, after Sertorius was killed by his own lieutenant, was able to gain control.

The social ills that plagued the late Republic (discussed in Chapter 8)—especially the city of Rome itself—naturally developed over time. Our sources for this decade reveal that some aristocrats were impoverished, some by debts contracted to support their new life-styles. The underclass in the city grew markedly. Grain distributions and the excitement of festivals and games drew them in, but some also came because they had lost out in competition with a growing number of slaves. Wars still brought in considerable numbers of slaves, who mostly worked the land of rich landowners. Through other means, including kidnaping by pirates, other unfortunates, sometimes well educated and trained, could be purchased as slaves in the marketplace. Upper-class households came to include many slaves, and richer persons possessed several villas, perhaps, besides their homes in the city. These, too, tended to have a permanent staff of slaves. Many such villas were located in the area near the bay of Naples, which was even then already prized for its resort atmosphere. Just to the north, rich Campanian land was filled with agricultural slaves.

The threat of slave revolt sent shivers down the spines of rich Romans. The ease with which Spartacus recruited thousands upon thousands of slaves from the region around Naples (though the numbers cited in our sources are surely exaggerated) was terrifying, and his remarkable ability to create an effective army from the motley horde was even more dreadful. Spartacus' forces crushed even consular-sized armies, and if he had not been double-crossed by pirates, whose ships he wanted to use, he would have escaped with his men to Sicily or perhaps to the eastern Mediterranean. But the revolt (73–71 B.C.) was put down, finally, by Crassus, who (probably) killed Spartacus. Crassus had to share the honors, however, with Pompey, who was returning from Spain with his army just as some of the survivors of the slave revolt attempted to flee north out of Italy. It was at this point that Pompey and Crassus approached Rome with their armies, asked permission to run for the consulate, and were allowed to do so. As for the (third) war with Mithridates, it was put into the hands of the consul of 74, a man named L. Licinius Lucullus, who had served as Sulla's legate in the first war. He had, at first, brilliant success, driving Mithridates out of Roman territory and then out of his own kingdom, even pursuing him into Armenia, whose king was Mithridates' son-in-law and ally. But Lucullus was unable to end the war.

Roman Government After Sulla

Once the more restrictive features of Sulla's constitution had been scrapped in 70 B.C., Romans might have expected some liberalization of the Optimate-dominated government. Many of the three hundred or so new members of the Senate (though the censors of 70 threw out sixty-four of these) must have come from families new to politics. In addition, there were hundreds of thousands of new citizens. Yet nothing at all changed: the political machinery, especially the elections, continued to be dominated by a remarkably small number of upper-class families because of their entrenched position and long experience as well as simple inertia. But there appears also to have been an increase in bribery in the elections; evidently the core oligarchs were determined to hold on to their power, whatever the cost.[1] Their opponents, the Populares, were

---

[1] The terms used to describe the Roman aristocracy can be confusing. The *patricians* were the old aristocracy; even when patrician families no longer had much power because family members no longer filled high office, they still retained high prestige. By the later Republic less than half of the original patrician families were politically active; some seem to have disappeared entirely. In this volume, the *oligarchy* (or the "inner" or "core" oligarchy) refers to the small group of aristocrats or nobles (some of them patricians, but most plebeians) who, through the Senate or through various types of political organization among upper-class families, were usually able to control the higher offices and, thus, the state. The term *nobiles* (nobles) describes a somewhat larger group that includes not only patricians and other core oligarchs but also less influential aristocrats and newer members of the nobility (New Men and their families). The term *Optimates* in the late Republic was applied to roughly the same group. Since not all senators were nobles, a still larger group of upper-class Romans may be designated by the term *senatorial families*. The leaders of the Senate were ordinarily members of families

not a charismatic lot. Pompey did not wish to play the role; Crassus was perhaps too involved in his business affairs; others had neither the necessary following nor the means to get it.

The little-heralded work of a single man, C. Cornelius, points up the corruption within the Optimate government. As tribune of the plebs in 67, Cornelius tried to get the Senate to initiate a law on bribery; eventually it did, but the legislation was much watered down. He tried to pass laws restricting the lending of money by private citizens to foreign states—the source of much profit for rich Romans, but also of great injustice. He tried to pass legislation forbidding the Senate from granting exceptions to the laws, a power it had arrogated to itself over a period of time. This law was vetoed by a tribune with Optimate sympathies. Cornelius eventually did obtain passage of a law requiring a quorum of at least two hundred men in the Senate for such action. Yet we know that this body continued casually to grant exceptions to the laws in the interests of powerful persons. As governor of Cilicia in 51 B.C., M. Tullius Cicero learned, for example, of several decrees permitting an illegal loan by Marcus Junius Brutus to the city of Salamis on Cyprus, passed when Cicero had been in ordinary attendance at the Senate but of which he was nevertheless unaware. Roman maltreatment of provincials seems to have been on the increase as Roman officials all too often mulcted their provinces.

One of Cicero's successful prosecutions helped him rise rapidly to prominence as the first orator of Rome. In the year 70 he exposed a rapacious governor of Sicily named Verres, who went into exile to escape sentence. Cicero's Verrine orations, like some others, were not delivered as published, but we may nevertheless learn much from them about provincial governance. A vicious cycle had developed. To obtain high office cost a fortune, which could be recouped by a lucrative governorship. But to recoup was not enough; provincial governors also wanted a gainful return for themselves. To get it, they might need to bribe jurors in order not to be convicted of extortion on returning to

---

constituting the core oligarchy; each generation, these families would place one or more members in high office. Such families were conservative and traditional, working through the cursus of offices (see footnote on page 32) and referring important decisions to the Senate.

The Populares, the opponents of the Optimates, were also upper-class leaders, but they gained political power through programs that involved passing laws through a citizen assembly. They made much use of the office of tribune of the plebs, presiding over the Plebeian Assembly, and they tended to ignore the traditions that gave great power to the Senate. They were not traditional, therefore, nor conservative like the oligarchs.

Some leaders—Pompey and Cicero are examples—were neither core oligarchs nor Populares, in part because they were not acceptable to the oligarchs and in part because they were ambivalent or wavering in their views.

Rome. It was illegal for an advocate like Cicero to take fees, but clients had to pay off somehow, often by including the orators in their wills; meanwhile, "loans" might be made to the orators.

Romans of the ruling class were as determined as ever to retain their power, but found it ever more difficult. The struggle occupied all their efforts. They had little time and scant inclination to work out the problems of the government or the provinces.

Pompey's Extraordinary Commands

The destruction of Carthage, the important naval power in the western Mediterranean, and the decline of Rhodes (as the result of Roman policy), the chief naval power of the east, led to a sharp increase in piracy. This uncontrolled piracy was only one instance of Rome's failure to bear her imperial responsibilities. Pirates even raided Italian coastal cities, some of which had to rebuild old walls in this period. Pirates had bargained with Spartacus to transport his army from Italy in 71, and although they double-crossed him, the pirate menace was clear. When piracy threatened the food supply of Rome itself, the Romans demanded action. A law (which was opposed by the core oligarchs) was passed in 67 B.C., granting Pompey an extraordinary, three-year command against the pirates, with an overwhelming force of both ships and men, and control over the whole Mediterranean littoral. The fact that his command overlapped that of other provincial governors and even, in theory, might involve sovereign states was deemed of no consequence. Pompey cleared the seas of pirates in just ninety days. It took somewhat longer to reduce pirate bases in Cilicia and elsewhere. Grain prices in Rome fell dramatically even as Pompey moved into action. Obviously speculators had held prices artificially high.

Pompey now got a new command, also given to him by a tribunician law, the Lex Manilia of 66, against Mithridates. He replaced Lucullus, whose position had been gradually undermined in the preceding years. Lucullus' story is worth noting. He had found the Roman province of Asia still suffering heavily from the economic burdens imposed by Sulla. The native towns had borrowed money from Romans (who else had capital?) to pay off the indemnity, and since interest rates were excessive, many still owed more than they had borrowed despite regular payments. Lucullus arbitrarily credited payments of interest against the principal and otherwise tried to help the provincials in a rare instance of an Optimate demonstrating concern for Roman subjects. But by doing so Lucullus created powerful enemies among the equestrian publicans in Rome. Lucullus had other problems, however, that led to his displacement. His troops, many of whom had been brought into Asia Minor by Flaccus in the time of Sulla, had served longer than was required by law, and now mutinied. The men also complained of Lucullus' severe discipline and claimed that he kept a disproportionate share of the spoils for himself. Clearly, the lower-class Romans who now filled the ranks of the army did not always find military service tolerable or profitable.

The fresh troops that Pompey brought to the war would be treated more generously. In a short time Mithridates was driven out of the province of Asia. He fled across the Black Sea and was soon killed. Pompey completely reorganized the provinces in Asia Minor, overturning all of Lucullus' arrangements, and he reestablished relations with the various client kingdoms. He also, quite illegally, took over the area of Syria-Palestine to the south. The old Seleucid kingdom centered in Syria was in tatters as various aspirants to power vied for control. Into this power vacuum Pompey moved without a struggle. In Palestine, where two brothers were fighting for the high priesthood and political control, the Romans besieged Jerusalem to persuade the natives to accept Pompey's decision as to which of the two should rule. Thereafter, the Jewish state became another of the client or puppet states of Rome under the supervision of the governor of Syria.

Pompey's triumphal procession at his return to Rome set new standards for display of wealth, spoils that he had taken from provincials in Asia Minor and from the inhabitants of Syria and Palestine. Pliny, a writer of the first century A.D., gives an impressive list of valuable objects carried in parade. He also says that Pompey deposited 200 million sesterces in the treasury, gave another 100 million to upper-level officers and quaestors, and 6,000 each to rank-and-file soldiers (a laborer could not earn so much in four years). Pompey brought many Jews to Rome as slaves. Philo, an Alexandrian Jew of the first century A.D., wrote that many of these slaves, in typical Roman practice, were later freed and so became Roman citizens. They established their own synagogues and culture in their residential area across the Tiber, just outside the city proper.

Cicero's *Concordia:* The Republic's Last Chance

While Lucullus' career was in decline and Pompey's approached its peak, others who would figure in this critical phase of Roman history were climbing the rungs of the *cursus honorum:* Cicero, Caesar, and the younger Cato. Cicero, a New Man, was the same age as Pompey, but the latter was the son of a rich consul; Cicero's father, though not without aristocratic friends at Rome, had never run for office in the city, and was only moderately well-to-do. Cicero thus attained the highest offices only through great ambition and effort. He rose because intense, hard work made him the best orator in Rome. He courted the populace on occasion, but he also made allies of influential nobles, primarily by defending them in politically motivated trials. He reached the consulship in 63 B.C. at the earliest possible age. Many who supported him genuinely thought him to be a high-level statesman; others were obligated to him because of his services or supported him because they did not like the alternatives.

Cicero was no revolutionary; he wanted to reestablish the ideal, traditional state. He called his goal the Concord of Orders (concordia ordinum, the "orders" being the nobles and equestrians). He hoped to broaden the oligarchy by lowering its resistance to infusions of New Men like himself from the equestrian order. The resulting concord would, he thought, be supported by all the boni—good citizens at all levels.

Cicero's great opportunity came in the year of his consulship, 63 B.C. He had the broad support of the equestrian order, and he gained that of at least a considerable segment of the inner oligarchy. Toward the end of the year he exposed a conspiracy and revolt against the state led by a dissolute patrician named L. Sergius Catilina (Catiline); a military campaign was needed to put the revolt down in 62, but Cicero had already ensured Catiline's failure.

Catiline's goals are not well known, but he advocated a cancellation of debts and expected to gain massive support both from the nobles and the lower classes. Neither joined him in large numbers, but Catiline's effort surely testifies to widespread economic distress. Nobles had fallen into debt by living beyond their means, and sometimes, like Catiline, through failure to obtain lucrative office; as for the lower classes, the city was filled with persons who subsisted on the edge of starvation, willing to listen to great promises. Day laborers in rural areas were no better off. Catiline's threat was thus real.

Cicero saw the suppression of the conspiracy as a great accomplishment that would finally weld together his paternalistic coalition; the fright given to the oligarchs and the rich equestrian moneylenders, he thought, had made them aware of the necessity for unity. But he was soon to be disappointed.

The aristocratic Republic could endure only if there was a de-emphasis on the powerful individual politician and strict adherence to the principle that offices should be held by more than one person. Cicero felt it was nevertheless necessary to give recognition to outstanding individuals, frankly allowing them honor and power, but within the system. Some oligarchs, however, had other ideas. Lucullus and M. Porcius Cato (the great-grandson of Cato the Censor), among others, wanted to curtail powerful individuals and to retain the narrow exclusiveness that had characterized the oligarchy in recent decades. Unfortunately for the Republic, their view prevailed over Cicero's concordia.

Pompey came home from his victories at sea and in the east at the end of 62. He disbanded his army and, as we have seen, celebrated his triumph with unprecedented lavishness. He expected from the Senate the prestige owing to a state hero, plus ratification of his arrangements in the east and a land program for his veteran clients. But this validation of his deeds in the east would also ensure Pompey's future power. Many of his arrangements in Asia Minor and Syria were political at base: he had put his adherents into important positions. Others were economic: in some instances Pompey had lent money, as to the kings of Cappadocia and Bithynia. The Senate, led by Cato, young though he was, refused Pompey all these things. He was furious but, for the time being, powerless.

Some important equestrians too were offended by the oligarchs. One company of publicans, no doubt depending on government estimates, had bid too much for the collection of taxes in the province of Asia; they wanted, with some justice, a renegotiation of their contract. The Senate refused, while Cicero bemoaned the breakup of his *concordia*. When Caesar returned from a governorship in Spain wanting both a triumph and the consulship, the oligarchs unnecessarily offended him by refusing to allow him both. They were to learn, at this point and again ten years later, that here was a man not to be trifled with. Caesar now put together an informal coalition of Crassus, Pompey, and himself, the so-called First Triumvirate, an anti-Optimate coalition that spelled the end of Cicero's hopes and those for the Republic as well. The Senate's obstruction produced the Triumvirate, whose specific intent was to get for each of the three what the oligarchs had denied them.

7 Failure of the Oligarchy: Caesar to Augustus, 60–30 B.C.

Unsolved Social and Economic Problems

THE FAILURE of the traditional oligarchy, which was dominated by a group of aristocrats—the self-proclaimed Optimates or *boni*, the "best" of society—precipitated the fall of the Roman Republic. Historians have often given the impression that the main lapse of the entrenched oligarchs was their failure to alter the machinery of the city-state so as to control the empire Rome had acquired. There is some truth in that view, although in their role as patrons to provincial cities or even to whole provinces, members of the Senate did to a degree represent the views of provincials in Rome.

The primary and most basic failure, however, involved problems affecting Romans and Italians more than provincials. Moreover, so many of these unsolved problems were social and economic in nature, political only in a secondary sense. Each such problem not addressed by the oligarchs offered opportunity to politicians who patterned themselves after the Gracchi. Though usually aristocrats themselves, the Populares were often willing to discard traditional procedures and ideals to achieve their public and personal goals.

A few examples will underline the theme. The disastrous decline of small farmers with concomitant rural distress brought no effective action from the oligarchy. The Gracchi and their followers, however, sought to alleviate the situation. Only Gaius Gracchus and others like him tried to do anything for the city's underemployed and often impoverished masses. The problems of a shrinking pool of potential draftees, with unhappy consequences both for the peasant-soldiers and for the quality of the Roman armies, were solved not by the oligarchs but by Marius. His solutions, all unintended, did much to weaken the old order. The injustice of continuing to deny the full equality of Roman citizenship to the Italians persisted until the oligarchs were forced by rebellion to allow the change. After citizenship was granted, only the Populares among the ruling classes supported legislation to spread the voting of the new citizens equitably among all the thirty-five tribes, and this legislation was slow in coming. The former Italians seem to have been discriminated against by the oligarchs even after that. These new citizens therefore tended to mistrust the traditionalists and to support the Populares.

The decline of the patron-client system and the movement of many of the rural poor to the cities meant that perhaps half the population no longer held a meaningful place in society and the state. After Marius' reforms of the army, many unpropertied plebeians found a place, and one of potentially great influence, in the large emergency armies of the last decades of the Republic. Their votes often supported those generals who, at least in some ways, looked out for their interests.

At last the only question was how stoutly the traditionalists would or could resist those hero-generals who were also Popular politicians ushering in a new order. The emergency armies required in the late Republic strengthened the generals and weakened the ability of the oligarchs to resist change. Yet resist they did. Under the leadership of men such as the younger Cato, they tried to control the generals and to shore up the deteriorating machinery of the state. But the oligarchs succeeded only in precipitating the civil wars that brought final political collapse.

Cato and his political friends sincerely wanted to free the state from the domination of successive, powerful military figures and to restore the old collegial principle under which aristocrats, each loyal to the group (as they saw it, loyal to the state) held the higher offices in turn. They believed that before Sulla, Marius, and the Gracchi there had been a time when individuals, even the most competent and powerful, were one and all subordinated to the state (group). But had such an age ever actually existed? The answer is a qualified yes, but long ago, in the days before Rome became an empire.

The efforts of the traditionalists peaked in the late 60s B.C., just as the younger Cato's career was getting under way. Cato and his group, as we have seen, tried to curb Pompey, Caesar, and some important equestrian tax farmers all at one time. The result they did not foresee was the creation by Caesar of an integrated opposition. The ease with which Caesar and his friends garnered popular support illustrates another fact to which the oligarchs were oblivious: they had almost entirely lost touch with the people.

Caesar's Early Career

From the beginning Caesar, a nephew of Marius, was a Popularis. While still a teenager he married Cornelia, the daughter of Cinna, a major opponent of Sulla. When Sulla, now become dictator on his return from the east in 83 B.C., demanded that Caesar divorce Cornelia, the young man brashly refused. Perhaps only his youth saved him from the proscription lists. Sulla did deprive him of a priesthood to which he had been chosen, and Caesar prudently decided to tour the eastern Mediterranean for a time, until Sulla's death. It seems that Caesar very early got permission of the people to move up the *cursus* at a younger age than allowed by Sulla's law. As aedile in 65, he borrowed heavily to put on lavish games and flamboyantly restored the banished trophies of his uncle Marius.

Meanwhile Caesar used his considerable skills as an orator to publicize his political set. For example, he instigated a prosecution in 63 that was really a public attack on the Final Decree. The suit was based on the alleged participation of the accused man, G. Rabirius, in the affair of Saturninus thirty-seven years before! Caesar got himself appointed judge of the court and condemned the man. Rabirius appealed, however, and the consul, Cicero, undertook the defense. Nothing came of it except that Caesar built up his popular image.

Also in 63, Caesar again borrowed freely to secure election as pontifex maximus. The position itself was probably secondary in Caesar's mind; the contest was an indication of his growing popularity. In the same year Caesar was elected praetor. At the end of the year he joined in the senatorial debate on what to do with certain prominent captives who had conspired with Catiline to overthrow the state. Caesar took a soft position against summary executions, emphasizing his opposition to the Final Decree; he advocated holding the prisoners until the emergency was over and then giving them fair trials. His view did not prevail—that of the younger Cato did—and Cicero as consul put several conspirators to death without trial under the Final Decree, an act he was to regret. Some Romans suspected that Caesar himself was involved in Catiline's conspiracy. Early in 62 he was actually suspended from his praetorship, but was soon reinstated. In 61, he went to Farther Spain as governor. His departure was hampered by creditors, who even attached his baggage. He borrowed from Crassus to pay them off. In Spain, he somehow managed to profit enough from campaigns against the provincial tribesmen to recoup his financial position.

In all his public actions Caesar followed a steady course, the aim of which was to establish himself as a Popular hero in the image of Marius and the Gracchi. Yet he did not at all neglect the customary methods for building a political base. He formed combinations and in every way possible put powerful men, both aristocrats and equestrians, under obligation to himself. Some of his subsequent acts as Dictator suggest that in Spain even in 61–60 he was already laying a foundation for later support by the Roman citizens there. Many of the citizens' associations (conventus) there supported him years after, in the civil war. As a reward he made them into formal colonies, which gave them preferred status. The same pattern developed in Illyria, which he later also governed.

The So-Called First Triumvirate

Caesar returned from Spain in 60 B.C., wanting to triumph and then to stand for election to the consulate. The oligarchs, by delaying a decision on the triumph, forced him to choose between the two honors. He chose the office, but he also created the informal coalition of Pompey, Crassus, and himself. Pompey joined with Caesar to get land for his veterans and official acceptance of his settlements in the east; Crassus (and the publicans) got a cut in the important tax contract for the province of Asia. The oligarchs in the Senate had blocked both measures. Thus was fashioned the informal coalition, the "first triumvirate." One Roman politician called it a three-headed monster. Cicero, who was invited to join the combination, would have none of it. Though unsympathetic with the tactics of Cato and the rest, he, like Cato, was a threat to the triumvirs.

The coalition was too strong for its opponents. Caesar's brains, Pompey's reputation, Crassus' money, so it has been noted, added up to formidable power. Caesar easily won election as consul for 59 and proceeded to carry out his end of the bargain. Significantly, he had to do it through friendly tribunes and the assembly, though he first tried to get action in the Senate. Ratification of the arrangements in the east left Pompey's friends assured of their posts and his loans to kings and municipalities in the area secure as well. Crassus benefited from the renegotiated tax contract. For himself Caesar wanted a lucrative post to follow on his consulship. He chose Cisalpine Gaul and by law—not by Senate decree—was given a five-year, extraordinary command of this territory and also Illyria. Transalpine Gaul was later added to his commands by decree of the Senate.

It was not easy for Caesar to get these laws enacted, even with tribunes as allies, and functioning through the shadow assemblies of the times, made up mostly of city plebs. The other consul, Marcus Bibulus, three of the tribunes, and of course Cato with the other core oligarchs all opposed Caesar, who used violence to override vetoes and obstruction based on claims of bad omens. Pompey did not approve the consul's tactics but went along with them, even permitting Caesar to imply that his veterans might join in the violence. Once Caesar got his command, he immediately began to raise troops, ostensibly for use in the province, but held near Rome. It was all too much for Bibulus and the Optimates. Fearing for his life—he was actually beaten at one point—Bibulus retired to his house and did not come out for the rest of the year. Wags called it the year of the consuls Julius and Caesar.

The Conquest of Gaul (58–50 B.C.)

The acquisition of Gaul was ultimately one of Caesar's most important actions. The extension of Greco-Roman civilization into this region and beyond helped set the course for the future Roman Empire and for Western Europe. We shall not discuss the brilliant campaigns of Caesar, nor detail his frequently barbarous treatment of both soldiers and civilians among them, or his rather generous and foresighted final settlement, in consequence of which the territory stayed quiet during the civil wars that followed and long afterward.

The conquest, well known to us through Caesar's own *De Bello Gallico* (*The Gallic Wars*) and other sources, seems to embody all the major motives that fed Roman imperialism. There was, first of all, a threat to Roman allies and to a Roman province, Narbonensis, which Caesar called "the Province," from roving tribes, looking as usual both for plunder and a place to settle. As was often the case in Roman expansion, unsettled conditions created a sort of power vacuum just opposite territory controlled by Rome. There was also the element of personal ambition—Caesar's and his staff members'.

Caesar certainly expected to gain personal profit from Gaul, and he expected to build up political patronage by seeing that those who served under him profited as well. These expectations were more than satisfied. In fact, Caesar somehow managed to bring back from Gaul enough gold alone to cause a 25 percent drop in its price as compared with that of silver. A reading of Caesar's account shows that he noted well the productivity of the land. Perhaps he thought less in terms of possible payment of tribute to Rome than of the density of population that the land could support, which might enable a strong power to develop next to lands dominated by Rome. Caesar always gave special attention to the richest grain-producing areas, partly as a matter of military logistics, since the army needed a secure supply of grain in order to function. Yet the Roman almost instinctively felt that such economically important regions ought to be under the permanent control of the Roman state.

The question of what role Roman businessmen played in the imperialism of the late Republic is difficult to answer, for specific evidence is hard to come by. Though their interests seem not to have been a chief influence, the business class and some of the upper class had unquestionably learned to exploit the provinces through tax farming, moneylending, and trade. Much of the active trade was carried out by Italians and Italo-Greeks who gained Roman citizenship about 90 B.C. Roman governors would hardly have been unaware of their interests. Caesar knew well, when he cleared some of the Alpine passes, that he was aiding Roman traders, who had been paying "tribute" to local tribal chiefs.

Even aristocrats, with their ethos against sullying themselves with such mercenary matters as trade and moneylending, nevertheless did so in the provinces, usually operating through agents, often freedmen or nonpolitical family members. They were especially active in the eastern Mediterranean. Marcus Junius Brutus, for example, Shakespeare's "noblest Roman," lent money to the city of Salamis on Cyprus. The city was suffering, along with the other municipalities on the island, from the exactions of the propraetor, Cato (Brutus' uncle), in 58–57. Brutus lent the money to the Salaminians at 48 percent interest. It was an illegal loan at an illegal rate of interest, which required passage of two or three special senatorial decrees permitting exceptions to the laws of the sort mentioned in Chapter 6. Brutus was discreet, of course, using agents. A few years later, when payment was understandably slow, Brutus' agent got Roman troops, who collected—after starving to death six of the Salaminian Council. Except for Cicero's report by private letter to his friend T. Pomponius Atticus after investigation during his later governorship of Cilicia and Cyprus in 51, we would know nothing of the matter. One may suspect that such disreputable loans were quite common, but it is possible that this was an exceptional case.

Certainly Caesar must have had intimate knowledge of how valuable Cisalpine Gaul and Spain as well had become to Rome. Though he says nothing to indicate that he expected Transalpine Gaul to be as important as the nearby older provinces, the thought may have lurked in the back of his mind. Gaul had no deposits of precious metals such as had drawn the Phoenicians and Greeks to the Iberian peninsula centuries earlier. But Caesar would have been well aware that Spain was increasingly renowned also for its horses, olive oil, wine, and other products. Emigration of Romans both to Spain and to the Province had been considerable for some years, as it had to Cisalpine Gaul even before the Hannibalic War. Such economic and demographic considerations surely influenced Caesar and his fellow Romans in their movement into Gaul and other areas with great potential.

Caesar's extraordinary command was renewed by law in 55 B.C. after a revival of the triumvirate. His conquests in a nine-year campaign included all of modern-day France, with parts of Belgium, Holland, and Western Germany. He made two inconclusive thrusts into Britain and probed across the Rhine. He achieved his victories through the disunity of the Gauls (which contributed to his much better intelligence information); quick marches often brought him into a rebellious territory before the Gauls were fully mobilized, and his swift movements kept them off balance. The superior discipline of the Roman troops—as well as the fighting ability of hired German cavalry and infantry—constituted another advantage. But Caesar was a superior general. His genius was evident in organization, especially of supply; in diplomacy, including a shrewd understanding of how the masses might be made to repudiate a charismatic leader if it seemed to their advantage; in his tremendous energy and demands on the energy of his troops, not only in the forced marches but in the hard labor involved in intensive fortification and siegecraft, and in unprecedented winter campaigns; and finally, in superior tactics in battlefield situations. The campaigns were not without grim aspects: Caesar sometimes followed a deliberate policy of terror, punishing whole populations in order to make them disenchanted with particular policies and leaders; he once cut off the hands of a number of rebels as an example to others; often he permitted unnecessary killing after a battle was won. Yet on balance Caesar showed more clemency than most commanders in antiquity when faced with similar circumstances. The whole was an astonishing achievement.

The End of the Triumvirate

It is perhaps remarkable that a political coalition aligning the ambitious Caesar and the egoistic Pompey should have lasted as long as it did. Pompey and Crassus disliked each other, but they reaped immediate benefits from their alliance. However, they saw Caesar accumulating wealth and a popular reputation on a long-term basis. Moreover, some of the persons who had looked out for Caesar's interests in his absence irritated Pompey, to say the least. One of these was P. Clodius Pulcher, a patrician who with the connivance of Caesar was adopted into a plebeian family and chosen tribune of the plebs for 58 B.C. In that year Clodius got rid of two potentially troublesome politicians, Cicero and Cato, exiling the former for putting citizens to death without trial in the conspiracy of Catiline and sending the latter off to take over the new province of Cyprus. Pompey did not like the persecution of Cicero, with whom he preferred to remain on friendly terms, and at length cooperated with those seeking his recall from exile in 57. Clodius seemed to delight in trying to pierce Pompey's shell of dignity or pomposity, whichever it was. Yet the marriage of Pompey and Julia, Caesar's daughter, helped to keep the two triumvirs on amicable terms, and Caesar had the good sense to patch things up in 56 by making arrangements for both Pompey and Crassus to have commands approximating his own, which was now extended.

The coalition began to weaken. Crassus was killed in 53 trying to conduct a major war against the Parthians while serving as governor of Syria. Julia had earlier died in childbirth, loosening the tie between Pompey and Caesar. The traditionalists under the leadership of Cato began to make renewed efforts to win over Pompey. At least some of them intended only to use Pompey to get rid of Caesar, after which Pompey would be discarded also. Pompey had command of Africa and the two Spanish provinces, but he was also given special charge of the grain supply at Rome and therefore could remain near the city, governing his provinces through legates.

Meanwhile Rome was degenerating into near chaos. Pompey had no authority in the city and violence prevented proper elections; organized terror was becoming routine. Clodius recruited a gang of toughs and ruled the political scene until a rival gang under T. Annius Milo was formed to counter him. At the beginning of 52 Milo murdered Clodius. Anarchy threatened the city. In this critical situation Pompey was made sole consul by the oligarchs and given authority to restore order. This he did, using the army and martial law—as was probably necessary.

Civil Wars, 49–45 B.C.

Final Breakdown Between Caesar and Pompey

In the same year Pompey, encouraged by most of the Optimates, began to move against Caesar. He had his own command extended, but not Caesar's. He passed a law that no one could run for office in absentia, as Caesar wanted to do. When he was reminded that all ten tribunes had recently passed a law to permit Caesar to do just this, he replied that of course Caesar was exempt from his law; but the question of his intent remained. Another law forbade anyone who held one of the high offices from proceeding immediately to the governorship of a province. The purpose was to spread about the governorships and make the magistracies less immediately profitable, which would make it more difficult to borrow in order to bribe the electorate. If elected to a second consulship, Caesar would afterward be forced to spend five years as a civilian, during which time he would doubtless be prosecuted on one charge or another; a conviction might derail his career.

The final descent into civil war revolved around the issue of whether

Caesar would be permitted to hold his province until elected consul for a second time. Caesar proposed a compromise: he would lay down his command and his army if Pompey would do the same. When Caesar's proposal was rejected, the Senate not only voted to replace him but also passed a decree that made him a public enemy if he refused to vacate his post. Thus threatened, Caesar made his fateful crossing of the Rubicon River, the southernmost boundary of his province, with a few cohorts—less than a tenth of his army. He hoped even after his invasion of Italy to negotiate a compromise. But most of Pompey's Optimate supporters saw Caesar as the destroyer of the traditional state and would brook no thought of compromise. The fate of Rome was to be decided by civil war.

Objectives in war are sometimes suffused with noble purpose, but none existed to justify this one. Caesar wished to maintain his own position, just as the oligarchs attempted to hold theirs. Perhaps a few persons, among them Cicero and Cato, were actuated primarily by principle, beyond ambition. Cicero, who supported compromise, had been on friendly terms with Caesar in recent years and did not believe that those on the other side were fighting for the Republic itself. At last he reluctantly joined Pompey's side as the most constitutional. Cato pressed for the struggle but secured passage of a Senate decree declaring that no Roman should be killed except on the field of battle, and that no city subject to Rome should be plundered. This ideal was often breached, and by those on Cato's side. By contrast, Caesar had quite early earned a reputation for clemency to his defeated opponents. But as the civil war dragged on and each victory brought not an end but only a new confrontation in some different place, Caesar's clemency wore thin; in the last two major battles many persons were put to the sword who might have been spared.

Caesar's Victories

In the first year of the war, Caesar's rapid movements kept Pompey and his supporters off balance. Caesar took over Rome before a defense could be organized and got the state treasury in the bargain, no small advantage. Pompey, in imminent danger of defeat and capture, moved quickly to Brundisium, a port on the Adriatic in southern Italy, and embarked with some troops for the opposite shore. Pompey had the navy and, besides the troops with him, seven other legions in Spain. Though he had given up Italy he seemed to have the advantage.

Caesar soon made the balance more even: collecting troops that had been scattered throughout his provinces, he marched into Spain and in a swift campaign, more of maneuver than of struggle, defeated Pompey's lieutenants at Ilerda. Caesar then returned to Italy, got himself elected consul (for 48) to regularize his position, and began to plan ways to get at

Pompey, who had established himself in a base at Dyrrhachium, in Greece. The consuls and a number of other officials had gone all the way to Thessalonica. Without control of the seas Caesar was to find the going difficult.

Caesar tried to send some troops by land through Illyricum, which nearly resulted in disaster. Though theoretically under Roman domination for a century, the Illyrians were intractable and dangerous. Caesar—or rather, Marcus Antonius, Mark Antony—also brought troops across the Adriatic by ship during the winter, when Pompey's warships would not be on intensive patrol. It was a chancy business. Nor was the danger over: Caesar could not adequately supply his troops. The result was that, though he "besieged" Pompey at Dyrrhachium, it was his own troops who suffered most. When he attempted in the spring to penetrate Pompey's defenses, his men were thrown back with heavy losses to one of his best legions. Caesar is reported to have said that if Pompey were not a loser he would have followed up the limited victory vigorously, and all would have been over.

In early summer of 48, his army starving, Caesar moved east into Thessaly, where the grain fields were ripening. He hoped for a showdown battle. Pompey wanted to delay until Caesar was further weakened and his own levies better trained. His Optimate officers, however, urged battle since Caesar was outnumbered two to one. In preparation, Caesar instructed some of his best infantry in tactics for use against Pompey's superior cavalry. This group would first rout Pompey's attacking horsemen and then overwhelm his unprotected left wing. All went as planned; the battle of Pharsalus was a resounding victory for the smaller but more professional force. Caesar was said to have stopped the killing as soon as he could, looking about the battlefield close to tears and saying, "They would have it so." Pompey fled to Egypt, only to be killed there by some Romans, at the instigation of Ptolemy before the pursuing Caesar arrived.

Caesar wintered in Egypt, where as everyone knows he became involved with the young queen Cleopatra, who was struggling with her brother for control of the country. The Dictator (he was given this title after his consulship expired) found himself besieged in Alexandria. Help came from allies along the eastern Mediterranean seaboard. In the spring of 47 Caesar made a quick thrust into Asia Minor, where Pharnaces, son of Mithridates, was attempting to restore the lost glories of the kingdom of Pontus. Then, finally, he returned to Rome, a city beset by financial problems, which had begotten political and military difficulties as well. He barely had time to face these before another major military campaign was upon him. Cato and some others had rallied all possible military resources in the province of Africa, held by a Pompeian.

Still without much of a navy, Caesar, again tempting fate and the weather gods, moved his men in the winter of 47–46 across from Sicily to Africa, established a bridgehead, and gradually built up his supplies. In a brilliant maneuver he forced the Pompeians into the open at Thapsus in 46 and once more won a complete victory. Cato, in command at Utica, was not in the fight, but gained a degree of immortality by the courage and style of his suicide.

Caesar now returned again to Rome, where he celebrated four magnificent triumphs (not over the Romans, of course; such a move would have angered even the urban plebs): his victories over the Gauls, the Alexandrians, Pharnaces, and King Juba of Numidia, who had been unwise enough to back the losing side at Thapsus. The unfortunate Vercingetorix was led in one of the triumphs and the sister of Cleopatra in another.

The war was still not over. Caesar learned that the sons of Pompey among others, still in control of the navy, once again were rallying, this time in Spain. The battle of Munda in 45 finally ended the matter. Neither the opposing troops nor the nearby city of Corduba, which had been their base, were treated gently after this battle. Sextus Pompeus nevertheless managed to get away with the fleet; from his base in Sicily he would plague Caesar and his successors for another decade. Caesar could now celebrate yet another triumph (over the Spaniards, of course) and at long last begin to lay plans for the future.

Caesar's Acts as Dictator

Caesar was not to have much time to plan and effect his reforms. Yet he managed to complete or get under way an astonishing number of projects. He advanced several laws to improve the structure and function of the Roman governmental system. He passed a law on bribery, the details of which are not known, but which seems to have been much needed. A colonization program provided land chiefly for civilians; there, too, the need must have been great.

The decade before Caesar's assassination, in fact, is filled with indications that Roman plebeians, both urban and rural, were economically hard pressed. Catiline's promises of cancellation of debt, as we have noted, had gotten the support of large numbers of the lower classes. Many were probably day laborers without land; it was these persons whom Caesar tried to help. Caesar's friend Clodius, who is usually presented as a demagogue/gangleader at Rome, may also have helped enlist the support of the dispossessed dregs of society in the city. As tribune in 58 B.C. he supported legislation for the benefit of the lower classes and is remembered as the first to supply free grain for them in Rome.

The violence of the city during the period cannot be blamed solely on political maneuvering, nor can the growth of the number of persons being given free grain be altogether the consequence of political pandering. There was real distress. Some of it resulted from crop failures owing to bad weather conditions, which contributed to grain shortages. A troubling cycle was established: cheap or free grain in the city drew in unfortunates from the country and in turn created a greater need, which could only be met by increasing the amount of cheap or free grain that was distributed. Much of the popular support built up by Caesar in his last years came from his genuine efforts to help these poverty-stricken citizens.

Caesar found 320,000 persons receiving free grain in the city. He began the task of reducing the number, primarily through his huge colonization program in the provinces, both for soldiers and civilians. The number on the grain dole shrank to 150,000. Caesar was generous to his veterans: they received large bonuses at his triumphs and on discharge, besides land. He also increased the pay of the army.

As always in civil war, the economy was thrown into chaos as the value of land and other property plunged. Debts were called in, and there were many sellers but almost no buyers. Some of Caesar's own followers advocated the cancellation of debt during the civil wars. Caesar compromised. Creditors were forced to accept property at prewar evaluations, and all recent payments of interest on such debts were credited against the principal. We are told that the action in effect canceled about a quarter of the debt. This very moderate measure shows that Caesar did not wish to offend the powerful moneylenders.

Property belonging to defeated republicans was confiscated and sold. Despite his clemency in other matters, in his need for money Caesar seems to have been a bit ruthless in making these confiscations. Besides, these persons were his deadly enemies.

Several building projects in Rome Caesar either completed or got well under way; others were planned. He began construction of a new and badly needed forum with a temple to Venus Genetrix. A large basilica rose across from the Curia in the older Forum. He had vowed a temple to Mars Ultor, and he planned numerous other projects, including the drainage of the Pomptine marshes south of Rome along the coast and of the Fucine Lake in the central Apennines, the building of a harbor at Ostia on the mouth of the Tiber, and construction of a new road across the Apennines to the Adriatic. It is possible that the Dictator expected these projects to provide employment for the idle poor.

One of Caesar's most important reforms was embodied in the Lex Julia Municipalis, known to us only through a fragmentary inscription. In some fashion not completely clear the law (or laws) attempted to bring much needed order to the patchwork of local government throughout Italy. New laws also regulated the provinces. A rule that governers were now to serve shorter terms was surely designed to prevent the rise of rivals. And various changes in the collection of taxes in some provinces probably made for greater efficiency more than for greater justice. Cuts in taxes in some of the eastern provinces after Pharsalus were probably temporary. Caesar bestowed citizenship generously in the provinces, bringing Gauls even into the Senate, which was much enlarged. He granted citizenship liberally also to physicians and scholars.

Within Rome, Caesar directed a scholar, Marcus Terentius Varro, to collect books for Rome's first public library. He doubled the number of praetors to sixteen and quaestors to forty. The number of aediles was increased from four to six. Caesar made frequent use of prefects, appointed by himself, for important governmental posts; sometimes they displaced elected officials. For example, prefects controlled the mint in place of the three *monetales*.

Caesar reformed the calendar in 46, importing for the task an Alexandrian astronomer (Egypt had used a solar calendar for almost three millennia). The old Roman system of adding an intercalary month every second year to fill out the regular calendar year of 355 days had been neglected, and the calendar was so badly out of correspondence with the seasons that the battle of Pharsalus was fought in August (then Sextilis) by the existing calendar, but it was actually early summer. In order to bring the civil calendar in line with the solar calendar, Caesar added days to equal a total of 445, making the year 46 probably the longest in

A model restoration of the Forum of Augustus at Rome. In the center is the temple of Mars Ultor (the Avenger), vowed by Caesar and constructed by Augustus as a filial act. (*Alinari/Art Resource, New York*)

history. The calendar Caesar set up, with a sixteenth-century modification, we still use.

The most significant changes in the government were naturally those that established Caesar's own position. Early in 44 he became Perpetual Dictator, a title that appears on his coins along with his bust. He was the first living Roman whose image appeared on the coins, though the sons of Pompey had been minting coins with their dead father's image on them. The Dictator was consul also. As is well known, he refused to be called king; when Antony offered him a crown at an annual religious festival, the Lupercal, he sent it to rest on the head of Jupiter, the only king the Romans had, he said. He had long been augur and pontifex maximus as well. The Senate voted him the proconsulship for life and perpetual use of the title Imperator. He was also given the powers of a censor (*praefectus morum*) so that he could freely control the citizen lists as well as those of the equestrians and the Senate.

Additional honors were showered on him (or were later falsely claimed to have been given to him), some surely by persons whose real motive was to bring odium on the new autocrat. It was said, for example, that a Senate decree provided that he could have as many wives as he wanted, and could sleep with whatever women he chose. Even those offered in serious vein seemed excessive: he was allowed to wear the triumphal regalia (the garb of the kings of old) and the laurel wreath always. He was in effect deified; a college of priests headed by Antony was set up to be in charge of the cult. His statue was placed in the temple of Romulus. Yet it is well to remember that, in the conception of most peoples of antiquity, no great chasm existed between humanity and deity. It was not Caesar alone who claimed to descend from the gods (both Venus and Mars, through descent from Iulus, the ancestor of Romulus). He was not, in fact, the first of the Julii to make such a claim. Romulus himself was, for the Romans, a man-become-god, just as Hercules and others were. Yet there is no doubt that these honors were ill advised, envied, and despised, and that the naked power so clearly displayed in all the titles and privileges—as well as in certain of Caesar's actions—caused even some of his closest supporters to waver.

One of Caesar's most serious errors was to publicize his quasi-monarchical power, as shown on this coin, where he is portrayed (the first living Roman to be so depicted on the coinage) and described as Perpetual Dictator.

About sixty upper-class Romans formed the conspiracy against Caesar; they included men whom he had forgiven for fighting along with the Pompeians and men who had long been close and trusted lieutenants. On March 15, 44 B.C., the great Dictator who had flaunted his power too openly was stabbed to death in front of the hall attached to a theater built by Pompey and near a statue of the latter. The deed, not followed through by the assassins—idealists who seemed to think one death would bring about the restoration of the Republic—would only result, after a period of wary maneuvering, in another round of civil war.

Resumed Civil Conflict

Mark Antony was consul with Caesar in 44, and another of Caesar's lieutenants, Marcus Aemilius Lepidus, was Master of the Horse—that is, second in command to Caesar as Dictator. Since the "liberators" (as the assassins called themselves) did not move against either and since Lepidus had a legion of troops near the city, the two quickly controlled the situation. Being realists, they soon came to an accommodation with the leading senators. All Caesar's acts both accomplished and projected were to stand; on the other side, amnesty was given the conspirators. The chief assassins nevertheless found themselves so unpopular with the urban plebs that they left Rome. Some of them had been designated to provinces; of these, two eventually decided their provinces were too insignificant. They seized others, and ultimately the Senate gave its approval to Gaius Cassius Longinus, who took over Syria, and Marcus Brutus, who seized Macedonia. Decimus Junius Brutus, a distant cousin of Marcus, had been designated by Caesar to have the strategically important Cisalpine Gaul—in fact Decimus had been made a collateral heir by Caesar—and he proceeded there.

After a time, Antony decided that he wanted Cisalpine Gaul himself. When the Senate resisted, Antony resorted to the familiar Popular pattern: he had a tribune call an Assembly of the Plebs and pass a law giving him that province. The Senate, now led by Cicero, among others, decided to oppose Antony and to support D. Brutus with arms.

Complicating the situation was the arrival on the scene of Caesar's grandnephew and chief heir, Gaius Octavius. Only eighteen years old at Caesar's death, he nevertheless left Macedonia, the site of Caesar's mobilization for the projected eastern campaign, and came to Rome determined to avenge Caesar. Once in Italy he learned that by the Dictator's will he was adopted as Caesar's son and heir. Once the adoption was legalized, he was known as G. Julius Caesar Octavianus. Caesarean veterans hailed him Caesar and offered their help. Octavius thus recruited a considerable entourage, one amounting to an army.

Antony not only had come to an accommodation with the assassins but he had also seized Caesar's money and papers. He refused to give the money to Octavius as heir on the ground that it was state funds. Octavius could hardly find him a satisfactory ally. But the leading senators, including Cicero, were anti-Caesarean. At Cicero's urging, however, the Senate decided to try to use the young "Caesar" and his irregular army against Antony, who by now had marched several legions to Cisalpine Gaul and had D. Brutus under siege. Octavian (as modern historians call him in this period) was made propraetor and sent north along with the consuls for the year 43 to fight Antony. It was hardly a secret that Cicero and the rest intended to get rid of Octavian once he had served his purpose.

In April 43 the armies of Octavian and the consuls, Hirtius and Pansa, brought Antony to battle and defeated him. Both consuls were slain, however, and now Octavian controlled the army. Instead of pursuing Antony, he moved toward Rome and "persuaded" the Senate to make him consul—before he reached age twenty. Then at last he followed Antony to Narbonese Gaul, a province controlled by Lepidus. The three did not fight each other but instead negotiated to form a second triumviral coalition. They made up proscription lists to get rid of their enemies; at the insistence of Antony, Cicero's name was included. The orator had indeed said many scurrilous things about Antony while trying to create an effective senatorial opposition to him. Along with numerous others, Cicero was soon killed (December 7, 43 B.C.), and his head and hands were hung from hooks in the Forum. D. Brutus had already been killed, by a Gallic chieftain who wished to please Antony.

It was not difficult for the coalition to gain control of Rome and Italy, nor was it difficult to get the Plebeian Assembly to legitimize them as Triumvirs for the Reconstitution of the State for a five-year period. The more difficult problems lay, first, in the east, where M. Brutus in Macedonia and Cassius in Syria had been scouring the whole area, collecting men and the material of war; and second, in Sicily, now held by Sextus Pompey, who still controlled the bulk of the republican army.

By late the next year (42 B.C.) Antony and Octavian were in Macedonia ready for a military showdown with Brutus and Cassius. Two battles at Philippi settled the matter. Cassius and Brutus were suicides. The Roman world was left to be divided up among the victorious triumvirs. Antony took the lion's share; Octavian clawed his way into second place. Lepidus was relegated to a poor third position. Antony took as his sphere the entire east, and after some maneuvering including actual struggle, left to Octavian the west, except for Africa, which went to Lepidus.

Reorganization and New Tensions

In the east, Antony confronted a multitude of problems. Brutus and Cassius had naturally put men they could trust in important positions at all levels where their authority reached. They had vigorously solicited the cooperation of allied states, client kings. Cleopatra, queen of Egypt, for example, despite her earlier association with Caesar, had furnished grain to the two. Antony now called on allies for loyalty to the new regime, overturned old arrangements, and substituted new. He replaced men of doubtful reliability and got state revenues flowing again in the new channels.

The Parthians also presented a problem, and a campaign seemed necessary—in good time, however. In 41, in response to Antony's peremptory summons, Cleopatra came to the triumvir's headquarters in Cilicia to give account of her policy. She impressed him with her personality, flair, and companionability, and he decided to winter in Alexandria. Unresolved problems could wait.

Octavian's problems in Italy and the west were as knotty. He demobilized veterans by the thousands, and this meant he had to find bonuses and land for them. Those families that had been unwise enough to support Brutus, Cassius, and the rest he wished to punish. To oversimplify, the two problems lent themselves to a single solution: land confiscated from the republicans could be granted to veterans. A rigorous and none-too-discriminating application of the principle made the triumvir quite unpopular in some quarters. One family that suffered loss of a farm (which was later replaced) was that of the young Vergil, who was to become Rome's greatest poet.

Octavian had trouble also with the consul of 41 B.C., Lucius Antonius, a brother of Antony. The dispute, abetted by Fulvia, Antony's wife, turned on the question of who was supreme in power, the triumvir or the consul; it involved the confiscated lands and the question of equal treatment for Antony's veterans. The confrontation degenerated into war. Thus, during the winter that Antony was in Egypt with Cleopatra, his wife and brother were besieged at Perusia by the army of Octavian. The latter won, but by then Lucius was no longer consul anyway. Octavian let Lucius and Fulvia go free but took harsh measures against the Perusians, Roman citizens though they were, who had given support to the consul. He also executed some senators and equestrians who had supported Lucius and Fulvia.

A conference was arranged the next year between Octavian and Antony after Antony at length found out about the winter war. Things were patched up; Antony even married Octavia, sister of Octavian (Fulvia had conveniently died) and took her with him back to Athens and his work in the east. Octavian was confirmed as ruler of all the west except Africa and was to send Antony soldiers to aid in the invasion of Parthia; Antony in turn was to send naval ships to help Octavian move against Sextus Pompeius, who still occupied Sicily.

Sextus was a real threat. For nearly two centuries Sicily had been a major source of grain for the city of Rome, and now this supply was lost. Moreover, Sextus' naval forces could prevent imports from Africa or Egypt. In one conference Octavian, Antony, Lepidus, and Sextus all met and came to a temporary settlement. But Sextus' power to choke off Rome's lifeline at will was intolerable to Octavian, who broke the agreement and attacked Sextus. The first efforts to invade Sicily met with disaster, mostly from wind and wave. Octavian's competent and loyal lieutenant Marcus Vipsanius Agrippa built a new fleet, trained new crews in an artificial harbor where they would be safe from Sextus' marauding ships, and in 36 B.C. defeated Sextus at sea. This victory was followed by an infantry invasion led by Octavian. Sextus fled east, only to be killed by an agent of Antony's.

Lepidus cooperated with Octavian in the attack on Sicily. As it happened, Sextus' army, after learning of the outcome of the naval battle, surrendered to Lepidus, not Octavian. Suddenly Lepidus found himself in command of enough legions to challenge Octavian. Here was heady opportunity to even the score. Octavian learned of Lepidus' incipient revolt and in a daring nighttime maneuver persuaded the legions formerly under Sextus to come over to his side. Lepidus capitulated and was kept under virtual arrest in an Italian town until his death in 12 B.C. Probably only the fact that he had been elected pontifex maximus in place of Caesar saved him from execution.

Toward a Final Break

The end of Sextus Pompeius' stranglehold and the prospect of a surer grain supply brought jubilation in Rome and along with it somewhat greater popularity for Octavian, who was given special honors, including some of the privileges of a tribune of the plebs. The date of the victory was made a holiday. The demobilization of so many troops brought its problems, however: as always, the veteran soldiers must be given land and bonuses, and this meant money. Octavian managed to find individual allotments of land for some in Capua; others he sent to colonies in Gaul.

In 36, the same year Octavian reduced Sextus Pompeius' Sicilian stronghold, Antony mounted an invasion of Parthia. He followed the strategic plan developed by Caesar, approaching through Armenia. South of Armenia, however, the Parthian cavalry attacked and destroyed Antony's siege-and-supply train. Without it, Antony's main army could not mount a major siege, and the Parthian cavalry did not allow adequate forage. It was necessary to pull out. Perhaps Plutarch was right in saying that Antony showed his best generalship in these difficult circumstances, but he got back with only a fragment of his army. In 34 and 33 he was able to retrieve the situation to a considerable degree, through tactics that Octavian declared un-Roman, involving the breach of a treaty made with the king of Media. Antony even celebrated a triumph—but in Alexandria!

We must remember that our sources all derive from Antony's enemies. Nevertheless, it does appear that Antony's will and vigor lessened after the Parthian debacle. He became more dependent on Cleopatra and less decisive in his moves against Octavian and the latter's skillful general, Agrippa. Too much wine and women, some said. Certainly he could still organize well and could yet command strong loyalty from his troops—at least until shortly before his decisive defeat at Actium.

Octavian maintained large armies in order to preserve a balance with Antony, though he could hardly announce this as his policy. To put a better face on things he used the troops to expand Roman dominions. He campaigned in Spain, Illyria, Dalmatia, and Pannonia, sometimes leading the armies personally to enhance his somewhat shaky military reputation, and so added large territories to the Empire. The spoils pleased the army, and the Roman populace, as always, enthusiastically greeted successes of this sort.

Agrippa masterminded most of the military successes of Octavian. He also cultivated public opinion in the city by his benefactions, especially as aedile in 33 (though he had already been consul). He repaired aqueducts and sewers, improved the public baths, made arrangements for gala festivals, and constructed public buildings; all of these activities, of course, gave employment to thousands in Rome.

Meanwhile Octavian publicly attacked Antony on various grounds, especially for his dalliance with Cleopatra. They were the parents of twins by now, born to her, actually, while Antony was living with Octavia. He returned to Cleopatra and formally married her; it was some time afterward that he divorced Octavia. Octavian felt threatened by Antony's recognition of Cleopatra's oldest child, Caesarion, as the true son of Caesar, and he also charged Antony with virtual treason for giving Roman lands—Cyprus, for example—to Cleopatra and for planning to give huge chunks of an expanded empire to his son by her, and others to Caesarion.

The war of words between the two triumvirs escalated throughout 33. Antony complained that Octavian did not share Africa (taken from Lepidus) with him, did not send the aid he had promised in his Parthian campaigns, and did not send any recruits to him. Octavian harped on Antony's shabby treatment of the loyal Octavia, implied that Cleopatra had somehow bewitched him, and made numerous other charges.

The year 32 presented some awkward moments to Octavian. He could no longer claim to be triumvir, for the command, originally voted for five years and then extended another five, ran out at the end of 33. Of course, so did Antony's command; but somehow the latter did not worry. He continued to call himself triumvir and to exercise his *imperium* as if it were still valid. Both consuls in 32 were pro-Antony. Octavian attacked them and they left Italy to join Antony; about three hundred of the senators (of around nine hundred) went with them. Obviously Octavian's propaganda was not completely effective. Ultimately Octavian tried to legitimize his position by requiring all able-bodied men throughout Italy and most of the western provinces to swear personal allegiance to him in an extension of the usual military oath.

Both Octavian and Antony pulled together money, men, arms, and ships. Octavian put on temporary but heavy taxes even in Italy, which had been exempt from the war tax for a century and a quarter. Free-holders had to pay a quarter of their annual income, and freedmen were required to contribute an eighth of their capital wealth. In some places riots broke out against these exactions. We know less about Antony's efforts to raise money, but certainly he accumulated great quantities of it in order to pay and to provision his approximately thirty legions and thousands upon thousands of sailors. Cleopatra of course helped substantially, contributing money, ships, and men to the cause.

Actium

Antony and Cleopatra chose Actium, a port city in western Greece across from the heel of the Italian boot, as their base of operations. Its bay could accommodate their huge navy, and there was space nearby for the legions. Octavian got together an army that was probably somewhat better than Antony's and a fleet that could rival his, though without the huge ships Cleopatra furnished.

Antony was curiously inactive at Actium during the first eight months of 31, allowing Octavian and Agrippa to cross over the Adriatic and besiege his position. Earlier in the winter of 32 Octavian might have expected that Antony would invade Italy, where he had even yet a great deal of support from all classes. Some among his troops blamed the deteriorating situation on Cleopatra. As typical Roman soldiers, no doubt they superstitiously condemned bringing any woman along on the campaign, let alone having her share command.

The battle of Actium was decisive. Intended as a naval showdown, it appears that the struggle was scarcely joined before Cleopatra, with a contingent of the fleet, sailed southward for home. Antony, seeing her

A "legionary" denarius of Antony, issued not long before the battle of Actium, 31 B.C., and showing the eagle of Legion IV plus standards. Much of Antony's coinage in this period was somewhat debased.

sail off, overtook her in a small boat and went with her back to Alexandria, virtually abandoning the navy and his untested legions. The navy and soon the army capitulated to Octavian.

The following year Octavian moved in force into Egypt itself. Cleopatra had been vigorously preparing to rally her forces, apparently on the Red Sea. She attempted to move her large warships across the sands on rollers, only to have them attacked and burned by desert tribesmen, who had seldom seen so delectable and vulnerable a caravan. Antony had lapsed into deep depression after Actium; he now bestirred himself as Octavian approached, but too late. Both he and Cleopatra were suicides. She had declared she would never be led in triumph at Rome.

The Mediterranean world now belonged to Octavian, soon to become Augustus.

8 Social Change in the Late Republic

The Urban Plebs

Historians BOTH OF ANTIQUITY and of modern times use the term "urban plebs" to refer to the city poor. In more precise historical usage, the Roman plebs included all nonpatrician citizens, rich and poor. For a long time, most upper-class leaders of the state were plebeians. In the first century B.C., for example, Cato, Pompey, and Cicero were all plebeians. Caesar, on the other hand, was a patrician. The composition of the urban plebs, the lower-class population of Rome, is worth noting, not only because politicians like Caesar appealed to it, but because its changing makeup helps explain social, religious, and political developments during the late Republic.

A most important impulse for continuing change in the city's population related to the liberal policy of the Romans connected with the institution of slavery. Educated and well-trained slaves were often freed, and freed slaves were granted Roman citizenship. This practice seems to have been unique to Rome. The first generation of freedmen retained legal obligations to their former masters and could not stand for office. In the next generation, however, they acquired full privileges of citizenship, though citizens of freeborn ancestry continued to view them as social inferiors. Freedmen had become numerous enough to create problems in the city even in the second century B.C. Shortly before his death in 129 B.C., Scipio Aemilianus railed at the mobs that heckled him for his attitude toward Tiberius Gracchus, calling them "stepchildren of Italy" whom he had "brought in in chains." Obviously he thought that most of the crowd were freedmen or even slaves; he could not have discriminated by their manner of dress. In an effort to neutralize their political potential, votes of freedmen were restricted for a time to a single urban tribe. After a generation or so, sons or grandsons of freedmen could acquire land in the rural tribal areas and be registered in the politically more important tribes even while residing in Rome.

Other noncitizens flocked to Rome also, drawn by the attractions of a great capital. Embassies, merchants and traders, even tourists accounted for a considerable proportion of the population. Probably no more than half the population of the city, slave and free, citizen and immigrant, was of old Roman stock in Caesar's time. The rest had come mostly from the Hellenistic east: Greeks, Syrians, Egyptians, natives of Asia Minor and other areas in the region. A Jewish community was established on the Janiculum, across the Tiber. A few Celts had come down from the north, and some Iberians from Spain. By now Rome had probably displaced Alexandria as the most polyglot city in the Mediterranean basin.

While Rome's population swelled with persons of foreign origin, many native citizens were settling the colonies in the Po valley and elsewhere. The Gracchan land assignations, along with later similar programs, also took at least some native stock from the city. The proportion of citizens of foreign origin in Rome therefore continually rose.

The city's lower classes formed the lowly base of the economic pyramid. Those of old Roman stock often fared less well than the freedmen, many of whom had useful connections and had acquired some wealth. Rome's proletarians usually held semi-skilled jobs that paid subsistence-level wages, about a denarius a day. For a family of four, about half that would be needed for food alone; the rest had to suffice for minimal clothing and miserable lodgings. The top floors of insulae—large apartment buildings with no water or sanitary facilities, always in danger of fire and occasionally of collapse, or the worst of other slum structures—furnished quarters for the poor.

After the precedent set by Gaius Gracchus the government did on occasion offer poor citizens grain at low rates. The land distribution programs provided sporadic help for some of the city plebs. Occasional largesse at the great games, bribes for votes in the electoral or legislative

assemblies, and regular small gifts from patrons to clients further supplemented incomes. In 58 B.C., the Popular tribune Publius Clodius for
the first time provided free grain for the city poor. His motives were
partly political, as is usually the case with welfare legislation, but
doubtless also compassionate. Even the conservative younger Cato had
earlier favored a similar program. Though Caesar reduced the number,
by the beginning of the Empire about a quarter of a million urban
plebeians regularly received free grain from the government.

Many of the city's plebeians were organized into groups, some of
which were comparable to guilds. *Collegia* and *sodalicia*, as they were
called, had existed from early times. The older clubs, social at base,
frequently had a religious aspect; many were primarily burial societies.
During the first century B.C., however, *collegia* of a new sort appeared,
formed primarily for political purposes, somewhat comparable to the
hetaireia found in certain Greek cities; indeed the new groups may have
been organized by citizens of Greek origin. Some of the clubs were more
or less for hire: among other things they made it easy to organize bribery
on a large scale for elections or legislative assemblies.

As noted in the preceding chapter, Clodius made extensive use of
these new political clubs for organized violence, and the Optimates
countered in similar fashion under the leadership of Milo. Such tactics
by the two groups terrorized the Forum. When, after a chance confrontation outside Rome early in 52 B.C., Milo murdered Clodius, the latter's
gang burned down the Senate house and miscellaneous other flammable
items handy in the Forum as a suitable pyre for their dead champion.
Rome itself was turned into a tinderbox ready for the spark. When
Pompey restored order he no doubt also curbed Clodius' *collegia*. Caesar had once found Clodius' clubs useful, but after he attained power he
outlawed all the local associations except the oldest.

To keep the city masses quiescent, something more was needed than
cheap grain, occasional private and public largesse, and bribes by office
seekers. That something was entertainment. Romans of all ranks went to
bed early and rose early. The workday began early also, and for many
workers it ended early as well. Add to this the enforced idleness of those
who had no work or not enough of it and the fact that homes were
unsatisfactory places to while away the hours, and it is easy to see that
the city plebeians, with time on their hands, would be hungry for
entertainment. If it was not provided, they might arrange it for themselves in a fashion displeasing to the magistrates. Entertainment for the
masses therefore became at once a public necessity as well as a means by
which magistrates might endear themselves to the lower classes in
Rome. The state itself did not adequately finance the presentation of the
games and festivals, so any aedile (or sometimes other officer or future
candidate for office) who wished to put on a crowd-pleasing spectacle

had therefore to scrape up money however he could. Sometimes he borrowed heavily, with his future prospects as collateral, in order to entertain on a suitable scale.

By the first century B.C. there were numerous official holidays crammed with action. They tended to be concentrated in the spring— April was the month most filled with spectacles—but some were observed even in winter. The five major religious festivals were those of the Great Mother (Cybele), Ceres, Jupiter (the *Ludi Romani*), Apollo, and Hercules (the *Ludi Plebeii*). Each lasted for several days and included processions, theater of several sorts, and other activities.

Gladiatorial games were growing in popularity but were not a part of any official, regular festival. They were presented at funeral games and by private individuals, especially candidates for public office. Yet more popular were the chariot races in the Circus Maximus. Located just below the Palatine Hill, in recent decades this race track has been excavated and landscaped in a partial restoration of the site, which still impresses the tourist. It could seat about 150,000 spectators and provided vantage points for perhaps 100,000 more. The rivalry of the various colors so characteristic of chariot racing in the Empire was only beginning. Much of the excitement doubtless related to the betting that accompanied the races. Wild animal shows also excited the mob, and already the Empire was being scoured for animals to cough out their lives before Roman audiences. Exotic species would in the future be brought in from distant countries at great expense. On occasion there was revulsion, however. Pompey once put on a spectacle of elephants; the crowd, normally bloodthirsty enough, was displeased at the butchery of these majestic and dignified beasts and let Pompey know it.

Roman theatrical performances seem to have declined in quality in the late Republic, in spite of the fact that in 55 B.C. Pompey gave Rome its first permanent theater, a magnificent stone building said to have

Chariot race in the circus. (*Alinari/Art Resource*)

been capable of seating forty thousand persons. An elaborately over-
done spectacle marked its dedication. The new, diverse population of
Rome—and of other major cities in the western Mediterranean—desired spectacles of the sort that seem depraved to modern sensibilities,
and people showed less appreciation for the higher types of tragedy and
comedy. As in our own day, popular culture often catered to the lowest
common denominator of taste.

Religion and the City Populace in the Late Republic

The flood tide of religious change in Rome belongs to the period of the
Empire. This shift originated in the Republic, however, relating in large
part to the changing nature of the city's population. Immigrants, no
matter how they came—whether as slaves or merchants or traders or
ambassadors—brought with them their own religions. Over a period of
time shrines and even temples began to be built in and around the city to
these new deities. Merchants in particular brought their native religions
with them. The worship of some Egyptian gods, for example, seems to
have come to Rome by way of Delos and other trading ports. Some
religious innovations were the result of the travels of Romans, especially men in the army.

Three Oriental deities important to the life of the city by the end of
the Republic were Cybele, Isis, and Mithra. The cult of Cybele, as mentioned earlier, was brought in at the end of the Hannibalic War, an
official import, not the bag and baggage of immigrants, even though the
latter were doubtless the most involved spectators at the spring processions that marked the Great Mother's rites. Devotees of Cybele (and
possibly of other deities) who could afford it underwent a purification
rite, the *taurobolium*, in which a bull was sacrificed on a grate and its
blood was allowed to stream over the celebrants standing below. The
native Roman temperament moderated the orgiastic character of the
goddess's ceremonies, and visitors to Rome in the early Empire remarked on how stately the processions were compared with those in
Asia Minor, Cybele's homeland. Moreover, the ranks of the priests of
Cybele (the *galli*) continued to be augmented mainly by foreigners who
showed their devotion to the goddess through public self-castration. We
know of only one native Roman citizen who thus became a *gallus*. Since
it was illegal, this man may have forfeited his citizenship.

The worship of Isis, an Egyptian fertility goddess connected with the
Nile, extended three millennia backward in time. In the Hellenistic age,
Isis was identified with Aphrodite by the Greeks who were dominant
throughout the eastern Mediterranean. She developed into a universal
goddess, omnipresent and omniscient, especially important to pregnant
women and also to travelers everywhere. Her worship was thus no
longer exclusively identified with Egyptians, and her devotees were

now a vast, ethnically mixed mass of people. The Senate still disapproved strongly of foreign shrines and temples within the sacred precincts of Rome, and five times in the middle years of the first century B.C. shrines to Isis were destroyed by Senate decree. They were usually rebuilt rather quickly. Mark Antony vowed a temple to this goddess but never had opportunity to build it. Not until the early Empire was Isis ensconced in a properly consecrated temple within the *pomoerium*, the city's sacred boundary.

The god Mithra derived from Persian Zoroastrianism as modified in the Hellenistic world, especially in Asia Minor. Roman soldiers, possibly of Sulla's army, certainly of Pompey's, brought back his worship. His cult was admirably suited to soldiers; Mithra was a man's god, from whose devotion women were excluded, or virtually so. There were seven degrees of purification. Holy days were Sundays (we derive the name from this religion) and December 25, the birthdate of the Sun (father of Mithra, or sometimes Mithra himself). Various other similarities to Christianity can be detailed but, in contrast, Mithra was distinctly a mythical, not a historical character. The cult statues displayed in the great museums of the world show the beneficent Mithra killing the sacred bull, from which he created all that is. The great flourishing of this religion lay in the future: the third century A.D. saw the widest expansion of Mithraism. But some *Mithrea*—half-underground chambers where the god was worshiped—in Italy, as in Ostia, for example, probably date to the late Republic.

Various other eastern deities, including the Jewish Yahweh (or Jehovah), also found their way into the Rome of this age. All were warmer than the more austere gods of the old Romans; all offered some personal contact with the deity; some, a system of morals; some, frenzied and emotional rites that brought a sort of comforting catharsis or other means of purification; and some, the hope of an afterlife.

The Rural Lower Classes

The Free Farmers

The conditions of rural society are much less well known to us than those in the city of Rome. The reason is simple enough: our chief sources of information are the writings of Cicero and others like him, who lived in Rome and who thought it the center of the universe. Yet Cicero realized full well that what Rome was and would become depended much more on the Romans and (former) Italians of the countryside than on the urban plebs. Caesar and other generals were even more acutely aware of the importance of the rural plebs.

The number of small farmers in Italy remained large despite both the attrition of population to the city and the increase in the number of slave-manned latifundia. The two basic factors that prevented the small farmer from declining into insignificance were the colonization of rich areas, especially to the north of Rome and on into the Po valley, and the distribution of land to individuals through various programs like that of Tiberius Gracchus in 133 B.C. At the end of the third century B.C. and during the second, large colonies were sent out, particularly into the Po region, which were at first Latin. Romans who joined such colonies in large numbers gave up their citizenship for "Latin right."[1] The areas involved were not contiguous with the *ager Romanus*. By the second quarter of the second century, however, Rome had begun to establish large-sized citizen colonies. So many thousands of Romans migrated into the Po valley that the demographic character of the region changed entirely. The area in fact became a conservative haven for old Roman customs as well as Roman stock.

Although individual land allotments held fewer persons than did colonial settlements, still an appreciable number of individual settlers helped offset the growth of the latifundia. The Gracchan type of program was less significant in the late Republic than the policy of awarding veterans land grants as a kind of discharge bonus. Veterans were given land all over Italy and eventually even in the rich areas of the *ager Romanus* to the south, as in Campania. Some settled outside Italy also, especially under Caesar, who placed many thousands of veterans (and civilians) on choice pieces of provincial soil.

Archaeological surveys confirm the continuing existence of large numbers of small holders in Italy in this period. Even in Etruria, where the latifundia were already numerous in Tiberius Gracchus' day, the stone foundations of numerous farm huts of the period testify to the persistence of small farmers there. Inferring their economic position is more difficult, but it cannot have been very good: small farmers are never really prosperous, and a single family, before the age of machines, was physically unable to produce much of a surplus. These farms, as earlier, would mostly have been subsistence operations whose goal was to attain the greatest possible degree of self-sufficiency. Little would or could have been produced for sale.

Small farmers with very little land often supplemented their meager incomes by providing labor for the larger landholders at harvest time and other peak work periods. However, the rise of the slave plantation and the use of contract labor gangs at harvest time reduced such opportunities. Public pasture land previously available to small farmers was also increasingly swallowed up either by lessees or by squatters, who

---

[1] See pages 43–44 for a discussion of Latin rights.

took over public land not formally leased out in a semilegal practice called *occupatio*.

More debilitating to Italian agriculture in the long run, especially to the small farmer, were bad farming practices, the consequence of both ignorance and poverty. The best Roman farmers understood the importance of allowing the land to lie fallow periodically; the recommended practice was to leave half of one's land fallow. Rudimentary crop rotation was understood as well. But the poorest farmers could not allow half their tiny holdings to be unproductive in any year, nor could they practice a system of crop rotation, whose immediate effect was to lower overall annual production of the most needed crops. Not even the larger farms had enough animal manure to keep the soil at a high level of tilth and fertility, though the importance of fertilization was well known. Something was known about composting also, but the practice was necessarily very limited. The result was that, in general, soil cultivated over a period of centuries gradually lost its productive capacity in spite of the best efforts of the farmers.

Similarly debilitating was the gradual deforestation of hills and uplands. This practice ravaged the land in antiquity; its effects are still noted in Greece, Italy, Spain, and elsewhere in the Mediterranean basin. The reasons for eliminating the forests were simple and practical: demand for timber for ships, lumber for building, and fuel for burning, coupled with a need for more pasturage and cultivable soil. The inevitable long-range results were the erosion of deforested hills, the choking up of river mouths, and the conversion of lagoons (especially along the west coast of Italy) into marshes. The emergence of swampy areas brought an additional and portentous consequence: the western coast of Italy became increasingly subject to epidemics of malaria carried by the anopheles mosquito. Although the disease had existed from an early time, some areas now slowly became almost uninhabitable. It must be reemphasized that declining production, deforestation, and the silting-up process were gradual. Their effects were beginning to be felt by the end of the Republic, however, and in later centuries help to explain the declining economic role of Italy within the Empire.

We have seen that the small farmers played a decreasing role in the citizen assemblies in Rome, since it was difficult for them to come in more than once or twice a year and most probably did not come at all. Except on rare occasions the city residents, many of them registered in rural tribes, dominated the assemblies. Nevertheless, the country poor—those who served in the army—ultimately had much more influence on Rome's fate than the somewhat parasitic urban poor. Roman generals knew that the sturdiest soldiers were not to be found on city streets. What we know of the recruiting areas in the late Republic and in the Empire shows that the soldiers who were the final arbiters in the civil wars and who later determined (with the prodding of their leaders) who the emperors would be came from rural areas.

The Slaves

The slaves of the peninsula, numerous as they were, lived lives almost as varied as those of the free population. The most intelligent slaves received training in childhood that made them valuable, sometimes even as managers of farms or businesses. They were allowed to accumulate money and often could purchase their freedom. Alternatively, many were rewarded for their service with emancipation, and as freedmen perhaps continued on a salary in their former posts. Some slaves, including the most attractive, served in the great households of the rich, and these too might lead relatively favored lives. (See Chapter 10 for a discussion of the slave populations of the large establishments at a slightly later time.)

Less well trained or untrainable (or intractable) slaves were routinely consigned to the rigors of the farms. Conceived of much as draft animals, they often received minimal care; some, as we know, at times worked in irons and lived in infamous *ergastula*, living quarters that were essentially prisons. Perhaps most rural slaves were well treated, but the labor itself, with confinement and utter boredom, made them potentially dangerous. The rebellion under Spartacus, briefly noted in Chapter 6, indicates as clearly as anything the unhappiness of these slaves. When Spartacus' early success against the Roman militia gave them a glimmer of hope, they joined him by the thousands. The decision was not easily made, for their lives were forfeit. No wonder most of them fought with Spartacus against odds to the end rather than submit to their fate. We cannot trust the reported statistics on the number of slaves who revolted then or at other times, but Spartacus' success against even a consular army implies that his army numbered many thousands.

Again in 63 B.C., when the patrician conspirator Catiline raised an army against the regime, an appeal to the slaves seems to have brought some of them into his rebel force—although the numbers must have seemed disappointingly small to Catiline. Of course, the ease with which slaves escaped to join Spartacus or Catiline might suggest that they were not confined under very tight security, and that those in rural bondage in Italy certainly could not be described as cowed and spiritless. In any case, Roman law and Roman officials invariably showed no mercy to rebellious or violent slaves. Nothing threatened masters more than news of a slave rebellion.

The Equestrian Order

The equestrian order developed out of the census class called *equites*, those citizens whose possession of property qualified them for service in the cavalry. After about 241 B.C. this class was apparently identical with that which furnished the first class of infantry. In the late Republic the amount of property required for a census listing in this class was a valuation of 100,000 sestertii. This probably had changed from 100,000 asses at about the time the denarius was revalued from ten to sixteen asses in the mid–second century B.C.[2] This amount would have seemed impossibly huge to a wage earner, who would have had to work a century or so to make so much money. To the richer Romans, by contrast, the amount must have seemed modest. The total number of persons in the class cannot have been very large.

From the days of the Gracchi, and to some degree even before, the equestrian order came to be sharply distinguished from the senatorial— that is to say, politically involved—members of the same census class. The distinction was legal, in the language of legislation such as that which put the permanent courts into the hands of the nonsenatorial equestrians. The staffing of the juries of these courts changed with the times. In the late Republic a compromise placed both equestrians and senators on juries. Yet the separation of the equestrian order as a group remained enshrined in law.

A rather common misconception holds that the equestrians of Rome were practically all businessmen, moneylenders, or tax collectors. Rather, most of them, like the families of Marius and Cicero, were residents of the Italian towns and cities, landholders who were often politically important in their own towns. Cicero's father, who has previously been cited as an example, had connections with important Romans—Marcus Aemilius Scaurus, the *princeps senatus* (the senator called on first for his opinion or vote), for example—but did not closely involve himself in politics at Rome. At Arpinum, however, he was an important person. The interests of these rural equestrians paralleled those of the ruling class in Rome. Such rural families provided a reservoir to replenish the senatorial ranks when necessary, as in Sulla's enlargement of the Senate.

One shortsighted weakness of the oligarchy of the later Republic was its failure to continue to admit substantial numbers of New Men from the formerly Italian upper classes into the governing elite of the state. These Italo-Romans supplied officers for the protagonists in the civil wars and with the rise of Caesar found their way increasingly into the higher posts of the government. By the time of the emperor Vespasian, himself of this background, most aristocrats had ancestors who in the late Republic had been Italians.

It is true, nevertheless, that the most visible and individually influential of the equestrians were those of the city of Rome itself. Of these, the most important were the publicans. Associations of publicans, organized somewhat like joint-stock companies, bid on the contracts for collecting taxes—tithes and customs—leased state-owned mines both

---

[2] See pages 67–69 for a discussion of Roman coinage.

in Italy and (primarily) in the provinces; and constructed ships, public buildings, and highways. Some were also moneylenders, businessmen, and merchants. They served on the jury panels of the permanent courts from the time of Gaius Gracchus, though they accounted for only a portion of the jurors after 70 B.C. In this role they exercised a degree of political influence even within the provinces, since the threat of prosecution before an unfriendly jury might serve to coerce a governor.

The equestrians' participation on the juries, however, does not alone explain their power. Historians of antiquity even now often do not recognize just how much the state needed this group of men. They provided much of the secondary organization of the government. Without their staffs of accountants, clerks, and other agents, the state out of necessity would have enormously expanded its own rather limited bureaucracy. Everyone knows about the Jews' contempt for the agents of the publican companies (these were always minor employees and not the important people whom Cicero referred to as *publicani*), and in general the opprobrium may well have been merited. Yet if the government had directly collected tithes and customs, built its own ships, roads, buildings, and so on, would the result have been any more humane or economical? There is certainly ground for doubting that a government bureaucracy would have been as efficient. The truth is Rome needed the upper-class equestrians because their companies functioned as a kind of extension of the state.

Rich equestrians exercised an influence on politics also. They made loans to politicians like Caesar; Cicero (who was a rural equestrian before he entered the Senate) became both a spokesman for the financial group and a defender of their interests. At times he defended them even when he disapproved of their demands, simply because he knew that the oligarchy could not function without their support. Though difficult to detail, equestrian dissatisfaction with the core oligarchy probably caused large numbers of them to support Caesar, which support in turn helped Caesar win his victories. The equestrians' revulsion against civil war and desire for peace, without which they could not prosper, later caused them to give general support to the man who might bring enduring peace. The equestrian order, that is to say, helped Octavian to become Augustus, the first emperor.

Titus Pomponius Atticus

A most prominent equestrian of the first century B.C. was Titus Pomponius Atticus (110–32 B.C.), the friend of Cicero. He was hardly typical—richer than most of his class, much too cultivated; he did not engage even in the fringe political activity, such as in service on juries or in public contracting, that occupied many equestrians. Yet he typifies the group in some ways, particularly in his instinct for survival in difficult times, which led him and other powerful equestrians to exert their influence very judiciously and evenhandedly in the direction of order and stability.

We know much more about Atticus than about other equestrians both because of Cicero's sixteen books of letters to him, spanning, with some gaps, the period from 68 to 44 B.C., and because Cornelius Nepos, a contemporary biographer, left a life of Atticus. Nepos was rather fulsome in his praise, as biographers often are. Atticus' wealth was inherited, partly from his father and, in middle life, from a rich uncle. In the middle 80s B.C., when civil war was in the making, Atticus invested much of his capital in Epirus and (probably) Greece and took up residence in Athens for two decades. This fact, plus his remarkable facility in the Greek language, accounts for his surname.

Atticus' early decision to detach himself from the political arena grew into a fixed policy, and he steadfastly refused to be connected with any faction in Rome. It might easily have been otherwise. He was related by marriage to the tribune Sulpicius, who had opposed Sulla and was slain by him. Nevertheless, in Greece Atticus became the close friend of Sulla, who, according to Nepos, was charmed by him. Adhering to his decision, however, Atticus refused when urged by Sulla to return to Italy with him, presumably as a supporter. Atticus could certainly have had a distinguished political career had he so desired; possibly, like his friend Cicero, he could even have attained the consulate. Instead he chose noninvolvement in any direct way; yet he was involved indirectly, through friendship, judicious use of money, and advice.

Atticus illustrates also the fact that some equestrians were approximately the social equals of the nobles, the officeholding aristocracy. He moved in high social circles; when Cicero refers in his letters to the richest of the core oligarchs, he describes them as "your friends." Besides his family ties to the patrician Sulpicii, his sister married Quintus Cicero, brother of the orator, and his daughter later became the wife of Marcus Agrippa, the chief lieutenant of Octavian/Augustus and mother of the first wife of the future emperor Tiberius. Though the consular nobles may have considered themselves a cut above Atticus, everyone surely recognized that only his decision to stay away from politics separated them.

Atticus used his wealth generously to support various individuals on all sides of the political arena even when, at times, it was dangerous to do so. For example, he helped some friends of Antony and Fulvia, Antony's wife, at a time when Antony's fortunes had dropped to a low ebb at Rome. This action probably explains why Antony eliminated his name from the list of the proscribed in 43 B.C.—a list that condemned several friends of Cicero, along with the orator himself. Atticus was at one point in danger from the oligarchs on the other side, however, some of whom felt that he should support the *boni* and oppose their "evil" opponents and attacked him because he remained unaligned.

He also played the role of benefactor in literary matters. He maintained a staff of skilled slaves and freedmen who helped research and publish works of Cicero and doubtless other authors. He himself served as Cicero's adviser and critic. He too wrote; we know of a chronological compendium of history, much used in his time and after.

In Athens Atticus used his money as any rich Roman (or citizen) residing in a provincial city would. He once distributed substantial supplies of grain to the Athenian citizens in a bad time, and on several occasions he either lent money to the city or guaranteed loans, at low interest. Probably there were many other such benefactions in both Athens and Rome. Yet Atticus lived a relatively simple life. His friend Nepos, who claimed he saw Atticus' daily account books, said that Atticus never spent more than an average of about 3,000 sesterces a month on his own household, even allowing for entertaining others. Nor did Atticus own even half as many villas as those Cicero acquired with only a fraction of his friend's wealth.

When the civil wars finally ended, Atticus and many other wealthy equestrians survived. Doubtless they had helped to finance both sides, but they managed to stay politically uninvolved. They perhaps lost something when Caesar reduced debts, in effect, by requiring prewar valuations of property used as collateral for loans, but they still had much wealth. Some, Atticus among them, retained also their *dignitas* and even their integrity. The support of such persons perhaps meant most when the war was decided and funds were needed to achieve stability. The influence of equestrians like Atticus probably tilted the balance more than we know.

The Upper Classes

Quite a lot of what we know about Roman society involves only the upper classes—at least, those members of the upper classes who held important office, or who wrote literary or historical works, or who were friends of Cicero and thus are mentioned in his letters (one of the most valuable sources of social information on the last decades of the Republic).

Obviously those at the higher levels of society had more of everything that people crave than those beneath them: money, prestige, and power. The continual expansion of the republican empire meant increased opportunity for officeholders and increased prestige for the small group of men who ruled most of the Mediterranean world. Yet the total number of top offices remained relatively small: however many provinces there might be, there were still only two consuls annually. The praetorship (there were eight praetors after Sulla, until Caesar doubled the number) was a plum worth having, especially since it usually meant a governorship. Failing that, a person could still hold up his head if he held a quaestorship or perhaps an aedileship, and had a seat in the Senate.

The total number of persons who made up the upper classes was perhaps larger than is often realized. One has only to browse through the lists of magistrates of the Republic to see the many names of persons about whom we know next to nothing—names that yet designate men who must have been important figures in Rome. We must always bear in mind that the accidents that have allowed some information to survive do not leave us with anything like a complete picture. Consider, for example, the list of the men known to have been involved in the conspiracy to assassinate Caesar. These men were surely trusted as absolutely safe for the Republic, that is to say, loyal to the oligarchy. Several of the names mean nothing at all to us. Yet they came from important families and formed an essential part of the politically oriented upper class. Nevertheless the men who held real power in the core oligarchy were few in number: that group was pretty exclusive. A New Man like Cicero or the son of a New Man, Pompey, might be quite important and yet not move within the inner circle either of society or of politics. On the fringes also were those men of secondary families who held important but lesser office. Beyond this sphere, many equestrians who were involved neither in government and politics nor in finance or business must still have enjoyed relatively high social status because they came from well-to-do old and respected families.

The most important reason for the failure of some members of old families to play what they might secretly have thought their proper role in the state was surely lack of money. Standards of luxury had increased rapidly for upper-class Romans. Cicero was a latecomer of a not particularly wealthy family, yet he had a townhouse on the Palatine Hill in Rome that cost more than 3 million sesterces. He also acquired seven villas of varying value outside the city, some in resort areas. These had, of course, separate staffs and their own maintenance expenses. Most of Cicero's money came from bequests; wealthy clients, grateful for acquittals the orator obtained for them in the courts but unable to pay a direct fee (which was illegal) left him money in their wills; meanwhile Cicero's credit was good since his future prospects were known. He had additional income from gifts, from his wife's dowry, and from farmland and urban rental property. The really rich Romans—Crassus, Lucullus, or Pompey, for example—had a great deal more than the parvenu Cicero. Romans of this and later times were astonished at how little money earlier figures of importance had had. They used to come see the small apartment Sulla had lived in as a young man and marvel at the small rental he had then paid.

Women in the Late Republic

In all periods of Roman history, we have much more information about the upper classes than the lower classes. The status of upper-class women and the conditions of their daily lives in the late Republic are fairly well known to us. In the city of Rome, women of this group were, by ancient standards, relatively free in their persons and their property, able to move about in the city and to attend various public events such as the games, theater, and sporting events. Such a range of activities was in considerable contrast to an earlier day: a consul of the mid–third century B.C. had divorced his wife because she attended public games without his permission.

Roman matrons possessed both prestige and authority more by cus·tom than by law. Their influence within their families often related to the wealth they controlled; widows especially were likely to have substantial wealth. The writer Cornelius Nepos, whom we have already encountered as the biographer of Atticus, contrasted the position of Roman women with that of Greek women in the preface of his collection of biographies:

> Who among the Romans would be embarrassed to bring his wife [uxor] to a dinner party? or whose wife [materfamilias] does not have first place at home and attend the [public] festivals?

Inevitably, it seems, some relaxation of moral standards accompanied women's freedom of movement and association. We know of some women of good family who illustrate this decline well enough. Best known is Clodia, who had several affairs with men other than her husband, including a liaison with the poet Catullus.

Women's control of wealth was possible not so much because of changes in the law as through the development of ingenious ways of getting around it. (It may be significant that the assemblies never formally changed the law.) Legally, the great power of the *paterfamilias* endured, so that by law he controlled the property of all family members. A daughter often married in her early teens and then came under the power of her husband. In practice, however, fathers in the late Republic treated daughters about as they did sons, and since most marriages were informal (by *usus*), wives did not come under their husbands' control as they had formerly.[3] Dowries were still given and used by husbands, but title to dower property remained in the hands of the wife's father—or, indirectly, the wife herself if the father was dead and she was under the authority of a guardian. Though the letter of the law made it difficult for women to inherit property and hand it down by will, the law could easily be evaded, and it was. Women whose fathers

---

[3] See also the discussion on pages 79–81.

were dead, or who had been emancipated by their fathers from the *patria potestas*, were assigned guardians, but these seem not to have supervised their wards' property closely. In fact, if a ward wished, she could compel a change of guardian, presumably to a more complacent one. When couples divorced, children went with the father because they belonged to his family. Illegitimate children, however, belonged to the mother's family.

The person of the late Republic who is best known to us is Cicero, and we also know something of his wife, Terentia. On one occasion, in Cicero's absence, she and their daughter, Tullia, arranged a marriage for the latter—one that Cicero himself did not much approve of. Terentia was wealthy in her own right, and since theirs was an *usus* marriage, she controlled her own property. Presumably she had a guardian, but we hear nothing of him. When Cicero was exiled and perhaps also at other times, Terentia handled some of his affairs as well, not always to his liking. She had her own financial agent, whom Cicero didn't care much for either. According to Cicero, Terentia's mishandling of his property led to their divorce. In an age when most persons who survived childhood (the period of greatest mortality) could expect to live to be perhaps forty or forty-five years old on average, Terentia lived to be more than a hundred.

Cicero, incidentally, seems to have loved his daughter more than his son and took responsibility for her financial situation even in marriage, when one of her husbands did not provide well for her (which may have been a not infrequent consequence of *usus* marriage). We know of other such strong bonds between Roman fathers and daughters.

Household slaves made possible this greater freedom of movement for upper-class women. In particular, the practice of employing wet nurses, usually slaves, freed women from the constant care of infant children. Wet nurses in fact had primary care of children for their first couple of years; other slaves helped look after older children as well. One should not infer that Roman parents took no interest in their small children, but the close relationship we expect between mother and child in today's society seems not to have been usual. Closeness often did develop, but at a later stage in the child's life.

Lower-class women were likely just as free to move about and go to public games and festivals as those of higher rank. However, without the security and influence that came with wealth (as well as household slaves to care for children), it is doubtful that they were as independent.

Upper-class women seem to have been better educated in the late Republic—though some, such as Cornelia, the mother of the Gracchi, had been quite well educated a century earlier. Several women of the first century who, like Cornelia, were both cultivated and influential are known to us. One such was Servilia, the mother of Marcus Brutus, who exercised both social and political influence.

Cicero (*Brutus* 58.211) mentions six women whom he had heard speak in public; Valerius Maximus (8.3) tells of women who were their own advocates in court. In 42 B.C., a year after the death of Cicero, Hortensia, daughter of the man who was the premier orator of Rome until he was displaced by Cicero in 70 B.C., made a public address that was attended by large numbers of men as well as women in which she attacked a plan of the triumvirs to tax women. The speech, and probably other agitation, caused the Triumvirate to cancel the proposed tax. Though little of their work survives, we also know of women poets and writers in this age.

Changing Mores Among Men of the Age

The greatest figures of the late Republic, such as Caesar and Pompey, were men of great military reputation. Even Cicero, though he refused commands after his praetorship and consulship, had done early duty in the military, and when he was a provincial commander in Cilicia he led a small military operation in the hope of earning a triumph. No longer did most upper-class young men serve in the army, however. In earlier centuries, all citizens who wished to be elected to public office had to serve a minimum of ten years with the army, but somehow, perhaps through a failure to enforce the regulation, the requirement was seldom met in the late Republic. The fact that the Roman army had almost no citizen cavalry in this period contributed to the change. The change likely relates also to the practice initiated by Marius and continued ever after of using propertyless persons to serve in the army. Citizens whose votes were important in the Centuriate Assembly, which elected the top officials of state, rarely served in the army. Other methods, therefore, were more effective in gaining name recognition among voters than army service. Only those upper-class young men who went along as junior staff officers on commands in the provinces or in other arenas got military experience. The writer known to us as Pseudo-Sallust said of young nobles who fought against Caesar in the civil war, "They know nothing of hardship, the enemy, or the military life" (*Ad Caesarem* 10.5.9).

The sociopolitical changes that led to the fall of the Republic may indeed relate to the Roman aristocracy's losing touch with the army. Preferring the easier life of the city, upper-class men gained voter recognition by service in minor offices such as moneyer, a post that in earlier times had been of little interest to scions of noble families.

The political and social conservatism of the upper classes was not unrelated to the increase in wealth characteristic of the age. Those who were rich enjoyed their villas, their many slaves and clients, their prestige. Cicero once remarked during the civil war of the 40s that these men were more concerned with keeping their fishponds (which supplied dishes for their gourmet appetites) than anything else.

Many among the upper classes were more sophisticated in Cicero's time than their counterparts had been even a century earlier. This sophistication showed itself in various ways, such as in their attitude toward religion and their intellectual pursuits. The changes came mostly through interaction with the Hellenistic east. The philosophical thought of the Greeks, for example, not only influenced some Romans toward one or another of the schools of philosophy but also impinged on their religious beliefs. They picked up the essential skepticism of Greek intellectuals almost by osmosis. The Romans already looked on religion as something to be used for state—or personal—purposes. The nobles continued to desire positions in the higher priestly colleges because of the prestige involved, and as aediles they put on ever more elaborate religious festivals. The purpose, however, had always been more political than religious, a fact that could hardly have escaped even the lowest class of citizens when they saw Roman officials manipulate the omens before a battle or use them to block legislation they opposed. The tendency of the lower classes to seek consolation in the cults of Oriental gods brought in by immigrants or soldiers surely related to this decline in basic religiosity among ruling-class Romans.

We must not overstate the decadence of the state religion in Rome during the late Republic, however. Religion was in the Romans' very bones; if with their minds educated Romans doubted the traditional gods, they nevertheless embraced the whole pantheon with their hearts. Moreover, religion and politics were completely intermingled; dedication to the state religion was an essential part of patriotism. Thoughtful Romans saw in the neglect of some aspects of the state religion one of the causes for the deterioration of the constitution.

Three intellectuals of the late Republic and early Empire, Cicero, Varro, and the historian Livy, all display this ambiguous attitude toward religion. Cicero professed himself a follower of the Academy, by which he meant that he was a skeptic, though he often seemed more Stoic than skeptic. His skepticism certainly extended to religion, yet he felt that religion was important, and not merely a sort of opiate of the masses. For Cicero, Rome's destiny was somehow inextricably entwined with augury, auspices, and all the rest.

Education in the Late Republic

As in many other aspects of culture, the Romans imitated and adapted Greek ways in educating their children. By the late Republic, the educational system that had developed comprised three tiers, roughly corresponding to elementary, secondary, and advanced levels. However,

Roman parents retained a strong personal role in educating their children, and the Roman state, unlike the major Greek states, never developed a system of state-supported schools. In the second century B.C., the biographer Plutarch tells us, Cato the Censor insisted on teaching his son himself. Roman mothers, too, taught their daughters personally.

Romans began to use tutors in the second century B.C.; they also sent their children to be taught at one or another of the available elementary schools (*ludi*) and soon grammar or secondary schools began to appear, offering instruction by grammarians (*grammatici*). Romans also began to select well-educated and trusted slaves to act as pedagogues to look after the children, conduct them to and from school, and help them with their homework. Teachers were paid fees based on their qualifications and reputation; since some teachers were slaves and charged very low fees, even lower-class Romans might attend elementary school for long enough to learn the basics. Education for children of upper-class families often involved parents, a pedagogue, a highly educated tutor, and teachers at the schools. Discipline was strict, in accord with traditional values; in the *ludi* students were flogged for infractions of the rules. The elder Cato, however, stern as he was in some ways, would not use corporal punishment with his children, and as we have seen, in the second quarter of the century, the playwright Terence held in *The Brothers* that a permissive education and upbringing with relaxed standards might well turn out a better human being than did the old, rigorous, and suppressive discipline.

In spite of his mistrust of Greeks and of the debilitating effects of Greek literature and philosophy on Roman morals, Cato eventually sent his son to Greece for further education. Cicero did the same a century later, but without Cato's misgivings. Thus a proper finish to the education of a Roman boy with promise might involve travel to Athens or Rhodes for work with Greek rhetoricians (*rhetores*) or philosophers there. Such higher-level education under Greek rhetoricians began to appear in Rome only toward the end of the second century. The Gracchi were said to have had some such training, and in the later Republic it was standard for upper-class sons. By Cicero's day, rhetorical training might be in Latin as well as Greek, but the Latin rhetoricians were long considered inferior. We have no evidence that girls attended the rhetorical schools; yet, as mentioned earlier, a few Roman women somehow became excellent public speakers.

Many conservative Romans had their doubts about the Greek rhetoricians, who, they thought, emphasized form at the expense of content and character. The *rhetores* taught a speaking style designed to persuade through polished rhythms and stylized techniques more than through solid content—a far cry from the methods of old Cato, who had held that good oratory was "a good man speaking" and emphasized the acquisition of a mass of factual knowledge; the words would come, he said. The censors of 92 B.C. (not unenlightened men: one was L. Licinius Crassus, a leading orator and statesman) issued an edict against the Latin rhetoricians who were imitating the Greeks, saying that young men were wasting their time with them, that what they taught was contrary to the *mos maiorum*. The Greek rhetoricians did not come under their ban, possibly because the censors recognized that it was important for Romans to achieve facility in reading and speaking Greek. The edict was not enforced for long, however, and Latin rhetoric, pretty much in the Greek style, continued to evolve as an essential part of higher education.

Roman rhetoricians were more pragmatic than Greek ones, however, and stressed substantive content. No one in the late Republic exercised greater influence on Roman education than Cicero, who advocated a curriculum for the education of an orator that included more than the typical foundation in language and literature; it required additional training in history, law, philosophy, and the sciences. And he underscored the traditional method of learning directly from Roman statesmen in the Forum.

Aristocracies characteristically inculcate in the rising generation of young men their obligation to serve the state. In Rome that sense of duty was strongly emphasized. As part of a young noble's education, his father would arrange with some eminent person to accept his son as a protégé, whether in the Forum or in the army (*tirocinium fori* or *militiae*). In the army the young man would both observe and participate as a junior member of the staff and tent mate of a senior officer; in the Forum, he would observe all phases of the work of his patron, who might perhaps be a man learned in the law (a *jurisconsultus*), dispensing advice about legal problems, or a great orator, composing speeches for delivery in the Forum or the Senate. Such young men were permitted to sit near the entry of the senatorial *curia* and listen to the deliberations of the Senate. Cicero, for example, was in his youth a protégé of Mucius Scaevola and in turn had protégés of his own. Such training may have been more important than rhetorical instruction in preparing young men for later participation in affairs of state. Lower-class children, after a couple of years in school, might learn a trade under their own parents or enroll as apprentices under masters in the trades that were to be their living.

Philosophy, Literature, Life, and Law in the Late Republic

One of Rome's strengths over the centuries lay in the sizable number of upper-class persons who devoted themselves to public service. We are familiar with the politicians and the generals, but there were others. With their usual pragmatism, Romans tended to gravitate to pursuits that somehow related to politics: if they studied philosophy they might be especially concerned with constitutional theory and the law; if they learned rhetoric, it was to improve their performance as speakers in the Forum. In literature Romans placed great emphasis on history, which they saw as especially useful in teaching the lessons of statecraft. Even their satire often had a political tinge.

The philosophical schools that had the greatest influence on the Romans were naturally those current in the contemporary Hellenistic east: Academic skepticism, Stoicism, and Epicureanism. The sophisticated skepticism of the New Academy had come to Rome as early as 155 B.C., when the head of the Academy, Carneades, came to the city with an embassy and lectured in public. His taking both sides of the question, What is justice? scandalized the elder Cato, among others, by dealing so cavalierly with such a serious topic. Cicero's Academic convictions were ambivalent, and no Roman ever became an important teacher of this school; however, it subtly affected the upper levels of Roman society for many decades.

Stoicism was much more directly influential. Panaetius, the house guest of Scipio Aemilianus and a member of the so-called Scipionic circle, popularized the teachings of the Stoic school in Rome. Among his pupils was P. Rutilius Rufus, consul in 105 B.C. and legate in the province of Asia in 97 or 94, whose career serves to remind us of that all too little publicized group of conscientious men of high integrity who made Roman rule—at least oftentimes—fair and palatable to provincials. Another pupil of Panaetius was the Rhodian Posidonius, whose influence on Roman thought and literature in the first century B.C. was pervasive. Stoicism powerfully influenced Cicero and the younger Cato, as it did Seneca and Marcus Aurelius in the time of the Empire. Romans were not much attracted by the cosmological teachings of the Stoics, nor even by such basic principles as the fatherhood of God and the brotherhood of man. However, the emphases on virtue as an end in itself, its own reward; on acceptance of one's fate with equanimity; and on duty, especially in the public service—all these appealed strongly to the Romans, whose notion of the *mos maiorum* already embraced these concepts. The Stoics merely articulated and ordered what most responsible Romans already believed.

True philosophical Epicureanism appealed to only a few Romans, among them Julius Caesar. A basic Epicurean theory was that the gods were unmindful of humans, who must then seek their own pleasure. In its degenerate form, the philosophy was taken to advocate a hedonistic style of life. This debased form of the philosophy spread rather facilely along a certain vein of the upper classes. Those who adhered to the original view of Epicurus, that only the virtuous man could be truly happy, were less numerous. The greatest exponent of Epicureanism among the Romans was a literary figure, Lucretius (ca. 94–55 B.C.), who wrote *On the Nature of Things*. Lucretius' poem, almost evangelical in tone, preaching to and teaching its readers, is nevertheless a fine work. He expounded the atomic theory of the origins of things as Epicurus had (based on still earlier philosophic thought) and taught a kind of chance creation followed by long periods of geological and biological evolution. A prime purpose of the poet was to free his readers from the fear of death. For him, it was a comforting thought that the end of life was to be the end of everything for everyone.

A contemporary of Lucretius was G. Valerius Catullus (ca. 84–54 B.C.), Rome's premier lyric poet. It is hard to imagine two poets more different. Lucretius was serious, contemplative, and apparently rather solitary; Catullus was capable of being serious but was more often frivolous, and he was gregarious and fun-loving. Catullus belonged to the young set that came to exemplify the charges of moral decadence in the Rome of his time. It would be a mistake, however, to conclude that the life-style of this rather small upper-class group was typical of all Roman society.

Catullus' best lyric poems were written in celebration of one of his love affairs, with Clodia (Lesbia in his verses), the beautiful if amoral sister of the politician Clodius. She was a widow at the time. Eventually she tired of the amorous poet; his works run the gamut from wild, ardent love to doubt and finally spiteful hate once he had fully felt her rejection. The simple intensity of feeling and fine flow of words have led discriminating readers to put Catullus' works with the best of all lyric poetry.

Romans often turned to the writing of history as a respectable ancillary occupation. The elder Cato in the mid–second century B.C., for example, published a book of history, *Origines* (of which we have only fragments). His writing he felt was as important as his study of the law and his service as Rome's leading orator. In the last quarter of the same century the official records (*annales maximi*) of the office of the pontifex maximus were published by the consular, Publius Mucius Scaevola and served as the basis for a number of works produced at the end of the century and later. None of the earlier ones remain. Other important historical sources too have been lost, including the memoirs of several important men. Sulla's memoirs, however, were available two centuries later to Plutarch (as were some other works of the period), and we have to rely on such secondary authors.

The best known historical work that survives from the last century of the Republic is the *Gallic Wars* of Caesar, a valuable work of history and literature as well as of style. Its fine, straightforward prose has caused it to be inflicted on many a schoolchild whose interest in the topic is nil; in its own day it may have been intended as propaganda for the politician's own cause.

Another historian of Caesar's time, Sallust (G. Sallustius Crispus, ca. 86–35 B.C.), typifies the genre better than does Caesar. Sallust was much

Cicero. (*Alinari/Art Resource, New York*)

imitated in his style, which may itself be an imitation of Thucydides. Besides a history of the period of the second quarter of the first century B.C., of which only some fragments remain, Sallust wrote a work on the Jugurthan War and another on the conspiracy of Catiline. The first portrays with exaggerated emphasis the decadence of the aristocracy. The theme is implicit also in the work on Catiline. Yet Sallust used excellent sources and wrote well and, despite his Caesarian sympathies, objectively. His pessimism and emphasis on decadence set a trend— almost a fashion—for future writers, who felt called on to take a similar moral stance.

The student may think of Cicero primarily as a politician and orator, but he was also a literary figure of great importance. He influenced the development of the Latin language more than any other single person, and his works have had a literary (and often a rhetorical or humanistic) effect on Western scholars over many centuries. He published his orations and essays in his own lifetime, but it is the letters—more than eight hundred of them, published only after his death—that have had most influence in modern times. They have also attracted the closest attention from historians, whether their interests involve primarily intellectual, social, economic, or political conditions. Polished and elegant in style, these letters are windows through which we glimpse the Rome of Cicero's day more intimately and directly than in any other Latin literature. Because we can see into Cicero's mind as into that of no other Roman, scholars have developed more emphatic views about him than about any of his contemporaries except perhaps Caesar. The tendency is to love the one and despise the other or vice versa, and often in most unscholarly manner.

Most of Cicero's orations in court cases display political overtones. Characteristic of his calling as an orator, he was not an outstanding legal expert, just as legal experts were not necessarily good orators. Those public-spirited men who studied the law intensively in order to give free, expert legal advice to all comers were called jurisconsults or jurisprudents. It was illegal for them to accept a fee, just as it was for trial lawyers to do so. The two greatest jurisprudents of the first century B.C. were Q. Mucius Scaevola, consul in 95 B.C. (the son of Publius Mucius Scaevola, consul in 133 and also a jurisprudent), and Servius Sulpicius Rufus, consul in 51. Much influenced by Stoic thought, the younger Scaevola made a beginning of rational codification of the law. Rufus also was a prolific writer, but none of his works have survived. The law at this time was rapidly changing, largely because of Rome's expanding territorial responsibilities. All Roman magistrates to a degree had the right to make law through their edicts. The urban praetors were most influential in this respect. The so-called formulary system, introduced some time earlier, was gradually replacing the older, much more rigid action system. A formula was, essentially, an instruction given by the praetor after a preliminary hearing before the judge who was to preside over the case, indicating that if the circumstances were found to be such and such then the decision should be such and such. Through the use of formulas, the praetors could fit the law to specific cases much more exactly. Considerations of equity entered into some cases: determination on the basis of what was fair rather than on specific law.

Another group of Romans made themselves expert in religious matters, as, for example, in the taking of auspices and omens. Because of the importance of securing favorable omens in guiding affairs of state, this was an important matter.

Public figures often had motives other than civic service: they wished to obligate important men to themselves, to build up a clientele in the usual fashion that would carry them to high office. Yet it remains remarkable that so many members of Rome's upper classes were willing to work so long and hard in service to the state for the sake of recognition. The tradition continued under the Empire, though the rewards then came from the emperor more than from the people. The upper classes of the late Republic, if we look at the picture painted by Sallust, were morally bankrupt and decadent; but a more accurate sketch will depict also those numerous jurists, scholars, and orators who, for the rewards of respect and recognition, dedicated themselves to the public service.

9 The Early Empire: Augustus and Tiberius, 27 B.C.–A.D. 37

The Pax Romana

IN NEITHER ANCIENT NOR MODERN TIMES have men disputed Augustus' greatest achievement: peace. People in his own time had lived through the years of the civil wars, with all their misery, uncertainty, and fear. To them peace, even at the price of restricted freedom for some, was as welcome as sunshine after long rain. A leader who could not only bring peace but also maintain it ranked in their eyes as a savior of humanity. The Hellenized Jewish philosopher Philo of Alexandria expressed the general feeling:

> This is he [Augustus] who . . . broke the chains which had shackled and pressed so hard on the habitable world, . . . who exterminated wars of both the open kind and the covert which are brought about by the raids of brigands. This is he who cleared the sea of pirate ships and filled it with merchant vessels. This is he who reclaimed every state to liberty. . . .[1]

---

[1] Philo *Embassy to Gaius*. Translated by F. H. Colson, Loeb Classical Library (Cambridge, Mass., 1956).

Looking backward from a perspective of many centuries, modern admirers of the first emperor have been most impressed by the length of time—two and a half centuries, except for brief episodes—that the pax Romana endured.

Peace became a consciously developed theme of the regime. The gates to the temple of Janus, closed only on the rare occasion when there was no war at all, were shut three times during Augustus' years, with public celebration. The Ara Pacis ("Altar to Peace"), constructed on the Campus Martius in the middle years of Augustus' reign, elaborated the theme in fine high-relief sculpture; the Augustan poet Vergil sang the theme in verse, seeing in Augustus the embodiment of Roman destiny, which was to put an end to chaos and to fashion a new golden age of peace and law. Many of the panels of the Ara Pacis, which may still be seen in a little museum on the Tiber opposite the remains of the mausoleum Augustus built, convey with powerful feeling the serenity of the age. Peace is also a theme in the *Res Gestae*, Augustus' summary and defense of his career. The document, largely preserved in inscriptions (in particular, one found in Turkey, called the Monumentum Ancyranum), indirectly expresses the theme by emphasizing the victories that brought peace. But this was the Roman view of things. Even Vergil saw peace as something that Romans imposed on others.

Peace alone was not enough, of course: in civil war rivals may be only temporarily subdued. For Augustus it was a great advantage, to be sure, that most Romans were weary of war. But he also understood that to endure, peace must be based on clemency, justice, and liberty. These

A relief from the Ara Pacis at Rome. The altar was erected by Augustus to elaborate the theme of peace. (*Alinari/Art Resource, New York*)

virtues, along with *pietas* and peace, became themes of the new age. Augustus did indeed show clemency for many of his defeated rivals—such of them as survived, at any rate. He may also properly be called just—evenhanded—in his treatment of Roman and provincial, upper class and low. Liberty he saw in the *Res Gestae* as the good that resulted from his defeat of the "tyrant" Antony; but he also attempted to restore at least a measure of that elusive commodity to members of the former ruling class by giving them an important role in the new order. As for the lower classes, their voting rights gradually disappeared during the Empire, both in the electoral and in the legislative spheres. However, peace probably brought more freedom of action and opportunity than any electoral process had provided in the past. The price the lower-class plebeians paid for security was their free institutions. But had they ever been really free?

The pattern was essentially repeated in the provinces. There Rome had granted the city-state units self-governing institutions that benefited a restricted ruling class. As for lower-class provincials, quite likely many of them enjoyed more personal freedom under the Romans than before, under their own rulers. Both at Rome and in the provinces, freedom did exist under the Empire for the lower classes, but it did not include the privilege of participating in governmental processes.

From Republic to Empire

In January of 27 B.C. Octavian took a new title that had been voted by the Senate: Augustus. The title suggested great dignity and authority, with religious overtones. It would be used by all emperors after him. The year 27 is often used by historians to mark the end of the Republic and the beginning of the Empire. Ironically, in this year also Augustus announced the restoration of the *res publica*, a term that transliterates somewhat imperfectly into English as Republic. Augustus certainly meant to restore many of the traditions of the old Republic and to continue the important offices, which would be held by men elected in the citizen assemblies. However, the Republic had been dominated by great individuals since the time of Sulla and earlier; even such a republican as Cicero had come to doubt that it could endure without a strong figure at the helm. It is therefore unfair to charge Augustus with completely cynical hypocrisy, as some have done, in his announced restoration. Quite probably he was consciously following Cicero's view, though in the matter of ultimate power for himself as the dominant leader he certainly went beyond the great orator's ideal type of the patron of the state.

No institution of the new state, not even the Senate, could be really free when confronted by the arbitrary power Augustus held in his grasp, even if in velvet gloves. Yet it is doubtful that Augustus fully understood this (at the beginning of 27 he was still only thirty-five); at any rate, most Romans were satisfied with the imitation of freedom projected by a princeps ("first citizen") who displayed tolerance and clemency. Augustus and at least a majority of his successors for two centuries were principes of that sort.

For Augustus and for all Romans, res publica meant much more than the political structure of the oligarchy of the Republic. The term embraced all public aspects of state, society, and culture, which were firmly rooted in the traditions of the past. A closely parallel expression was mos maiorum, the customs of the ancestors. In many ways Augustus did try very hard to restore the old ways. He reconstituted priesthoods, some of which had gradually deteriorated; he rebuilt temples and revived the historic sacrifices and festivals. He tried to restore the old morals, passing several laws in the attempt. Sumptuary legislation, in the pattern of earlier laws stretching back a couple of centuries, aimed to limit how much individuals might spend on banqueting and the like. Conspicuous consumption and ostentation the princeps also dampened somewhat by his own modest manner of life.

Augustus' Legislation on Women and the Family

In 18 B.C. (with changes in A.D. 9), Augustus had rather strict laws on adultery enacted. The laws were applicable to both men and women, but they seem to have affected women especially. Though in early Rome adultery could be punished severely within the family, only now did it officially become a crime. Condoning adultery also became a crime. In the late Republic, several well-known men continued to live with adulterous wives (Lucullus and Pompey, for example); but Augustus' law required upper-class men to divorce wives guilty of adultery.

As defined in law, adultery was extramarital sex involving a married woman. For a married man to engage in sex with an unmarried woman was not termed adultery, and sex by men with slaves, lower-class women, and actresses was not a crime. However, Augustus' laws made it a crime for any man and upper-class unmarried woman to have sex, regardless of whether the male was married or unmarried. This crime was termed fornication (stuprum); however, the penalty was the same as for adultery: exile.

Augustus had to enforce the law on adultery even against his own daughter, Julia, and her daughter of the same name as well: both were banished. Clearly, Augustus felt that adultery threatened the social fabric of the state; it damaged the family, that most important constituent unit. Especially in the upper strata of society the family had lost cohesiveness under stress of prosperity and the freer sexual mores of the late Republic. Augustus' moral laws were, as one might expect, often fractured, but they had some effect on open behavior.

Paradoxically, the new affluence made it difficult for many upper-class families to raise more than a minimum number of children. Child-rearing cost a great deal, especially because each girl required a dowry and each boy an inheritance if children were to take their proper places in society at the level these families tried to maintain. Augustus often gave large presents of money to heads of families in distress. As a rule the man involved was about to lose his rank—usually senatorial—because he could not meet the minimum property requirement, 1 million sesterces; but Augustus' motives were not solely political.

The princeps made it clear that the normal life-style of the upper class should include marriage and children: he hoped the upper classes would increase in numbers. He taxed unmarried persons of marriage-able age, even widows and widowers, and he permitted men with children to hold office earlier than childless candidates. Another law of the period gave special status to women of all classes who had three children or more (four for freedwomen): they were no longer required to have a guardian and thus became financially independent.

In both the Republic and the early Empire women were permitted to attend most public events, including theater and gladiatorial games, but Augustus forbade their attendance at athletic contests, probably because Rome had adopted the Greek practice of nudity for participants in such games.

Yet Augustus' measures to maintain the great families largely failed. In the next several decades, many such families vanish from history. This disappearance may reflect only the withdrawal of the scions of great families from political activity and thus from the records from which we fashion history. (Did they consider it all a charade or did they just shirk the army and provincial service ordinarily required?) However, it is likely that most such families simply died out.

Augustus furthermore allowed men and women—except those of the senatorial order—to enter into formal marriage with ex-slaves. But at the same time, the princeps apparently thought that the practice of granting freedom to slaves was diluting the body of citizens excessively, so he had a law passed to establish thirty as the minimum age for such manumission. Exceptions were allowed in the case of relatives or ped-agogues, and of slaves who were freed in order to marry the patron. (This last instance usually involved a man and a slave woman; curiously, only women who were themselves freed slaves could manumit a male slave, probably her former fellow slave, in order to marry him.) Freeing edu-cated or trained slaves at age thirty seems to have become almost stan-dard procedure.

The Augustan Image in Art and Architecture

Long before Octavian became Augustus he recognized the importance of public image. On millions of coins he presented himself as *divi filius*, "son of the divine one," Caesar. He built a temple to Caesar in the Forum and in various ways nourished the imperial cult. (Predictably, the provinces later echoed the trend: temples to Augustus and Roma were built in Pergamum and Ephesus, for example, and a similarly dedicated altar was erected in Lugdunum [Lyons] in Gaul.) He completed the new forum begun by Caesar, with its temple to Venus, and built another forum himself, dominated by a temple to Mars, which had been vowed by Caesar. These two deities the Julian family claimed as ancestors, through Aeneas and Romulus.

Octavian/Augustus especially venerated the god Apollo as a patron deity. Apollo was a god of pure light, of morality, order, discipline—qualities the princeps wanted to restore in the Roman people. He could also be a god of victory. The Romans had first established a festival to Apollo, with games, during the Second Punic War, and Octavian believed that Apollo had brought him victory in the critical battle near Actium. He enlarged the temple to Apollo there and established regular celebration of games. On the Palatine Hill in Rome he erected another temple to Apollo, completed in 28 B.C., next to his residence. Nearby he placed a colossal statue of the god. The story was told that he sited the temple after lightning struck the spot, where Octavian had planned to build a new palace for himself. (The complex also housed a library, one of several now in the city.) Later in life, Augustus is said to have melted down eighty silver statues that had been erected in his honor and used the proceeds to provide gold objects in this temple. Still another temple of Apollo, remains of which can still be seen near the theater of Marcellus, was refurbished during Augustus' reign. Until his death, Augustus himself lived in rather simple style in his unpretentious residence near the temple of Apollo on the Palatine.

The theme of victory and triumph was elaborated in other new structures; though some had existed earlier, triumphal arches are seen as essentially a creation of the Augustan age. The first constructed in honor of Augustus was put up in the Forum about 29 B.C. to celebrate the victory at Actium. It was later enlarged to honor Augustus' "victory" (mostly negotiated) over Parthia. This triple arch is represented on a coin issued in about 17 B.C. Other triumphal arches were built in Italy and the provinces. A basilica dedicated to Neptune and celebrating the naval victories of M. Vipsanius Agrippa, Augustus' lieutenant, son-in-law, and designated successor, formed part of an elaborate complex that also included baths and the Pantheon (the existing structure was rebuilt by Hadrian more than a century later). Early in his reign, Tiberius added two triumphal arches honoring his son Drusus and his nephew Germanicus to the Forum of Augustus near the temple of Mars.

The Theater of Marcellus, which was built by Augustus and named for his nephew and first-designated successor. (*Alinari/Art Resource, New York*)

In keeping with his desire to restore the old, public religion of Rome, Augustus not only observed all the traditional festivals and found enough patricians to fill the priesthoods, but he also repaired almost all the ancient temples. Most had been built in brick; now he reconstructed them in marble, favoring a simple, unelaborated style in building that art historians term "classic."

The emphasis on the peace Augustus secured for Rome, best seen in the Ara Pacis, has already been stressed. The Roman ideal of piety, too, involving attitude and action not only toward deity but also toward family, has been mentioned as one of the virtues Augustus intended to mark the age. Aeneas, claimed as Caesar's ancestor, was the very symbol of piety; hence the popularity of statuary depicting Aeneas bearing his father Anchises from doomed Troy. Probably Octavian early on meant to project this quality when he returned to the Hellenized cities of Asia Minor works of art—many no doubt religious—that Antony had taken. In this as in many other ways Augustus thus established himself as a patron of provincials. In Italy and Rome also he visually displayed his patronage to the people.

He took care to see that the best art, in particular statuary of Greek origin, was displayed in temples or other public buildings where all could see it. Some temples became almost public museums of art. The new temple of Apollo on the Palatine, for example, was filled—and surrounded—with fine statuary, mostly by Greek masters of the fourth century B.C. The cult statue of the god in the temple was done by Scopas, and a four-horse chariot carrying Apollo and Diana, a work of Lysias,

Coin of Caesar. On left, the goddess Venus, from whom the Julii claim descent. On right, Aeneas carrying his father Anchises, a widely used symbol of piety, which is a common theme in artifacts from the Augustan period. (*American Numismatic Society*)

adorned an arch at the entrance. In the area of the temple was also a colossal bronze statue of Apollo surrounded by four oxen, the work of Myron. Such art might be found at other public buildings as well. At the door of the public baths built by Agrippa, for example, stood the famous statue of a young man with a bather's scraper, attributed to Lysippus.

Gradually, in a way not planned in an overall sense, Augustus began to mold an image that conveyed not merely the greatness of the Julian house—or of himself—but rather of eternal Rome, the great imperial city. The Romans had, of course, for centuries absorbed Greek culture, collected Greek objects of art, and adopted Greek architecture in a piecemeal, fortuitous manner. Now, under Augustus, the visual aura of majestic grandeur that has endured to our own day first took shape. Doubtless Augustus still made use of Greek artists and architects, but the general direction and conception was Roman and reflected a new age.

The Emperor as Patron

Augustus adopted the role of patron in constructing public buildings and displaying art objects. But of course he was patron in many other ways. He served as patron to provincials through the benefits he offered them: peace with noninterference in trade and commerce; a corps of governors, mostly capable rulers who supervised adequately; and career opportunities even for members of the lower classes in the army.

Naturally he became patron to the whole army. From recruitment to retirement, he saw to soldiers' needs, providing them with good wages and occasional, quite lucrative largesse. For some, army service opened the door to jobs in the civil government. In the city of Rome, through the presentation of games and circuses, distributions of grain, and again,

Athlete using a strigil, or scraper, to remove oil from his body. This statue is a copy of the one placed by Marcus Agrippa in the baths he constructed in Rome. (*Alinari/Art Resource, New York*)

largesse, Augustus was the patron of the whole population. The latter reciprocated by cheering him in public (incidentally adding a measure of security); the army, of course, did his bidding and, since it usually approved his leadership, allowed no successful rebellion.

Members of the upper classes could embark on prestigious and lucrative public careers only with the approval of Augustus, so they were in effect his clients also, though the nobles especially resented the fact of their subordination. But by treating them well, the princeps made the situation palatable. Those on good terms with Augustus would make requests on behalf of their own clients, which would be honored; thus the favor came from Augustus, but by way of the noble making the request, who thus preserved his status as a patron. To use an example from a later period, we know that the younger Pliny several times requested from the emperor Trajan appointments, citizenship, and other favors for sons of friends or citizens of his hometown in northern Italy. Trajan invariably granted them. The element of mutuality in the patron-client system was also maintained. Roman aristocrats primarily reciprocated imperial favors by being loyal, accepting Augustus as princeps and first patron. Most were willing to do so as long as they could retain a comfortable life-style, some prestige, and a few shreds of dignity.

The system was not vastly different from that which had existed during the late Republic. The important commanders of armies and governors of provinces had long had the authority to allot subordinate positions to sons of clients or friends (or to sons of those whom they wished to make their friends). Some, such as Pompey and Caesar, had operated as patrons on almost as grand a scale as Augustus himself now did. Augustus and most of his successors in the period of the Principate handled their enormous power as patrons with good sense and some grace as well.

The Distribution of Power

The Government

The major bases of power in any government lie in the army, in finance, and in the chief offices. Augustus dominated all these areas; but he knew well the history of the later Republic, and he consolidated his power with great caution. He had learned from Caesar's fate that power should not be held too openly, and he thus adhered more closely to the traditional forms than Caesar had. In Augustus' early years the people by and large continued to elect the chief officers of state, as they had in the Republic. These officials performed duties assigned in the traditional manner by the Senate, which also controlled the old treasury in the Aerarium Saturni. Part of the army was commanded by these elected officials. However, Augustus for some years held one of the consulates. Later, in 23 B.C., when he ceased to be consul, he was given what was called *maius imperium*, meaning that his *imperium*, or right of command, outranked that of any other official. Moreover, most of the army was under his command, and he controlled all recruitment and retirement besides. Furthermore, he had a great deal of income at his disposal that did not filter through the Aerarium Saturni at all. He had in addition the powers of a tribune, which gave him the authority to convoke both Senate and assembly; occasionally he exercised the old powers of censor without actually reviving the office.

Augustus thus masked his great power. Whereas Caesar had been Dictator, Augustus liked the title *princeps*, with its republican origins. The title Augustus, conferred by a complaisant Senate, implied a personage of great influence, dignity, and semidivine qualities. Later on he was styled by the Senate *pater patriae*, "father of his country," an epithet he stressed on coinage. His behind-the-scenes power affected elections: he did not always specify favored candidates, but when he did, sometimes openly canvassing for his choices, so far as we know they always won.

The Senate was hardly a free body despite the carefully maintained appearance of freedom. The most powerful senators were always somehow tied to the regime. Those who wished full careers could advance most rapidly, or perhaps could advance at all, only if they had the good will of the princeps. The positions conferring the greatest prestige—especially in the command of troops—were those held by the princeps' deputies or legates. These were appointed by him, not elected; the Senate neither gave them their assignments nor allocated them funds.

Yet in some ways the Senate was technically more powerful than it had been during the Republic. Its decrees gradually acquired the force of law: the emperors enforced them, since the Senate enacted the measures they desired. The most important matters recommended to it were first screened by the princeps, with the assistance of a kind of cabinet, at first unofficial, the *consilium principis*, a body that always included some of the chief senators. Even in the greatest days of the Republic, attendance at the elective and other assemblies had never reflected more than a small fraction of the citizens eligible to vote. Now, during Augustus' reign, such assemblies began to consist more and more only of city residents. The units called prerogative centuries, composed entirely of senators, voted first in the elections; since the other centuries followed like sheep, the senators decided the voting. Tiberius (probably) eliminated the pretense; in effect, elections simply became a function of the Senate.

The body also acquired new judicial power, both over its own members and over others in cases involving high crimes. In addition it served in some instances as an appeals body. By the reign of Tiberius the Senate was fulfilling these judicial functions, albeit somewhat haphazardly. Tiberius tried to raise standards by sitting in on some Senate trials. The historian Tacitus, an old senatorial conservative in sentiment, declared that this practice was good for justice but bad for freedom—meaning the Senate's freedom, of course.

Certainly the Senate did not behave like a free institution under Tiberius (14–37), though he began his reign with an appeal to senators to share the heavy burdens of his post. The worthies tended to make decisions on the basis of what they thought the princeps wished rather than on any independent judgment. Thus in the later years of Tiberius many persons were tried and condemned for *maiestas* ("treason") against the emperor, on trivial charges. Tiberius had earlier several times personally quashed such charges, but he should have stopped these trials altogether. The procedure was inherently bad: the Roman legal system had never included public prosecutors, depending instead on private citizens to bring charges against those guilty of crimes. The accusers or informers (*delatores*) were rewarded from the estates of the persons condemned. Though *delatores* might also be punished for making false accusations, some persons seem virtually to have made a career of informing. The atmosphere thus created was quite repressive.

The emperors put some of the most important and sensitive administrative posts into the hands of officials called prefects, mostly drawn not from the aristocracy but from the equestrian order. Such men often owed all to the princeps and thus were likely to be more loyal than the nobles. The highest ranking prefects included the governor of Egypt (other major imperial provinces were governed by legates); the praetorian prefect, who commanded the Praetorian Guard; the prefect of the grain supply at Ostia, Rome's port; the prefect of the *vigiles* (police and fire units) at Rome; and the urban prefect, who governed the city of Rome for the emperor. The latter was a senator. Equestrians also supplied the imperial procurators, who looked after the financial matters of the princeps all over the Empire, commanded the fleet, and governed small provinces.

Imperial Finance

Although the old treasury in the temple of Saturn survived and the Senate in time-honored fashion continued to appropriate from it for the traditional purposes, most of the Empire's wealth gradually came under the control of the princeps. A new treasury was established, the *aerarium militare*; supported by a new sales tax levied in Italy and by an inheritance tax, it was designed to ensure bonuses and retirement benefits for soldiers. Of course it was completely controlled by the emperor. Most of the imperial provinces that required legionary forces produced no net income for the Empire, and tax monies raised in those provinces remained within the provincial treasuries (*fisci*) for local expenditure. Naturally the governor (that is, the emperor) or his representative controlled these funds, and doubtless rendered account on paper at Rome.

Only one of the new provinces yielded a considerable surplus—primarily of wheat—and that was Egypt. This province was somehow different from the rest and under the special care of the emperor. As we have seen, it was governed by an equestrian prefect, and senators were not allowed even to visit it without special imperial approval: history had demonstrated clearly how a leader with an army could turn the country into an easily defended independent kingdom. The income from this rich province was of course under imperial control.

The emperor's property itself, the *patrimonium*, came to be so large that it too was an important element in the imperial financial structure. The early emperors accumulated property rapidly. Every important person felt it an obligation, if not an actual honor, to include the princeps in his will. Properties confiscated from upper-class persons condemned of high crimes usually remained in the control of the emperor. Gifts added to the whole. Possibly income from Egypt also swelled the total. It is doubtful that the person—probably a freedman—

The emperor Augustus in ceremonial armor and commanding pose. (*Alinari/Art Resource, New York*)

who kept the accounts for the imperial household thought it important to distinguish property of the Empire from that of the princeps.

Procurators looked out for the emperor's financial interests even in senatorial provinces. As every reader of the New Testament knows, some played a role in the smaller provincial areas where they served as governors. In addition, some prefects appointed by the emperor controlled important funds or financial operations. Whatever overall financial planning was done took place in the imperial offices (we do not know anything in detail about it, however). Thus in indirect but quite open ways, Augustus and Tiberius set a trend that was to continue until virtually all important public funds were controlled by an official appointed by the emperor and responsible only to him. By the second century A.D. there had evolved, probably out of the office originally in charge of the *patrimonium*, a central treasury at Rome, the *fiscus*, which became the chief treasury of the Empire.

The emperors also closely controlled the coinage. Coins were struck to meet current expenditures; there was no conception of manipulation of the money supply to control the economy. The coins were issued in gold, silver, bronze, and copper. (The bronze and copper coins usually have the inscription SC, indicating they were authorized by the Senate, but that authorization was only formal.) The gold coin, the aureus, weighing about forty-two to the Roman twelve-ounce pound, was tariffed at twenty-five denarii. The latter, struck at the old standard, eighty-four to the pound, were the standard silver coins, and were issued in huge quantity. The sestertius, worth four asses and one-quarter the denarius in value, was usually brassy in appearance and often a beautiful coin; larger than the gold and silver coins, it gave the engraver freer scope for his art. The dupondius, worth two asses, was sometimes struck in brass and sometimes in copper; the as and its fractions were copper coins. Enough has been said of coin types to indicate that the coinage was used for propaganda as well as for purely monetary purposes. It is not certain, of course, that the types were personally approved by the emperors, but in general the emphases are the same as those known from literary sources, inscriptions, art, and architectural monuments.

The Military

Emergency armies only loosely controlled by the central government, each soldier sworn to obey his commander, had helped to bring down the Roman Republic. Augustus therefore decided to keep a standing army that would eliminate any need for such emergency armies. He also controlled all recruiting and retirement arrangements. Troops took an oath of loyalty to the princeps rather than to the men who exercised actual command in the field. Augustus also served as commander-in-chief of most of the legions since through his legates he governed the provinces in which they were largely stationed (not all: some were still commanded by proconsuls appointed by the Senate, such as, early in Augustus' reign, in Macedonia, which was a senatorial province, and in Africa).

Augustus managed to rule his dominions, to hold off threats to the frontiers, and even to extend them vastly with an army of only twenty-eight legions, later twenty-five, plus auxiliaries. Theoretically each legion contained 6,000 men, but they were usually somewhat under-manned. The number of auxiliaries was comparable to that of the legionaries; therefore, the size of the army in Augustus' day was around 250,000 men. Toward the end of his reign the legions were distributed as follows: in Spain, once the conquest of the peninsula was completed in 19 B.C., a reduction to three; in Gaul, none, small units only; in Germany, along the troublesome Rhine frontier, eight; along the Danube and in Macedonia, six or seven; in Syria, three or four; in Egypt, three; and in all the rest of North Africa, only one, with other units.

That this army should have been equal to such tasks indicates how few troops were required within the center of the Empire and how effective the legions were on the frontiers. Such an army seems extremely small for an empire so far-flung, made up of a population of many millions (just how many is extremely uncertain; perhaps, say, somewhat more than 50 million) of such diverse groups, and with frontiers so long and exposed. Yet this was about the maximum number the Empire could support without adverse effects on the economy. When at the famous battle of the Teutoburg Forest in Germany the Roman general Varus and three whole legions fell to the German Arminius (A.D. 9), Augustus did not try to reconstitute the lost legions. He simply called off further expansion into Germany, consolidated the frontier on the Rhine, and managed with fewer legions.

Part of his problem may have been recruitment rather than finance. The legionaries were Roman citizens only, drawn mostly from Italy. Were too few citizens willing to go into the still arduous army service? Such service offered advantages. Wherever the legionaries served they constituted a privileged class. For one thing, they were citizens; in most provinces there were still few such. Moreover, they were representatives of the dominant power. Also, their pay compared favorably with the local wage scales, and they could look forward to a generous retirement settlement. For some few persons the army could become the stepping-stone to a distinguished career. Men who became centurions often displayed such abilities as to mark them as candidates for higher posts in the government. The chief centurions of legions often advanced to rather important military tribunates and then, occasionally, to procuratorships or prefectureships.

Auxiliaries were drawn from the noncitizen classes all over the Empire. Though paid less than the legionaries, required to serve longer, and qualifying for smaller bonuses on retirement, many in the provinces were attracted to military careers. One reason was that on retirement they received citizenship. Both auxiliaries and legionaries were often settled in colonies that enjoyed the Italic Right, the *ius Italicum*—that is, its residents were free of taxes and other usual obligations. Such communities in the provinces were naturally Latin-speaking, and although the cultural level was not high they became quite important as centers of Romanization. These colonies served an acculturization role most significantly in the western areas and along the Danube. Army service tended to become hereditary, the sons of retired soldiers enlisting in their turn. The role of the Italians in the army gradually declined, perhaps in part because of the availability of citizen recruits from the colonies or elsewhere in the provinces and also because of an increasing disinclination of Italians to commit themselves to twenty years of army service.

Augustus established a new and prestigious branch of the armed forces, the praetorian guard. Commanders had long used praetorians to guard their headquarters, the *praetorium*. Though not a personal bodyguard, the guard in a sense served the traditional function and thus was based on precedent. Its size (nine cohorts, one double-sized), however, was extraordinary. Moreover, the fact that their commander usually stayed in Rome meant that these cohorts were stationed in Italy—and later, under Tiberius, just outside Rome itself. The troops therefore served to prevent outbreak of any sort against the regime. They could be and occasionally were used as a sort of reserve for emergency service in critical situations in the provinces. Mostly, though, they acted simply as an elite guard, superloyal to the princeps. Praetorians were of course citizens, and for two centuries were drawn only from Italy. They served a shorter period than the legions (usually sixteen years) and received both higher pay and larger bonuses on retirement. The guard also served as a means of social mobility, for praetorians of promise might be promoted to officer rank in the legions.

Freedmen too found opportunity in the imperial military service. They made up the ships' complements of the fleet. Augustus established two major naval bases, both in Italy: one at Misenum on the Tyrrhenian Sea and the other on the Adriatic side, at Ravenna. The most competent freedmen, however, surely stayed out of the navy, finding more lucrative careers in small business and industry, at least in Italy.

Freedmen also served in another new organization of a semimilitary nature, the *vigiles* of the city of Rome. These seven cohorts functioned both as firemen and police in the city, which in the late Republic had suffered from the lack of such units. Augustus formally organized Rome into fourteen *regiones* and into smaller districts, called *vici*; each cohort of a thousand men was responsible for two of the regions.

Augustus used his army rather vigorously for some years. He, or rather his chief lieutenant, Agrippa, campaigned in Spain until the entire peninsula was more or less under Roman control, by 19 B.C. At the same time he brought under Roman dominion the vast areas in the northeast, just south of the Danube, which the Romans called Noricum, Pannonia, and Moesia; here the Danube became the frontier, except that Thrace for the time remained an independent client state. Exploratory thrusts eastward across the Rhine into Germany at first went well but came to a sudden halt after the disaster that overtook Varus' army in A.D. 9. At the same time a rebellion had to be put down on the extended northeastern frontier. Augustus thereupon, as we have seen, made the Rhine and the Danube his frontiers and followed a generally passive policy during the last years of his life.

Tiberius, who in most ways tended to follow the policies of Augustus, took the same route. He had to restrain Germanicus, his nephew, who as commander in Germany seemed determined to seek Varus' fate. In the east, the Parthians to some degree occupied the attention of both Augustus and Tiberius. Augustus wanted to regain the three eagles captured by the Parthians in 53 B.C. when they overwhelmed Crassus' ill-fated expedition in the desert. But he recovered the eagles through diplomacy backed by the threat of force. Tiberius too avoided a major confrontation. Peace in the last half of the reign of Tiberius helped make it possible for him to accumulate a substantial surplus in the treasury.

Creating a Unified Imperial Society

We have seen that, especially within Rome and Italy, Augustus molded an image of grandeur for the Empire, an image of which most Romans could be proud, and helped draw the people together. The princeps was also able, to a considerable degree, to unify the whole empire, chiefly through the military and the imperial cult.

The army had always played a social as well as a military role. Augustus needed only to extend the recruiting practices of the late Republic (including enlisting troops from provinces and allied states) to make the army a vehicle bringing provincials into a close relationship with the new regime. Legionaries were recruited from citizens both within and outside Italy; auxiliaries (who served mostly in smaller, cohort-sized units) were drawn from all over the Empire. They were paid less than legionaries and were expected to serve longer (twenty-four rather than twenty years), but like the Romans, the provincials found the army an attractive career, particularly because of the possibility of promotion, which could bring advancement in social status as well.

Army service appealed to provincials even more when they received Roman citizenship on discharge. Augustus was not as liberal in granting citizenship as his successors, who made such grants routine. But the

The theater at Merida in southwestern Spain. The town was originally called Emerita, indicating that a veteran colony, established by Augustus, was there. The theater was built by Agrippa, in about 24 B.C. (*Ancient Art and Architecture Collection*)

discharged soldiers were a force promoting Romanization: they knew Latin, participated in activities of the Roman state religion, and usually lived in colonies with special privileges. The veterans thus tended to be loyal supporters of the Empire who spread Latin culture in the areas where they were settled.

Even during the Republic, members of the Roman aristocracy had forged links between themselves and the upper classes in the provinces, and Augustus continued the practice. Republican army commanders had also used their positions to build political and social influence: Caesar, for example, asked Cicero whether he wished to send his protégés to Caesar's army in Gaul, where he promised to take care of them, doubtless by making them junior officers and cutting them in on the spoils. Augustus of course did the same, but he also often asked upper-class officials of provincial cities to recommend to him persons for such appointment—say, as military tribunes in the auxiliary units. These individuals too might go on to higher service, sometimes in civilian positions.

Thus the army provided for both citizens and provincials a degree of social mobility that constituted a unifying force linking thousands of families to the new order. A good soldier might rise through the ranks to become a centurion; occasionally a centurion might continue to rise, perhaps to the military tribunate, or even to become an imperial procurator or prefect. Along the way, many of these—even some centurions—accumulated enough wealth to enter the equestrian order. The army, then, even though now highly professional and controlled through a monolithic command structure, was a significant social and political institution, not merely a military one.

Another cultural institution whose growth began almost accidentally also became a solidly unifying force: the imperial cult. We have seen that Octavian/Augustus emphasized, immediately after the death of Caesar, that he was the "son of the divine one" in order to assert the legitimacy of his succession. The cult quickly caught on in the provinces more than in Italy, especially in the east, where the populace had accepted the idea of monarchs as deities from the time of Alexander. In Egypt, in fact, the pharaohs had been gods for three thousand years.

Midway in his reign, Augustus apparently began to see possibilities. Though he officially discouraged the worship of himself, he encouraged worship of his adoptive father and allowed some veneration of himself outside Rome. He organized prestigious councils in the eastern provinces (at least), one of whose functions was to nourish the imperial cult, and colleges of priests called *augustales* were organized, in Italy and elsewhere, again to support the cult.

Thus, not only by bringing peace and playing the role of patron of all, but also by extending opportunity and privilege, Augustus did much to cause people throughout the Empire to feel that they were a part of Rome.

Partners in Prestige: The Upper Classes

It is a tribute to Augustus' wisdom that he shared with the Roman nobles the façade of power but not its reality. Some of them who were not satisfied with prestige alone were of course frustrated. The historian Tacitus reflects well that frustration. But most accepted the situation. Tiberius continued the policy but, characteristically, with less finesse and, consequently, more resentment on the part of some members of the upper classes.

Augustus' early attitude contrasts somewhat with that of the last half of his reign. Early on he did not, apparently, make use of the scions of the old aristocratic families, choosing rather to elevate relative unknowns to prominent positions. Often these favored ones were descendants of Italian families, citizens only since the Italian war of 90–89 B.C. Once assured of his position, however, the princeps tended to give more important posts to old-line aristocrats—such of them as had survived the civil wars. He also made several marriage compacts involving his relatives and the great families. His own marriage with Livia had brought connections not only with the Livii but with the patrician Claudii. His granddaughter Julia was married to an Aemilius Paullus; his nieces, the daughters of Mark Antony by Octavia, to a Claudius and a Domitius; another niece, Octavia's daughter by Marcellus, he married to an Aemilius Lepidus. To some extent Augustus was simply doing the natural thing, making the best marriages for his relatives, but he seems to

Onyx cameo from the early reign of Tiberius. Top, Augustus, now deified and being crowned is flanked on the right by the gods of the sea and the bountiful Mother Earth. To his left is Roma; at the far left is the future emperor Tiberius descending from his triumphal chariot after his victory over the Pannonians. Next to him is Germanicus. Bottom, Roman soldiers erect a trophy and deal with Pannonian prisoners. (*Vienna Kunsthistoriches Museum*)

have deliberately sought a reconciliation with the old aristocracy. Having lost much in the new order, the Roman nobles, conciliated in this and other ways, were for the most part content to bask in the warmth of their secondary place in the sun.

The emperors also supported the upper classes in the provinces, here following what had been the policy of the government of the Republic. Local government functioned with considerable autonomy in the city-states that made up the fabric of the provincial system. But what Rome encouraged was the formation of little oligarchies, not democracies, with popular assemblies that elected officials from among a restricted class of eligible persons. The upper classes of the provincial cities were often on terms of friendship with Roman nobles. As we have seen, provincial aristocrats might be rewarded for their good service in local government by seats on the provincial council, which carried little power but much prestige. And they might be rewarded with Roman citizenship.

In the west Augustus and Tiberius were less generous to the native stock. Tribal organizations were set up in the less settled areas in place of the city-states of the east. Though Julius Caesar had given not only citizenship but even Senate appointments to a few Gauls, Augustus chose not precisely to reverse the policy, but at least to apply it with great deliberation. Yet in the west as well as in the east the primary effort to tie provinces to the central government with bands of loyalty mostly involved the upper classes.

For citizens, the most precise definition of the highest rank was political rather than social. The senatorial class is thus most often mentioned in the sources. The nobles were primarily those descended from the older *nobilitas*, though sometimes now the term was synonymous with the senatorial class. Members of the class wore the broad stripe (*latus clavus*) on their togas; sons of senators wore the stripe by right also, since they were expected to follow in their fathers' footsteps. Occasionally the princeps granted the right to wear the senatorial symbols, perhaps to someone who sought a senatorial career, or to a man who deserved special distinction. There was also a very limiting census qualification of 1 million sesterces in property.

The equestrian order was more amorphous. In one sense it included all citizens who met the technical census qualification, now 400,000 sesterces in property, whether they lived in Italy or in some provincial city. The term might also refer to a more restricted portion of the order: those men who at some time in their lives had served, if only on paper, in the cavalry—"held a public horse"—and who ordinarily went on to political careers. Sons of senators were normally included in this group until they were elected quaestors and entered the Senate. For this group Augustus revived the old practice of an annual parade or review, a ceremony of dignity and honor.

The equestrians wore the narrow stripe (*angusti clavus*). Their sons began their political careers with a lower office than did the sons of senators and could not normally aspire to the highest ranks. The highest posts available to men of this class were the prefectureships already discussed. The prefectureship of Egypt was most prestigious: it compared to the senatorial *legatus pro praetore*, for the Egyptian governor commanded three legions and controlled property of great value. The post of praetorian prefect at Rome grew in power and importance also, so that by the mid–first century A.D. its importance rivaled that of the Egyptian prefecture.

Many of those who qualified for the equestrian census, especially those away from Rome itself, were businessmen who put much of their wealth into land as the most stable and sure investment. Moreover, some who remained equestrians, as, for example, Augustus' friend Maecenas, moved in the highest social circles. The number of equestrians in the Empire cannot be determined; it was quite small relative to the total population, but the number must have increased in the early Empire. Augustus and his immediate successors created conditions under which trade could flourish: peace, little governmental interference, and reasonable levels of taxation. The government intervened and exercised restrictive controls only over the grain supply.

Being a patrician still conferred social status, though no political distinction remained. Acting on a precedent established by Caesar, the early emperors on occasion created new patrician families because of declining numbers, perhaps chiefly to provide aristocrats eligible to hold the old priesthoods that Augustus carefully reconstituted.

Literary Figures of the Early Empire

Artists and writers naturally reflect their own times; not even a Lucretius lives in a vacuum. And so it was during the Augustan period, in which literature flourished so richly that it is called the golden age of Latin literature.

The historian Livy (Titus Livius, 59 B.C.–A.D. 17) approved of Augustus and his general aims and yet felt a strong nostalgia for the great days of the past. He helped generations of Romans—and others since—not merely to understand but to feel the crises their ancestors surmounted through the simple virtues. How profoundly Livy's *History of Rome* impressed the Roman mind in his own day is illustrated by a story told by the younger Pliny, of the Roman citizen residing in Spain who came to Rome solely to lay eyes on the great historian and, having seen him, paid no attention to anything else in the resplendent world capital but returned home immediately.

Livy's strong attachment to the old ways and his admiration for the great figures of the Republic might have seemed dangerous to a more paranoid princeps than Augustus. The emperor, in fact, once called Livy a Pompeian, and possibly Livy did not take his history further—it came down, in 142 books, to about 9 B.C.—because of the sensitivity of the material. Still, Augustus seems to have been wholly tolerant of the historian and of others holding similar views; after all, they both saw many things alike, and Livy must have approved wholeheartedly of the princeps' attempts to restore old virtues and mores. The enormity of his task sufficiently explains the historian's failure to go further. Indeed, his toil was heavy enough to excuse many of the weaknesses of his work, which include occasional contradictions and failure to make use of the most basic source materials. His achievement has stood high enough not only to survive but even to triumph over all criticism.

In a sense, the premier poet Vergil (P. Vergilius Maro, 70–19 B.C.) sang in verse what Livy narrated in prose—the rise of Rome to become, through the strivings of virtuous men, the ruler of the Mediterranean. But whereas Livy was pessimistic about his own times, which contrasted sharply with the greatness of the past, in his mature work, the

Aeneid (which he left unfinished at his death), Vergil held that a new era, a golden age, had come with the Julii. At one time he may well have shared Livy's uneasiness, though not his despair. His earlier works, the *Eclogues* and the *Georgics*, are romantic almost to the point of being escapist, turning to rural themes, the idealization of the sturdy, virtuous Roman farmer, when the troubles of the times seemed to defy solution.

Horace (Quintus Horatius Flaccus, 65–8 B.C.), writing flawless and facile lines, dwelled on less exalted themes than those of Vergil. His *Epodes, Satires, Odes,* and *Epistles* deal with everyday joys and concerns as well as with the faults and foibles of ordinary humans. Though Horace was the son of a freedman from Apulia, he got a good education at Rome. He was in Athens when Brutus organized opposition to the triumvirs; caught up in republican enthusiasm, he fought on the losing side at Philippi. He was basically apolitical, however, and not only was forgiven but soon became a supporter of Octavian. Several of his *Odes* and *Epodes* deplore the carnage of the civil wars and laud Augustus as the one who restored peace along with all the neglected virtues: piety, patriotism, justice, restraint, modesty.

It was Maecenas, the trusted lieutenant of Augustus and patron of the arts, who brought Horace into the good graces of the emperor. Descended from a reputedly royal Etruscan line, Maecenas was too voluptuous in his tastes for Augustus and did not formally hold high office, but he was enormously useful nevertheless. He encouraged Vergil and gave aid to Horace. The latter seems to have lost property (as Vergil's family had lost a farm in northern Italy) because he embraced the losing cause. But Maecenas got for him a fine farm in the Sabine country not far from Rome, which gave Horace a living and the independence he required.

Though none of them came from a noble background, these three major writers reflected in their works an upper-class viewpoint, which they had acquired through education. Roman upper-class society freely accepted them because of their literary achievements. Horace sneered at the upstart rich military tribune, though he also poked satirical fun at nobles and equestrians. Both Vergil and Horace played the part, surely sincerely, of propagandists for the Augustan regime. When Augustus put on the great Secular Games in 17 B.C. (celebrated each century, or *saeculum*, calculated at 110 years), Horace wrote the *carmen saeculare*, which included fulsome praise of the emperor. Yet any fair appraisal must concede that Augustus' considerable achievements, coming as they did after so much war and destruction, deserved recognition in contemporary literature.

Though less important to the political historian, the work of the Augustan poet Ovid (Publius Ovidius Naso, 43 B.C.–A.D. 17) casts light on a dissolute social scene in the capital. Ovid came from an old equestrian family and might have been expected to climb the political ladder or at least to have joined Maecenas' circle near the center of power. Instead he chose to drop politics after a small beginning; he stood apart from the regime as a member of a loose set whose behavior and morals undercut Augustus' public policy on these matters. One of his best known and probably most read poems is his *Ars Amatoria—The Art of Love* or, perhaps more exactly, *The Art of Seduction*. He married well— three times—and moved in some of the same circles as the emperor's own daughter Julia, who was later exiled for adultery. Ovid himself was exiled in A.D. 8 for an undisclosed offense, perhaps involving Augustus' granddaughter Julia, to Tomis on the Black Sea, and there he lived his remaining years, constantly complaining about his miserable fate and appealing to return.

Ovid's important works also include the *Metamorphoses*, a valuable compilation mostly of somewhat romanticized Greek mythology, and the *Fasti*, a calendar of activity at Rome, unfortunately only the first six months of the year. As poetry it lacks the quality of Ovid's other works, and it does not convey deep feelings toward religion and the gods as well as do the works of Livy or Vergil or Horace, but for the social historian it provides a wealth of information on ancient festivals and brings understanding of various aspects of Roman religion.

Farms and Farmers

Vergil and Horace, like many another poet before and since, portray rural life not merely as pleasant and beautiful but as idyllic, somehow ministering to the deepest needs of humanity. Throughout the history of the West this theme of the romanticized glories of life in the country has recurred many times in art and letters. In application, however, the desire to return to the soil, brought on by the beauties of spring and the excitement of the first growth of plants, often peters out under the hot July sun when the weeding needs to be done. Farming in ancient times was not only hard but sometimes brutish, and we must remember that Horace and Vergil wrote as absentee landlords and slaveholders.

Some farmers obviously prospered and sent their sons to be educated in the city—perhaps even to Rome or Athens. But more commonly they struggled hard, prospered little, and put small store in education. They were provincial, suspicious of foreigners, narrow in their views. Moreover, rural life had its perils: bands of robbers, disease, drought, flood. Every farmer needed a sharp lookout, two or three strong dogs, and high walls to enclose house, barn, and yard against night prowlers.

The problems that had beset Roman agriculture during the Republic continued into the early Empire: a decline in small holders, further increases in the number of *latifundia*, and the trend toward tenant farming, with all the evils that go with absentee landlords. These reports

Mosaic depicting pastoral scene. (*Alinari/Art Resource, New York*)

may be exaggerated since the colonization programs in the Republic and the Empire, especially for veterans, reestablished thousands of small holders in the Italian countryside, many of them permanently. Slaves were harder to come by, and thus more expensive, in the peace of the early Empire, which must have posed a deterrent to the continued growth of the large *latifundia*.

Southern Italy began the decline that has endured to our own day during the early Empire. Seneca describes the countryside of Apulia as deserted, and the Greek cities no longer flourished. A combination of deforestation and perhaps climatic change may have been factors. In the central areas of Italy farmers did well. They did not grow much grain, of course; that was imported, at least into Rome and the coastal cities. The region produced an increasing number of fine wines fermented in vats fed by the vineyards of the area; olives remained important. Close to the cities truck gardening was most profitable. In some areas pigs, cattle, poultry, and sheep (whose wool naturally was in demand) multiplied.

In the west central region, from Rome southward, in all the most pleasant areas of the Alban Hills and particularly near the Bay of Naples, the rich built villas both as stopping places for themselves and their friends when traveling and for annual respite from Rome's summer heat and daily grind. These villas took much land out of cultivation and produced little except for the output from truck gardens tended by slaves. Such estates increasingly included fishponds, whose catch tempted the palates of their owners. The north of Italy and especially the Po valley flourished. There the rich soil produced an abundance of grains, fruits, and animals. Wool was high in quality and relatively cheap. Augustus gave greater security to the area, clearing several of the passes over the Alps. In one campaign in the vicinity of the Great and Little St. Bernard passes he killed thousands of native Salassi and sold thousands of others into slavery. To protect the passes he planted a colony called Augusta Praetoria, now Aosta. The Brenner Pass, debouching into Verona, had been clear for some years. Greater security meant greater prosperity for the entire area as trade through the passes stimulated the growth of towns. The communities of the region burgeoned, nourished by the strong agricultural base. Verona, Cremona, Padua, Mediolanum (Milan), and other towns grew into cities.

We know less about rural life in the provinces than about that in Italy. Undoubtedly the provinces too enjoyed a share of the prosperity and stability of the new age. Provincials could also enlist as auxiliaries in the Roman army, whose various privileges, including Roman citizenship after twenty-four years, attracted many provincial young men to military service.

Rome relied heavily on the province of Africa (gradually extended east to Cyrenaica) to produce grain and oil, which were relatively easily transported to Italy, to meet urban needs. The climate of course made these suitable crops, but the policy restricted farmers' freedom to grow the most advantageous crops for local markets. Moreover, absentee landlordism especially afflicted Africa, with a few Roman families gaining control of vast acreages. Nevertheless, the archaeology of the area indicates a general prosperity continuing into the next century and even later.

Egypt, like Africa, was required to provide Rome with grain; presumably it continued as it had for centuries on end to be the chief source of grain also for many areas in the Mediterranean east. Roman control of Egypt, although in some ways less restrictive than that of the Macedonian dynasty during the Hellenistic age, yet largely maintained the arrangements under the Ptolemies. The lot of the lower classes was as grim as ever: producing for landlords (who were often absent), whether owners, renters, or the state, while themselves living the barest of existences.

Elsewhere in the eastern Mediterranean, Greece moldered but still produced grain on the plains of Thessaly along with oil and wines. Tourism and educational opportunities in Greece brought some money to the region, and creation of artworks continued to be important. Asia Minor had not recovered fully from the economic burdens stemming from the Mithridatic Wars, which had continued during the civil wars. Each successive war had seen the entire eastern Mediterranean stripped of money and supplies. A lack of capital caused by debt to Roman bankers slowed recovery. Farther south, Syria and Palestine too had suffered from internal problems and the Roman civil wars. The area soon revived to a degree and exported dried fruits, nuts, and manufactured products (the last including, notably, purple-dyed fabrics mostly sent to Rome).

To the west, Spain and Gaul prospered. The rich farmland of Gaul produced abundant crops of grain and, increasingly, vines, along with lesser products. Spain still furnished Rome with most of her precious metals, and the province was also beginning to export to Rome and elsewhere a superior quality of olive oil as well as wines, horses, and products such as drugs and other metals.

Industry

Italy was for most of this period a strong exporter of certain manufactures. Arretine pottery, a glossy red ware usually made in relief molds, dominated the market for ceramics in the western Mediterranean. Glassware and some bronze ware produced in the Naples area were widely sought after. Bricks were produced in great abundance, especially near Rome, but of course were not exported. Bronze and copper ware were fabricated at Capua; Puteoli now (rather than Etruria) smelted much of the iron needed in Italy and for export. By the end of this period, however, small industries had already sprung up in the western provinces, especially Gaul. Workmen imitated the Arretine pottery and Italian metal goods and competed with the Italian manufacturers. The costs of transportation from Italy, labor costs, and other factors put the Italian products at a disadvantage, despite the somewhat lower quality of provincial wares. But the consequences of this competition belong to a later period.

Cast of an Arretine bowl showing scenes of the harvest, vintage, and a Dionysian festival. (*Courtesy Museum of Fine Arts, Boston*)

No really large industry developed in Italy or anywhere else in the Empire. We know of some potteries that were quite large, it is true. At Arretium, north of Rome, the center of Arretine production, one pottery had a mixing vat that would hold ten thousand gallons. The business must have employed scores if not hundreds of persons, but it was exceptional. It is, in fact, rather puzzling that something more like mass production did not evolve. The small workshop-cum-salesroom prevailed as the typical production unit. Even lead water pipe, which in the cities might easily have been standardized in size and manufacture, was always expensively custom-made by each plumber-installer. As for textiles, spinning and weaving remained mostly a household activity. In the cities, materials were sent out to professional fullers for finishing.

A lack of capital partly explains the failure to develop more economical means of production. Trade was more profitable than manufacture if the gods of storm and sea looked on one's ships with favor. For greater security and prestige, even if with a smaller return, capital was put into land. The small, family-controlled workshop/salesroom most suited the artisan businessman of the ancient world, who did not usually aspire to more than a comfortable income, and who prized his independence of action. If he accumulated extra capital he was more likely to invest it in land than to expand his production facilities.

As a consequence of this attitude the Empire failed, even in a long period of peace and general prosperity, to develop a sizable middle class. Such a class existed, to be sure, but it was far too small to play an important role. Its members were the men who entered the world of trade and commerce or took up banking and moneylending. The group of landholders who were neither poor nor rich shared the interests of the landed upper class, and it furnished the manpower for the middle positions in government and the army. Individual members were occasionally rewarded with upward political and social movement. But the Empire lacked a class whose first concern was large-scale manufacture, whose members ardently sought to increase production through continually applying capital to develop increasingly efficient methods. We must remind ourselves, however, that we in the modern world, misled by the ready availability of fossil fuels, tend to have an overly simplistic view of how quickly and easily the processes of manufacture can be improved.

Economic Policy in Tiberius' Later Years

Though some Romans might have called Tiberius stingy, it is no doubt fairer to say that he was thrifty, and he was so throughout the Empire. On rare occasions, however, he could be generous with his accumulated reserves. When in A.D. 17 an earthquake in Asia Minor devastated Sardis and other cities of the area, he remitted their taxes for five years and made substantial grants of money also. He deposed and brought to trial a rapacious governor of Asia. Another governor who was overly eager in the collection of taxes he warned to "shear his sheep, not skin them."

In Italy Tiberius was able to cut in half the sales tax that supported the military treasury. During a grain shortage in Rome a couple of years later (A.D. 19) he spent liberally from the treasury to bring emergency supplies. In a monetary crisis in 33 he made 100 million sesterces available from the treasury for low-rate loans. And when fire ravaged the Aventine and adjoining areas in 36 he made a similar sum available for rebuilding the burned-out areas. Some of his generosity was made possible by the continued growth of the personal wealth of the emperor. Yet like his predecessor, Tiberius lived comparatively unostentatiously, and he sometimes refused inheritances when there was a legitimate heir.

Tiberius' policy of thrift, which was to leave 2.7 billion sesterces in the treasury at his death, in some ways depressed the economy, especially in Rome, which of course was highly sensitive to changes in the levels of state expenditure. Absent from Rome for the last decade of his reign, Tiberius put on many fewer games and festivals in the capital and spent less on those staged. The results were felt not merely in the boredom of the lower classes but also in the pocketbooks of the people. In an economy that almost exclusively uses precious metals as currency, thrift—saving—by both public and private persons can easily depress the economy. Bullion thus withdrawn from circulation decreases the money supply unless there is an equivalent production of the precious metals through mining. (The production of metals in Rome would also have had to compensate for attrition through normal loss of coins, through their export in the Empire's usual adverse trade balance with the east, and through use of precious metals in jewelry, statuary, and the like.) Thus Tiberius' accumulation of this huge sum in the treasury probably contributed substantially to the financial crunch of A.D. 33.

The End of Tiberius' Reign

Tiberius' son Drusus died (perhaps from poisoning) in 23, and after 26 Tiberius withdrew from Rome altogether, taking up residence on the island of Capri and ruling almost entirely through his praetorian prefect, Sejanus. The sources present Sejanus as an unscrupulous and ambitious man who engineered the deaths of Drusus and two of the sons of Agrippina and Germanicus so as to eliminate claimants to the succession in preparation for his own takeover. By contrast, some scholars have suspected that Sejanus was merely Tiberius' tool. In any case, in 31 Tiberius belatedly learned of Sejanus' machinations; Sejanus' former wife told him that the prefect had even made away with Drusus. Moving cautiously, Tiberius had Sejanus deposed and executed. The remaining six years of Tiberius' life were embittered. Trials for treason marred those years, and the Romans felt neglected. There were stories of depraved sex orgies, with the old emperor as voyeur, in the imperial palace on Capri. The provinces were little affected and in general seem to have been well governed throughout Tiberius' reign. But men rejoiced when the old recluse died—smothered in his bedclothes, it was said, by his new praetorian prefect, Macro—in A.D. 37.

10 The State and Society from Gaius to Domitian, A.D. 37–96

THE ROMAN STATE as constituted by Augustus endured for several centuries, but it slowly changed in character. The old traditions held over from the Republic faded in influence. The ruling classes gradually if grudgingly accepted a role subordinate to the office of the princeps, and in some ways the role was merely an extension of it. How graciously each generation of aristocrats acquiesced in their reduced role depended primarily on the personality of each emperor and how gracious his attitude was toward them. Unfortunately, several of the emperors proved inept in the delicate social and political relationships involving scions of the great families.

Not surprisingly, a good many conspiracies were hatched, even against the better emperors. For a century or more in the early Empire men hoped and plotted to restore the oligarchy called the Republic. But even when conspirators managed to assassinate an emperor, they did not succeed in bringing back the Republic. Most conspiracies were nipped in the bud by the executioner's sword. Such executions depleted the ranks of the old families. The changing composition of the ruling classes, with the new families all owing their positions to the emperors, partially explains the growing subservience in the Senate. These gradual changes within Rome, however, meant little outside Italy.

A Political Sketch

Gaius (37–41)

Even though Augustus had forced Tiberius to adopt Gaius' father, Germanicus, and apparently intended him to succeed his stepson, Gaius had little reason to hope for the throne until late in Tiberius' reign, when Drusus, son of Tiberius, died (or was murdered) and Sejanus' hopes were aborted. Thus Gaius was both young (in his middle twenties) and politically inexperienced when he acceded to power. Nevertheless, he had definite ideas about his position—ideas that did not correspond to general expectations. His father, Germanicus, had been personable and popular. As a child Gaius had traveled about with him—it was in Germany that he got the nickname Caligula (Little Boot)—and thus he came to be identified with him. Both Gaius' father and grandfather, Drusus, brother of the emperor Tiberius, were thought to have had republican leanings, but not Gaius. Nothing was further from his mind.

Gaius' mind was, to some extent, unhinged, possibly by serious illness early in his reign. His acts, which appear to be factually established, cannot be explained so as to make his conduct seem entirely rational. Yet we must allow for exaggeration and hostile reporting. It has been quite plausibly conjectured that Gaius resented the straitjacket of expectations he had inherited, and that he intended instead to rule in the manner of the Hellenistic monarchs. Caesar perhaps had had similar intentions; at any rate, the pattern was familiar to all educated Romans, and it explains Gaius' insistence on deification and worship. Augustus had resisted such worship in Rome, though he allowed worship of himself along with Roma in the provinces, and he was deified formally after his death. Tiberius, as in almost all things, followed Augustus' precedent. Gaius' different attitude may at first have engendered little more than amusement in the capital, along with sardonic comment, but in the provinces there was little objection to the idea of the emperor as god, except in one: but for Gaius' assassination there would have been rebellion among the Jews. Only the resistance and procrastination of the governor of Syria, P. Petronius, at the risk of his own life, kept the lid on open revolt in Judea. Gaius had ordered his image set up in the Temple in Jerusalem, as a god, and Petronius, fearing rebellion, delayed the work for many months. Only the death of the emperor prevented Petronius' execution.

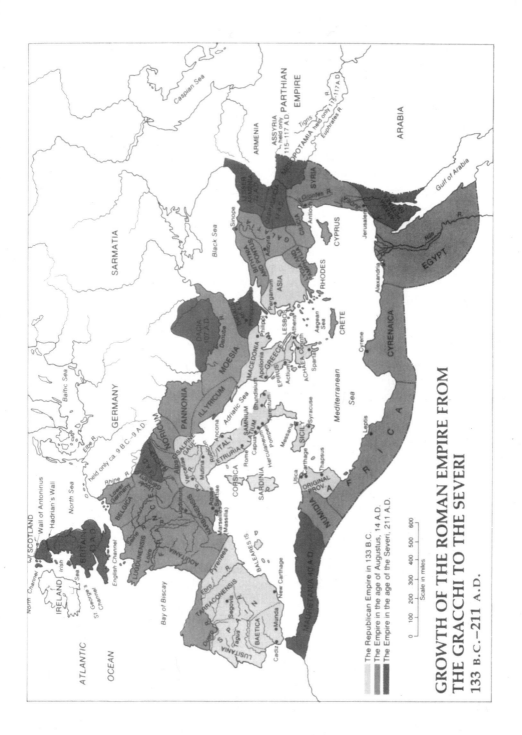

GROWTH OF THE ROMAN EMPIRE FROM
THE GRACCHI TO THE SEVERI
133 B.C.–211 A.D.

The Republican Empire in 133 B.C.
The Empire in the age of Augustus, 14 A.D.
The Empire in the age of the Severi, 211 A.D.

0   100 200 300 400 500 600
Scale in miles

How does an apologist account for Gaius' great expedition north to the English Channel where, the sources say, he eventually lined up his troops, told them to gather seashells, and then returned home to celebrate a triumph as if they had indeed invaded Britain as he planned? One major purpose of the expedition was to put down a conspiracy headed by one of his generals in Germany, who had control of a large legionary force; the secondary objective, the invasion of Britain, was aborted because of the complete unwillingness of the troops to venture into what they considered the shadowy limits of the inhabited world.

But the building of a bridge of ships about three miles long across the Bay of Naples does not yield any rational explanation. Did Gaius want to impress a visiting Parthian embassy by building a bridge like that of Darius the Great but longer? Perhaps. Had his bizarre sense of humor concocted a huge practical joke? One source suggests he did it because someone important had once said that Gaius had about as much chance of being emperor as of riding his horse across the Bay of Naples. It was in any case an enormously expensive whim.

One may choose simply not to believe that Gaius really said he intended to get his horse elected consul, to show his contempt for the Senate; it is surely best to discount as mostly gossip or rumor the stories of his sexual vagaries, including incest with his three sisters. But no apologetics can exonerate him of extravagance. Gaius found a full treasury at his accession; in three years of tax cuts, games, gifts, and general carousing he managed to spend most of it. Confiscation of the estates of those judged guilty of conspiracy helped to replenish it, but not enough. Still, his spending did no real damage; in fact, piling up bullion in the manner of Tiberius was likely more injurious to the general economic welfare. And the provinces—except Judea—were little affected one way or another.

Gaius was murdered in a conspiracy between a prefect and several tribunes of the praetorian guard.

Claudius (41–54)

That Claudius, the uncle of Gaius and the brother of Germanicus, would accede to power was even less expected than that Gaius would. Afflicted with some sort of paralytic disability that made him ungainly, Claudius had been an embarrassment to both Augustus and Livia, Claudius' grandmother, who had kept him in the background. He had a good education, however, and displayed an intellectual bent. He studied and wrote history (dealing with the Etruscans and the early Empire) and was interested in linguistics. The great Livy seems to have advised and consulted with him. He had held no important office until Gaius let him be consul for a couple of months.

It was the praetorians, afraid because Gaius had been slain by one of their own officers and looking out for themselves, who put Claudius in power. One source says that the praetorians encountered him accidentally as they rampaged through the palace following Gaius' assassination. Claudius, hardly a free agent, agreed to serve. However it happened, a very bad precedent was set: not only was an emperor installed by soldiers without even the consent of the Senate (which meanwhile was debating how to achieve a restoration of the Republic), but the guardsmen also demanded and got from Claudius what amounted to a huge reward—15,000 or 20,000 sesterces per guardsman. The money must have come from Claudius' own personal fortune.

The sources say that Claudius was too much influenced by women and freedmen, and there is some truth to the assertion. There is no doubt, however, that in important matters of state policy he was his own man, and as a matter of fact he seems to have thought matters through quite well. Some rulers mindful of history and transfixed by past traditions have adopted a stubborn conservatism. Not Claudius. He accepted Livy's view of the Republic, that Rome rose to greatness because of a willingness to learn from others and to accept others on an equal basis into full citizenship and participation in the state. He avowed an intention to follow in the steps of Augustus, but he seems to have followed Caesar rather more. Twice Caesar had briefly invaded Britain; Claudius acquired it as a province. Caesar wanted to build a port at Ostia; Claudius did it. Caesar wanted to drain the Fucine Lake; Claudius did it, with less than complete success. Caesar rather liberally extended the citizenship to Gauls as he made Cisalpine Gaul part of Italy, and even admitted some into the Senate; so did Claudius, in the case of some Transalpine Gauls.

The motivation for the conquest of Britain, as for any major imperialist expansion by the Romans, involved a mixture of reasons. The Romans thought the Britons stirred up dissatisfaction among their subjects on the continent, and conquest would presumably take care of that. But reasons more purely economic, such as opportunities for Roman businessmen, may have existed. Moreover, the historian Tacitus implies that one major objective was acquisition of the gold and silver mines in Britain. Other known mineral wealth on the island included lead, tin, and coal. Cornwall's tin, it is thought, had drawn Phoenicians to Britain centuries earlier. The Romans probably never mined these minerals in sufficient quantity to profit from the conquest. There was no great quantity of gold; some silver, copper, and tin were mined, however, along with much lead. And the coal was used extensively in the next century, mostly for heating by, for example, Roman troops stationed along the walls built in the north. There was too much sulfur in the coal to make it desirable for the smelting of iron ore, which was also found in some quantity in Britain. The Spanish mines long continued to furnish most of Rome's silver, copper, and lead. If the invasion of Britain was mounted in the hope of economic gain, that gain was not realized: in spite of the income from the numerous state-owned mines (regularly leased to private persons or companies), or from trade or agricultural production, the outlay for the legions required there must have put the governors' books into the red.

Claudius reorganized the civil administration of the government. The earlier emperors had quite naturally followed the usual aristocratic familial procedures, whereby freedmen of their households often managed property and other concerns of their patrons. Augustus, in effect, used them as civil administrators of the Empire. Claudius formalized and extended the system. It is often fashionable to decry the growth of administrative bureaucracies, and it is surely true that those who staff them in every age tend to become as interested in advancing their own positions as in seeing to the affairs of state. Yet such a service is absolutely necessary. Surely Claudius' rational ordering of the services ought to be accounted a positive good.

Four of Claudius' talented if grasping freedmen headed up major departments with clearly defined areas of responsibility. Here was the origin of the charge that freedmen too much influenced the emperor. Two of these freedmen, Pallas, the financial department head, and Narcissus, head of correspondence (and thus of routine provincial matters), became both powerful and rich. The great power delivered into the hands of such freedmen, and at times into the hands of imperial slaves, made them very important figures. Their social position was therefore much enhanced; a senator might even wish to be seen walking along the street with one of them. Other aristocrats who would not so demean themselves resented the situation and transferred their hatred to the emperor.

There were conspiracies against Claudius, though it is difficult to credit the figures given in the sources for the number of grandees the emperor is said to have executed for such plots—tens of senators and scores of equestrians. At any rate, the gradual disappearance of the older families for one reason or another continued; others replaced them.

Despite an impressive number of good things that may be said about Claudius' reign, it is easy to focus on his faults, on his freedmen, and on the two women who were his wives in this period, Messalina and Agrippina.

There seems no reason to doubt the accounts of Messalina's extravagant parties and her affairs with various men. She developed an infatuation for a man, G. Silius, a possible candidate for the throne in the event of a sudden vacancy, and she reportedly "married" him at a party in Claudius' absence. Claudius' freedman Narcissus, whom Messalina had earlier offended, persuaded the emperor to order her execution. Thus left wifeless Claudius, whose sexual appetite was said to have been unimpaired by his physical disability, cast about for a suitable replacement. He eventually settled on the younger Agrippina, his own niece, sister of the previous emperor. It is questionable whether the marriage was his idea or hers. The outcome was significant: Claudius adopted Agrippina's son, Lucius Domitius Ahenobarbus, by her previous marriage and thus he became Nero Claudius Caesar. Claudius' own son by Messalina, called Britannicus, was displaced and murdered by Nero after his accession.

Nero (54–68)

The younger Agrippina, Nero's mother, was the daughter of the elder Agrippina, who was the granddaughter of Augustus by Agrippa and Julia. Nero was thus the great-great-grandson of Augustus—and Agrippina never let her young son (he was sixteen when he became emperor) forget that it was her pedigree and influence that brought him to power. She expected to be a regent for him in his early years but was frustrated in her ambition, first by Nero's advisers Seneca and Burrus and later by Nero himself. Eventually (in 59) he decided to do away with his mother, whom he saw as some kind of threat to himself.

Nero is remembered as almost the archetype of the tyrant, not only for his matricide but also for his persecution of Christians at Rome. The Christian religion had its beginnings in Judea during the reign of Tiberius. Jesus was accepted by some of his fellow Jews as the Messiah (in Greek, *Christos*), the savior-king of Judaic prophecy. His death at the hands of the Roman governor Pontius Pilate in about A.D. 30 was probably ordered to prevent unrest among the Jews; most of their leaders did not see him as the Christ. After a period of slow growth among Jews and Hellenized Gentile proselytes (Jewish converts) within Judea and surrounding areas, Christianity, as it was soon called, began to spread among other Gentiles, especially in Asia Minor and Greece, primarily under the missionary leadership of Saul or Paul, an apostle or personal messenger.

Not until the Jewish revolt of 66–70 did the Jewish Christians, for their own safety and for other reasons, begin to separate their religion from Judaism. Christians could thus no longer claim to be a sect within Judaism, which was officially recognized by Rome and granted certain legal privileges. Without official sanction, Christians faced eventual conflict with the Roman state.

Nero's persecution of Christians only indirectly involved the illicit status of the religion. The persecution, sharp but short and localized, came in 64 after a great fire had destroyed more than half the city of Rome. Nero saw in the disaster an opportunity to improve the appearance of the city—and to build for himself a vast new palace on the Oppian Hill across from the Palatine. The behavior of the fires, which often seemed to spring back up after they had been extinguished, had already convinced the populace that the fires were the work of arsonists. The announcement of the plans for rebuilding, which came so soon after the conflagration, aroused suspicion that it was Nero himself who had burned the city. To put down the rumors (for which no hard evidence exists), Nero pressed the investigation. Someone persuaded him to make scapegoats of the Christians.

The fires may well have been set, but by whom is still a mystery; surely not by Christians, or by Nero either, though he may have been moved to dramatic declamation by the lurid and grandiose sight. Nero provided funds to help private persons rebuild, and he set up a fire code requiring building setbacks and such to make the reconstructed city safer from fire. Yet his new palace, the Golden House, took up about a quarter of a square mile of the most valuable land in Rome.

The emperor Claudius had had a morbid fascination with the bloodier combats at the games. Nero was less bloodthirsty than his adoptive father, favoring Greek-style games and tending to neglect the depraved spectacles the city crowd increasingly demanded. Though he became suspicious and executed some persons who probably had not actively joined in any conspiracy, he did so partly because real conspiracies had taught him to fear. The most notable conspiracy against Nero was headed by the reputable noble Gaius Calpurnius Piso in 65 and involved several high personages. It was discovered and came to nothing. Piso and others committed suicide. Some of those done to death by Nero in connection with this and other conspiracies are familiar and respected: Lucius Annaeus Seneca, the Stoic philosopher who had been his tutor and served him well in the government for several years; Petronius, writer and critic of the regime; the poet Lucan; and Corbulo, the most renowned general of his time.

Certainly Nero was a megalomaniac who vastly overrated his own abilities and accomplishments. A hundred-foot-plus statue of himself attired in the accoutrements of Apollo was placed in the vestibule of his new palace. Nero became obsessed with art and in particular with his own singing and lyre playing. He gave public performances at which it was dangerous even to be inattentive, much less go to sleep as the future emperor Vespasian once did. The latter got off with a rebuke since he was both a good general and a social nobody. Nero felt he was truly among his own when he made a tour of Greece, participating in the great games—all held during the same year, out of the usual order, in honor of the royal participant. The emperor won almost all the laurels—the ancient equivalent of first-place gold medals—more than eighteen hundred "victories" for everything from lyre playing to chariot racing. In return he freed Greece from tribute, but since he was near the end of his reign the award was short-lived.

Nero's record as an administrator was not so dismal. He chose good men for important jobs in the provinces, the best examples being Vespasian for the Jewish rebellion and, earlier, Corbulo for a general command against the Parthians, where the struggle involved the control of Armenia. Partly by war and partly by diplomacy Corbulo achieved a satisfactory compromise settlement. Nero had no drive for martial glory, the bloody route that most megalomaniacs in high places pursue. He should probably not be blamed for the rebellion in Britain under Boudicca, a native queen, though his minister Seneca may have helped perpetrate it through huge loans there at predatory rates of interest. The rebellion in Judea that broke out in 66 was primarily the result of long-standing hatred between Jews and Gentiles in the area. The precipitating incident involved Jew-baiting in the Roman provincial capital, Caesarea, and also Nero's recent decision not to permit Jewish participation in the local government. Yet it seems less Roman misgovernment than the complete impossibility of governing to everyone's satisfaction that caused the revolt.

Nero did depreciate the coinage (see the section on economics below), and he was personally extravagant, but there is little evidence of irresponsible economic policy. Still, if a fraction of the stories recounting the persecution of innocent Christians is true, if indeed men like Seneca and Corbulo were guiltless of treason, and taking into account that Nero killed his own mother, Agrippina, perhaps Nero deserves his popular reputation as an appalling tyrant.

The "Year of the Four Emperors"

Nero's artistic performances; his preoccupation with the construction of his Golden House; his trip to Greece, with all its peccadillos; and in particular his alienation of powerful army officers, partly through neglect and partly through his treatment of Corbulo, who was suspected of conspiracy and forced to commit suicide, caused the emperor's fall. Generals in the provinces began the rebellion; the last straw was the defection of the praetorian guard. Nero committed suicide in the summer of 68, when he was still only thirty-one years old. The Senate had already declared him deposed and sentenced him to die. Since Nero was the last of the Julio-Claudians, the Senate and the praetorians accepted the man who led the revolt, Servius Sulpicius Galba, as the new princeps.

The new emperor was an elderly man in his seventies, an aristocrat of an old family. With his own army from Spain, where he had been a provincial governor, the support of some troops in Gaul and of one of the powerful Rhine armies, plus the backing of the Senate and the praetorian guard, he seemed to have a solid base. One would not have guessed that there was to be a succession of ephemeral emperors.

Galba quickly committed a number of errors. He alienated some of the upper classes when he attempted to reverse many of Nero's arrangements, he lost the backing of the guardsmen and many others as well by his choice of a successor, and he refused to pay what had been promised in his name to the praetorian guard. Besides, the other armies had learned how easily a new emperor could be created and how profitable the deed might be.

In January 69 the legions of Lower Germany were persuaded to renounce their annual oath of allegiance and a short time later to acclaim as emperor their general, A. Vitellius. Before the news arrived in Rome the praetorians had already killed Galba and elevated their choice, M. Salvius Otho; thus the stage was set for civil war. The Vitellian commanders managed to get their troops through the Alpine passes before spring fairly arrived—and no doubt sooner than Otho anticipated. The latter energetically marshaled his forces into the Po valley, near Cremona. If he had waited, his army would have been augmented by a strong contingent from the Danubian frontier. But with bad judgment he chose to fight immediately, and lost; in April he committed suicide.

Vitellius punished some of his captured opponents, executing a good many centurions, a distinct error that caused many army officers to look to their interests elsewhere. In his short reign, if his ancient biographers are right, he seems to have been more concerned with his gourmet meals than anything else. He was said to have spent fantastic sums on exotic foods. Meanwhile, other army officers were ambitious also, and other legions disliked the way the German legions had taken over. Though Vitellius did not pay the legionaries large bonuses because of the state of the treasury and his own extravagance, they profited by treating Italy as conquered territory to be despoiled.

The governor of Syria and the prefect of Egypt, both commanders of substantial armies, got together to nominate as emperor the commander of a third army in the east, Titus Flavius Vespasianus, who was engaged in suppressing the Jewish rebellion. Vespasian had by this time overrun the northern areas of the country and was mounting a siege of Jerusalem itself. He may have been influenced by a Jewish captive, one Flavius Josephus (the historian), who had prophesied to Vespasian that the general would one day be emperor. Vespasian always claimed July 1, when the first troops took oath to him, as his accession date, but it was October before the decisive battle took place—again near Cremona in the Po valley—and about a year after that before the new emperor actually arrived in Rome.

The battle for Vespasian's ascendancy was fought by Danubian troops; disappointed earlier not to have arrived for the first battle of Cremona against Vitellius, they hurried to Italy without waiting for the contingents from the Syrian or Egyptian forces. They took the disorganized army of Vitellius by surprise and in a hard-fought and bloody battle that lasted many hours, the Danubian troops at last won a complete victory. They, too, moved south to Rome, living off the country as they went. Meanwhile a separate little civil war devastated the capital. Vitellius agreed to abdicate, but in December his troops attacked Flavian supporters on the Capitoline Hill, where the great temple of Jupiter Optimus Maximus was burned. When the Vespasianic troops came from the north they killed Vitellius. Rome, Italy, and the rest of the Empire, having tasted the evils of chaos and civil war, now were ready to let the latest emperor have a chance to reestablish order.

The Flavians

Vespasian (69–79)

Despite some remaining embers of civil war, as well as other problems, the military was soon fully under control. Vespasian had been accounted a good general, and most other possible military claimants to the throne were gone. The rest had chosen not to enter into competition. The new emperor left the war against the Jews in the hands of his oldest son, Titus, who sacked Jerusalem in 70. Contrary to Titus' intention, the temple Herod had rebuilt and embellished went up in flames. Thousands of Jews died in the fighting and more in the long siege, and other thousands were sold into slavery. Some went to Rome and helped build the Flavian Amphitheater, popularly known as the Colosseum, which rose on the spot where Nero had placed a reflecting pool for his Golden House.

Along the Rhine a rebellion of Gauls and Germans took on the proportions of a war of liberation. A Romanized Batavian named Civilis, under suspicion of sedition before the war began, led an uprising when in the absence of the great Rhine armies the Roman frontiers were left thinly defended. Trying to make it a general rebellion, he persuaded some free Germans and some Gauls already serving in the Roman auxiliary forces to join with him. But most of the Gauls refused to aid him, even when news of the burning of the Capitol gave hope to enemies that Rome's end was approaching. By reinforcing the Rhine the Roman commander Q. Petillius Cerialis, a relative of the new emperor, split the rebel territory in two. He soon accepted the former auxiliaries back into Roman loyalty. Next, in 70, he reduced Civilis' headquarters at the captured Roman camp of Vetera, and finally he made peace on easy terms with the Germans. Perhaps the failure of most of the Gauls to join in the struggle indicates that they had become too civilized and soft, but it is in any case a tribute to the original settlement of Caesar and to subsequent Roman policy that the tribes were not eager to take up arms for freedom.

In the second year of his reign Vespasian closed the doors of the temple of Janus in Rome as a sign of peace. Pockets of resistance held out in Judea, however. The most celebrated of these was atop the mesalike fortress of Masada, on the Dead Sea. Not until 73 did the Roman circumvallation and laboriously engineered assault reduce that desperately defended outpost.

Vespasian, though a military man, did not increase the number of permanent legions, but returned to the former number as soon as possible. He did strengthen the naval flotillas on the Rhine and the Danube. The milestones uncovered by archaeologists and happenstance proclaim him a great road builder. One of his more important roads connected the Rhine and Danube frontiers through a newly acquired territory in south Germany. The route had obvious military significance. Italy now supplied few recruits, and those mostly for the praetorian guard and other special units. Most legionaries were recruited from the citizen population of the provinces.

Vespasian asked the Senate to confirm to him the powers Augustus had held, demonstrating in this and other ways his intent to restore the old partnership—to play the role of princeps, not tyrant. Inevitably his equestrian background affected his outlook, as it did his choices for the depleted ranks of the Senate. Into the Senate and the lower governmental ranks as well he ushered many new persons, mostly from old Italian families, some from provincial backgrounds. That he chose well is indicated by the fact that the great emperors of the next century derived from families who were brought into the aristocracy under Vespasian. Naturally the low-born emperor had difficulty with some old-line aristocrats, who resented both him and his New Men.

Vespasian's greatest problem was economic. He found the treasury bare, yet immense sums were required not only for the routine expenses of empire but also for reconstruction in Rome and other cities. The temple of Jupiter on the Capitol, in ruins, was only the most conspicuous example of this need. Cremona, once a flourishing city, had been destroyed; and in many other places the devastation and spoliation had reduced Italian cities and towns to a depressed state. Vespasian met the economic needs by heavier taxation, even in the capital. When he put a tax on urine collected from the public latrines by fullers for use in bleaching cloth, his son Titus protested he was going too far. Vespasian, who was noted for his dry sense of humor, held a denarius under his son's nose and said, "This doesn't stink, does it?" Doubtless the provinces groaned under the added tribute. Vespasian instituted a complete survey of privileged communities all over the empire, probably intending to revoke some undeserved privileges and increase revenues. Greece lost the immunity to taxation granted by Nero and was again made subject to tribute. Some estates given away by his predecessors were taken back for the patrimonium. But Vespasian also economized; he embarked on no new expansive ventures, except that he did resume the conquest of Britain. Before the end of his reign he was able to reduce taxation to its former levels and still leave the treasury in a healthy state of solvency.

Titus (79–81)

Vespasian had been practical, hardworking, effective. He died with the humorous comment that he was on the point of becoming a god—referring to the now usual practice of deifying dead emperors. His son Titus was tremendously popular, and there was great rejoicing when he assumed power. There had been no doubt of the succession: Vespasian had made it quite clear, despite criticism, that he intended to establish a dynasty. Titus was associated with him in the government almost from the beginning, at times serving with him as consul. (Unlike the Julio-Claudians, all the Flavians served as consuls on an almost annual basis.) Titus' own popularity naturally helped ensure that there would be no difficulty with the succession.

In spite of his desire to please everyone and his tendency to spend more freely than his father, Titus might have been a good princeps if he had lived; his reign lasted less than two and a half years. Unfortunately, it is remembered more for disasters than for anything else. The year 79 saw another destructive fire at Rome, followed by plague; and most

The Flavian Amphitheater, popularly called the Colosseum because of the colossal statue nearby. Originally, the statue was of Nero, but after Vespasian became emperor, the head was replaced with that of the sun-god Apollo. (*Alinari/Art Resource, New York*)

important for us today, a violent eruption of Mount Vesuvius, near Naples, which buried Pompeii and Herculaneum, partially preserved them for rediscovery by the world in excavations that continue today.

In 80, Titus dedicated the great Colosseum with games lasting more than three months, which were tremendously pleasing to the Roman mob but excessive even by Roman standards. He also made a part of Nero's Golden House into public baths. Other sections of the palace, a symbol of Nero's extravagance and of the belief that he had caused the burning of Rome, were simply abandoned. Covered over by fill for the baths, part of the palace was preserved and may still be seen by tourists.

Domitian (81–96)

On the untimely death of Titus, his younger brother Domitian came to power without difficulty. Our sources portray this emperor with venom as an unfeeling tyrant, a characterization Domitian doubtless deserved to some degree. Yet perhaps his most heinous offense was that he stripped off the façade of the Principate, exposing the Senate and the upper classes for what they had become—dependents and servants of the emperor. He kept his own counsel for the most part, trusted no one fully, and through his less than winning personality presented to the world an image that was easy to despise. Stories of his cruelty further explain this revulsion. Like the emperor Gaius, he was deified in life and addressed as *dominus et deus*, "Lord and God." He had reason to be mistrustful, even fearful: he snuffed out several conspiracies before the successful one that finally took his life.

It is possible that a bit of charm, an outgoing personality, a diplomatic and deferential attitude toward the Senate, a greater effort to please the crowd—these qualities may have been all that Domitian required to be accounted one of Rome's better principes. He was industrious and conscientious in his responsibilities. The men he chose for high position seem mostly to have been excellent people. He was not extravagant, but made good use of public funds.

Along the Danube frontier where the most serious problems with outside invaders arose Domitian was, however, not totally successful. Ultimately he made the most troublesome leader, Decebalus, king of Dacia (approximately modern Romania), a Roman friend and ally by granting him an annual subsidy—as had at times been granted earlier to the king of Armenia. He then strengthened the Danube army and built permanent forts at strategic points. He also recalled Agricola (Tacitus' father-in-law) from Britain and called off any effort to expand into Scotland. To the more jingoistic of Roman critics these actions were reprehensible: Rome, they thought, had always been greatest during times of expansion. In his policy, however, Domitian followed the example of Augustus, who learned from a long and expensive series of campaigns that expansion was not always the wisest course. Trajan, as we shall see, was to change that policy. And Trajan is accounted the greater ruler; but in these matters at least it is possible that Domitian was right.

Local Government: Italy and the Provinces

Rome was doubtless the most interesting and exciting city in Italy, but in matters of self-government the cities and towns away from the capital had a great advantage over the metropolis. The situation in the city of Rome was somewhat comparable to that of Washington, D.C., today, where the federal government overshadows and to a considerable degree displaces local institutions.

That local government was alive and well in the Italian cities is clearly indicated in the inscriptions painted everywhere on the walls of Pompeii. Individuals, neighbors, and religious groups solicited support for candidates ("All the worshipers of Isis urge you to vote for . . ."). In particular, members of the various craft and service occupations were active in elections. Mule drivers, fruit sellers, dyers, garlic dealers, goldsmiths, perfumers, barbers, fishermen, and many other groups all proclaimed candidates.

As for the candidates themselves, they must have wanted to serve, for not only were they unsalaried, but they were expected to spend their own funds, perhaps to present shows or to build or repair a public building or to donate free oil for the public baths. In many towns such obligations were specific and required. We do hear of times when prominent citizens had to be urged to put their names forward, but usually the local aristocrats who held the top offices felt sufficiently paid off in honor.

Most Italian towns had four top officials—a board of two men, *du-umviri*, with judicial authority, and usually two aediles, who were in charge of finance and the treasury as well as the marketplace, temples, and festivals. Lesser posts were sometimes held by men who did not rank high on the social scale. Every five years the *duumviri* took a local census and performed other tasks analogous to those of the Roman censors in the days of the Republic. Each city also supported a variety of priests, some of whom by now ministered to the imperial cult. The *augustales*, formed in the reign of Augustus and devoted to the cult of the reigning emperor, were rich freedmen who thus gained a modicum of status despite their rank.

The major institutions of the cities were the assembly of all citizens, which elected the officials, and a kind of senate made up of ex-officials like the Senate at Rome. This organization, ordinarily called the curia, usually contained one hundred members, or decurions. Election day could be a lively time: we hear of riots during elections at Pisa in this period. When such irregularity occurred, the emperors usually intervened by appointing prefects to govern the offenders for a time.

Wide variations existed in the government of provinces, but most had a similar system of oligarchical self-government with officials and a town council comparable to the Italian curia, all drawn from the upper classes, and a body of citizens who served as an elective assembly. In the western provinces tribal organization sometimes played a role. But even there Roman policy encouraged urbanization and thus the establishment of self-governing oligarchical institutions. Though they ruled an empire, Romans still considered the city-state the proper unit for local affairs.

Local officials and decurions in the provinces were often awarded Roman citizenship, which naturally added to the luster of their position. Yet obligations accompanied the honor; officials had to see to the order and functioning of public places—temples, gymnasia (used by philosophers, teachers, and others), and market areas. Especially in times of shortage they had to seek supplies of grain and oil. They were expected to serve in the priesthoods, to serve on juries, to go abroad on embassies. Local tradition invariably required high officials to provide public benefactions at their own expense. In addition, Rome used local officials as instruments of central policy. In a general way the local

The Temple of Jupiter, fronting a forum at Dougga, Tunisia. Provincial towns such as this tended to build public structures similar to those in Rome, including temples, basilicas, theaters, arenas, and baths.

oligarchy was expected to keep things under control for Rome. More specifically, the local governing class supported the imperial cult, aided in the collection of taxes, and raised auxiliaries to serve in the Roman army. These obligations perhaps lay lightly enough on the shoulders of the leading citizens of provincial cities in this period, but in times of trouble in the future, such responsibilities would weigh heavily indeed. Other local obligations that were normally not too irksome included the upkeep of some roads, usually by adjoining property owners, and bridges. Main roads were as a rule built at imperial expense.

In Italy as in the provinces the cities tended to mimic Rome in many ways. Citizens almost everywhere wanted aqueducts, basilicas, temples, theaters, and arenas. The remains of these structures, still to be seen all over the area of the defunct Empire, testify to the economic health of the times as well as to the efforts of the provincial citizens to make their cities into small-scale Romes.

The Economy of the Early Empire

The greatest single blessing for the economic life of the Empire was the era of peace that Augustus had secured. The devastation of the civil wars of 68–69 was confined mostly to Italy, though the contemporary struggles in Judea and Gaul of course disrupted the economies of those areas. Everywhere else the single political administration, coinage system, safe sea routes, and a continually improved road system all contributed to a healthy economic structure throughout the Empire.

The road network, finely conceived and engineered, helped to hold the Empire together politically and militarily. Its importance in trade must not be overstressed. Farmers of course found the stone-paved or graveled roads useful in getting their products to local markets. But only objects of high unit value could profitably be transported more than a few miles overland. No bulky items would normally be sent, for example, from Italy to northern Gaul (or vice versa) through the Alpine passes overland. Grain could be transported from almost any seaport in the Mediterranean to Rome by ship cheaper than an equivalent amount could be transported overland as little as seventy-five miles by cart or pack-donkey.

Neither must it be thought, though there was internal peace, that the roads and seas were completely secure. Local officials had charge of security along the roads, and they did not always suppress the highwaymen who infested some areas. Nor were the seas always completely safe from piracy. On balance, however, conditions remained favorable for traders. Except for the grain trade, which was government controlled at Rome and to some extent at other cities, commerce was neither closely controlled nor excessively taxed. Port dues and customs were no real impediments to traders. They were harassed more by pirates, but their worst enemy was the weather. The large number of ancient ships found by modern underwater archaeologists—only the tiniest fraction of the total number lost—testifies to that fact.

Social Benefits of Economic Opportunity

Investigating the various crafts and skills pursued by lower-class Romans of the age, a modern scholar has concluded: "The first and second centuries of our era saw a revival of industrial life in the Roman world in both town and country. More freemen were probably engaged in the trades and crafts than ever before, and it was perfectly possible for shrewd and very ambitious *opifices* to acquire a fortune, retire from business, and vie with men of higher birth. . . ."[1] Deriving her information almost altogether from poets of the time, she lists some of the important products that came to Rome: from India, pepper, gold, ebony, ivory; from China, silk; incense from Arabia, dyes from Phoenicia, spices and perfumes from Syria; from Cilicia, saffron; timber and marble from (among other places) Phrygia and Bithynia in Asia Minor. Foodstuffs such as grain tended to be brought in imperial ships, though oil, *garum* (a prized fish sauce), and other items came from western provinces mostly, and especially from Spain, in private vessels also.

The traders who risked their capital in ships rather than placing it in the much safer and more prestigious investment, land, did not usually content themselves with bringing oil and wine or the like from Spain; they wanted to deal with valuable products of the sort mentioned above. And then, once they had made their pots of gold, they usually wanted to put it in land rather than continue taking risks. Thus in trade as in small industry (see Chapter 9), little effort was made to invest capital year after year for improving production and efficiency.

There was considerable progress, nonetheless. In the building industry, for example, astonishingly complex and effective cranes were invented for hoisting heavy stone, and in the harbors ingenious devices aided in loading and unloading vessels. Yet the very concept of capital investment in labor-saving equipment that is so integral a part of the modern business world never developed in ancient times.

The Structure and Importance of Public Spending

The effect of state spending on the economic prosperity of the various regions of the Empire has received little attention. Income came from all parts of the Empire in proportion to local productivity, but certain

---

[1] E. H. Brewster, *Roman Craftsmen and Tradesmen of the Early Empire* (New York: B. Franklin, 1972), pp. 31ff.

geographical regions saw a great deal of government expenditure, others very little, and the economic consequences were considerable. The effects of monies coming into the capital city itself have been noted well enough: it is often said that Rome imported tribute and exported government. However, other areas too benefited from a disproportionate share of state spending.

The income of Rome came mostly from two taxes, a poll tax (*tributum capitis*) and a property tax (*tributum soli*). Italy and provincial towns enjoying the Italic Right were exempt from these imposts but, like other areas, paid customs duties, sales tax, and miscellaneous other taxes such as the charge for manumitting slaves. On the other side of the ledger, expenditures were for goods and services, salaries of civil service and other government officers, building, and the military. Military spending for salaries of the soldiery, equipment, troop ships, warships, and military bases surely constituted by far the largest single cost category of the state, exceeding all other outlays combined. Proportionately large sums thus went to areas where military bases were located.

No elaborate credit structure existed, as in the modern world, whereby the state could increase or decrease the supply of money in given areas according to perceived economic needs. Thus the supply of money in any region might depend heavily on government expenditure in that region. Total expenditures were limited by the total received from all forms of taxation plus income from government-owned property, especially mines.

The government could not, as modern governments do, simply print money that has value in proportion to demand for it to buy goods and services. Later emperors did do something similar: decrease the value of the metal in coins. And as in modern times, inflation resulted when too much currency was issued.

Though Rome drew funds from all over the Empire, she spent most of them either in Rome and the vicinity or on the frontiers, at the fringes of the Empire, where the legions were. The legions thus tended to bring prosperity to certain provinces at the expense of others. Provinces such as Greece or Asia—even Italy itself apart from the Po valley and the region between Rome and the Bay of Naples—suffered a constant net drain of funds. The situation was somewhat analogous to that of estates owned by absentee landlords who took as much as they could in profit, returning very little in continuing capital investment. Partly because of this situation, by the end of the first century some of the older, interior provinces were characterized by stagnant or declining economies while the newer provinces prospered.

We have noted how Augustus disposed his twenty-five legions. Under Claudius the Romans invaded Britain and afterward had three legions posted there most of the time until the abandonment of the province in the early fifth century. The process of enlarging the province and at the same time putting down rebellions continued through the reign of Domitian and long after. In Spain, however, one legion instead of the former three sufficed. Domitian reinforced the Danube frontier. Through the whole period the greatest concentration of troops was on the Rhine (four legions each in Upper and Lower Germany) and on the Danube (six to eight legions in the four, later five provinces involved). Under Vespasian two legions were stationed in Cappadocia. Elsewhere, one legion was maintained in Judea, Syria had three legions, Egypt now only two, and Africa only one.

Though the Gallic provinces had few troops, they nevertheless benefited greatly from military expenditure because of the supply routes and because the bulk of the supplies for the German legions came from the Gallic provinces. Archaeological discoveries at Augusta Treverorum (modern Trier), a flourishing colony in Belgica on the Moselle River, exemplify the benefits enjoyed by provincial cities located on important supply routes for the great armies of the Rhine. The whole area near the Rhine prospered over several centuries.

The Gallic provinces and Spain as well seem to have been productive enough, mainly in agricultural products, to remain economically healthy; Spain was not seriously affected by the withdrawal of two of its three legions. The Danubian provinces suffered from the incursions of tribes across the river, especially in the latter part of the period, so that any economic benefit from a favorable balance of state funds hardly mattered. In Egypt expenditures for the province's two legions did not balance the heavy flow of money and goods—particularly wheat and paper—to Rome. In grain alone, Egypt furnished enough to feed all of Rome's several hundred thousand persons—perhaps as many as one million—for one-third of each year.

Within Italy the prosperity of Rome radiated outward to some degree. Despite Claudius' tremendously expensive effort to build a harbor at Ostia, much of Rome's shipping came in to Puteoli on the Bay of Naples and proceeded north via the Appian Way to Rome. Moreover, much of the coast from Rome to Sorrento south of the Bay of Naples was prized as resort territory; many rich Romans owned one or more villas in the region. These villas contributed less to the real economy of the area than is sometimes supposed, but nevertheless they did something to spread the wealth.

Coinage of the First Century

As in the Republic, coin types to some degree reflect official policy and thus are useful to the historian. Augustus displayed on his coins his favorite titles—for example, the inscription PATER PATRIAE, "father of his country"—and also called attention to events he considered important, as when he regained from the Parthians the legionary eagles lost by

A denarius of the princeps Augustus, inscribed PATER PATRIAE, one of the titles he was given by the Senate and which he obviously liked to flaunt.

Crassus and marked the achievement with a coin type labeled SIGNIS RECEPTIS. Coinage in precious metals, the standard silver denarius and the gold aureus, worth twenty-five denarii, Augustus apparently controlled himself. For the sake of propriety he minted them all in Lugdunensian Gaul. The Senate nominally controlled minting of the brass or bronze sestertius (four to the denarius) and the other smaller copper coins, which were usually marked SC, "by decree of the Senate." Later in the first century, however, the emperors began to mint in Rome, and the SC legend on the lower coinage (or the occasional absence of it) probably meant little or nothing.

Nero's money is especially interesting both for the coin types and for the fabric of the coinage. Early on, soon after Claudius' death, Agrippina appears with Nero, in the dominant position, on the obverse of the major coins. Later she and Nero get equal billing, appearing face to face. Then Agrippina's bust is relegated to the reverse of the coin, leaving Nero to dominate the obverse in the manner customary since Caesar. Finally the queen mother is banished from the coins altogether, reflecting the decline of her power over her son.

Nero was also the first of the emperors to devalue and debase the coinage. The denarius had been minted to a standard that varied little from about the end of the Second Punic War. Nero reduced it in weight from about eighty-four to the pound to about ninety-six to the pound, and he also debased the silver content from virtually pure metal to about 90 percent silver. Thus the new denarii contained only about three-fourths the weight of silver of the old ones. The gold aureus, though not debased, was reduced in weight to a standard of about forty-five or forty-six to the pound as compared to the earlier forty to forty-two.

Confronting busts of Nero and his mother Agrippina, issued early in Nero's reign. Agrippina is shown on the right, in the dominant position; this coin (and others) reflect Agrippina's ambition to serve as regent for her young son. (*Ancient Art and Architecture Collection*)

The meaning of the debasement is not as simple as might appear. It is easy to say that an extravagant Nero needed money and decided to ease the strain on the treasury in this way. But there remains the problem of the smaller devaluation of the gold as compared to the silver: there must have been some change in the relative value of gold and silver, the latter having increased in comparative value. Furthermore, later emperors' debasement of the currency seems to have been done in part because of an appreciation in the value of silver. The value of gold and especially of silver increased because of loss of coins through attrition (the half-life of silver coins was only about twenty-five years), through an adverse balance of trade with the East, and through other uses of precious metals. The chief cause, however, was inadequate supply as production from the major mines declined and demand for currency increased. The supply of bullion—the only currency—being low, the intrinsic value of silver coins appreciated.

It is thus possible to argue on the one hand that Nero merely took measures to increase the money supply in a time of need. Or, on the other, it may be suggested that since gold changed value less than silver the Empire now went on a gold standard, and that the debasement of the denarius was thus relatively unimportant. This latter view, however, assumes that it was always possible to take twenty-five denarii to the treasury (or somewhere) and obtain for them one gold aureus, which is unlikely. On balance, what happened may be explained by a combination of these views: there probably was a shortage of currency and it probably caused both gold and silver to rise in value, silver the more; but Nero probably devalued the currency more than these circumstances required in order to gain a temporary advantage for the treasury. And thus he set a bad precedent that would often be followed by future emperors.

Upper-Class Intellectuals: Uncertain Loyalties

Anyone connected with a university in the twentieth century well realizes the importance of intellectual or academic freedom in the search for better ideas and ways of doing things. The very process of research, writing, or teaching involves criticism of the status quo and a consideration of junking it in favor of something else. In first-century Rome such freedom of thought and action existed only at the will and good nature of the emperor. Sometimes there was little restriction and sometimes, depending on the personality—or whim—of the reigning princeps, there was a great deal of restraint, whether active or indirect.

Even during the age of Augustus, when authors generally favored the regime, awkward situations arose. Historians especially, of any age, may feel the lack of untrammeled freedom, for their works will be read with a view to the present: the manner in which the past is treated often implies criticism or approval of the present situation. The historian Livy, for example, probably took his work no further than he did because of his mixed views on Augustus. Gaius Asinius Pollio (76 B.C.– A.D. 4), another great historian (whose works are unfortunately altogether lost), had been one of Caesar's commanders, had supported Antony and in general Augustus as well. Yet he tread on shaky ground as he asserted a critical independence; even those who attended his salons perhaps sometimes feared they were exceeding bounds. The poet Horace, addressing one of his odes to Pollio, spoke graphically of the situation:

> Thou art treating of civil strife . . . a task full of dangerous hazard—and art walking, as it were, over fires hidden beneath treacherous ashes.[2]

Pollio's major work, covering the years of the civil wars from about 60 to 42 B.C., was much used by later writers.

Pollio is also noted for having established the first really public library in the city of Rome. That of the Antigonids, brought back from Macedonia by Aemilius Paullus in the second century B.C., had perhaps been available for most scholars, as also another similarly brought from Greece by Sulla; but Pollio's was regularly and widely available much as

---

[2] Horace *Odes* 2.1. Translation of C. E. Bennett, Loeb Classical Library (New York: 1929).

a public library is today. The number of such libraries increased during the first century until there were five, but one of these may have suffered damage in the Neronian fire and another burned in the fire of A.D. 80.

The dilettante historian Marcus Velleius Paterculus (19 B.C.–A.D. 30?), who had served as an army officer under the future emperor Tiberius, could hardly have offended anyone, even though he did manage to admire a suspiciously broad spectrum of the great figures of the late Republic. His work—mostly extant—merely sketched the history of the state, for one thing: for another, he saved his greatest admiration for the emperor Tiberius himself. The tone of his work offsets that of the works of the later historian Tacitus and the biographer Suetonius; the former hated Tiberius and cleverly vilified him, whereas the latter, though he treated Tiberius much more objectively, yet incorporated unbelievable stories of his perverse sexual behavior as an old man in secluded semiretirement on the island of Capri.

More courage was demanded of Aulus Cremutius Cordus, a historian who lived and wrote under Augustus and Tiberius; who praised the republican heroes Cicero, Cassius, and Brutus; and resolutely refused to flatter Augustus. Sejanus seems to have instigated his prosecution for treason: the unfortunate man committed suicide in A.D. 25, and his books were burned. His daughter courageously reissued them at some later date. They too no longer exist for our firsthand judgment.

The most important works of younger Seneca (ca. 4 B.C.–A.D. 65), the minister of Nero, are essays and letters reflecting his Stoic views. The philosopher rises to a more lofty ethical plane in his writings than he managed to reach in his personal life. He extols the simple life, for example, but he became enormously rich and lent out money at high rates. In fact, by then moneylending had become so usual that Seneca did not keep it secret, as Brutus had in the late Republic.

Seneca bewailed the mores of the age:

> All intellectual interests are in abeyance; those who follow culture lecture to empty rooms, in out-of-the-way places. The halls of the professor are deserted; but what a crowd there is in the cafes! How many young fellows besiege the kitchens of their gluttonous friends! I shall not mention the troops of luckless boys who must put up with other shameful treatment after the banquet. . . .[3]

He also wrote tragedy of a peculiarly one-dimensional type that seems to have been intended for presentation through reading at a literary salon rather than for performance. Yet perhaps because of its availability, his work strongly influenced the great Elizabethans in the most flourishing period of English drama. A tragedy of this period

---

[3] Seneca *Epistles* 95.23.4. Translation of Richard M. Gummere, Loeb Classical Library (Cambridge, Mass., 1953).

once ascribed to Seneca but actually written by an unknown author soon after Nero's death is the *Octavia*, which sympathetically sets forth the plight of the daughter of Claudius whom Nero married, then rejected and ultimately executed. One lesser work generally thought to have been Seneca's may have been damaging to him: the *Apocolocyntosis*, a scathing satire written soon after the death of Claudius. The fantasy lampooned the efforts of the dead emperor, recently proclaimed a god in the usual fashion, to join the other deities. No doubt the young Nero read it and laughed heartily. But how did the mature Nero feel about it? Did he think that Seneca would as easily write satire about him also? Did he suspect that this little work reflected Seneca's real feelings about the institution of the principate? After all, Seneca had also written bad things about Gaius and indeed about the principate itself. Perhaps it helped convince Nero that Seneca was involved in the Pisonian conspiracy.

Similarly, another author of Nero's age, Gaius Petronius Arbiter, seems to have incurred the emperor's wrath by his writings. His *Satyricon* is not now intact; the largest fragment, the dinner of Trimalchio, tells of a new-rich bumpkin of a freedman who tries to play the role of an educated patron. He puts on a lavish dinner party, invites several intellectuals (who attend for the sake of the food), and dominates the conversation, committing hilarious blunders of language and ignorance. Some modern scholars have seen in this work implied criticism of Nero; perhaps Nero saw that too. At any rate, both Petronius and Seneca were told to commit suicide soon after the Pisonian conspiracy. We do not know whether they might actually have been involved.

A poet who wrote on a historical theme, Lucan (39–65), the nephew of Seneca, found first restriction and then, also, death for his pains. His epic work, the *Pharsalia*, on the civil war between Caesar and Pompey and Cato, glorified republican heroes and themes. Perhaps partly owing to simple jealousy, Nero forbade the young poet to read his works in the salons that Asinius Pollio had made so important a part of the intellectual world. Lucan later joined the Pisonian conspiracy and thus inexorably came to the hour when he had to take his own life.

Even a second-rank poet, the Stoic A. Persius Flaccus (34–62), may have offended Nero by his austere and obscure satires. Possibly both Lucan and Persius suffered in the emperor's esteem because their Stoic teacher, the freedman L. Annaeus Cornutus had dared to suggest that Nero's plan to write an epic poem on Roman history was too grandiose; Cornutus was banished for his temerity.

The Stoic Focus of Disloyalty

High-level opposition to the principes of the first century centered in the small but close-knit group of Stoics; a few Cynic philosophers also joined in the disapprobation. The basis for their opposition apparently lay both in a sentimentalized view of the Republic and in a concept, less philosophical than political, that government should be in the hands of the best men (or the best man), which of course meant the old oligarchy, naturally led by themselves. Seneca was an important figure among the Stoics at Rome despite his service in Nero's government. One of his comments serves to point up the sentiment that drove the group: "If you set a high value on liberty, you must set a low value on everything else."[4]

The republican heroes of these dissidents were the younger Cato, Brutus, and Cassius. In the *Pharsalia* Lucan made Cato a Stoic martyr to the cause of freedom. A Stoic senator of Nero's time, P. Clodius Thrasea Paetus, wrote a life of Cato that has not survived, but we can perhaps infer his attitude in the life of Cato by Plutarch, who used Thrasea. Cicero, who well understood Cato's shortcomings, would scarcely have recognized the man he knew. The veneration of Cato became almost cultic; groups of people gathered secretly to celebrate his birthdate. Thrasea irritated Nero most by his silence. He walked out of the Senate when that body basely congratulated the emperor, after the murder of Agrippina, on his "escape" from his mother's conspiracy. Later he withdrew again, and he stayed out of the Senate for three years. A remark of Juvenal's (*Satire* 5) may indicate that Nero and other emperors after him who moved against the Stoics had reason to suspect real conspiracy. Juvenal says that Thrasea and his son-in-law, Helvidius Priscus, used to celebrate the birthdays of the Cassii and the Bruti with garlands on their heads (such as a Roman might wear for sacrifice). Thrasea was accused of treason and chose to forestall the inevitable by suicide.

Nero was the more fierce in his tyrannical behavior because he was frightened by the extent of the Pisonian conspiracy, which included several high officers in the praetorian guard as well as many members of the upper aristocracy. If the assassination had been planned for a few days earlier, it would surely have succeeded, and the history of the Empire might have been very different.

Helvidius, along with Arulenus Rusticus and his brother, Junius Mauricus, after Thrasea's death headed up the opposition—once Helvidius returned from the exile into which Nero had sent him. They and others of their way of thinking not only vexed Vespasian but perhaps actually conspired against him as well. We are not as well informed about such conspiracies as we are of the Pisonian plot against Nero, but Vespasian was goaded into reluctant reaction: about 75

---

[4] Seneca *Epistles* 104.34. Translation of Richard M. Gummere, Loeb Classical Library (Cambridge, Mass., 1953).

Helvidius Priscus was executed—we are told that Vespasian tried to reverse the order but not in time—and other philosophers were expelled from Rome. Domitian, with characteristic heavy-handedness, in 89 not only expelled philosophers from Rome, as his father had, but even from Italy; three or four years later he executed a man who eulogized Helvidius and his son and he banished others, Arulenus Rusticus among them.

Such blanket expulsions of philosophers naturally injured completely innocent men. Among those unjustly sent away from Italy by Domitian was Epictetus, who had risen from slavery to become a Stoic philosopher and whose *Discourses* emphasize attainment of happiness through action of the will regardless of anything external. Another whose banishment was Rome's loss was Dio Chrysostom, a friend of Vespasian and later, under Trajan, an enthusiastic supporter of the Empire. Yet another exile, Apollonius of Tyana, was less of a loss to Rome. Part philosopher, part mystic, he gained a reputation as a performer of miracles. Future pagan admirers would set him up as a rival to the Christians' Jesus.

Notable Women of the Period

Our understanding of the status of women in the first century is shaped by what is known of the wives of the early emperors—including Messalina and Agrippina, both wives of Claudius, and Poppaea, the wife of Nero—as well as by the portraits of the vain and cruel women in the works of Juvenal. But we also know of women possessing both high character and great influence who played important if secondary political roles or participated with their families in intellectual resistance to the growing power of the emperors.

To be sure, more evidence survives of women of not-so-high standards in that age—as well as of masculine criticism of women who stepped outside traditional bounds. Seneca, for example, wrote:

> [Hippocrates] remarked that women never lost their hair or suffered from pain in the feet; and yet nowadays they run short of hair and are afflicted with gout. This does not mean that woman's physique has changed, but that it has been conquered; in rivalling male indulgences, they keep just as late hours, and drink just as much liquor; they challenge men in wrestling and carousing; . . . they devise the most impossible varieties of unchastity, and in the company of men, they play the part of men.[5]

---

[5] Seneca *Epistles* 95. Translation of Richard M. Gummere, Loeb Classical Library (Cambridge, Mass., 1953).

Seneca's own mother, Helvia, had been a remarkable woman. The elder Annaeus Seneca was a well-known rhetorician who doubtless influenced their son, but it was Helvia who had given Seneca a love for philosophy, and she used her influence to help him in his political career. We have three letters that he wrote to her from exile (apparently at the instigation of Messalina) during the principate of Claudius, which show the respect and affection that characterized their relationship.

Several women, intellectuals in their own right, took part with their husbands in the resistance. The elder Arria, for example, was the wife of one Caecina Paetus, who was caught in a conspiracy against Claudius. Paetus decided to commit suicide, but when he hesitated at the actual plunge of the dagger Arria took the knife, gave herself a mortal thrust, and handed it back to him, saying, "Paetus, it doesn't hurt." Nor was she only intending to follow her husband in a wifely martyrdom: she herself had been involved in the plot. It was their daughter, also named Arria, who was the wife of Thrasea Paetus. Like her mother she shared her husband's views and, like her, wished to follow him in death, but she was dissuaded. Their daughter, Fannia, wife of Helvidius Priscus, in turn shared his exile and almost his death. She herself was later exiled and her property confiscated for her role in encouraging men to carry on the tradition of opposition.

Another worthy woman, Domitilla, niece of Domitian and wife of Gaius Flavius Clemens, forfeited her son's chance of being chosen by the emperor as his successor when she and her husband refused to give him blind support. But she and Clemens were attracted to monotheism— Jewish or Christian, it is uncertain which—and suffered the penalty for "atheism": death for Clemens, banishment for Domitilla.

We know little of women who in some way fashioned careers for themselves, but we do know of several who were trained physicians, apparently specializing in gynecology. Numerous lower-class women were midwives. We know also of women, especially in rural areas, who practiced folk medicine. Women engaged in business to some degree, no doubt hampered by the requirements of guardianship—though more women fully controlled their financial affairs than they had earlier. Some owned ships, though we do not know whether they were directly involved in mercantile trade.

Lower-class women and of course slaves were often trained to per-form personal services, most often cooking and catering, spinning, weaving, dyeing, dressmaking, hairdressing, and wet-nursing. Some were entertainers: they sang, played music, danced, acted—or engaged in prostitution, a regulated profession that in the Roman mind differed little from other kinds of entertaining. We do hear of women who worked in trades normally thought of as masculine, such as shoemaking and silver-working; they even fought as gladiators on occasion.

Senatorial Supporters of Empire

By no means did all thinking men and women of the upper classes turn against the first-century rulers. Gaius Plinius Secondus, known as the elder Pliny (23–79), for example, found it possible to serve the state and follow the path of the scholar as well. His compendious *Natural History* was less likely to give offense than history or political philosophy, dealing as it did with topics such as astronomy, mining and metallurgy, and so forth. Pliny was commander of the fleet at Misenum when Vesuvius erupted in 79. He took some ships close to Pompeii, partly from scientific curiosity and partly to help fleeing refugees if possible, only to die himself, asphyxiated by volcanic gases.

Gnaeus Julius Agricola advanced to high office even under Domitian. His most important service was as governor of Britain, where he extended both imperial boundaries and civilized settlement. It was rumored, however, that at the end of his career his life was in danger from the capricious Domitian. But all of our information is slanted, especially that coming from Agricola's son-in-law Tacitus, whose *Annals* and *Histories* suggest that several emperors of the first century were some species of monster.

The greatest support for the principate came from the formerly obscure persons raised to important posts by the various emperors, particularly the Flavians. Lacking any family traditions of power and independence, these servants of the state were deeply obligated to the emperors who had elevated them. As the Senate came to be filled with such men, the very concept of freedom changed. No longer did it mean an independent Senate, as in the Republic. Freedom to most senators of this age meant no more than the right to be respected, consulted, and permitted to do and say what they pleased within reasonable limits—a restricted notion of freedom, indeed, but the system offered nothing more.

The new families enrolled among the upper classes did, however, provide a needed balance. Out of their rural, colonial, or provincial origins often emerged the solid virtues, the frugal habits, and something of the spirit that had made Rome great. According to Tacitus (*Annals* 3.55), the emperor Vespasian did much to set the same tone.

Lower-Class Worlds

The Slaves

At least until Nero, the emperors lived in constantly increasing luxury and affluence, with the great families imitating royalty as much as their means permitted. The general prosperity made possible by the pax

Romana was concentrated at the center of the Empire. On a lesser scale it extended to the cities of the provinces as well, and to a small degree radiated out to the countryside. One form of the new prosperity, however, was the development of ever larger domestic slave establishments among the wealthy.

Slavery was debilitating to all of ancient humanity. Sexual exploitation and practices such as concubinage made it especially damaging to that most important social unit, the family. Worst of all was the personal degradation suffered by the slaves of inconsiderate or cruel masters, who lived in endlessly humiliating situations.

Though we have some census data for citizens (however difficult to interpret), we have none for slaves. Estimates of the slave population of ancient Rome are made on the basis of scanty literary evidence and archaeological finds. Slaves may have accounted for 30 to 40 percent of the total population of Italy in the first century A.D.; in the eastern provinces and in Africa the proportion of slaves to free citizens may have been even greater, while in the northern provinces it was probably smaller. In numbers, these percentages translate to perhaps three million slaves in Italy and twenty million or so in the Empire at large.

Doubtless the city of Rome itself harbored the greatest concentration of slaves. Residents on occasion remarked that it was well that the slaves dressed like lower-class citizens and therefore could not realize how numerous they were. Slaves were used in all tasks and trades. Even such craftsmen as cobblers or proprietors of plumbing shops might have a few slaves, as memorial inscriptions show. Slaves might be trained as skilled accountants, educators, physicians or midwives, managers.

Slaves and freedmen rarely competed directly, since many slaves probably were purchased in order to cut costs in providing services to their owners. However, occupations that might have been desirable and remunerative for lower-class persons were dominated by slaves or freedmen, thereby greatly restricting opportunities for the urban plebs. Similarly, slavery made it difficult for urban plebeians to establish small business enterprises and rise to more comfortable situations. Rich people were not likely to spend very much in patronizing small contractors or caterers of any sort: they simply acquired enough slaves to take care of all (or almost all) of their needs, so that the large households were in many ways as self-sufficient as a medieval manor. The enormous amount of capital tied up in the institution of slavery might easily have been used in more productive ways.

The largest number of slaves served in the imperial establishment. Archaeologists have uncovered a single latrine for servants in Domitian's palace that had seats for sixty people. (Such toilets usually had a continuous stream of water flowing below the seats.)

Information from ancient cemeteries provides specific detail about the slaves in the household of Augustus and his wife, Livia, and indeed

Public lavatory at Ostia. The Romans provided excellent public toilets, often with constantly running water, in all cities of any size. (*Ancient Art and Architecture Collection*)

in several other great houses of Rome that maintained large numbers of slaves. A few miles south of Rome on the Appian Way, the *columbarium* (repository of the ashes of the cremated dead) of Augustus' household, mostly slaves, was discovered in the eighteenth century. The total number of persons buried there was not less than six thousand. Some had died young, making extrapolation of the normal size of the imperial slave establishment difficult, but certainly it was large. Of the total number, about one tenth, or six hundred, had been personal servants of Livia. A whole corps of slaves attended to Livia's personal needs: hairdressers, persons in charge of her bath, perfumers, keepers of jewelry, no less than eight goldsmiths. (We must remember that this evidence comes from burials; she may not have had that many servants at one time.) Those who saw to Livia's clothing had very detailed tasks: one slave maintained only her dresses of the royal purple; another, morning dresses; still another, clothing worn on state occasions. One slave kept (and probably made) her sandals; she presumably had two or three others for different types of shoes.

Other *columbaria* of great households in Rome tell a similar story. The Statilia family, important in the reign of Augustus and later—

Messalina, wife of Claudius, was a Statilia—had a huge retinue of slaves and freedmen. All phases of making clothes, from carding wool to weaving and sewing, was done in the house. Such self-sufficiency, which one would expect on a country estate, had become usual in the large urban households as well. Some household slaves were used in economically productive ways, but most were not. For example, Statilius kept many Spanish riding horses, and a number of servants maintained his stables.

According to Pliny, the largest number of slaves attested for any of the great households was 4,116 (*Natural History* 33.135). But it is doubtful that many Romans owned anywhere near that number. Probably few senators had more than fifty or so to serve in their townhouses.

Away from these great houses, slaves performed more socially useful tasks. Some slaves became persons of influence and comparative wealth. Slaves and freedmen even held important managerial posts, not only in small businesses, but in contracting corporations. In Rome, for example, slaves usually managed the huge complexes of warehouses along the Tiber; in the suburbs, they ran brickyards, tile yards, and the like; in the rural areas, they often managed farms, vineyards, and orchards.

Most production slaves, however, were ordinary laborers who lived under miserable circumstances. They were worked as hard as possible and given barely enough food and clothing to keep them alive and in condition to function satisfactorily. Slaves who worked the mines and quarries had perhaps the bleakest lot; ordinary farm laborers, who sometimes worked in chains, were not much better off. Free day laborers without land worked when they could on others' farms and were better off only marginally—if at all—than agricultural slaves.

Many Romans treated their slaves well, especially *vernae*, slaves born in the household, or *alumni*, those acquired as babies or small children. Good treatment of course only ameliorated an irredeemably bad institution. Often decent treatment was seen as simply a means of keeping slaves quiescent and hardworking; after all, owners had to live with and depend on household slaves. A law of the early Empire that we know to have been applied more than once provided that if a household slave killed his master, all the slaves in the house were to be executed since it was presumed that the slave's intent would have been known to at least some of the others.

Nevertheless, both Roman practice and Roman law in some ways treated slaves more leniently than did those of earlier civilizations. Manumission of educated slaves became common as early as the middle Republic, and these freedmen by law became Roman citizens. They did remain clients of their former owners, however, and though they were citizens they could not run for office. But children born to freedmen were full citizens, though they might (like the poet Horace) feel some social disadvantage because of their lowly ancestry, and they were unlikely to be admitted to candidacy for high office.

Manumission was unlikely though not unknown for rural slaves who served as laborers; philosophers, physicians, teachers, trained slaves in personal service, and managers of farms or businesses much more commonly received their freedom. In Augustus' time a law forbade freeing slaves, with some exceptions, before age thirty, which then became the usual age slaves were manumitted all over the Empire. Augustus also restricted the growing practice of freeing slaves at the death of the master: only a limited number could be so freed. He also put a tax on manumissions; we can only guess at his motives.

Slaves were permitted to own property themselves, usually in money (*peculium*), and they sometimes ran schools, owned small businesses, even owned other slaves. Slaves who accumulated money were often allowed to purchase their own freedom, and sometimes they could also purchase the freedom of another slave, frequently a spouse. Slave marriages were in some ways protected in law, though not so completely as to prevent families from being broken up through sale. The law did not permit masters the unrestricted right to mistreat slaves—at least, not to kill them. In court, slaves had little standing. When called as witnesses or when accused of crimes they were routinely tortured before they gave evidence. In practice, therefore, slaves probably had little recourse in the courts, no matter what the law.

As we can tell from later law codes, many court cases involving slaves concerned the question of whether they were slave or free. During the high Empire a principle of law evolved that, in the absence of evidence to the contrary, it should be assumed that a person was born free. A humane principle indeed, but without a powerful patron to press the case, few slaves can have managed to obtain their freedom, whatever the circumstances of their enslavement.

Life in the Capital

In a number of ways Rome was a safer and more satisfactory place to live during the early Empire than in the late Republic. Augustus had divided the city into fourteen regions, each with its own minimal governmental forms. He had established *vigiles*, the combination police and firefighters, with one station for each two regions; we know of a few substations, apparently located in especially troublesome areas. The city had plenty of water—most of it of quite good quality—brought in by a complex and growing system of aqueducts (Claudius built two). The only area not well supplied in the first century was the Janiculum, across the Tiber from the city proper. In the next century, Trajan would remedy that situation with still another aqueduct. Sanitary drainage, though inadequate by modern standards, was as good as that of the major cities of the West more than a millennium and a half later.

The *vigiles* could not make the city completely safe from fire or crime. In Nero's time, Seneca wrote that it was safe to walk alone anywhere in the city (*De Clementia* 1.8.2). However, it was best to avoid the unlit streets after nightfall. Juvenal's third *Satire* (written decades later) explains why: some bully of a mugger would beat and rob the man who could not afford to have a retinue of servants along with him. Even at home one could not be safe:

> When your house is shut, when bar and chain have made fast your shop, and all is silent, you will be robbed by a burglar; or perhaps a cut-throat will do you in quickly with cold steel.[6]

Moreover, other dangers lurked from the windows of the high apartments that lined the streets:

> See what a height it is to that towering roof from which a potsherd comes crack upon my head every time that some broken or leaky vessel is pitched out of the window![7]

Destructive fires, as we have seen, wrought major devastation on two occasions in the first century. We can only imagine how many less destructive fires went unreported in our sources. Nero's plan for reconstruction after the great fire of 64 included wider streets, improved distribution of water, and buildings better designed for fighting fires when they occurred, but all this did not prevent the major fire of Titus' reign.

Safe or not, Rome was expensive. Rentals were high. Juvenal again provides us with a graphic example:

> If you can tear yourself away from the games of the Circus, you can buy an excellent house at Sora, at Fabrateria or Frusino, for what you pay in Rome to rent a dark garret for one year.[8]

And the same poet tells what the cost of living could mean to a person of little means:

> It is no easy matter, anywhere, for a man to rise when poverty stands in the way of his merits; but nowhere is the effort harder than in Rome, where you must pay a big rent for a wretched lodging, a big sum to fill the bellies of your slaves, and buy a frugal dinner for yourself.[9]

---

[6] Juvenal *Satire* 3.302–305. Modified translation of G. G. Ramsay, Loeb Classical Library (Cambridge, Mass., 1959).

[7] Ibid., 269–271.

[8] Ibid., 223–225.

[9] Ibid., 164–168.

The poorest of the lower classes at Rome—if, indeed, the welfare system was so managed as to select the most needy—were aided in their efforts to survive by distributions of free grain. For centuries an average of about 200,000 persons received this dole, not merely as a privilege but as a hereditary right. Whatever they could gain from their labor would yet provide only miserable lodgings and a minimum of other necessities. Occasional largesse from the emperors or from officials or even private persons helped also at times.

The city was noisy. Traffic had long been a problem; Caesar, in fact, had forbidden vehicular traffic in downtown Rome during the daytime hours. Deliveries of heavy freight were thus made at night, and the grinding of iron wheels on protesting paving blocks and the swearing of the teamsters made sleep difficult. The days brought other clangor and clamor, Many of the activities that take place indoors in modern cities were street-based in ancient Rome. Hawkers of goods, craftsmen, barbers, butchers, and even bankers all used the streets to conduct their business. Add to the scene the crowds of people who were often outdoors simply because their living quarters provided little more than a place to sleep and were inadequate for that, and one can begin to imagine the sights, sounds, and noisome smells of the great metropolis.

Yet there were compensations. Rome was the most exciting place in the world, at least in the view of most of its inhabitants. Varied entertainments added spice to urban life. The great public baths provided, for a small fee, places for welcome afternoon baths and also served as social centers where Romans could play games, get a massage, buy hot food, or just talk with friends. Many lower-class Romans belonged to *collegia*—clubs of different types, some like craft guilds, others more specifically religious or social. (As mentioned earlier, clubs with political tendencies had been banned by Caesar.) Most *collegia* provided aid to members, often in the form of arrangements for proper burial, and all gave a sense of identity within a social group.

Life in the Provinces

It would be impossible to generalize very much about the circumstances of the lower classes in provinces so diverse as, say, Egypt, where most families worked in serfdom for the state or great landowners, and Britain, where most workers probably toiled as independent small holders. Nor is there space for surveying conditions in each of the provinces. Earlier it was suggested that most members of the lower classes in Roman territories found their lot improved over their circumstances prior to absorption by Rome. Peace had its blessings, and since the Romans were mostly conscientious and orderly in their administration, and local governments were largely allowed to function as they had before Roman conquest, probably most lower-class provincials had as much freedom as before, with generally better economic conditions.

At times, of course, Roman subjects felt strongly their inferior political position. When noncitizens found themselves in confrontation with Roman citizens, before Roman officials, they were at a disadvantage. Or if the provincial governor showed bad character or greed, little could be done despite the existence of provisions for bringing suit in the admirable Roman court system. Perhaps few officials were venal in proportion to the total, but we know of several.

One particular area of abuse was the frequent bad treatment of the populace by Roman soldiers. John the Baptist, in the Bible, is reported to have told soldiers to be content with their wages, implying that often they were not and that they made up for it by extortion. The poet Juvenal, writing for a Roman audience about a universal problem, gives insight in his sixteenth *Satire* into the sort of incident that was common. One benefit all soldiers had, he declared, was that civilians would never dare to attack them. If, however, a civilian was beaten up by a soldier, the former could not hope for redress. The reason? All such redress had to be sought within the camp, for no soldier could come before a civilian court. Even if the case should be heard by a centurion who was a strict disciplinarian, as many of them notoriously were, and he should decide in favor of the civilian, Juvenal says the complainant would simply have made an enemy of the soldier's whole cohort and could expect even more brutal treatment in the future. Juvenal adds that it was easier to find someone to give false witness against a civilian than to find anybody to testify to the truth against a soldier. Yet, it will be remembered, army service was available to selected provincials, whose enlistment as auxiliaries brought citizenship, among other benefits, at discharge.

Public Entertainment: Games and Circuses

Emperors and kings have always found it prudent, especially when they rule from large capital cities, to try to keep the lower classes in their capitals reasonably happy and amused. Failure to do so has helped bring about the fall of rulers from Nabonidus in Babylonia in the sixth century B.C. to Louis XVI in eighteenth-century France. To a degree the urban plebs were useful to the principes. The capital was the backdrop of the imperial stage, and the plebs provided a sort of chorus for the imperial drama—or was it perhaps their role to serve as appreciative audience, applauding and cheering at proper intervals? No state would seem great and powerful without a chief who emerges from time to time in full panoply for some state occasion, the success of which is pointed up by huge cheering crowds.

Great state occasions are not simply for show; they are the warp and woof of the state. In Rome many such occasions had a religious significance. The success with which public spectacles are carried off in some measure testifies to the essential health of a regime. Nor had the great festivals of Rome been invented by the emperors; most were inherited from the Republic, along with the facilities. Two great circuses, the Circus Maximus and the Circus Flaminius, had existed long before the caesars. Gaius, Nero, and Domitian all added new facilities. Nero's circus on the Vatican is now partially covered by the Basilica of St. Peter. A permanent stone theater did not exist until Pompey built one in the first century B.C. Augustus added another, called the theater of Marcellus, after his nephew, remains of which still impress tourists today. The great festivals carried over from the Republic lengthened and grew more elaborate. Others were added: Nero and Domitian both established quinquennial (five-year) games celebrating their reigns; birthdays of the emperors tended to become festival days.

The major festivals in Augustus' reign, all of long standing, were those of Cybele, Ceres, and Flora in the spring; games in the summer to honor Apollo; and in the fall the *Ludi Romani* and *Ludi Plebeii* celebrating Jupiter and Hercules. Augustus added games to Venus Genetrix, tutelary deity of the Julian family. The total of such holidays reached about 77 under Augustus, increased to 87 under Tiberius (who added a festival dedicated to Augustus), and continued to rise until about 175 such days were marked in the official calendars of the fourth century A.D. Of course, not all Romans could be idle on holidays. If they did not work they got no pay. The workday began quite early and ended early; workers could labor a few hours and have time for some excitement after that. Moreover the hawkers, vendors, and others worked even harder on festival days.

In the first century the most entertainment time was allotted to theatrical performances, even though the classical theater was in decline; more appealing to the crowds were farces, mimes, and pantomimes. However, by far the largest crowds attended the horse and chariot races. The teams each had a distinctive color, and the blues, the whites, the reds, and the greens all had their rabid partisans. For some reason the greens were dominant throughout most of this period. Those who have seen the old motion picture *Ben Hur* can begin to appreciate the excitement of the chariot races.

Caesar began a practice occasionally followed by later rulers of putting on naval combats in an artificial lake he constructed along the Tiber. There were often boat races. Other types of performances included those seen in modern circuses: acrobats, jugglers, rope-dancers, fire-eaters, trained beasts, and so on. Animal fights or fights between men and animals (the men were usually condemned criminals) were often staged. Gladiatorial combat, later often thought to epitomize the Roman games, was not a part of public spectacle until the late Republic. However, showings put on by private persons—earliest at funeral

This model, a part of the city of Rome as it was about A.D. 200, shows the Circus Maximus, scene of the horse and chariot races. In the upper left is the Flavian Amphitheater or Colosseum; between is the Palatine Hill, with residences of the emperors.

games—had already become common, and public showings increased steadily during the early Empire. The emperor Claudius, who had a bloodthirsty streak in his character, pandered to the demand for such displays, exhibiting many pairs of gladiators. He also put on a naval combat in grand style at the dedication of the works draining the Fucine Lake, bringing criminals from all over the Empire to serve in the crews— nineteen thousand men on each side, many of whom were slain.

Of the gladiators it should be said that while theirs was doubtless a demeaning, cruel, and bloody "sport," yet some attained notoriety and even wealth. The successful ones owned the finest decorated armor (probably not used in combat) and were frequently besieged by admiring women. Even freeborn men, on occasion of high social status, entered the gladiatorial ranks; others who did not still trained themselves in gladiatorial fashion. A few women are known to have fought in the arena. The practice reached a peak in the third century, when numerous prisoners of war were available for combat.

Titus set the record for length of celebration in the first century at the dedication of the Flavian amphitheater in 80; games of all sorts went on for 100 days. Trajan's Dacian triumph early in the second century exceeded that, lasting 123 days.

The festivals and games no doubt permitted the crowds to let off steam and perhaps prevented general unrest, although the argument is debatable, somewhat like the question of violence on television. Perhaps these crowd demonstrations to some extent substituted for the loss of the more orderly expressions of opinion through the ballot in the now defunct assemblies. But disturbances frequently occurred at the games that required coercive measures to quell. The emperor Gaius, irritated one time when the noisy crowds began to enter the circus in the middle of the night, had soldiers clear the circus; a good many of the revelers were killed, several of equestrian rank. Activities on the fringes of the arenas and circuses required policing, and gambling and sale of wine caused much trouble.

The emperors or their official representatives often made distributions of food and money at the festivals. It was probably Nero who first began the practice of throwing tickets into the crowd good for prizes, sometimes valuable ones.

Italian and provincial cities, particularly in the west, imitated Rome in the matter of games as they did in government and architecture. As in Rome the crowds at the games were often rowdy. In Pompeii a few years before its destruction a gladiatorial contest brought on such riots that imperial authorities suppressed the games entirely for several years. This bloody affair is reported not only by Tacitus (*Annals* 14.17), who dismisses it as "typical of such country towns," but it is also vividly portrayed in a wall painting from Pompeii that has survived the centuries. Puteoli was the scene of similar riots. Criminals were in many places routinely executed either by being forced to fight with each other to the death—after which the victor was killed—or by combat with starving and fierce wild animals. Whatever Christians may have done to the Roman Empire, their ending such bloody spectacles deserves praise.

11 The High Empire: The Good Emperors and the Severi, A.D. 96–235

IN MANY WAYS the second century was the greatest age of Rome. Perhaps no nation in any age has managed to put into its highest office a succession of five men of higher caliber than the Five Good Emperors who ruled between A.D. 96 and 180: Nerva, Trajan, Hadrian, Antoninus Pius, and Marcus Aurelius. Competent, conscientious, and hard-working, they performed at a consistently high level. In unprecedented fashion they assisted systematically in the welfare of orphans and the poor, organized the civil administration along rational lines, and controlled state expenditures carefully, for the most part avoiding personal, extravagant show. Like their predecessors they too took up their allotted role as absolute autocrats. But they acted with advice from the governing class and usually without the arbitrary coercion often characteristic of rule by one person. In their time the Empire continued to be the Principate, not the Dominate.

The Empire attained its largest size in this period, with boundaries on the east in Mesopotamia and on the west limited only by the Atlantic.

Almost uninterrupted internal peace prevailed, while the wars on the frontiers were usually limited to necessary operations. Even the military campaigns of the most warlike emperor of the five, Trajan, were not motivated by greed for power. Though Christians occasionally endured persecution, the populace generally enjoyed considerable personal—though not political—freedom. We have the written testimony of several notable men of non-Roman stock singing the praises of these intelligent, urbane emperors and the Empire they ruled. Conditions of life in Rome and in cities all over the Empire—housing, sanitation, public facilities—were superior to those in the ages that followed until the nineteenth century.

Broadened Participation in Government

Particularly notable in this period is a trend that began in the days of the Republic: the circle of active participants in government continually widened. In the last century of the Republic the Romans had extended the citizenship to all Italians, and with it the right to hold the highest offices. By the time of the Flavian emperors, formerly Italian families held most of the dominant positions in government and society. The imperial succession itself well illustrates the trend: first came the Julio-Claudians, drawn from older Roman families; then the Flavians, drawn from formerly Italian rather than old Roman stock; after them the Good Emperors, all but the first of whom also derived from Italian families that by then had been citizens for generations but had migrated from Italy to Spain or Gaul; finally the Severi, of neither old Roman nor Italian stock, though citizens to be sure, with roots in Africa and Syria. Most other emperors to the end of the Empire derived from provincial families. Particularly in the military but also in the central administration a class of officials arose that, like the emperors, had ever less familial connection with Rome and Italy. Widening privilege continued in the gradual extension of the citizenship until, by 212, almost all free persons in the whole Empire were Roman citizens. This broadening of the circle of participants in government did not, however, bring with it any democratization in governmental structures.

Romanization of the Provinces

Other continuing changes in the nature of the Empire accompanied the gradual extension of privilege. One of these was the Romanization of the Empire. It is debatable whether areas became Romanized because of the extension of privilege or that privileges were extended to areas because they became Romanized. In the east, where Greek culture had long been dominant, neither statement is quite correct. Everywhere else, most notably in Spain, the provinces of Gaul, the Danubian provinces, and North Africa west of Egypt, the Latin language and Roman ways penetrated, paving the way for the extension of citizenship and other privileges. The term *Romanization* may mislead. A hybrid civilization developed in the provinces, melding both peoples and cultures with an overlay of Latin language and Roman ways, which gave the appearance of Romanization.

Romanization resulted in a growing intimacy between the provincial cities and the central administration. The local officials and the members of the governing city councils found themselves more and more the agents of the central government, particularly in the collection of taxes. Local obligations added to the expenses laid on officeholders.

In the early Empire, service as an official brought great honor locally as well as Roman citizenship; thus upper-class provincials long sought positions or at least did not object to them. Gradually, however, local office came to be regarded as a burden, and eligible persons often sought exemption from such service. In the second century A.D. those exempted from having to serve in local office included veterans (at first for five years, later for life), philosophers, rhetoricians, teachers, and doctors. Notable among those refused exemptions were poets, primary school teachers, and accountants. By the middle of the century it was necessary to limit the numbers exempted. In the larger cities, for example, no more than ten doctors, five rhetoricians, and five schoolteachers could be exempted.

An unplanned consequence accompanying the increased responsibilities of provincial officials for services to the Empire was less local freedom as power gradually became centralized in Rome. The imperial system eventually nearly destroyed local government.

Provincial Cities: Degrees of Privilege

How provincial citizens might enter government service and rise to positions of importance depended on the municipalities in which they lived. These municipalities did not all enjoy the same privileges, even when most or all of their citizens were Roman citizens. Some cities were "free" and ran certain of their own affairs without much interference from the provincial governors. Some were "free" and "immune," so that in addition their citizens did not pay one of the two major taxes collected everywhere outside Italy, the *tributum soli*, a land tax, and the *tributum capitis*, a head tax based on a property census somewhat like a personal property assessment. Some few of the most favored cities had also the Italic Right (*ius Italicum*), with the same financial privilege as Italy itself, and paid neither of the two major taxes. Though not all communities given the title of *colonia* possessed the *ius Italicum*, probably all the true colonies of Roman citizens, usually veterans sent out to settle on land in the provinces, were granted this most coveted privilege, as well as a few favored municipalities elevated to colonial status.

The colonies of veterans seem to have provided their citizens with the best opportunities for government service. And like the cities that grew up around the major army camps, the colonies also did much to Romanize the areas where they were located. Even noncitizens recruited from the provinces, who received the citizenship only on discharge, ordinarily acquired the Latin language plus, usually, a Romanized attitude in religion, dress, and general view of the Empire. By this time veteran colonies served as important recruiting grounds since sons frequently followed their fathers in the military career. Men of ability could rise, often quickly, in the army. The military in fact first allowed a few select lower-class citizens to move into lucrative civil careers.

Under the Severi the number of offices available to men who rose through the military increased at the expense of the senatorial aristocracy, which therefore faded in importance. As for the Senate itself, though it remained an important body under the Good Emperors, by the end of the Severan dynasty it was well on the way to becoming little more than a glorified city council for Rome. Imperial decisions made with the advice of the emperors' *consilium* and implemented by the praetorian prefects replaced senatorial decrees, which by then were no longer a major source of law. Roman senators continued to compose the aristocratic elite of the Empire, but careers were forged elsewhere. A senator out of office was little noticed.

Portents of Decline

This generally bright picture of the Empire under the Good Emperors renders all the more disquieting the apparent fact that, despite the best efforts of the superior leaders of the second century, the decline of Rome had already begun. Culturally, the signs are clear. In literature this century saw the end of the silver age of Latin literature and the opening of what one scholar has called the Silver Plated Age.[1] Architecture reached a peak early in the period and began a slow decline despite certain technical advances. Roman law entered the so-called classical period of its development—while at the same time the government deliberately began to apply the law unequally according to social status.

Symptoms of decline seem quite noticeable in the economic sphere: deterioration at the center continued, with trouble also in several of the

---

[1] Tom B. Jones, *The Silver Plated Age* (Sandoval, N.M.: Coronado Press, 1962).

provinces. By the end of the period, state revenues covered necessary expenditures only with difficulty, and only with stress on the provincial upper classes responsible for collecting taxes. The coinage continued to reflect the economic strain as silver coins were increasingly debased throughout the period. By the end of Marcus Aurelius' reign the denarius was worth only about 60 percent of its value in the age of Augustus; by the time of the last Severus, Alexander, it was worth about 50 percent at best.[2]

Circumstances no emperor could control contributed to the decline, including a series of bad crop years over large areas because of weather, plague, depopulation, and unwanted foreign wars. So strong an empire should have been able to endure a few bad years more successfully. There is almost no accounting for the failure of spirit, the slackening cultural response, in what seemed a great age.

Nerva (96–98)

After Domitian was assassinated in a palace conspiracy the Senate moved quickly to name a successor, Marcus Cocceius Nerva, a rich senator in his sixties, who had some knowledge of the law and considerable governmental experience. Though he ruled barely over sixteen months, Nerva certainly deserves to be classified with the Good Emperors. He might well have been only the first of a series of ephemeral rulers during another time of civil war since neither the praetorians nor the army had had a hand in his selection. The troops were quieted by largesse paid to the praetorians and probably to the whole army as well as to the city plebs. In addition, a new program was passed as law— incidentally, by a body calling itself an assembly of the Roman people, the last such ever held—that distributed land to other lower-class Romans. Nerva generously helped finance at least this latter measure with his own wealth.

He carefully maintained amicable relations with the Senate, swearing not to put any senator to death without judgment of his peers, an oath repeated by each of the next several emperors. He allowed open criticism, even by one of the consuls, who thought he was being unnecessarily lenient with wrongdoers under Domitian's reign. Indeed, the senators were in a vengeful mood, passing a *damnatio memoriae* against Domitian, by which all official references to the former emperor were eradicated, from monuments and the like. They were also eager to

---

[2] In weight of silver; the price of the silver may have been higher than before, so that the actual depreciation of the currency may have been somewhat less, by percentage, than these figures indicate.

prosecute Domitian's lieutenants. Even the amiable Pliny the Younger made ready to prosecute the man who earlier had prosecuted the Stoic philosopher Helvidius Priscus. But Nerva, wishing to put an end to bitterness, refused to permit such proceedings. He took care to honor the *damnatio* but had certain of Domitian's acts specifically reconfirmed to avoid awkwardness.

Nerva had no son, and thus there was no question of his establishing a dynasty—the sore point that had set the intellectual community against Vespasian. But this made the choice of an heir apparent the more important, especially since the emperor was not young. Any selection that would vastly displease the army, the praetorian guard, or the Senate might again cause a crisis, with two or three candidates backed by different armies fighting for the purple. Nerva did not even pick a relative. With excellent judgment he chose Marcus Ulpius Trajanus, a second-generation noble (his father had been elevated by Vespasian) who was not only a senator of note but also an excellent general. He was at the time governor of Upper Germany and therefore in command of one of the largest armies. All the powerful elements of Roman politics accepted the choice. Only three months later, while Trajan was still in Germany, Nerva died.

Trajan (98–117)

The younger Pliny, in his *Panegyric* delivered about 100, may have first termed Trajan *optimus princeps*—here at last, the "best citizen" whom the Stoics and other opponents of the Flavians had argued should be selected for the highest office. The intellectual community indeed, and the Senate as well, seems to have accepted this view of Trajan. Trajanic coin types later bore the appellation as an official, honorific title. Like Domitian, Trajan was addressed as *dominus*, but the *et deus* was left out. Trajan's origin in Italica in southern Spain seems not to have aroused any doubts.

Most Romans liked the new emperor because of his amiable personality and flexible administrative style. Domitian had been hated and feared, but Trajan was respected and admired. No important constitutional change in the position of the princeps gained him popularity. Indeed, Trajan's power was as absolute as Domitian's and he used it in some ways, particularly in the provinces, that Domitian had not. However, Trajan did repeat the oath of Nerva never to put senators to death without trial by their peers, and what is more important, he treated them with respect, even deference, and made use of them both in formulating and in carrying out his policies.

Despite the good-humored courtesy and common sense displayed by Trajan, he strongly desired efficiency in government and did not hesitate to take extraordinary measures to bring about improvement. Pliny furnishes a good example. Bithynia, in Asia Minor, was a consular province controlled by the Senate. Through bad management the financial affairs of a number of its cities had become badly disorganized. Trajan got Senate approval to take over the province and sent the senator Pliny as governor (110–112), with orders to intervene in the affairs of the city-states of the province and restore financial order. The practice was continued both by him and by his successors. Moreover, Trajan sent "correctors" to various places, including even the free cities of Greece, again in the interest of efficiency, and perhaps as well of sound government free of corruption. Yet it has been often said that freedom includes the freedom to make mistakes, and Trajan's interventions, though beneficial locally—as well as to the imperial treasury—meant enlarged power for the central government and less freedom in local matters. Even under an enlightened princeps, the tendency toward centralization of power was inevitable and relentless.

New Conquests: Extended Frontiers

For many years the tribes north of the Danube had tested Rome's defenses along that river, occasionally sweeping across it, bent on plunder. Domitian had strengthened the military on that frontier and had even

The spiral reliefs of Trajan's column in Rome depict in successive scenes the beginning and progress of the Dacian campaign. (*Alinari/Art Resource, New York*)

led campaigns in person. Twice he lost whole legions and parts of other units. He had eventually stabilized the area of the lower Danube by making Decebalus, king of Dacia, a Roman "ally" and giving him a subsidy. Trouble continued on the middle Danube, however, and Nerva campaigned against the Suebi there.

Trajan attacked Decebalus. Whether he had failed to behave like an ally or whether Trajan simply felt that the arrangement made by Domitian was impossible is not known. In fact, for details of Trajan's Dacian Wars of about 100–101 and 105–106, historians must rely on scraps of information. The magnificent relief sculpture spiraling upward around the column that Trajan erected sometime later in the new forum he built in Rome offers further evidence. One scene shows the 3,300-foot bridge the Romans built across the Danube, a wooden superstructure on twenty great stone piers, some remains of which still withstand the swift currents of the river. The roadbed was destroyed after only a few years to prevent easy crossing of the stream by enemies. Though the accomplishment was Roman, the architect, Apollodorus, was a Syrian with a Greek name.

These major wars demanded extensive mobilization of men and resources. It was claimed that Trajan captured a great treasure in the war that, with other spoils and income from the Dacian gold mines, more than paid for the war. Gold does seem to have become gradually cheaper in relation to silver. If truly a profitable war, it was probably the last such fought by Rome. After the first war Decebalus remained king, but his territory was reduced. He soon rebelled. After the second war he committed suicide. The territory now became the Roman province of Dacia, a Roman salient across the Danube preventing easy movement along the river by foes and dividing them. This province—which was later subdivided—was, however, in an exposed position and proved difficult to defend. By now nine legions with large numbers of auxiliary units were stationed along the Danube frontier.

Soon after the end of the Second Dacian War, Trajan moved into the Near East and took over the Nabatean kingdom on the death of one of its client kings. He made part of the kingdom a separate province, called Arabia Petraea, comprising approximately the Sinai peninsula with some adjacent territories. Since he stationed a legion there, his motive in the venture may have been the defense of the important trade routes connecting with the Arabian peninsula to the south.

With these victories, Trajan took the name Dacicus, celebrated record-length games in Rome along with a triumph, and spent enormous sums on a donative for the urban plebs. He soon was engaged in extensive building projects, to be surveyed later in the chapter along with some of his economic measures and welfare programs. But after a time he again turned his attention to the east. There Rome had long had problems with Parthia. Nero, it will be recalled, had sent his greatest general, Corbulo, to the east and, after a combination of campaign, maneuver, and diplomacy, had come to an agreement. The chief difficulty then, as for Trajan later, was the kingdom of Armenia. Since it was strategically located at a geographical pivot between the two spheres of influence, neither the Roman emperor nor the Parthian king could permit the other to control the area. Nero's compromise had permitted a relative of the Parthian monarch to become king, but he received his coronation from Nero himself in Rome, with all that implied.

When the Parthian king, Chosroes, put his nephew on the Armenian throne without consulting Rome, Trajan launched a major war designed both to weaken Parthia and to provide a permanent solution to the recurring problem of control over Armenia. After extensive preparations he sailed east in 113.

During the next three years Trajan's armies occupied Armenia; then moved south into Parthia; captured Ctesiphon on the Tigris, a Parthian capital; and at one point penetrated all the way to the Persian Gulf. Trajan was aided by division within Parthia. However, there were no defensible frontiers and Roman garrisons could not be put in all the key points of such a vast area. The Parthian monarch kept up the fight in every way he could, from direct attack to guerrilla tactics to stirring up opposition in territories occupied by Romans.

The very elements conspired against Trajan, who was almost killed in a devastating earthquake at Antioch in the winter of 114–115. Rebuilding the city would require great expenditures. Moreover, a serious Jewish rebellion demanded attention. Beginning in Cyrene and Egypt, it spread to Cyprus and even to Roman-held sections of Mesopotamia. Gentiles were said to have been slaughtered by the hundreds of thousands; doubtless the figures can be discounted, but the toll certainly was appalling. Trajan of course took measures to put down the rebellion—if that is the right term to describe the bloody reaction to a long series of events that had goaded the Jews beyond endurance. Roman troops were in turn soon slaughtering the Jews in equally appalling numbers.

But Trajan did not live to see the end of either his Parthian grand venture or the Jewish revolt. He died in Cilicia, on the way back to Rome.

Hadrian (117–138)

P. Aelius Hadrianus, a distant cousin of Trajan's, also came from the Spanish town Italica. Trajan is usually portrayed as the conquering imperialist and Hadrian as the peaceful builder—and so they were. Yet Trajan, in Italy at least, built as much as Hadrian did, and the latter gave close and continuing attention to the army. Hadrian did end the wars as soon as he could, even giving up territories Trajan had won in

Mesopotamia, and then adopted a generally defensive stance every-where. A number of factors may have shown Hadrian the necessity of such a course. In the east, the rebellions within Mesopotamia, the signs of Parthian revival, the difficulty of setting defensible boundaries, and the Jewish-Gentile struggle all indicated a need to draw back and con-solidate small gains. Perhaps Hadrian saw that the costs of Trajan's campaigns had grown completely out of proportion to any possible long-term benefits.

Hadrian's own rather uncertain position may have influenced him. Trajan had acted as guardian to him and had favored him in several ways, giving him an important army command in the Dacian Wars and later appointing him governor of Syria, the logistical base for the Par-thian War. But Trajan had never formally adopted him or otherwise specifically designated him as his successor until just before he died. There seems little reason to doubt the story told by Plotina, Trajan's wife, that the dying emperor did announce the adoption and intended succession. No other likely candidate existed; Hadrian was the nearest male relative of any importance, and some years before he had married Sabina, a grandniece of Trajan. Probably Hadrian already had the em-peror's signet ring, with all that it implied, before Trajan's illness. Sto-ries circulated of an attachment between Plotina and Hadrian, and little love seems to have existed between Hadrian and his wife. The rumors caused mutterings and grumblings back in Rome.

The Senate had little to do with the choice of the new emperor. Some senators raised questions about Hadrian's legitimacy, either on the ground of improper dynastic succession or philosophical doubt that here was another *optimus princeps*, the "best leader" for the post. A conspiracy led by some of Trajan's chief administrators and generals developed in 118 and was put down, with several executions, by At-tianus, the praetorian prefect, a man also from Italica who had earlier served as a second guardian for the young Hadrian. The executions of senators in the case, without the approval of the Senate, brought Ha-drian much ill will. He disavowed any involvement in the executions and replaced Attianus. Eventually the Senate accepted the new emperor and deified the dead one, but relations between Hadrian and the Senate continued to be strained.

Static Frontiers

Although Hadrian abandoned most of Trajan's conquests in Meso-potamia, he did retain territory in northern Mesopotamia to guard the flank of Armenia and provide additional buffer area for the important administrative and economic center of Antioch in Syria. He set up additional forts to protect the north-south trade routes down to the Red

Sea on the east side of the great rift that includes the Jordan valley, and he increased the legions in this sector of the Empire to ten. He completed and strengthened the *limes*, a frontier collection of forts and walls, that linked the Rhine and Danube rivers across what is now mostly southern Germany. In Britain he built a wall twelve to twenty feet high, eight feet wide, and seventy miles long across the entire island in the north. He improved the defenses of North Africa in various ways. For Hadrian the days of Roman expansion were obviously over.

This peaceful policy, however, involved no weakening of the army. Hadrian reorganized the units, altered their tactical dispositions, and set up new training maneuvers, so useful that they were still in use at least a century later. He visited most of the units personally and shared their strenuous training. In several ways he improved the lot of the common soldier and saw to it that officers were not overly privileged. By now the legionaries were drawn mostly from the provinces; greater use was made of noncitizens in a larger number of auxiliary units. The legions became more closely identified with a given area, and replacements were usually enlisted locally. Legionaries could thus live lives somewhat like those of civilians. Ultimately this fact gave the troops in an area a more homogeneous and localized character, which was perhaps unfortunate. At any rate, Hadrian vigorously attempted to keep his army strong and battle-ready, something not easily done when decades went by without major combat. The troops worked regularly on building projects, roads, and combat exercises.

Hadrian's wall in northern England, which stretches some seventy miles from sea to sea. (*Archiv für Kunst und Geschichte*)

The Provinces

Hadrian traveled over all the vast extent of his Empire more than any of his predecessors, making two extended tours of four and five years besides other shorter journeys. These were not mere travels but inspection trips, during which he visited the army posts and participated in training exercises. Every major city was the beneficiary of some public building or road or bridge or aqueduct, sometimes constructed in a sort of matching funds program financed partly through local subscription.

For this emperor, the provinces were the Empire; the city of Rome was for him perhaps more than a symbol, but his attitude was clear enough. Naturally this view did not endear him either to the Roman Senate or to the urban plebs, although the latter actually had little reason to feel neglected, for Hadrian gave them the usual games and largesse and engaged besides in huge construction projects in the capital. However, the real government traveled with the emperor, and nothing could more clearly indicate to the senators their subordinate role. Even when Hadrian was at Rome he was often out at his new villa near Tibur, which was also a center of government when he was there.

Illustrative of Hadrian's emphasis on the Empire as a whole, the complex of buildings at Tibur included areas reflecting specific provinces, with special emphasis on Egypt. One feature of the villa, significantly, was a map of the Empire, done in mosaic. Hadrian seemed to get along quite well without the Senate—indeed, without the capital.

Centralization of Administration

Hadrian took particular interest in improving the efficiency of government in all its phases, which resulted in greater direction from the emperor and his staff. The emperor also regarded the sensibilities of the Senate aristocrats in most things. In the imperial finances, for example, he carefully preserved the old treasury controlled by the Senate, the Aerarium Saturni. But as much as any emperor before him he was responsible for accelerating the process by which the various treasures (fisci) in the provinces, the patrimonium, or personal holdings of the emperors, and the other repositories of funds were gradually converted into a single treasury of overriding importance, the fiscus. The Aerarium Saturni had long been overshadowed by the various properties and sources of income controlled by the emperors. Hadrian appointed a special advocate of the treasury (advocatus fisci) to safeguard the legal interests of the fiscus—possibly meaning all imperially controlled repositories of funds—in court suits. This action helped to bring about a single administration of the finances of the Empire.

The civil bureaucracy was in general enlarged and rationalized. Fewer freedmen were employed in positions of responsibility, in accord with a trend going back to Vespasian; they were replaced by men of the equestrian class. The formalizing of ranks, salaries, titles, and so on, which had its beginning with the Flavians, developed extensively in Hadrian's reign. Careers were now organized according to specific patterns. One unfortunate adjunct to the bureaucracy deserves mention. Hadrian began to make use of a group of imperial agents called *frumentarii*, whose primary duties had lain in procurement of supplies for the army, to collect confidential information on officials, provinces, and the like. This usage created (though in some form it must have existed before) the secret police of eventual infamy.

Imperial properties all over the Empire got attention from Hadrian. Important even in the reign of Augustus, the *patrimonium* must have grown to immense size by the second century. Nero had confiscated a large number of properties; for example, six large landowners were said to have controlled half of the province of Africa, and Nero took all their holdings. Confiscation of private property, in fact, was one of the standard ways by which the more improvident emperors balanced a budget that was out of control. The income from these properties was a most important component of the imperial revenues. To ensure their efficient management, Hadrian appointed a new imperial procurator to that specific task. From this time there was doubtless a strong tendency to regularize practices on the various estates. Some scholars see in the developments of this period, particularly in the system of treating tenants on imperial estates called *coloni*, the growth of a system that led to medieval serfdom.

Italy itself, whose population still consisted mostly of citizens from old Roman and Italian families (except for Rome and its environs, where much of the population was of foreign origin), had to a degree resisted the centralizing pressures of the emperors. Caesar and Augustus to some extent had rationalized the hodgepodge of municipalities, colonies, and allied states that made up the peninsula. Hadrian undertook to reorganize its legal structure. He divided Italy into four parts and placed officials over them for judicial administration. The officials were senators—consulars, in fact—but the measure disturbed the senators, perhaps because the more important among them were patrons of Italian municipalities: the new arrangement infringed on the autonomy of these municipalities and doubtless on the patrons' influence as well.

In Rome itself Hadrian did not hesitate to change the legal machinery. Praetors had for centuries issued an annual edict that governed law and legal procedure. Hadrian in 131 employed expert jurists under Salvius Julianus to come up with a "perpetual" edict. Promulgated by himself and presumably changed only with imperial consent, it symbolized the imperial encroachment on prerogatives and the decline of power of the old republican officials, and thus of the Senate itself. The actual change in the edict, which had been carried down from year to year in such a way that it was virtually perpetual in nature already, surely was unimportant. One other consequence of this reform was that praetorian prefects, as representatives of the emperor, began to do some of the work previously done by the praetors. Selected jurists gained new status (and new salaries) and sat regularly on the emperor's *consilium*. After this time praetorian prefects were often jurists. Some of the greatest of them would hold this position under the Severi.

Hadrian's Last Years

Hadrian's final years were unhappy ones. He increasingly felt the tension between himself and the Senate, deriving from his distant person-

The Roman Forum, view from the Palatine Hill. In foreground, columns of the temple of Castor and Pollux; on left, remains of Caesar's basilica; above left, the arch of Septimius Severus; above right, the curia or Senate. (*A. Devaney, Inc., New York*)

ality, his long absences, his greater—or more open—exercise of power. A conspiracy hatched among some of his relatives, and to make matters worse, in the east the Jews once more broke out in rebellion against Roman rule.

The conspiracy, in 136, involved Hadrian's ninety-year-old brother-in-law and his eighteen-year-old grandson. We know little about it. It is likely that the older man attempted to get the grandson designated successor to the sick Hadrian and, failing that, tried more direct action. Hadrian forced the two to commit suicide and threw others—some of them senators—into prison, probably intending to execute them. The Senate was furious, suspecting that Hadrian meant to break the imperial vow not to put senators to death without trial by their peers.

The Jewish rebellion was partly Hadrian's fault and partly caused by the operation of the same factors that had made Palestine the most difficult of Rome's provinces to govern from its acquisition. When the emperor was traveling in the east in about 130 he decided to rebuild Jerusalem and plant a Roman colony there called Aelia Capitolina. The site of the ruined Temple, he apparently decided, should be the location for a temple to Jupiter. The outraged Jews lashed out in rebellion in 132 under the leadership of a man calling himself Bar Kochba, Son of the Star. The slow but methodical repression decimated the Jews. Survivors were banished from Jerusalem and surrounding areas.

Hadrian's first choice as successor died before he did, and he therefore chose another, known to us as Antoninus Pius. He also designated the young man called Marcus Aurelius as successor in the second generation. On his death, the Senate wanted to pass the *damnatio memoriae*, but Antoninus dissuaded them and even got the usual decree deifying the dead emperor.

Antoninus Pius (138–161)

Though born in Italy, Antoninus came from a family that had long resided in Nîmes, in southern France. Perhaps his ancestors were original members of the colony of veterans that Augustus had established there. Antoninus had risen to the consulate and had served as one of the four consulars in charge of the judicial districts that Hadrian set up in Italy. Antoninus got his surname, Pius, because of his strong filial defense of the dead Hadrian and because of his insistence on the latter's deification.

For information on the reign of Antoninus we are reduced to a very bad biography (in the *Historia Augusta*); scraps of literary information, as in the letters of Marcus Aurelius; evidence drawn from legal materials; and miscellaneous inscriptions, coins, and so forth; plus, of course, the artifacts turned up by archaeologists. (The literary evidence is almost as sparse for Trajan and Hadrian.) The most remarkable feature of the evidence for Antoninus is not how little there is, but rather its uniform tone of praise: almost nothing that could be called criticism or reproach survives. Even the Christians, who had just complaints about others of the Good Emperors, found little bad to say about Antoninus.

The interest in judicial affairs evident in Antoninus' earlier career carried over into his reign. Our limited information tells us that he was concerned with the courts in the provinces; he emphasized that provincial governors must be accessible. Furthermore, in the interests of foreign residents he reorganized, at least in one province but probably more, the administration of the courts at the judicial levels below that directly supervised by the governors. In Italy he used eminent jurists, for example Salvius Julianus, in his council, and he personally intervened in court cases that seemed to establish important precedents, always in a direction that moderns would find enlightened. One instance may be noted: the principle that in cases of doubt as to whether someone was free or slave, the person should be considered free. To conciliate the Senate, Antoninus did reverse the change in the judicial system in Italy set up by Hadrian; in the next reign, however, it was restored.

Restraint characterized Antoninus' life-style, his methods of administration, and his principles. Not only did he live economically, but he was the sort of man who would labor along with a group of workers in the first of the vintage and then join with them in their simple meal. Young Marcus Aurelius, from whom we learn this anecdote, was much impressed with the modesty, forbearance, and yet firmness in the right that Antoninus displayed.

The emperor found it unnecessary to engage in any serious warfare, though he did undertake a campaign in Britain, where he pushed the frontier a bit to the north and then built a new wall, this one of turf, some thirty miles long, less than half the length of Hadrian's Wall. Hadrian had traveled incessantly, benefiting the provincial towns where he traveled, perhaps, but also no doubt seriously burdening them with the expenses of entertaining him and his court. Hadrian had also offended the Senate by his peregrinations, which seemed to show contempt for that body if not for the very city of Rome itself. Antoninus traveled little, to the gratification of the Roman grandees, perhaps partly to save on court expenses. He did not, however, skimp on games and circuses for the Roman plebs; no emperor was likely to do that anymore.

In Italy, Antoninus remitted the "crown gold," an accessions tax that had developed from the practice of giving gifts of golden wreaths to new emperors. Possibly he was able to reduce taxes somewhat even for the provinces. Those were fortunate days, with long periods of peace on the frontiers under a sensible and frugal emperor who left a well-filled treasury to his successors.

Marcus Aurelius (161–180)

The well-known Stoic propensities of Marcus Aurelius illustrate how different was the position of intellectuals in the time of the Good Emperors. In the previous century Nero, Vespasian, and Domitian, all had executed some prominent philosophers and exiled others. Now came an age in which such men were not only officially tolerated but even encouraged. For Marcus Aurelius, the Stoic philosophers were his mentors and heroes, and he exemplified their teachings in his own life. His chief tutor in early life, M. Cornelius Fronto, was not a philosopher but a rhetorician, the most celebrated orator in Rome in this age. Some of his correspondence was with Marcus Aurelius himself; though it shows a petty disappointment that the adult Marcus preferred philosophy to rhetoric, it is an important source of information to us.

One of Marcus Aurelius' teachers, Rusticus, was a descendant of the Stoic of that name done to death by Domitian. The emperor had also been greatly influenced by Epictetus, the former slave and Stoic teacher whom Domitian exiled. Perhaps he learned of Epictetus only through his admirers, who wrote down the simple but powerful teachings of the freedman. As a quite young man Marcus studied with the Stoic Apollonius and learned from Sextus of Chaeronea, nephew of the great Plutarch. His own *Meditations*, written toward the end of his troubled reign, mark the emperor as a philosopher in his own right, though the work hardly qualifies as one of the more important Stoic documents of antiquity. Through the centuries the *Meditations* have been read by many for their moral and inspirational value. The work portrays a serious, contemplative, and hardworking man who saw himself as, above all, a public servant.

Associated with Marcus Aurelius as co-ruler was Lucius Verus, son of the man who was Hadrian's original choice as his successor; Hadrian had requested Antoninus to adopt Lucius along with Marcus. Antoninus apparently intended to leave Marcus alone on the throne, but the latter insisted on equal power for Lucius. The sources indicate a strong contrast between the two co-rulers; Lucius seems to have loved luxury and the banquet hall more than duty. It was perhaps fortunate for the Empire that he died in 168.

Marcus Aurelius would have preferred a reign like Antoninus' in which full attention could be given to internal matters. But possibly Antoninus had been too peaceful: all along the frontiers, tribes and peoples awaited any sign of weakness before they burst across the borders in search of easy spoils or a permanent home within the Empire. (It should be noted that peaceful, small-scale immigration poured in almost continuously.) Marcus was forced to fight a long war against the Parthians in the east (Lucius was the first commander in this war, though little inclined to active generalship); an even longer series of wars against a multitude of tribes along the Danube frontier, most important of which were the Quadi and Marcomanni; and other less serious wars in Spain and Egypt. Each conflict began with serious losses and ended with success, but only after hard fighting and heavy casualties.

The Parthian struggle was heralded when the Parthian king, in the manner of his predecessors, attempted to acquire full control over Armenia. A major mobilization, strong reinforcements, and actual invasion of Parthia finally forced a solution satisfactory to Rome. By that time serious irruptions along the Danube frontier required still more recruiting and reinforcement. The emperor commissioned at least two new legions and several auxiliary units. He ultimately determined to establish new provinces north of the Danube, with mountain ranges marking the new frontiers in place of the river. If he had lived to carry through his plan, the frontier would have been shortened considerably, and the history of the later Empire might have been different. But he could not complete his task and his son abandoned the effort.

Perhaps the plan was too grandiose for the resources, human and economic, of the Empire. The recruitment problem was even more troublesome than usual, for troops returning from the Parthian War had brought back some sort of epidemic disease. The unreliable literary sources unanimously proclaim this plague a devastating blow to the Roman world, indicating losses of as much as a third or one-half the population in some areas. Studies based on epigraphical army records, however, do not corroborate any such disaster. Yet it is probably wrong to discount too much the testimony of the ancient writers; doubtless they wrote in hyperbole, but the plague must have taken many lives in many places, a serious matter in an already underpopulated empire; in some rural areas, lands were abandoned.

Of course the great military effort was expensive. Marcus Aurelius dramatized the degree of sacrifice called for; he displayed a large number of imperial treasures, from jewelry to gold-threaded dresses of his wife, Faustina, in the Forum of Trajan and then put them up for sale in a kind of auction.

Against all challenges Marcus struggled valiantly, despite a physical affliction that affected his chest and stomach. He had trouble sleeping. From his personal physician, the famous Galen, he got a prescription for what seems to have been opium; predictably he became dependent on it. No clear evidence exists, however, that it seriously affected his ability to perform his tasks before death, possibly from plague, overtook him in 180 on the Danube frontier.

Commodus and the End of the Principate (180–192)

The accession of Commodus, son of Marcus Aurelius, to the principate at age eighteen has been viewed as Marcus Aurelius' greatest mistake or his greatest tragedy. Marcus probably expected his young son to mature into a more stable person. Besides, he could only have excluded Commodus from the succession by killing him. Toward the end of his life, Marcus realized both that Commodus was inadequate to his task and that his own death was approaching, yet he did not attempt to change the succession so as to preserve the traditions of the previous century. No doubt he thought that his advisers and administrators would help Commodus govern effectively. He did ask Commodus not to give up the plan to enlarge the northern Empire and improve the frontiers.

Despite his dying father's request, Commodus immediately negotiated a settlement of the northern war. This move may not have been a mistake: the effort was great for the Empire, reeling under blows from wars, plague, and the widespread drought and famine of these years, which we hear about so much. For some decades little trouble occurred along the affected frontier, so Marcus Aurelius' campaigns were not wholly wasted.

Our sources uniformly portray Commodus in a bad light. He was too much influenced by personal servants and favorites; he allowed his praetorian prefects who functioned as prime ministers to tyrannize over the Senate, Rome, and the Empire, while waxing rich; and he did not control the praetorian guard itself, which grew dissolute and insolent along with its commanders. When anything went wrong, however, and there was public outcry, it was Commodus' technique to sacrifice the prefect. He wanted nothing to disturb him in his own extravagant and depraved life. The young emperor was not given much of a chance to mature in his duties. In his third year he was nearly assassinated in a conspiracy that included Lucilla, his sister, and a number of senators, most of whom were peremptorily executed in a style quite uncharacteristic of the age of the Good Emperors. It is interesting that at this point two future emperors, both then serving in Syria, were relieved of their posts but not otherwise mistreated. These were Pertinax, the governor, and Septimius Severus, a legionary commander. Both were given new positions after the fall of the prefect Perennis.

What Commodus did to the Senate—or allowed his prefects to do— was probably the worst feature of his reign. He permitted his personal servant Cleander to sell offices, even the consulate. In 190 there were twenty-five consuls. Thus the highest office held by senators was reduced to a mockery. However unbalanced the partnership, the Senate had previously served as a constitutional check on the power of the emperors, or principes. Commodus exposed the senators' utter powerlessness by administering as he pleased without reference to the Senate, and so vastly reduced the body's prestige and usefulness. The first of the Severi would be able to ignore it or manipulate it almost with impunity. Confiscated properties helped to finance Commodus' continued extravagances.

Another conspiracy succeeded, this one involving Marcia, Commodus' concubine (a Christian, it was said), and others. Commodus, who was big and strong, fancied himself Hercules; he had had himself sculptured in stone with appropriate garb, the lion skin and club, and he had participated at public games as Hercules and in several other roles. At last he planned to appear as consul on January 1 in the costume of a gladiator. But his wrestling partner, bribed by the conspirators, strangled him on New Year's Eve, 192.

Disorder and Civil Wars (193–197)

The troubled situation on January 1, 193, threatened to dissolve into civil war, just as in the months following Nero's assassination in 68. The successor, Pertinax, chosen by the Senate, was much like Nero's successor, Galba, the right man at the wrong time. Pertinax, the son of a freedman, had forged an extraordinary career, rising to become consul. An able administrator and general, he was noted as a disciplinarian. Money was a problem for him as emperor. He did not give the praetorians all they expected—"only" 12,000 sesterces a man—and, even worse, tried to discipline them. After a few weeks they turned on him and killed him. Then they brought two would-be emperors at the same time to different gates of the camp and got them bidding for the guards' support. The winner, Didius Julianus, bid 25,000 sesterces a man, several years' wages. The amount was not really so extravagant: Marcus Aurelius and L. Verus had paid 20,000 as a gift upon their accession— though that was disgraceful enough. But the virtual auction of the imperial office repulsed both the Senate and the Roman people. The city mob began to riot. Somehow a kind of appeal was made to the governor of Syria, Pescennius Niger, to come to Rome to straighten out matters and presumably to become the new emperor. Naturally the situation produced other claimants supported by other armies. Besides Septimius Severus, governor of Upper Pannonia, the eventual winner, there was a third major candidate, Clodius Albinus, governor of Britain.

Severus made some sort of deal with Albinus, recognizing him as caesar and apparently adopting him. Then he moved on Rome with his army (of the major armies, his was nearest the city), posing as the avenger of Pertinax. The praetorian guard, which had already executed Julianus, surrendered and was completely discharged; the former guardsmen were forbidden to stay within a hundred miles of Rome. A new guard was formed from legionaries, and doubled in size. One of the regular legions was stationed in the Alban Hills just south of the city. Senate and people were generally complaisant, and Severus was soon ready to move east to meet the most important threat to the new regime, that of Niger. With support from the other Danubian and the Rhine armies, he confined some of Niger's forces in Europe within the fortress city of Byzantium. The next year he defeated Niger himself decisively at Issus in northern Syria, site of a battle five hundred years earlier between Alexander the Great and the Persians. He made a sweep across the Euphrates as a warning to the Parthians, and ended with a long siege of Byzantium. Meanwhile the Senate voted a triumphal arch for Severus, which still stands in the Roman Forum.

By this time, to legitimize his rule Severus had arranged for the dead Marcus Aurelius to "adopt" him, and he now styled his older son, Bassianus, Marcus Aurelius Antoninus. History knows him as Caracalla, from the Gallic-style cloak he liked to wear. The pseudo adoption perhaps implied that the new emperor would follow in the steps of the Good Emperors; preserving such a line would reassure many persons, including senators. However, Clodius Albinus saw a dynasty in the making that left him out. He crossed the English Channel and mobilized all the troops he could command in central Gaul. The eventual struggle was decided near Lugdunum, where Severus' victory meant that the Empire was his (February 197).

The Military Monarchy: The Severi

Under Septimius Severus the Empire began a new age, the "military monarchy," which brought an end to the principate and its lip service to some of the more important traditions inherited from the period of the Republic. Severus did indeed take the Antonine name, and he posed as Marcus Aurelius' successor. But he much reduced the prestige and power of the senators and the Senate, relying instead on his military officers and the army as the basis for his power.

The change was apparent early: when he got back to Rome after disposing of Clodius Albinus, he arbitrarily executed several senators who, presumably, had favored Albinus. Nor did he then or later take the oath of the Good Emperors not to execute senators without trial by their fellows. The highest military and administrative positions formerly reserved for senators now went to personnel who had risen through military service alone. Moreover, the judicial powers of the Senate were largely shifted to the (now two) praetorian prefects. These, of course, had always been creatures of the emperors.

For centuries the Roman nobility had been defined through officeholding; since the highest military and administrative positions went mostly to army officers who were not senators, the Roman aristocracy became largely a military group not specifically identified with the much-weakened Senate. The earlier sense of partnership between the emperor and the Senate—along with the restraint that the arrangement had at times imposed—no longer existed as politics came to play a role secondary to that of the military. In the new order, senators were in no position to be effective patrons of young men seeking to rise in government service. Patronage now rested firmly in the emperor himself, and secondarily in his staff officers.

From an early date Severus made it clear that he would be succeeded by his sons. Caracalla was made consul at age thirteen; Geta, a second son, had to wait until he was fifteen. By then both were "caesars," a term that had come to indicate an heir apparent. The certainty of Severus' intentions perhaps kept down conspiracies. The praetorian prefect G. Fulvius Plautianus, however, who exercised tremendous power for several years, often conflicted with Severus' wife, Julia Domna. Eventually he went too far and was killed, perhaps by Caracalla's machinations. At Severus' death in 211 while on campaign in Britain, no obstacle impeded the peaceful succession of the two brothers. Severus is supposed to have advised the brothers to stick together, to take care of the armies, and to worry about nothing else.

The first part of his admonition was a vain hope. Caracalla and Geta hated one another, and the elder brother had perhaps attempted to kill Geta even before the death of their father. In fact, according to some accounts he tried to hurry Severus himself off. Their mother, Julia, tried to keep them reconciled, but Caracalla soon killed Geta (212) and ruled alone.

Caracalla has a bad reputation, somewhat like that of Nero or Domitian, and on the whole it is probably justified. Aside from his vagaries and occasional tyrannical behavior, he is remembered on the positive side chiefly for the construction of his tremendous baths, the vast ruins of which still impress the traveler to Rome, and for his giving Roman citizenship, probably in 212, to almost all free persons in the Empire who did not already have it. The sources are unkind enough to suggest that he took the latter step because he wanted to collect a larger accession tax, which was paid only by citizens. But the action could have simplified imperial administration, especially of legal matters. It certainly did not equalize the legal treatment accorded to all, which was apportioned with a bias that rested on social and economic status, all citizens being classified as *humiliores* or *honestiores*, approximately lower class and upper class—not so very different from the administration of justice almost any time in history, but then officially recognized.

Caracalla went east toward the end of his five-year reign. He visited Egypt, where he was in some way incensed at a public demonstration by the Alexandrians—who had the reputation of being almost totally ungovernable—and killed many of them. He then prepared for a Parthian war, apparently seeing himself as a reborn Alexander. Caracalla had executed Plautianus' successor, Aurelius Papinianus, one of the great classical jurists. His new prefect, learning that he too was to be liquidated, assassinated the young emperor in 217. This was M. Opellius Macrinus (217–218), the first equestrian to seize the throne. He did not

On the left is Julia Domna, first of a series of powerful women in the Severan dynasty. Her husband, Septimius Severus, on the right, perhaps hoped she would be a restraining influence on his son, Caracalla. It didn't work.

show much aptitude for the position, but for a time there was no focus of opposition. Julia Domna's sister, Julia Maesa, shortly engineered an upset.

The Severan Women

The Julias had come from the city of Emesa in Syria, of a family of high priests to the god Elagabalus, the local Baal. Julia Domna enjoyed many years of influence during the reigns of her husband and sons, initially because Severus was impressed with her horoscope, but later because of her abilities and the force of her personality. Unfortunately, soon after the overturn of Caracalla by Macrinus she herself died, apparently of cancer. Her sister, Julia Maesa, had two grandsons by her daughters Julia Soemias and Julia Mamaea. The elder of these, the son of Soemias, was Bassianus, who, though still in his early teens, held the hereditary high priesthood. It was decided to give him an aura of legitimacy by claiming his illegitimacy. Accentuating his resemblance to Caracalla, his mother, Soemias, said that he was really the son of the former emperor. The ruse worked, less perhaps because of any merit than because Macrinus was disliked and no other successor appeared in the vicinity of the army. Bassianus, whom we know as Elagabalus, was hailed as emperor by some troops, and after a battle Macrinus was killed. It was said that Julia Maesa herself rallied the soldiers at a critical moment and led the victorious charge. The Senate accepted the third emperor in a year, sight unseen.

Elagabalus turned out bizarre. He brought an image of the Emesan Baal, a sun god, to Rome with him and "married" the god to the moon gods of Carthage. Meanwhile, the Syrian priest displaced the pontifex maximus in rank. Elagabalus himself turned to debauchery. His sexual quirks offended even the tolerant society of the times. He married males and females, including one of the vestal virgins. His male sexual partners, inexperienced in government, he installed in high office. He offended the all-important soldiery by appearing in public wearing rouge and various other sorts of female adornment. Julia Maesa was unable to control him at all and simply took the best way out: she prepared her other grandson to take over when, inevitably, Elagabalus was assassinated, along with his mother, in 222, after a rule of four years.

M. Aurelius Severus Alexander was the son of Julia Mamaea. Since Severus Alexander, as the last member of the dynasty is known to history, was a mere stripling of thirteen or fourteen years at his accession, a regency comprising a cabinet of the Senate dominated by Julia Maesa until her death in 226, and then by Julia Mamaea, ruled in his stead. These remarkable women as nearly approached imperial office as any women in Roman history. The administration began well; the great jurist Ulpian (Domitius Ulpianus), for example, became praetorian prefect. If the army could have been persuaded to put up with this arrangement for any extended period, the government might have functioned well. Since the reign of Marcus Aurelius, however, a continuous series of wars had been conducted. Probably these were easily within the capacity of the Empire to control, but they required strong military leadership. Julia Maesa could conceivably have even played the role of general, as she supposedly had in the charge against Macrinus near Antioch in 218. But she died early in the reign—and was consecrated a goddess. Alexander attempted to command the armies personally, but without great success. His mother helped as much as she could. They fought against Ardashir, the founder of the new Persian Sassanid dynasty that had replaced the Parthians in about 227, but with only partial success. Called back west to a new threat from across the Rhine, they and their advisers chose to negotiate rather than fight. Many of the army officers showed disgust with Alexander and with female influence over the army (Mamaea had presented herself not only as Mother of Augustus but also Mother of the [army] camps and of the Senate, and finally Mother of All Humankind). The generals engineered the assassination of both Alexander and the queen mother in 235. Ulpian had been murdered earlier. Half a century of virtual chaos was to follow.

The Economy in the High Empire

Earlier in this chapter some of the disquieting indications of decline were considered, but the economy of the Empire in its greatest age

deserves a longer treatment. Interpretation of the scattered evidence left
to us is extraordinarily difficult. In the rare statistics available, as, for
example, on income from land, we often can ascertain nothing of the
land's quality, whether the figures given deal with gross or net profit,
and so on. Yet certain trends stand out clearly.

As might be expected, the political centralization of authority in the
period brought correspondingly greater control over economic matters.
We have seen this tendency before, both in Trajan's financial "correctors," whom he sent in to stabilize certain provinces, and in the special
authority of Pliny the Younger, as governor of Bithynia, to examine the
financial affairs of cities and on that basis decree necessary improvements. Hadrian's *frumentarii*, the prototype of the secret police as they
traveled about the Empire, naturally sent back information on which
central decisions were made affecting all. Imperial financial officials,
the procurators in charge of the emperors' affairs in the provinces,
tended to encroach on the powers both of the provincial governors and
local officials (with some consequent friction), naturally contributing to
the trend toward centralization.

By the middle of the second century, if not earlier, the central government began to take over the operation of state-owned mines in the
provinces—in Noricum, for example—instead of auctioning off to publican companies the privilege of working them for private profit, as in
the past. By the time of Marcus Aurelius the state also began to collect
customs duties in the ports directly instead of through publican companies. In each instance the motive was, of course, greater efficiency,
with a larger profit for the state. Yet the publican companies, despite the
bad reputation some of them had earned and doubtless deserved, had in
general served the state well. It is doubtful that the government bureaus
set up to take over the mines and the customs functioned more effi-
ciently in the long haul, but initially at least the central treasury probably benefited.

In the cities the emperors—notably the Severi—exercised greater
control over small industry as well as over the artisan class by restricting
the old corporations (*collegia*) of workers and in some places requiring
the formation of new ones. This movement paralleled the reduced freedom of the *coloni* in the countryside, whose status was degenerating
toward serfdom.

The more intense, state-controlled exploitation of silver and gold
mines not only reflects the growing metal shortage and concern for an
adequate money supply but also points to a clearly established infla-
tionary trend, gradual during the period of the Good Emperors but
sharper after the death of Marcus Aurelius. Prices of staple items went
up at least 75 percent from about the middle of the first century to the
end of the Severan dynasty in 235. Wages, as usual in the ancient world,
lagged a bit; even the soldiers, whose pay had been doubled by the time
of Septimius Severus (as compared to the first century, before Domi-

tian), found their wages buying less during much of the second century. The occasional huge donatives (as at accessions) more than redressed the balance. however.

At the same time, the silver coinage was gradually cheapened, with some lightening of gold currency as well. Nero, it will be recalled, initiated the process, adding lead to the nearly pure silver and reducing the weight of both gold and silver. From that point on, at periods difficult to determine by weighing surviving coins since there is some normal variation in weight and composition, silver coins were slowly debased further. As has been noted, by the end of the reign of Marcus Aurelius the standard silver denarius contained perhaps 60 percent as much silver as it had in the early Empire. By the time of Severus Alexander the comparable figure was about 50 percent. The latter ruler also reduced, again, the weight of gold coins. In the chaotic period following his reign the debasement accelerated wildly.

We must not assume, however, that the debasement of the coinage corresponded exactly with a real cheapening of the currency. The problem is not that simple. The debased coins may actually have been almost as valuable as before. Part of the reason for the lessened quantity of silver in each coin, it seems certain, was that production of silver declined, at least relative to need, and bullion became relatively more valuable in terms of the amount of basic foodstuffs it would buy, for example. Gold declined in value as compared with silver, perhaps because of the gold of Dacia. It would be more accurate to say that silver outstripped gold in the inflation race.

Large quantities of silver as well as gold were exported to purchase imported goods. Probably the largest quantities went to the east, especially India, for such items as spices and silk cloth. Except for precious metals, Rome had few exports acceptable to eastern traders, and thus a considerable imbalance of trade developed. The trade imbalance involved not only the east: much precious metal was also exported to Germany and other areas across the Danube, where it was hoarded as wealth rather than used as currency. So long as the Spanish, British, and other mines produced an adequate quantity of precious metals, this adverse balance of trade meant little. But when silver and gold came into shorter supply the effect was more serious. Moreover, international traders would not accept debased coins; they insisted on the older, pure silver ones—or on bullion (which was weighed, as probably the silver coins also were)—which meant that imports, already expensive, became relatively more costly still. The shortage was compounded by the inevitable hoarding both of the better coins and of bullion; doubtless the use of precious metals for statues, jewelry, and other art objects contributed to the problem.

The degree of debasement of silver coins was greater than was called for by the rising market value of silver bullion, however. Thus the value of the silver in a coin of Severus Alexander was less than the value of the greater amount of silver of a coin of Augustus, even allowing for the increased value of the metal. During the intervening period the money supply had therefore gradually expanded artificially to meet the growing expenses of government and of frontier defense. This trend led to a mistrust of the currency, a psychological attitude that caused some to refuse to accept it at face value, just as international traders refused to accept it at all.

Inflation must always be paid for by somebody. In this case the costs would not be accepted—for long—by soldiers; the army was too necessary. Nor would it be paid for by government workers, who could gain a sympathetic ear from the administration. The economic victims were primarily small farmers and tenant farmers. City laborers also were hurt. Prices for their labor and for manufactured products rose, but not in proportion to the rise in prices of the commodities they had to buy.

Even early in the second century, under Trajan and Hadrian, we hear of agricultural land going out of production. Possibly it was fringe land, and likely it was land that had declined in production through overcropping, especially of cereals. But abandonment of land had become serious. In some places Hadrian offered land free to anyone who would occupy it and bring it back into production, granting remission from taxes for a period also. Yet the problem remained, which meant that (1) the prices of products that farmers had to buy inflated more rapidly than the prices of farm products; (2) these lands were so depleted as to make them unprofitable; or (3) the exactions of tax collectors or absentee landowners made farming impossible at times. Usually a combination of the three factors contributed to small holders' abandoning their farms.

Imperial budgets during most of the age must have been manageable, but when, especially in wartime, they became intractable, further debasement of the currency usually paid for excesses of expenditures over income. Confiscation of the property of rich opponents provided an occasional alternative in the later decades of the period. Higher costs resulted in large part from the increases in the size of the army from the time of Marcus Aurelius. Another factor was the continuing growth of the imperial administration—the burgeoning bureaucracy. The latter problem looms as large in the twentieth century as it did in ancient Rome. It often seems necessary to create new departments of administration; it never seems possible to dissolve them.

Italy: State-Supported Welfare and the Economy

As long as Rome was the center of government it served as a stimulant to the Italian economy. Salaries paid to government employees and to the guardsmen not only put a great deal of money into circulation, but also many emperors took a special interest in the well-being of the peninsula through special enactments. Trajan, for example, passed a measure requiring that candidates for high office have a third of their wealth in Italian real estate. For a time at least, this policy increased the value of all property close to Rome. The Campagna, the countryside around the capital, had been in decline but revived somewhat because of the measure. Wealthy Romans who owned estates in the resort areas around Naples and Puteoli, the port city to the west of Naples, spent large sums on elaborate villas and the like, maintaining the prosperity of that part of Italy despite the shift of a considerable segment of the import trade to the artificial ports built by Claudius and Trajan at Ostia.

The emperors of this period also favored Italy in the establishment and development of the alimentary institutions. The *alimenta* were first conceived and put into practice by private persons; Nerva and Trajan brought the government into the picture on a regular basis. We know of fifty such institutions in Italy, and there must have been many more. They worked like this: the government furnished a capital sum, which was then lent to major property holders within the territory of the town concerned. Interest on the loans was used to support, in perpetuity, needy children—sometimes specifically orphans. The capital sums lent to the landowners may occasionally have been needed for improvements to the land, which in some instances increased productivity. Some landowners who received money, however, were pressured into taking it. The loan remained a permanent obligation on the property, naturally reducing its value. Even so, the system continued to expand within Italy and on a private basis in some of the provinces.

Boys were ordinarily preferred in the *alimenta*, but girls were accepted also in some places. The original intention was probably to bolster future military manpower, but the goals became broader in time. The chaotic period after the death of Severus Alexander destroyed many such programs, but some lasted at least to the end of the third century. The widespread building programs (of Hadrian especially) throughout the Empire and the establishment of the *alimenta* in Italy perhaps served, somewhat like the so-called pork barrel legislation of the U.S. Congress, to spread government expenditures more evenly throughout the peninsula, with attendant beneficial economic effects.

The general picture of the economy in Italy away from Rome nevertheless remains spotty. In the central and southern portions some of the ills that later plagued the economy had been felt even earlier, as already noted. Deforested uplands were eroding, and the erosion had begun to do secondary damage by choking up river mouths, producing swampy lands that harbored malaria-spreading mosquitoes. Some of the land lost fertility through overcropping of cereals. There was never enough manure for fertilization and, although crop rotation was understood, it was imperfectly practiced throughout Roman history. The *lati-fundia* seem to have declined in favor of tenant farming, with the evils of absentee landlordism continuing as before.

The Po valley, with its enormously productive soil, continued to be prosperous. The close connection with several economically developing frontier provinces such as Noricum and Raetia immediately to the north and the Pannonian provinces to the northeast gave the area's producers and merchants opportunities that they were not slow to develop. The trade was two-way, but army payrolls made it possible for the frontier provinces to buy more than they sold.

Industry in the Po valley also continued to grow throughout the period. This was not the case in central Italy, however. In Etruria, Latium, and Campania, metal goods, glassware, and ceramic manufacturers gradually lost out to new entrepreneurs in the western provinces who imitated the Italian products—already mentioned, for instance, was the famous Arretine ware, a type of red pottery with relief decorations, made at Arretium—and undersold their competitors so drastically that Gallic pottery was exported even to Italy.

Though Italy was noted for its wine, Italian producers also began to face competition from the western provinces. Italian olive oil likewise gave way to imported products to a considerable degree. The competition in these areas came especially from Spain, which must have nearly dominated the Roman market. The wine and oil came by ship—the only long-distance means of transportation that was at all feasible—in cheap, mass-produced amphorae. The pots, not worth keeping, were thrown away, and broken sherds piled up near the docks on the Tiber until they formed a hill, Monte Testaccio, that covers so many acres that archaeologists have studied the pottery stamps and inscriptions for many decades. The sherds show that most of the amphorae arrived full from Spain and that the flood of such imports began early in the period we are considering.

The decline in Italian agriculture and industry, though it must have affected the economy of the peninsula even in the palmy days of the Good Emperors, was masked by the artificial stimulus of state income so long as Rome was the effective center of government. In the third century and after, however, the decline would be more marked.

Buildings and Construction in the High Empire

Rome and Italy

Although signs of economic deterioration in the Empire and especially in Italy appeared in this period, we must not overemphasize the decline.

True, Marcus Aurelius chose to auction some imperial treasures in order to finance the northern wars, and slight debasement of the coinage continued even under this careful emperor. But the coinage was still generally sound, and perhaps the auction was primarily a gesture to emphasize the need for sacrifice. Marcus Aurelius later bought back all the items from those purchasers who wanted their money back. And despite the cost of the wars, nothing indicates that he left an empty treasury to his son. Certainly he found it possible to pay enormous bonuses to his troops and to stage lavish games for the Roman populace.

One sign that the Empire continued to be generally prosperous despite economic weak spots was the tremendous amount of construction that the emperors as well as private builders of the period managed to finance, especially in Rome and Italy.

Trajan's Forum and the market complex or shopping center built in conjunction with it constituted one of the grandest building projects—perhaps the largest single one—ever carried through in the capital. The magnificently conceived forum contained an open area bordered by colonnades forming great semicircular porticoes, a magnificent basilica used for the courts, a Greek library and a Latin one, a temple, and of course the famous column with its spiral relief sculptures picturing the great general's Dacian campaigns. The top of the 127-foot column was in later antiquity supposed to mark the crest of the hill that had been removed to clear the site. We now know that the leveling that was required was not that great, but certainly it was a tremendous earth-moving project. Adjacent to the forum itself Trajan constructed a new shopping center with hundreds of shops on four levels. Altogether, the monument was worthy of Rome and of this great princeps. The architect, the Greek Apollodorus of Damascus, designed and supervised the construction not only of the forum but also of most of the major building under Trajan. The architect was haughtily disdainful of Hadrian's projects later, and Hadrian first exiled and then executed him.

Trajan built the city's tenth aqueduct, which brought water to the Janiculum, across the Tiber. Some of its substructures underlie the present building of the American Academy in Rome, and its water still supplies a fountain built by Pope Paul V, in 1605, high on the brow of the hill overlooking the city, at night arguably the most beautiful of the many fountains in modern Rome.

Outside Rome Trajan constructed extremely important works also. At Ostia, where the artificial harbor built by Claudius had proved inadequate, he spent a tremendous sum to excavate a new hexagonal-shaped inner harbor, which was connected to the Tiber by a canal. The dock facilities there, surrounded by covered colonnades, must have been as attractive as any ever built. To the north of Rome along the coast Trajan formed another artificial harbor at Centumcellae, modern Civitavecchia. A third such facility, this one portrayed in relief sculpture on the

One of the hemicycles of Trajan's forum. At the top, baths and the remains of the great market constructed in conjunction with this forum are visible. The large area in the foreground was surrounded by a colonnade. To the left were Greek and Latin libraries flanking Trajan's column (see p. 239) and a magnificent basilica; beyond was a temple. (*Ancient Art and Architecture Collection*)

emperor's column, was constructed across the peninsula on the Adriatic, at Ancona. Like so many Roman building projects, these testify as much to Roman engineering ability as to architectural genius.

Hadrian too built extensively in and around Rome. The Pantheon, though originally constructed by Augustus' lieutenant Agrippa, was completely rebuilt after it was destroyed by lightning and fire in 110 and thus is essentially the work of Hadrian. The interior is an elevated hemisphere; the distance from wall to wall, about 144 feet, is about the same as the distance from the floor to the 27-foot aperture in the dome, which is still one of the largest masonry domes in existence. Hadrian's mausoleum, called by the Italians the Castel Sant' Angelo, across the Tiber not far from the Vatican, still wears the military accretions acquired in medieval wars, when it was used as a fortress. It was intended not simply as a tomb for Hadrian but for all the imperial family for many years. (The mausoleum Augustus had erected in the Campus Martius on the city side of the Tiber, also impressive, was now full.) A third great structure in Rome conceived and built by Hadrian was the temple of Venus and Roma. Placed between the Colosseum and the Forum on a platform large enough to contain three football fields abreast, it was a double-apsidal building of great size, in the Greek style though not of classic proportions.

The mausoleum built by Hadrian, with Tiber in the foreground. Originally, the cylindrical structure sat atop a cube. Some of the structures attached were built during the Middle Ages, when it was used as a fortress; this is reflected in its modern name, the Castel Sant' Angelo.

Out toward Tiber and the Sabine Hills Hadrian constructed a whole governmental center ("Hadrian's villa"), which was noted earlier in this chapter. This tremendous complex of buildings took years to complete. So much constant building around Rome of course contributed materially to the economic well-being of the city. Huge brickyards grew up close to the city. It is curious that owning brick- and tile-making plants was considered quite respectable for Roman aristocrats, who in general felt that direct involvement in business was demeaning. Because brick making developed in connection with farming, it was in its origins an essentially agricultural industry and so retained a propriety that other manufacturing did not possess.

The other emperors continued to embellish the city with buildings. Marcus Aurelius put up a large temple in the Forum in honor of Antoninus and his wife, Faustina, and his column with sculptured spiral relief like that of Trajan still stands in the Piazza Colonna along the Via del Corso (ancient Via Lata). Septimius Severus, among other things, put up most of the complex of the imperial palace on the Palatine, the ruins of which loom over the Circus Maximus in the valley below. He also brought an aqueduct over to the Palatine; the lead pipes that had earlier supplied the promontory were evidently unable to take the pressure necessary to force the water up so high. Southeast from the Circus Maximus Caracalla built the massive baths his father had planned, with their tremendous barrel vaults and cross-vaulting. Later, even in decline, Rome continued to amass structures. The most impressive of these were the baths of Diocletian and the great basilica in the Forum started by Maxentius and completed by Constantine.

Visiting the ruins of Rome today, studying the plans of the public fora and buildings, and using imagination while gazing at the scale-model reconstruction of the ancient city in the Museo della Civiltá Romana, one can catch a glimmer of the sense of magnificence, grandeur, and permanence that the city and the Empire it symbolized inspired in the old Romans. No wonder they called it the Eternal City.

The Provinces

Though Rome and Italy were relatively favored in the building of cities and harbors, the provinces also benefited by a tremendous amount of construction throughout the Empire. Emperors, local governments, and private persons financed such building. Roads especially, which were crucial to the political, military, and even social welfare of the Empire, formed a network of scores of thousands of miles. In Roman Britain, a province of only moderate size and importance, more than five thousand miles of Roman roads have been identified.

These roads were built along natural routes, of course, and often over preexisting roads. But Roman engineers straightened many of the old routes and laid out numerous new ones. The roads naturally varied in the quality and permanence of construction. In most cases the Romans favored deep and careful preparation, both for retaining the roadbed and for drainage. The crowns were usually finished off with paving stones and curbed; along the route stood permanent milestones, which aided in systematic maintenance as well as being informative to the traveler. On difficult mountain routes the Romans did not hesitate to drill tunnels through solid rock; in marshes they elevated roadbeds on causeways. The major routes were those arteries that were both militarily significant and critically important to the imperial post system. The official post maintained way stations for officials and imperial messengers, making possible rapid communications through the huge and sprawling Empire.

The high roads were usually twenty or twenty-four feet wide, narrowing in mountainous areas. The narrower routes in the mountains reflect not merely the greater difficulty of construction but also the fact that most traffic over them involved asses or mules with backpacks rather than the wheeled vehicles often used at lower elevations. Such mountain roads were often only eight feet wide.

The most extensive network of roads was in Europe. A single route about sixteen hundred miles long connected the Danube and Rhine frontiers from the Black to the North seas. Another continuous road of about the same length stretched from Rome to Gades in southern Spain. A traveler could select from a number of routes how to go from the Bosporus to the Pillars of Hercules, or Gibraltar. A three-thousand-mile route stretched along the coast of North Africa; several branches useful both for trade and for the military extended south into the Sahara. Though improved, many miles of these roads were not paved. In Egypt east of the Nile the Via Hadriana (whose name indicates its chief planner) connected Berenice, a port on the Red Sea, with Alexandria in an important link in the eastern spice trade. The ancient coastal route still provided the main artery along the eastern Mediterranean coast through Palestine, Phoenicia, and Syria. Trajan began the interior road north from the Gulf of Aqaba, which provided a more satisfactory alternate route for eastern trade in spices and other luxuries. From a sea terminus at Aqaba this road ran through the remarkable rock-cut city of Petra, on to Amman (the ancient city of Philadelphia), then northwest to Damascus, or on a more northerly course, to the great caravan city of Palmyra and then to the Euphrates River. Land routes to China and the Persian Gulf fed into the trade centers along this road. Silk became a major import from China. The ancient routes on into Asia Minor through the Taurus Mountains were of course maintained and improved by the Romans—or on the Roman system, at least. Local governments and private property owners were required to maintain many roads.

Hundreds of graceful bridges, causeways rising above marshes or atop retaining walls on steep slopes, and rock-cut tunnels along mountain routes marked the course of the road system. The bridges, usually of solid rock, arched over streams and chasms that obstructed convenient travel. Many of these bridges survive intact, and still more partially so, all over the former Empire. The greatest number in one place is of course at Rome, where several arches of the eight ancient bridges survive: the Milvian Bridge to the north, arches on both sides of the Tiber island, and a span of the Pons Aemilius, which probably replaced the ancient wooden Pons Sublicius, the oldest of the Tiber bridges. The most spectacular bridge anywhere was probably that erected by Trajan that spanned the Danube just down from the Iron Gates in modern Romania. Only some of the piers survive. However, the same architect again, Apollodorus, built a similar bridge in Spain across the upper Tagus. Three arches still stand of the original eighteen; the bridge was some 1,300 feet long. Another great bridge, across the Tagus at Alcántara, stands intact (though it was torn down and then rebuilt during the Spanish Civil War in this century). The six soaring arches, 90 feet in diameter, stand 158 feet above the river. The total length of the bridge, however, is only 640 feet. Other notable bridges were built in the east:

The bridge built by Trajan across the Tagus river at Alcántara, in southwestern Spain. The central arch, which is 90 feet in diameter, lifts the road 158 feet above the river. (*Scala/Art Resource, New York*)

north of Antioch in Syria fourteen arches (of twenty-four) still remain of the 1,000-foot bridge that spanned the Adana River.

Sometimes the Romans combined bridges and aqueducts, as in the much-visited Pont du Gard north of Nîmes in southern France. The aqueduct, lifted on arches superimposed on a lower tier that supports the bridge, is no longer in use, but the bridge still serves local traffic. A similar combination, equally graceful, spans a stream near Barcelona. Surviving arches of aqueducts are yet found in many former provinces. Most notable perhaps is the Augustan aqueduct at Segovia in Spain, carried on lofty tiers of granite arches superimposed one above the other across a main street of the city; until recently it still carried water (through modern pipes) into the city. Other fine remains of aqueducts in Spain stand near Tarragona and at Mérida.

The aqueduct that supplied the Roman city of Trier (Augusta Treverorum, French Trèves) was about fifty miles long, as was that at the colony founded by the Romans on the ancient site of Carthage. Roman officials, imperial and local, worked assiduously throughout the first two centuries A.D. to meet the needs of all the important cities of the Empire for communications, a water supply, and public buildings such as the arenas, theaters, temples, and basilicas, ruins of which are scattered from Bath in England to Palmyra in Syria. North Africa—even in areas that are today desiccated—still shows impressive remains of

The aqueduct at Segovia, Spain. It was constructed of granite without mortar in the first century A.D. and was still in use until very recently. (*Archiv für Kunst und Geschichte*)

structures built during the Roman occupation, especially in the first and second centuries. Septimius Severus, a native of the city of Leptis Magna, built a whole new precinct there, including a forum and a basilica.

Herodes Atticus, Private Benefactor

A number of major public buildings of the period were erected with money raised partly or wholly from private sources. Rich citizens underwrote the costs of some quite munificent structures. Perhaps the best-known private benefactor of the age was Herodes Atticus, the rich Athenian Sophist. Atticus possessed a vast family fortune acquired mostly by his grandfather Hipparchus, who made his money in various ways, including industry, trade, and farming. Somehow he came under the condemnation of the emperor Domitian, who executed him and confiscated his lands. Either a considerable amount remained, or perhaps Nerva restored the lost property. Hipparchus' son, also called Herodes Atticus and also a Sophist, entered the Senate, possibly under Nerva, as many Greek and other provincials did in the early Empire. The elder Herodes Atticus achieved praetorian status, then was made legate of Judea, and was finally awarded the consulship, possibly in 104. The younger Atticus, born around the turn of the century, lived until 177 or 178; he was a friend of Hadrian and one of the teachers of both Lucius Verus and Marcus Aurelius.

Atticus erected several public structures in his home city, Athens, more or less carrying on where Hadrian had left off. Best known of these is the Odeion, a magnificent concert hall, the remains of which may still be seen near the Acropolis. He also financed buildings in several other cities, among them an aqueduct with nymphaeum at Olympia and a reconstruction of the stadium at Delphi. The tradition of privately financing some public service or building somewhat ameliorated the bad consequences of a system in which otherwise the rich might have become ever richer at the expense of the poor. Imperial confiscation of the property of the rich, especially under the early emperors Gaius, Nero, and Domitian, also played its role in checking the accumulation of wealth among the great families.

From Augustus to Severus Alexander, almost all the emperors built something of note in each of the provinces: if not a triumphal arch or bridge or aqueduct, then at least a series of milestones, testifying to the continual building and rebuilding of roads over long centuries. Even the ruins of these monuments after the neglect of nearly two millennia still evoke admiration and awe.

12 The High Empire: Cultural Vicissitudes

ONE THEME of the historian M. I. Rostovtzeff in his great work *The Social and Economic History of the Roman Empire* is that higher civilization can be disseminated widely to the common people only at the expense of its unhappy dilution and decay. Almost no one in modern America wants to accept such a thesis, with its implications for our own civilization. Nevertheless, in the high period of the Roman Empire, when the upper-level system of education reached its peak, with well-paid professors and polished lectures; when more Romans than ever before were well-educated, cultured persons; when the city of Rome was the most cosmopolitan and sophisticated city in the world—the greatest age of Roman culture was already past.

Perhaps the loss of political freedom for the governing, educated classes (which, stated baldly, marks the distinction between the Republic and the Empire) brought with it a concomitant loss not only of intellectual freedom, but also of intellectual vitality. The best literature produced in the High Empire was that in which writers protested against the times. In a work of history, such a protest might take the form of a comparison of some great emperor like Trajan with a predecessor such as Domitian. Dissidence was more easily expressed through satire. Even though stability and general prosperity made possible a broader education and a more numerous intellectual elite, the Roman Empire at its height was culturally stultifying.

What caused the stagnation of culture in the second century? The increasingly monolithic form of government, with its dependent social structures, must surely have played a role. Direct repression or censorship from on high was, to be sure, not frequent; however, government and society were subject to a great deal of informal pressure toward conformity. An upper-class person who had any hope of a career or even of continued high social status could hardly afford to offend the powers above by patronizing some free-spirited author. The prevailing rhetoric, characterized by eloquence rather than substance as a means of persuasion, was most suited to the times. It was far less dangerous, at parties or salons, to laugh at satire directed at misfits or women or pompous men of little influence than to abet biting political satire like that of Lucilius more than two centuries earlier. Yet such self-censorship may be only a small part of the explanation of the decline of Roman culture. At times in history cultural wellsprings have run dry for no discernible reason; originality fades as mediocre work that is only superficially different supplants masterpieces of civilization. Perhaps the brightest minds give their attention to something other than cultural creation. Problems of decline and fall are nearly always so complicated as to defy simple explanation.

Education in the High Empire

Lower-class education was probably not much affected by the transition to Empire. Since the city of Rome was a world capital into which flowed enormous sums of money, the consequent general prosperity may have made it possible for a larger number of children of this lower stratum to get an education. We must yet assume a considerable degree of near illiteracy at these levels; but the graffiti of Pompeii in the first century A.D. are often addressed to mule drivers or potters or other groups not likely to have had the advantage of formal education. Most persons must have been able to read, write, and figure at an elementary level.

Scattered references to children of the middle group in society indicate that they knew, certainly, how to read and calculate. Some rose to affluence as Petronius' Trimalchio did, but they learned little of the gentler arts. Their training fitted them for the marketplace rather than the Forum. The details of this level of education for boys who would be merchants, traders, small manufacturers, and the like, are becoming better known. Handbooks used in such schools, still mostly unpublished and untranslated, taught how to write letters, for example, or calculate at a practical level. Some early Christian letters follow the pattern of the handbooks, implying that the writers must have received this sort of middle-level education—though not, of course, in Rome.

Upper-class education did undergo change. Along with greater sophistication in the social sphere and a more complex system of social and political relations went an emphasis in education on polish and elegance as well as on what would later be referred to as the liberal arts. A proponent of the concept of liberal education in the twentieth century will find it hard to criticize the trend; surely any life is enriched by an introduction to arts and letters. But in the Roman Empire these changes instead reflected the decline of the old order. What critical need was there for the old system, with upper-class sons acquiring formal training from statesmen and jurists, poring over the course of Roman history, the development of the constitution, the law? Great decisions were now made in the emperor's *consilium* or in the even narrower confines of the emperor's own chambers, where only a few trusted advisers participated in the decision-making process—or in some obscure office, by anonymous bureaucrats. Important speeches might still be made in the Senate relating to trials or even conspiracies, but they only seemed trifling compared with the great orations of the past, which were still read. Rhetorical training to produce polished gentlemen thus became more important, the pragmatic elements of earlier education less important. Education might now turn out a sophisticate whose wit and learning would make him a welcome member of any social group. Incidentally it might yet help him toward a career in public affairs.

The change must not be overstated. Scions of members of the expanded aristocracy in the Empire still observed in the Forum, made notes, and discussed issues, as the great historian Tacitus informs us in his *Dialogue on Oratory*. The most important of the Latin rhetoricians now brought Latin authors into their courses of training, and any study of Vergil necessarily brought with it exposure to the older ideals. Moreover, some *rhetores* still followed Cicero, as we may see in the work of Quintilian, a Roman of Spanish background, the most important teacher at Rome in the first century A.D. Probably the most serious students were the sons of former Italian families or of old but undistinguished Roman stock. Opportunities opened to such families in the new order, and fathers ambitious for their sons doubtless pressed hard for a proper education for them.

One of the latter, from a previously obscure family, became emperor in the person of Vespasian. He had been given a good education by his parents—certainly he had studied Latin and Greek literature, though he seems not to have been much exposed to philosophy (or at least he had little taste for it). Under Vespasian more than ever before careers opened to men of ability. A proper education got them off to an early start and presumably sharpened the qualities that brought them to the attention of the emperor. Vespasian also first began the practice, extended under his successors, of paying state salaries in what we may term chaired professorships of both Latin and Greek literature. Quintilian, appropriately, was the first to receive such an appointment, at the excellent salary of 100,000 sesterces a year.

Just as the emperors of the second century came mostly from families that had settled in the western provinces, so several of the rhetoricians and literary lights of the early Empire came from those areas. Among those from Spain besides Quintilian were the elder Seneca, rhetorician and historian; his son, the minister of Nero and a Stoic philosopher; and his grandson by the latter's brother, Lucan the poet, all of Corduba; and the poet Martial. From the elder Seneca and later sources we learn that educational trends in the provinces followed those of Rome. *Rhetores* there, as in Rome, emphasized the practice of declamation on invented, sometimes fanciful topics (*controversiae*). Probably the schools in the Gallic provinces and Spain were good enough, but it was the practice for those who could afford it and who were ambitious for their sons to send them to Rome for a year or two of finishing.

During the second century Hadrian and other emperors increased the subsidy for professorships, and some were established even outside Rome, for instance in Athens. Possibly local funds in a matching arrangement helped pay salaries in such cities. Hadrian also arranged retirement benefits for teachers, and he built an athenaeum in Rome for the rhetoricians. Antoninus Pius upgraded the status of rhetoricians, grammarians, philosophers, and physicians by granting them immunity from certain taxes. The rules applied all over the Empire, but the number of persons in a given city who could receive such benefits was limited.

M. Cornelius Fronto, the teacher of Marcus Aurelius, illustrates the trend. Born in Numidia, he combined teaching with a political career, rising even to the consulate. He must have been a sound scholar to have retained the respect and affection of his star pupil; yet Marcus Aurelius turned away from his field for philosophy. And it is apparent from their correspondence that Fronto, like the rest, chose to emphasize language and style more than content. Neither Cicero nor Quintilian would have approved.

Upper-level education in the high Empire, then, put much stress on rhetoric and declamation. The older teaching of subject matter doubtless continued, however, and ambitious young men yet learned in the Forum or on military campaign. If the case of young Marcus Aurelius is not atypical, the total educational experience of promising young men must have included a sampling at least of more than one school. Perhaps one might study rhetoric and practice declamation, then later attend lectures in philosophy under some (most likely Greek) master. Then one might also attend one of the law schools. These latter were now more formally organized. Gaius in the second century and Paulus in the early third both wrote *Institutes* or textbooks for formal teaching of law, and all the great jurists taught, whatever else they did. Other instruction was available in architecture and engineering as well as in music, mathematics, and language. It was possible, in second-century Rome, to get a broader education under more competent masters than ever before (except perhaps in oratory); and yet, somehow education as a whole had declined in quality. Perhaps higher education had become more an end in itself than a preparation for life: the most highly educated persons were qualified more for professorships than for anything else.

The most highly educated Christian apologists of the period received their training in this system. Although the earliest of the Christian writers owed little to the Greco-Roman educational curriculum, the Apostle Paul had received an interesting combination of training that included upper-level Greek and Jewish education and also, doubtless at an earlier age, work in the middle-level, practical educational system mentioned earlier. More typical of the well-educated Christian publicists were Apollos (mentioned in the New Testament), the Hellenized Jewish Christian of Alexandria, the same cosmopolitan city that had produced the Jewish scholar Philo; and the later second- and third-century Christian writer-scholars Clement and Origen.

In the west, Tertullian exemplifies the educated Christian writer in the high Empire. Born and educated in Carthage in the broad manner in law, philosophy, and rhetoric, once converted he turned his training to the production of high-flown and occasionally turgid apologetic works in which he attacked pagan culture. Later Christian writers in the west, through Jerome, Augustine, and beyond, all owed something to the educational structure painstakingly built by Greek and Roman mentors over a period of centuries and essentially preserved through the third-century barbarian invasions, civil wars, plague, and financial collapse.

In the chaos of the third century some imperial edicts aimed to safeguard the rights of teachers. Probably they testify only to the crumbling of the special benefits that had come to the profession during the high Empire. After the restoration of order by Diocletian, the emperors kept up their interest in educational affairs. Apparently it became usual for them to make appointments to chaired professorships all over the Empire, as Constantius Chlorus is known to have done at Autun. Julian, in the middle of the fourth century, attempted through strict controls to exclude Christians from important teaching posts, holding that they could not possibly have a sympathetic understanding of the literature they thought pagan. Later in the century Theodosius set up a sort of university at Constantinople, with a staff of thirty-one. Justinian, in the sixth century, in an excess of Christian zeal closed down all the famous old schools at Athens, including those of Plato and Aristotle, the Academy and the Lyceum.

Later Silver Age Authors

As the Empire reached and passed its peak, the quality of Latin literature declined—even under such a ruler as Hadrian. What role the political system might have played in this decline is quite uncertain. Even a radically different political form might have meant little to literature.

Latin literature had a practical aspect in this age, which was surely little affected by the constitution or by the current ruler, whether princeps or tyrant. Thus Columella, the Roman of Spanish birth who continued the tradition of agricultural writing during Nero's reign, was safe from the strictures that that jealous emperor visited on Lucan. Though one of the twelve books of the *De Re Rustica* was in verse, it was not good enough to excite jealousy. The work mainly served as an agricultural handbook, including a rural calendar with sections on trees, vines, beekeeping, and so forth. Similarly, the *Natural History*, which the elder Pliny dedicated to Titus in 77, was unlikely to give offense to any emperor. Not that Pliny's compendium was entirely practical—for example, he gave the color of the eyes of five emperors—but he emphasized facts of nature, and the various excursuses deal with uncontroversial matters. So also Frontinus, writing mostly in Domitian's reign after a military career that saw him governor of Britain under Vespasian, did not offend even the imperious Domitian. He wrote a book on land surveyors (we have only excerpts), another on military affairs (lost but used by Vegetius, a writer probably of the late fourth century), and another military work, the *Strategematica*. Frontinus served under Trajan as director of the waterworks. The Latin, *curator aquarum*, makes the job seem important, as indeed it was; the eminent Marcus Agrippa first held the title under Augustus. Besides the city distribution system, this official oversaw scores of miles of aqueducts outside the city. Based on his experience, Frontinus wrote *De Aquis Urbis Romae*, which is a major source of information still.

Another category of literature was completely safe because it was so purely literary that it had little to do with the real world. Seneca's tragedies might be mentioned here—unless, contrary to most scholarly views, the *Octavia*, dealing with the daughter of Claudius who was Nero's unfortunate wife, was indeed one of Seneca's plays. The tragedies are based on common stories from Greek myth or legend. Apparently they were meant to be read at Nero's salons rather than performed. Except for historians of literature and linguists, most persons consider them dull, although in the history of literature they are quite important owing to their influence on later writers, such as the great masters of Elizabethan England, centuries later.

Nero's repressive measures following the conspiracy of Piso, which brought death to Lucan, Seneca, and Petronius, doubtless had a dampening effect on authors. Writers in the years immediately following, and especially those publishing in the reign of Domitian, were often inconsequential. Valerius Flaccus' epic the *Argonautica*, written under Domitian, contains some of the best poetry of the age, but Jason and the golden fleece were romantically long ago and far away. Statius' highly polished poetry of the same period is by and large not bad even if overmuch influenced by rhetorical style. The epics the *Thebaid* and the *Achilleid* deal mostly with the world of heroes and gods in the manner of Valerius Flaccus. Other poems—especially the major extant work, the *Silvae*—treat of real-life events and are thus of some value to the social historian. A notable aspect of Statius' work is his flattery of Domitian. Flattery had long been a part of Roman literature from Cicero's speeches (if not earlier) on, but Statius' brand smacks of an unlovely insincerity: the author alludes to planned works on Domitian, for example, which he probably never intended to write.

Silius Italicus, in the *Punica*—an epic treatment of the history of the Second Punic War—dealt with more sensitive matter in an unobjectionable way. Also written under Domitian, the work follows Livy closely, but with inoffensive rhetorical embroidery. The longest surviving Latin poem, it is often tedious, with its long speeches in the style of the time. It would not have survived, of course, without some merit. Interestingly, the work begins with Hannibal's oath, and the Carthaginian emerges as more of a hero than Scipio.

Martial and the Social Set

Social and economic historians find a mine of information in the *Epigrams* of the poet Marcus Valerius Martialis. A native of Bilbilis in Spain, Martial came to Rome in the reign of Nero and spent about the last thirty-five years of the first century A.D. there. He became a member of a group that included several participants in the conspiracy of Piso, and he himself was perhaps saved from involvement only by his relatively recent arrival. He turned to poetry—mostly epigrams, but some longer poems also—and became quite popular. His often salacious and obscene quips, masterfully crafted so that the point is often delivered with sudden impact in the last word, did not require intellectual effort on the part of the reader. Martial was not rich and had to get along any way he could—which was not bad compared to the life-style of most Romans, but miserable compared to that of members of the upper class with whom he hobnobbed. Around the turn of the century, thanks to the generosity of the younger Pliny and a Spanish patron, he returned to Spain and was able to afford a comfortable retirement.

Martial bemoaned the lack of a latter-day Maecenas who might adequately subsidize him, though some of his patrons did send substantial annual gifts—an important facet of Roman social life. Still, he lived from hand to mouth and at times had to scrounge dinner invitations or hint for a new toga. He found it necessary to play the role then expected of clients: he came at dawn, sometimes cold and shivering, to his patron's house, and rather ungratefully received the small cash payment (sportula) that had become customary. This sum, perhaps a denarius or five sesterces, the largesse of the rich to their less important clients, helped keep bread, cheese, and cheap wine on the table. Falernian wine, for such a client, was beyond reach—except when on some special occasion a dinner invitation was also forthcoming.

The sportulae, both cash payments and special feasts, became an important feature of upper-class society not only in Rome but also in the major provincial cities. Rich leaders occasionally gave sportulae to all the citizens of a town, the amounts varying according to status—decurions, for example, receiving three or four times as much as common citizens. The emperor Claudius referred to games he gave for the populace as sportulae, and indeed the games and circuses were, in effect, the benefice of a super-patron to a huge mass of clients.

Martial could hope to make some money from the sale of his books. However, copyrights did not exist, and he once wrote that some of his works had even been read at a salon or dinner party by a host who himself claimed authorship. The poet's complaints about his low income as compared with others' reminds us of the plaints of intellectuals of our own time: a cobbler who pleased his customers and so got included in some of their wills had ended in a more comfortable situation than he; the winner of a race in the circus got more in one day than he might receive in a year.

Martial's satirical and sarcastic epigrams had the kind of punch he sought only through his treating themes that lent themselves to such a style. His work thus reflects not the usual but the unusual, even the bizarre. Many of his poems deal with sex—every imaginable variety, very explicitly set down, sometimes naming names, leaving the impression that heterosexual monogamy had almost disappeared from the lives of the Roman social set. The works of the younger Pliny and others partially offset this undoubted exaggeration; still, an indelible impression of moral decadence emerges from Martial's lines.

Martial wrote quite a lot about food, sometimes giving whole menus. For many Romans, dining sumptuously had become one of the chief ends of life. The poet gives whole menus; from such works modern scholars have compiled Roman cookbooks, and some of the dishes appeal to modern tastes, though sow's udder, cooked rare with the milk—a gourmet entrée for a fancy dinner at Rome—has not caught on with twentieth-century palates. One whole book of Martial's epigrams consists of couplets on specific food items, from beans to truffles.

Martial flattered Domitian shamelessly. The lines may reflect a genuine attitude, since that emperor gave way to the cruel streak in his character only at the end of his life, after conspirators tried to kill him.

The poet later hailed Nerva and Trajan, but spoke of the end of Domitian's reign only as a hard and difficult time. Certainly Martial bears witness to Domitian's popularity at one point (probably) in midreign when the emperor gave some games and received a prolonged ovation.

The Romans Martial portrays come alive through his verses: the pretty fellow, depilated and smelling of balsam, who was an idle sophisticate and gossip; the magister of the elementary school, bawling at his poor pupils even before dawn, waking the sleepy poet nearby. The baths, the great social centers of Rome, are animated by the intrigues and idiosyncrasies of Martial's characters.

It is not easy to determine the poet's attitude toward women, nor to be confident that his verses seriously reflect his or anyone else's views. Incidental remarks may demonstrate real views more than specifically directed verses. For example, when Martial writes that he likes best the woman who is a prostitute, always willing, and cheap besides, he is probably only trying for laughs. He seems generally to accept women as social equals; wives, however, he implies, should accept a secondary sex role, not complaining about concubines or youthful man-slaves. To be sure Martial would, with typical jest, grant wives equal opportunity to cheat on their husbands. One rather enigmatic epigram on the subject is worth quoting:

> Let the matron be subject to her husband, Priscus;
> In no other way do woman and man become equal.[1]

Tacitus and Pliny: Upper-Class Career Politicians

Tacitus and Pliny the Younger not only present to us in their writings much of what we know of the nature, feelings, and aspirations of upper-class Romans of the age, they are also themselves specimens—perhaps not altogether typical—of their class. Both came of old Roman stock, though not of the older aristocracy, from families that had migrated to northern Italy (or, in the case of Tacitus, perhaps Narbonensian Gaul); both probably got their early education in their home cities but came to Rome for finishing, Pliny under the famous Quintilian, Tacitus under Marcus Aper and Julius Secundus. They were of similar age: Pliny was born in 61 or 62 and Tacitus about five years earlier. Each developed a considerable ability at oratory to advance his career. Tacitus first held important office under Vespasian, Pliny a bit later; and both managed to advance their careers under Domitian, whom they came to hate. The consulate came to each at the end of the century. They were friends;

---

[1] Martial *Epigrams* VIII, 12. Translation of Walter C. A. Ker, Loeb Classical Library (Cambridge, Mass., 1968).

some of Pliny's letters are addressed to Tacitus. Their writings, however, are vastly different. Tacitus is remembered primarily as a historian, though he wrote other works, such as the *Dialogus de Oratoribus*, a chronicle of the decline of oratory that must have been used by the *rhetores* in their schools despite its pessimistic tone. Pliny is noted for his *Letters*, carefully composed in polished, literary style, and for his *Panegyric* of Trajan.

Without specifically criticizing the principate, Cornelius Tacitus in his *Dialogus* deplored the petty themes of the speeches of his own day, in contrast with the great orations on public policy or war or important legislation of the late Republic. This sort of ambivalence about the Empire saturates Tacitus' other works as well—chief of which (in order of composition) are his *Histories* and *Annals*, which, in inverse order, covered the period from the death of Augustus to the death of Domitian. Tacitus thought it possible, even with the loss of independence under the Empire, for men of his class to act with courage, determination, and moral integrity. His model was his own much-admired father-in-law, Julius Agricola, memorialized in a biography that elaborates the theme. Tacitus' other major work, the *Germania*, an important source of information on the Germans, holds up the primitive virtues of these half-civilized tribesmen as an example to his own decadent age.

Moralizing on sex, the historian contrasted the behavior of Romans of his age with that of the Germans:

> Their life is one of close modesty, with no seductions of arena-spectacles, no provocations at dinner feasts to corrupt them. They know nothing of secret billets-doux between men or women. . . . No one there laughs at vice, nor dismisses it . . . as the spirit of the times.[2]

Tacitus admired any people who would fight for their freedom; with overtones for his own age, he wrote,

> The German fighting for liberty has been a keener enemy than absolutism of Arsaces [the Parthian king].[3]

Tacitus looked with a jaundiced eye at what the Empire had become after Augustus. He displayed not only bitterness but unreasonable bias against Tiberius and his successors, reaching a kind of crescendo with the "monster" Domitian. None of the imperial butts of his sharp phrases was as bad as he said, and it is inexcusable that the historian pretended to understand what Tiberius thought, without any evidence whatever. However, Tacitus' virtues as a historian were many: he used his sources well and was accurate in his presentation of facts; he had considerable

---

[2] Tacitus *Germania*, 19. Translation of W. Peterson, Loeb Classical Library (New York, 1914).

[3] Ibid., 37.

psychological insight into his subjects; and with his compressed style he often produced epigrammatical sentences that compare favorably with those of Martial. One of the more famous such remarks is this summary characterization of Galba in the *Histories:* "All would have agreed that he was capable of ruling—if he had never ruled."[4]

A speech the historian put into the mouth of Galba, on the occasion when that emperor adopted a man expected to be his successor, clearly reflected the thinking of Tacitus as well as of others of his class. The speech acknowledged that the Empire could never return to a republican form: the need remained for a *rector* or *princeps.* But the principate had earlier been handled as if it was a "sort of heritage" (*quasi hereditas*). The new system of selecting emperors was a "substitute for freedom" (*loco libertatis*) that would turn up the "best" persons for the job. Written in the reign of Trajan, this passage and others show that Tacitus agreed with Pliny's view of the new ruler as the *optimus princeps.* In the same book the historian spoke of that "rare and happy time when you can feel what you wish and say what you feel."

Tacitus thus shared some of the views of the philosophers who had opposed Vespasian and Domitian because the hereditary principle had resulted in the formation of a new dynasty. But the martyred Helvidius Priscus, though admired by the historian, was not his ideal. He favored men who spoke out, who acted, not those who opposed in passive silence. And despite his longing for the old freedom, in essence forever lost, he approved the Empire and shared Vergil's conviction that Rome had a destiny to rule men well. Further conquests he doubtless approved as a fruit of the old military virtues. Freedom could not be reconciled with Empire; all that could be hoped for was a succession of good emperors who would respect the independence of the ruling class. Had Tacitus lived for a hundred years, he would not have been displeased.

While Tacitus, in semiretirement, was writing his *Histories* and later the *Annals*, G. Plinius Caecilius Secundus advanced in his political career, serving as prefect of two of the imperial treasuries and sitting on the emperor's *consilium.* Then, as an imperial legate, he set out to govern the province of Bithynia in about 110 and died there in service a couple of years later. From the tenth and last book of his letters we learn much of the imperial governance of provinces, of the uses of the imperial post, of the financial disorder and bad planning in the province. And, incidentally, we learn of the large number of Christians in the area and how they were treated. The earlier books of his letters tell us something of social life and of the various requests for letters of recommendation and the like that a man in his position as patron received.

---

[4] Tacitus *Histories* I, 49. Author translation.

Pliny wrote much of his landholdings and the income from his property—or lack of it, for in the manner of some of the well-to-do persons he continually deplored the low return from his farms. Yet it has been estimated that his net worth was 15–20 million sesterces, including about five hundred slaves, and that his annual income exceeded 1 million sesterces.[5] Most of this income was from land, though substantial legacies from friends helped. One interesting feature of his letters, which were intended for publication, is his casual mention of lending money at interest. In the days of the Republic, moneylending would have been kept at least semisecret as hardly a respectable activity. In both periods, such loans would probably not have been handled directly, but indirectly, through a freedman, banker, or other agent.

Although Pliny owned several villas in northern Italy, his area of origin, and in Rome and Ostia, he lived without extravagance, using substantial portions of his wealth to benefit others. As expected of scions of important municipal families, he was a patron to his hometown, Comum, where he set up an alimentary fund, provided money for improvement and operation of the baths, funded a library, and paid part of the salary of a teacher. Still another fund established pensions for about a hundred of his freedmen in Comum (whom he had apparently freed late in life). Once these beneficiaries had died, the remaining funds were to provide an annual banquet for the citizens. Pliny may have been more generous than most, perhaps because he was childless.

Juvenal: The Satirist as Social Critic

Decimus Junius Juvenalis, born in the latter years of Nero's reign at Aquinum, was a friend of Martial and must have been influenced by him. Like Martial, he lived hand-to-mouth as a client of important Romans. Juvenal's sixteen Satires were published in the reigns of Trajan and Hadrian, after Martial had returned to Spain. Rhetorical, moralistic, and pessimistic, the Satires present a somewhat sordid picture of an upper class in decline, in sharp contrast with the favorable impression we gain from Pliny's Letters. Like Martial's epigrams, the Satires on occasion describe the vices of upper-class Romans in such detail that they must often have been read more out of prurient interest than for any moral benefit.

One of the most quoted sections of the tenth Satire comments sadly on the state of the Roman populace in Juvenal's day:

---

[5] R. Duncan-Jones, *The Economy of the Roman Empire* (Cambridge: Cambridge University Press, 1974), pp. 21ff.

> What of the mob of Remus? . . . the people who once bestowed every-
> thing—imperium, the fasces, the legions—now anxiously content
> themselves with just two things—bread and circuses.[6]

In the poet's view, the one thing that ruined the Roman people was
luxury. From the sixth *Satire:*

> We endure the evils of long peace: luxury, more savage than war, has
> laid its hand on us, the revenge of a vanquished world.[7]

The overwhelming influx of foreigners, attracted by the new wealth, had
flooded the city with corruption. Greeks attracted especially caustic
criticism: they were like comic actors, Juvenal said, splitting their sides
at your jokes, given to insincere, outrageous flattery.

Juvenal saw decadence everywhere. He excoriated the gluttons who
squandered whole fortunes on delicate foods, the aesthetes who must
have the most diaphanous silks for their tender skins, the husbands and
wives who cheated on each other (Juvenal seems not to have known of
many stable marriages), the prostitutes of both sexes, poisonings, mur-
ders, informing. The satirist held a somewhat Stoic conviction that
crime takes its own toll, inflicting punishment through an inescapable
psychic guilt.

Some of Juvenal's blackest pessimism he reserved for women, whose
depravity he depicted in the sixth *Satire.* Chastity among women did
once exist, he said—in the days of cavemen! Will Hibernia be satisfied
with one man? No more than she would be with one eye. Censennia,
who brought her husband a large dowry, uses it as a license to carry on as
she wishes before her spouse's face, since if he divorced her he would
have to return the dowry. If one finds a wife of good family, she taunts
her poor husband interminably with her hauteur. While the mother-in-
law lives a husband can expect no peace; she will aid and abet her
daughter's extramarital affairs. The satirist somberly reported on savage
women who took out their frustrations on their slaves; one cruel wife
had a miscreant beaten half to death for some minor infraction while she
made up her face. One curl out of place could bring a flogging. Rich
women, Juvenal said, would not endure having children: they could
afford the fees and the strong drugs of the abortionist.

The poet told of a burlesque of the mysteries of the Bona Dea (Good
Goddess) at which the women burned with passion, and another at
which they ended by urinating on the statue of Chastity! Here Juvenal
made his famous remark on the suggestion of some that wives be kept at

---

[6] Juvenal *Satire* 10, 72ff. Modified translation of G. G. Ramsey, Loeb Classical Library
(Cambridge, Mass., 1959).

[7] Ibid., 6, 293–294.

A noble matron of the Flavian period. (*E. Richter/Roma*)

home with doors locked. "Who will keep watch over the guards?" he asked.[8]

The satirist also condemned those women who "boldly go about the whole city, interfering in men's affairs, talking with the generals," anxious to be the first to learn any news from China or Parthia, and, incidentally, gossiping about the smallest domestic matters. The woman who dominated an intellectual conversation at dinner Juvenal could not stand. Was he a little jealous, perhaps?

The satire's climax comes with the story of one Pontia, who poisoned her two children and, when confronted, admitted the crime, saying she would have done the same if there had been seven of them. Only once did Juvenal sound a really sympathetic note for women: in the second *Satire* he put into the mouth of the prostitute Laronia an amusing speech in which she defends herself against the twits of her male competitors.

Obviously Juvenal is not to be taken at face value. Moreover, at times, such as when he tells of the activities of women and of foreigners, the poet unintentionally bespeaks a climate of relative social freedom that by twentieth-century standards seems good. It is fortunate that we have

---

[8] Ibid., 345ff.

Statius and Pliny to reflect for us a healthier society than that portrayed
by Martial and Juvenal. But we cannot read the satirists of this age
without retaining the impression that prosperity, power, and a government that had often been dominated by persons who set sad examples—
the Gaiuses and Neros and Messalinas and Agrippinas—had indeed
profoundly affected for the worse Romans of all stations, but particularly the upper classes.

Suetonius: A New Age

Though born only a few years after Tacitus and the younger Pliny, who
was his friend, the Roman biographer Gaius Suetonius Tranquillus
reflected a new age. For him and his generation the excesses and the
tendencies toward tyranny of some of the Julio-Claudian and the Flavian emperors were curious and fading history, not a bitter and personally resented immediate past. Suetonius' *Lives of the Twelve Caesars*—
Julius Caesar through Domitian—came out about 120. Less pessimistic
than Tacitus as well as less penetrating, Suetonius is entertaining, objective, less judgmental as he discusses in rather stereotyped form the early
lives, influences, and omens or prophecies for each of the early emperors, and then recounts the major events in the lives of his subjects.
His critical acumen suffers by comparison with Tacitus', but the biographer does supply frequent quotations from basic sources—for example,
letters of Augustus to Livia asking what they are to do about poor,
handicapped young Claudius—which allow modern historians to do
something more than criticize an interpretation based on facts known
only through the author, as they must often do when using Tacitus.

The younger Pliny took a friendly interest in Suetonius and obtained
for him one of his early appointments. Suetonius held three secretary-
ships under Hadrian, including the *ab epistulis*, in charge of correspondence, and must have had access to the official archives. Even after he
was fired for some breach of manners toward the empress Sabina, Suetonius may still have been able to use the imperial files. Hadrian was not
really fond of Sabina—he much preferred the company of his young
friend Antinoüs until the youth's untimely death—and surely he was
more concerned with proper form than anything else: it seems unlikely
that he took any further action against his cabinet officer.

The new generation, impressed with the superiority of the more
recent emperors, was ready to believe the worst about the rulers of the
past. The stories that Suetonius tossed in liberally, almost casually, of
the errant sexual excesses of these emperors must have derived from
confidential memoirs, perhaps set down years after the facts, rather than
on any official records. Though our own jaded age finds sordid tales
easy to believe, it is yet difficult to accept Suetonius' picture of, for
example, Tiberius' alleged lewd and disgusting behavior during his

years of retirement in old age on the island of Capri or of Agrippina's allegedly seducing her own son, Nero. Yet Suetonius mostly wrote as one who did much research in good sources. His works have a mixed effect: on the one hand the emperors are humanized, shown to be individuals who struggled with difficult tasks; on the other, many of the twelve seem bizarre and the Empire lucky to have survived.

Suetonius apparently lived into the reign of Antoninus Pius and wrote a number of other works. Besides the biographies of the caesars we have only some sketches remaining from his *Lives of Illustrious Men*, the subjects of which are grammarians, rhetoricians, and poets, including Terence, Vergil, and Horace. Suetonius himself was something of a *grammaticus*, as we can tell from the titles of some of his lost books; and he wrote in Greek as well as his native Latin. The lost books would have added much to our scanty information on the mid–second century, especially those on Roman manners and customs and on the festivals.

With Suetonius' death comes the end of the silver age of Latin literature; there follows a decline both in quantity and quality of literary output. Yet Suetonius was much imitated in following years by other biographers like Marius Maximus, whose works have mostly disappeared. Still later, the author (or authors) of the *Scriptores Historiae Augustae*, dealing with several emperors beginning with Hadrian, followed a similar format. Christian writers also used Suetonius as a model; so too did Einhard in writing the life of Charlemagne in the ninth century. Suetonius' influence continued, like that of Cicero, Seneca, and others, through the Renaissance and into the modern age.

Apuleius

A Latin writer of the later second century is Apuleius of Madaura in North Africa, who received his early education in Carthage. He studied also in Athens and Rome, and had some pretensions as a philosopher and rhetorician. The most important of Apuleius' works is a sort of novel, the *Metamorphoses*, commonly called *The Golden Ass*. It is the story of a young man who dabbles in black magic with the help of his girlfriend and accidentally turns himself into an ass. He can be changed back only by eating fresh roses—but doesn't manage to get any before the season is past. He therefore remains an ass for a year, which is chockfull of amusing and unbelievable adventures. He is beaten, petted, feasted, and starved before the goddess Isis brings about his restoration.

The social historian and the religious scholar both find much of interest in Apuleius. He describes everyday scenes from the lives of the rich and the poor: for the palates of the rich, imported fish dishes garnished with fine sauce, marinated beef, or peppered fowl, with fine wines; for the poor, barley fried with cheese or a simple crust of bread.

The rich sleep on beds with down bolsters and coverlets of linen dyed with Tyrian purple or cloth of gold; one poor man sleeps on straw under a rough lean-to, even in winter. The rich wear fine linens or sheer silks; the poor, cast-off, torn, patched mantles of coarse material. The stories themselves are of course fantasy, but the settings often have the impress of reality: townspeople, aroused by the arrival of a large company of travelers in the middle of the night, assuming they are thieves and setting dogs on them; slaves mistreated at a sweatshop bakery; local officials giving traditional and expected largesse to the citizenry.

Apuleius describes several of the gods in the form and costume in which they were conceived and popularly portrayed. The reader can almost be a spectator at a couple of religious processions, so well are they pictured in words. With some scorn the writer tells of one band of "priests" of the Dea Syria, little better than beggars, who went about bearing the image of the deity, beating drums, clanging cymbals, playing flutes, wearing painted faces and elaborate vestments, pounding on doors, demanding gifts. Apuleius presents the goddess Isis (with her consort Osiris), by contrast, as omniscient and benevolent, almost a composite of all the major goddesses. Some of the well-known male divinities, such as Mithra, for example, are only her lieutenants. The emphasis on a female deity hardly implies any generally enlightened attitude toward women, however. Apuleius mostly presents them in traditional roles, and regularly refers to them as the "weaker" sex.

Several writers of the first and second centuries compiled interesting and occasionally significant stories or anecdotes, probably intended as sourcebooks for orators and rhetoricians. One such writer in the second century was Aulus Gellius, whose work, in Latin, called *Attic Nights* because it was composed in Attica, is mostly extant. Amusing as the work is, it nevertheless symbolizes the decline of Latin literature. It is a haphazard, motley collection, even though it is put together with pleasant style.

Greek Authors of the High Empire

Greeks who wrote about Rome—at least those whose writings have survived—tended to be accepting of the dynamic, brash state that had risen to conquer the world. Perhaps they responded to the Roman tendency to admire all things Greek. Even in the second century B.C. Polybius had been impressed with the constitution of the Roman state, which he had written about at some length. In the latter part of the first century B.C. Dionysius of Halicarnassus, who lived and wrote in Rome after about 30 B.C., was similarly admiring of the Romans. His *Roman Antiquities*, written mostly to explain Roman history to a Greek audience, parallels Livy, yet diverges at times and provides a useful supplement. Dionysius' contemporary, Diodorus of Sicily, in his *World History*, emphasized eastern Mediterranean civilization much more than that of the newcomer, Rome, and displayed less regard for that state, which had subjected Sicily to so much bad government during his time.

The major Greek writers of the high Empire mostly felt themselves a part of the universal state that was Rome, as indeed they were, not only intellectually but, for many of them, politically as well. It is therefore artificial convention to treat of the Greek writers as if they were in a completely different category from their Latin colleagues. They did indeed have a somewhat different background, but in manner of education, training, and outlook they belonged to the same cosmopolitan group.

Surely the most popular biographer who ever lived was the Greek Plutarch, who lived from the middle of the first century into the middle years of Hadrian's principate. His *Lives*, mostly presented in pairs, a Greek and a Roman with similar careers, has been influential down to modern times. Shakespeare, for example, used Lord North's translation of Plutarch as the basis for his plays on classical themes, and the moving spirits both of the French and American revolutions were obviously familiar with his work. Napoleon's early orientation toward the east reflected his fascination with Plutarch's life of Alexander the Great. In his own time, Plutarch's other works—the extant ones are grouped together in a collection usually called the *Moralia*—may have been more popular than the *Lives*. The parallelism in the biographies symbolizes the cultural and intellectual partnership of Greece and Rome.

Though Plutarch spent most of his life near his home in Chaeronea, he did travel to Rome, where he lectured and studied. He made close friends among Romans in high places and may have been given an official post in his home province, Achaea. The works give the impression of a very civilized person. His biographies show that he was more interested in people than in politics; in consequence, modern historians often bemoan the lack of detail on political history or chronology. But Plutarch remains a mine of information on people, religion, philosophy, and other social and cultural topics.

Three Greco-Roman historians of the high Empire examplify that category of Hellenized persons who, as Roman citizens, participated in both Roman society and Roman government. They show us how Rome was becoming less and less narrowly Roman as it gradually assumed the nature of a world state.

Arrian (Flavius Arrianus), a native of Bithynia in Asia Minor, was a Stoic who studied under Epictetus, probably in Epirus after the latter was exiled from Rome by Domitian. We still have part of his book, *Discourses of Epictetus*, and a handbook on Epictetus' moral teachings as well. Of his historical works the most important is his *History of*

Alexander, the best life of that general we have (Plutarch's life of Alexander is next in importance). After he acquired Roman citizenship he was governor of Cappadocia under Hadrian, and he held the consulate during the reign of Antoninus Pius.

Appian (Appianus) of Alexandria also lived during the second century. The only imperial office he held, as far as we know, was a procuratorship in Egypt, under Antoninus Pius. He wrote an extensive history of Rome down to Trajan, of which somewhat less than half remains. Mostly organized by the wars the Romans fought as they rose to dominance, the work is nevertheless not narrowly military. It has many lapses: the chronology is weak, and Appian did not completely understand the constitution of the Roman Republic. The best and most useful segment is *The Civil Wars,* in five books, dealing with the period from the Gracchi to the late Republic.

Finally, we have much of the work of Dio Cassius, like Arrian a native of Bithynia, grandson of a man called Dio Chrysostomus, the Golden-Mouthed, who was a noted rhetorician and philosopher and was lionized at Rome, especially under Nerva and Trajan. Dio Cassius became a senator in the late second century, near the end of the reign of Marcus Aurelius, then praetor, and during the Severan dynasty served twice as consul (last under Severus Alexander in 229) and three times as proconsul, governing Africa, Dalmatia, and Pannonia. His *Roman History* covers the period from the mythical beginnings to the date of his last consulship. Only the books dealing with the first century B.C. are pretty well intact; for the rest we have occasionally substantial fragments that are sometimes useful in helping to fill in gaps in our information, especially for the high Empire. The work is excessively rhetorical, containing more, longer, and more fanciful speeches than are usual in the works of other ancient historians; some of them are really essays of political philosophy.

In the *Deipnosophists,* a Greek compilation like that of the Latin writer Gellius, the Hellenized Egyptian Athenaeus collected the kind of anecdote or story, amusingly composed, that might have been the subject of conversation at banquets or symposia. The miscellany is important for its wealth of quotations from earlier authors, mostly comic playwrights and poets but also historians and others. Athenaeus published his work about the turn of the third century. Another second-century writer (in Greek, though his native tongue was probably Aramaic) deserving of brief notice is Lucian of Samosata. A sort of latter-day Sophist, his satires, mostly in the form of dialogues, have been so much admired in our own age that some of them have been included in Great Books courses.

A second-century rhetorician, Aelius Aristides, a Greek from Mysia, eulogized Rome in one of his orations, emphasizing precisely the theme of this section: that Rome was no longer just Roman but a worldwide empire offering benefits for many who were neither Roman nor Italian. Some of the fifty-odd extant speeches have a historical emphasis (mostly Greek). One group gives interesting detail of the author's efforts to obtain help from the god of healing, Asclepius, for a persistent and difficult physical ailment. The answer came to him in a dream.

This survey is by no means a complete list, even of authors of the high Empire whose major works are mostly extant. A great many technical writers flourished; Claudius Galen, for example, a second-century native of Asia Minor, wrote philosophical and, more important, medical works in Greek. Galen had studied both philosophy and medicine in Smyrna, Corinth, and Alexandria and was a physician for gladiators in Pergamum. About 162 he went to Rome and was introduced into Roman society by a consular. He returned to Pergamum on the outbreak of plague but came back to Rome in 169, later becoming court physician to Marcus Aurelius. He engaged in scientific research, adding much to knowledge, of human anatomy and the circulatory system, probably based on dissections of apes.

Great jurists—a few of whom will be discussed under the heading of law—were busy writing digests and histories in the period. And Christians wrote works some of which deserve the name of literature; Tertullian's works are rhetorical, and in some ways typical, products of the age. But these, too, are reserved for discussion elsewhere.

Religion in the High Empire

In the second century B.C. Polybius had said that the Romans were the most religious of all peoples, and the Romans themselves felt that their piety had contributed much to their political success. During the Empire some of the oldest, most primitive deities were remembered, if only dimly; others were worshiped with archaic ceremonies of almost forgotten meaning. The state gods, neglected during the civil wars of the late Republic, again received official attention, and a variety of new gods, brought in mostly from the Hellenistic east, replaced the earlier ones no longer worshiped. Seeing the multiplicity of temples, shrines, festivals, priestly colleges, liturgies, sacrifices, and private devotions, an observer would have thought that the Romans were as religious as of old.

Historians familiar with the tendency of imperial states of the earlier Near East to promote the worship of their major gods in step with their political expansion might have expected the Romans to require their chief deity, Jupiter Optimus Maximus of the Capitol, to be worshiped with Roman rites all over the world. But the Romans were slow to spread the Jovian cult, despite the seriousness with which they took their religion. Probably the reasons are the same as the reasons why Latin literature did not immediately sweep through the eastern Mediterranean: the older, more advanced cultures of the east had their own religions as well as literary heritage. Moreover, the process of religious syncretism characteristic of the Hellenistic world had already produced composite deities; the Roman gods simply fitted into the pantheon that had already developed. Jupiter was thus also Zeus, the Egyptian Ammon, and so on. The peculiarly Roman features of Jupiter's worship could have no great effect on the world.

Ultimately the Romans did advance one cult, which took on some of the characteristics of a universal religion and became a political tool in the interest of stability—a symbol of loyalty to the state and its rulers. This was, of course, the imperial cult, the worship of the emperor-as-god. There was nothing new about such a cult: the pharaohs of Egypt had been worshiped as gods for more than three thousand years, and the concept of the hero-become-god had roots that went back at least to the legendary Sumerian king Gilgamesh in the third millennium B.C. From Alexander the Great onward, deification of kings had become usual in the Hellenistic world. Great men among both Romans and Greeks often traced their ancestry back to a deity. That Julius Caesar, who claimed as his ancestors Aeneas, son of Venus, and Romulus, son of Mars, should have been exalted by his followers, doubtless with his approval, as in some sense divine was thus not remarkable.

Augustus, as we have seen, made much of his "divine" father by adoption, Caesar, and he permitted temples and shrines to be constructed both in the eastern and the western provinces where subjects venerated Augustus himself also, along with Roma. Augustus was officially deified at his death, which became the standard practice; occasional exceptions occurred when Caligula and Domitian in the first century and Commodus in the second demanded recognition as deities in their lifetimes. The provincial councils, made up of upper-class men, gave much attention to the imperial cult; so also did the *augustales*, priestly colleges of freedmen. Other priestly colleges included rites to the emperors in their regular observances: and the army too made much of the cult, for example, in oaths and through observing birth dates. The imperial cult thus touched the lives of persons in all social strata. The proper observance of its ceremonies became a symbol of patriotism as well as of piety.

From earliest times the Romans embraced—eagerly, at times—foreign gods and rites. During the Republic their religion changed under the impulse of Etruscan and Greek influence. In the late Republic and early Empire, a host of new gods and goddesses associated with eastern mystery religions came into the city. Mostly accompanying immigrants, these new deities probably did not find many devotees among native Romans and Italians at first, as archaeological discoveries seem to indicate. In the early period foreigners, especially of Greek origin, tended to settle in enclaves on the Aventine Hill. Indeed, their settlement in this location may have had official sanction. Later, in the early Empire, the Janiculum received new colonies of immigrants. There and in the Trastevere nearby the ruins of temples to their gods have been found. Inscriptional remains indicate that the foreigners sometimes organized themselves in clubs. Among the various groups on the Janiculum, the Jews seem to have been quite numerous; at least two synagogues have been found there.

The new gods included Isis, the Egyptian goddess who was especially looked to by women in connection with childbirth, and her consort, Osiris; the Dea Syria; Cybele (brought in at the end of the Second Punic War) and her male consort, Attis; and Mithra, of Persian origin, whose cult penetrated the Mediterranean world through Asia Minor. Particularly important among soldiers, Mithra was especially venerated along the frontiers, at the major army posts. In general these deities were served with initiation ceremonies and rites involving mysteries known only to the initiates, usually with some sort of purification process. The cults brought a hope of life beyond the grave, and each, it seems, developed a code of ethics. Devotees were caught up in a relationship with the deity much more personal than in the older Roman religion except, perhaps, for the connection with family and household gods. Since these religions were not monotheistic it was easy to hold on to the old and add the new.

Christians: Aliens in the Empire

Christianity was obviously the most important Hellenistic import into Rome, where it flourished despite sporadic repression, finally to become the official state religion—the universal religion of Toynbee's thesis—and displacing all the rest.

The roots of the Christian religion lie in Judaism; the cultural background of earliest Christianity is illustrated through our knowledge of the Pharisees as well as the Essenes, the sect that produced the Dead Sea Scrolls. John the Baptist, Jesus himself, his apostles and other disciples, and all their earliest converts were Jews or Jewish proselytes who thought they were somehow fulfilling the Hebrew law, not breaking away from it. The new teaching caught on best with the Hellenized Jews and proselytes outside Palestine, so that it was perhaps inevitable that the emphasis soon would be on converting Gentiles.

For a time the Christians wished to be considered Jews since the Jewish religion was *licita* (officially recognized) and its adherents granted certain privileges—such as, for example, exemption from army service. But after the Jewish revolts in 66–70 and later during the reigns of Trajan and Hadrian, Christians preferred to emphasize their separateness. The gulf between the two groups was by then virtually unabridgeable anyhow. Christian leaders had decided years before, in a conference at

Jerusalem, that converted Gentiles would not, in effect, have to become
Jews in order to be Christian. There was peril, however, for members of
an unapproved (*illicita*) religion. Possibly by the time of Nero, and
certainly by Domitian, Roman policy decreed that to be guilty only of
the name Christian—that is, to have committed no crime other than
joining the sect—was to incur the death penalty. Pliny's letters to Trajan
from Bithynia, where there were many Christians, and Trajan's reply
show that this policy had long been established, though Trajan wanted
no widespread campaign to enforce it.

Yet Christianity spread. Strongest for a century or so in Asia Minor
and Greece, it also took hold in Rome itself and in the western provinces. In some ways the other Hellenistic religions had helped pave the
way. The similarities—the shared concerns with celebrating the mystery, ritual purification, and the promise of an afterlife—made Christianity acceptable. Many found it superior. Central in the religion was
Jesus, a historical rather than a mythical figure, who was enormously
appealing. His teachings as presented in the books soon known as the
Gospels (Greek, *Evangelia*) attracted many. Complete well before the
end of the first century, these were in tone and content elevated—
though written in the language of the people and in a style the *rhetores*
sneered at.

Even Stoicism may be said to have prepared many for acceptance of
Christianity. The new religion contained much of the best in Stoicism
but without its sternness and with the added message of love and
forgiveness. The Christians sometimes made specific appeals to Stoics,
which can be seen in the speech of the Apostle Paul to the Athenians
(Acts 17). An early apologist for Christianity, Justin (ca. 100–167), himself originally a student of several philosophical schools, made such
appeals through comparing and harmonizing Christianity with Stoic
doctrine; he did the same with Platonism. Justin moved to Rome and
taught there for a time until he was denounced to the authorities by a
jealous philosopher rival and tried before the urban prefect Q. Junius
Rusticus, ironically a Stoic himself as well as a teacher of the reigning
emperor, Marcus Aurelius. Recognizing in Justin a broadly educated
person, Rusticus urged him to reject his Christianity. Justin refused.
Imperial policy had not changed; to be a Christian—and to refuse to
recant—was worthy of death. Justin has henceforth been known as
Justin Martyr. At Lugdunum a decade later in Marcus Aurelius' reign,
many persons were tortured and executed in various ways, such as by
wild beasts. In that instance a general public outcry against the Christians had caused the unusual, widespread persecution. Even a Rusticus,
even a Marcus Aurelius would not reconsider the question of whether
the existing law and policy were just; they would only enforce them.

By the time of Tertullian, toward the end of the second century,
Christian literature began to be composed in the style of those trained in

rhetoric. Still, it remained difficult for highly educated people to become Christian. Saint Jerome (who lived in the latter half of the fourth and the early fifth centuries) confessed that his first exposure to Jewish prophetic literature—and doubtless the Christian works as well—repelled him, as he compared them with the incomparable, polished style of Cicero, whose works he loved. Moreover, there was a spiritual gulf between Christian and pagan: much in the Roman world offended the dedicated Christian. The Roman religion inseparably intertwined all sorts of events; the festivals, the games and circuses, the theater, all involved ceremonies the Christian could not be a part of. So strongly did the associations carry over that some Christians argued that flute music was in itself sinful! Everywhere they saw obscenity, loose sexual morals, skepticism, philosophical materialism, and just uncaring hedonism. Some Christians retreated into social isolation. The separationist tendency went back to Jesus; though he advocated obedience to authority (such as in paying taxes), he emphasized something beyond: the kingdom of heaven. Later authors of the books that ultimately comprised the New Testament continued the emphasis. Christians "are not of the world," John quotes Jesus as saying.

Yet the early Christians in some ways not only tolerated the Empire, they approved of it. Jesus had taught men to "render unto Caesar the things that are Caesar's." Paul, who was proud of his Roman citizenship, was quite clear on this point, advocating complete obedience to imperial and local authorities. In many ways devout Christians must have been excellent citizens. Yet intellectually, culturally, and socially, the Christians were in some important ways aliens. "We have not here a lasting city: but we seek one that is to come," wrote the author of the Epistle to the Hebrews. After Nero, largely of necessity, Christians began to set up almost a state within the state made up of people who did not believe in the gods, did not bow down to the emperor or his image, would be inclined not to participate in important governmental institutions—including, for many, the army—and thus generally rejected the whole social and cultural undergirding of the Empire. Tertullian might complain all he wished about Christians being convicted though not guilty of any real crime. To the Roman governing classes they seemed a threat to the whole order of things. And indeed, ultimately they were.

Roman Law: The Classical Period

Just as Roman society from an early period was saturated with religion, so also it was suffused throughout with the law. Literary sources for the period of the kings, even though suspect in detail, indicate that great development of law occurred in that age. The Twelve Tables, traditionally dated to the middle of the fifth century B.C., show the centrality of law to the state in the early Republic. One of the central features of the patron-client system, a social structure that antedated the Republic, illustrates the importance of law even for the lower classes: the major duty of the patron to his client was to represent his interests at law. So familiar were Romans with legal terms and usages that the comic playwrights of the second century B.C., Plautus and Terence, made puns—understood by the common people, one assumes—based on rather obscure legal terminology.

In the centuries after the Twelve Tables, as Rome evolved into a republican empire, the legal system that emerged permitted flexibility and growth to fit the changed situation (see Chapter 5). The sources of law, besides statutes and, informally, senatorial decrees, included the edicts of the various magistrates—the two praetors in Rome, the urban and the peregrine praetors being the most important—as well as the new rulings made possible by the evolution of the formulary system. Roman contact with the laws of other states, especially in the provinces but even in Rome itself, brought modifications as well. These changes are illustrated in Roman commercial law, which developed mostly from Hellenistic models.

In the Empire the sources of law inevitably changed along with the structures through which it was applied, while its theoretical development took new channels as well. The emperor influenced the law both directly and indirectly. Through his *consilium*, for example, he controlled most of what came to the floor of the Senate. The Senate, in fact, became a primary source of new law, since the princeps now enforced its decrees as law: they were, after all, mostly his decrees. The assemblies withered both as elective and as lawmaking bodies, both of these activities being taken over by the Senate. From the time of Augustus, the policy decisions made for those provinces that the emperor directly controlled tended to be applied also in the consular provinces. By the second century if not earlier, the princeps or his agents controlled all the provinces, and a degree of uniformity existed. Imperial opinion—reached with the aid of a growing imperial staff, of course—had the force of law. Imperial edicts such as the famous Constitution of Caracalla in 212, which gave citizenship to all free persons in the Empire, became increasingly important in the high Empire.

Praetors gradually waned in importance as formulators and supervisors of the law and of the courts. By the time of Hadrian, jurists serving as imperial advisers influenced the development of the law more than praetors. By the end of our period, the praetorian prefects in many ways controlled the legal machinery—which explains why several of the prefects were renowned jurists. The edicts, completely stabilized from the time of Hadrian on, were changed only on authority of the emperor. Even outside the imperial bureaucracy, the influence of the principes can be seen. Thus the opinions of certain named jurists were designated by the emperors as authoritative. This practice continued; however, when the procedure was reformulated in the Theodosian Code (438), the jurists named as authoritative were then men long dead.

Some of the classical jurists turned out by the two major (private) schools of law deserve mention. Salvius Julianus was the distinguished lawyer whom Hadrian asked to compile the permanent praetorian edict; Gaius, who flourished in the middle of the same century, drew up a textbook, the *Institutes*, that was tremendously influential then and later, both among Greek and Roman jurists. Papinian (Aemilius Papinianus) capped his legal career with the office of praetorian prefect, which he held from 203 until 212, when he was executed by Caracalla because he did not approve of Caracalla's murder of his brother, Geta. Papinian seems to have been moved by humanitarian concerns, as indeed were many jurists of the period. It is ironic that these great men were formulating legal principles governing universal human rights at a time when the political structure of the Empire was sinking toward absolutism.

Two understudies of Papinian, who seem to have been praetorian prefects at the same time, were Paul (Julius Paulus) and Ulpian (Domitius Ulpianus). Ulpian is usually considered the last of the great classical jurists. Paul's voluminous writings made him famous in his own time. Ulpian had a greater reputation in later times. He is the most quoted of the jurists in the Justinian Digest, about a third of which comes from his works. Both of these jurists were perhaps less original than Papinian; their primary work was that of synthesis—an important aspect in the work of ordering the law.

The great edifice of the law was to be, perhaps, the most important of Rome's bequests to the later world. Most influential in western Europe after the fall of Rome was the Theodosian Code of the early fifth century. But the most imitated and studied code of law in history is the formulation by a group of lawyers headed by Trebonian under the eastern Roman emperor Justinian. The *Corpus Iuris Civilis*, as it is called, issued in 534, contained a Digest of opinions of jurists, the Institutes, a textbook based on Gaius, the Code itself, and the Novels, or newer additions. Studied in medieval and early modern times to the present, this code served as a model for many of the nations of western Europe in the modern age and also for South Africa, Japan, and portions of Canada and the United States. Indirectly the principles of the Roman law, though perhaps not the procedures, have also strongly affected the development of the Anglo-Saxon common law, which is the basis of the legal systems in most English-speaking nations.

The classical period of the development of Roman law came at the very end of the high Empire, when economic and political deterioration was already insidiously at work. When Ulpian was assassinated by some praetorians in 233, the Romans had only two more years of relative peace before the onset of crisis and near chaos that wracked the Roman world for half a century. The structures of law and government that had been so painstakingly erected in the previous centuries were to suffer grievously; yet they stood strong enough to prevent complete collapse. Diocletian and his immediate successors were able to shore up the battered foundations so that the Empire could exist for yet another two hundred years. The law, naturally, did not cease to develop; and indeed much of the actual legislation of the Justinian Code is of later date. But the great age of development based on analysis and formulation of the values inherent in the law was over.

13 Final Centuries: A World in Decline

T HE LATE TWENTIETH CENTURY has seen the decline and near dissolution of the Soviet Union, one of the most extensive states in human history. Such decline has happened many times before, and the causes are often inherent in the internal structure rather than the result of foreign conquest.

The Roman Empire, in its last centuries, faced numerous invasions from without, especially in central and eastern Europe, but its inability to respond adequately related more to internal failure than to external threats. The seeds of ultimate decline had lain from the beginning in the centralization of power at Rome and the gradual destruction of local initiative along with the continual erosion of local freedom. Increasingly top-heavy and inflexible, the central government found itself unable to cope with the serious problems of the age.

So long as the Empire defended the frontiers and maintained internal peace the price, considering the alternatives, may not have been excessive. But the system made it easy, eventually, for pretenders to power to mount civil rebellion and for invading armies to make early headway; no longer were there strong and loyal local government units that might check conspirators or hold off invaders.

The brief civil wars after the deaths of Nero and Commodus had been difficult enough to contain; the convulsions that began with the death of Severus Alexander were complicated by frontier incursions and went on fitfully for half a century. The Sassanid state that bounded the easternmost provinces presented a series of challenges to Rome. The new state was infused with two concepts straight out of the Persia of Darius the Great, seven hundred years before: Zoroastrianism and imperialism. The Sassanids wanted to reconquer all territories that had once been Persian—including Roman Asia Minor, Roman Syria, and Roman Egypt. Other peoples, less civilized but no less determined, awaited only the opportunity to flood across the Roman frontiers on the Danube and the Rhine.

The political, economic, social, and cultural consequences of these internal and external problems changed the Roman world. Diocletian and Constantine managed to restore peace and recover some of what had been lost. Curiously, most citizens of the Roman world still supported this centralized government; none of the occasional rebellions had the character of national uprisings. After Constantine the Empire became Christian, which in turn changed many things, some profoundly. But the patched-up structure could not, after the fourth century, withstand unending barbaric invasions; the Empire broke in two, and at length into several pieces. Some of these fragments long remained important, especially in the east. In the sixth century Justinian, from his base at Constantinople, almost managed to reunify the whole. The effort was too great, though the eastern Empire endured for almost a thousand years. In the west, during the fifth and sixth centuries, the structure collapsed, changed, dissolved—or reappeared in new forms. But Eternal Rome, mother of the nations, was no more.

In this chapter we sketch some of the more important events and discuss broadly the social, economic, and cultural changes that accompanied the decline.

Half a Century of Distress and Disorder (235–284)

Most Romans—certainly those who lived in the larger cities, near the great roads, or along the northern or eastern frontiers—must have felt their world falling apart in the years following the assassination of the last of the Severi in 235. A succession of generals sought and gained transient power through civil wars, invasions disrupted the frontiers, trade virtually collapsed, farming activities declined over broad expanses, inflation turned rampant, and social structures bent to accommodate the new conditions of life.

Many of the more deleterious trends marking this chaotic age had their roots in the earlier Empire; the disorder accelerated their growth. Centralization of power in the emperor during the period approached absolutism: military emperors tended to control the administration just as they controlled their soldiers. Rome remained the ceremonial capital, but the real center of government was located wherever they moved. The emperors could not have conferred with senators far away in Rome even if they had been so minded.

Routine affairs of civil government were dealt with by the bureaucracy. Headed by a class of officials completely dependent on the emperor, it nevertheless functioned as an almost independent entity, not always responsive to the imperial officials who headed its departments.

Septimius Severus had made a drastic change at the top when he gave over to the equestrian order—mostly military men—positions previously reserved for the senatorial nobility. A culmination of this trend may perhaps be discerned in an action attributed by one source to the emperor Gallienus (259–268) of debarring senators from any military command. Actually, it seems, the change was gradual. Though it still meant something to be a Roman senator, by the end of the century the most important positions went to others.

Financial problems that became acute in the recurrent crises of the age had existed earlier. The abandonment of land by tenants, a serious problem, was a feature of an earlier age, for example, though the reasons then surely were only taxes and exactions of landlords, whereas deserted lands now must often have resulted from the depredations of ill-supplied Roman soldiers on the march and, even worse, ravaging by invading semibarbarians. Art, architecture, and literature all suffered in this time of troubles, though they had begun to decline a century before. What all this adds up to is a truism: problems, including weakness of structure, always exist and are accentuated by crises such as civil disorder or foreign war.

Of the Barracks-Room Emperors, as the rulers from Maximinus "Thrax" the Thracian (235–238) to Diocletian (284–305) are called, we know enough about fifteen of them to write short biographies; thumbnail sketches can be put together of about that many more emperors or would-be emperors of this period. But there were yet other claimants to the throne, one of whom is known solely from the coins he struck. Several of these were quite competent and might have enjoyed long reigns in a more peaceful time; a few were, as well, men of culture, fit to have served in the high Empire as principes, "first citizens," rather than as absolutists. We shall look at only a few of these often ephemeral emperors, with their problems, as typical of the whole.

In the seven-year period 238–244 there were seven major claimants to the throne, including Maximinus; Gordian I, the latter's son; and also his grandson. The last three were all proclaimed emperor in 238. Gordian III was only thirteen years old at the time. Maximinus campaigned against the Alamanni east of the Rhine, and against the Dacians and Sarmatians on the Danube frontier. He was killed in 238 before he could respond to a Persian incursion into Roman territory. The Empire he left faced internal financial problems, which Maximinus had temporarily resolved in part through the familiar tactic of confiscating opponents' property. He had also initiated a persecution of Christians, possibly because Alexander had rather favored them.

Gordian III (238–244) became sole emperor now, for both his father and grandfather had been killed earlier. He was under some senatorial influence, and he attempted to reduce somewhat the power of certain imperial administrators, especially the procurators. With the help of a capable praetorian prefect, Timisitheus, he defeated the Persians and coped with other crises. But Timisitheus died and his replacement, a general called Philip the Arab, the son of an Arab sheik, killed Gordian and himself assumed the purple.

Typically in this age, Philip (244–249) was a thorough Roman in spite of his birth. He gave his son the title of Augustus also; and the empress, Otacilia, who figures prominently on the coinage, seems to have been important in his administration. Philip celebrated in 248 the completion of a thousand years since the founding of Rome. It was not an auspicious year. The general who had been sent by Philip to deal with the Goths killed the emperor in 249 and himself took over.

The new emperor was Decius (249–251). All the major problems of the age beset him in his short reign: internal administrative difficulties; financial decline with uncontrollable inflation; invasion, by the Goths in particular; a series of events that would mean the loss of Armenia to Persia; and plague, which again made inroads on the already depleted population. Decius also was reviled by the Christians because he was the first emperor to decide that they represented such a mass of potentially disloyal citizens as to require persecution throughout the Empire to eliminate the internal threat they posed. Citizens everywhere had to appear before local officials, swear sacred allegiance to the emperor, and carry with them signed statements in proof of this obeisance. Those who refused to submit were mostly Christians. Punishment for noncompliance varied with the attitudes of local officials. Christians rejoiced when Decius was killed by the Goths in warfare on the lower Danube.

Overwhelming problems continued to dog the emperors of the next three or four decades. Valerian (253–260) and Gallienus (253–268), father and son, of distinguished family, highly educated, generally competent, faced both a barbarian thrust into Asia Minor that reached even to Ephesus, where the famous temple of Artemis, one of the so-called Seven Wonders of the Ancient World, was destroyed, and a Persian invasion under the energetic King Sapor, which penetrated to Antioch, possibly twice. Valerian lost a large army in upper Mesopotamia and was actually captured (260). The Persians made much of the coup: the image of Valerian on his knees before Sapor appeared on coins and was also engraved on rock-face reliefs.

Gallienus, in the west, could do nothing about the Persians. In 258 the Alamanni had broken into northern Italy itself, breaching the imperial defenses in the north-central area; the Franks, a newly formed tribe, were streaming across the Rhine; and the Saxons on the northern European coasts were beginning to disrupt trade in the English Channel. Meanwhile, a new incursion of Goths across the Lower Danube overran Dacia and parts of Macedonia and Greece; they ravaged even Delphi and Athens. We are told that Gallienus also had to confront eighteen or more challengers to the throne. To add to the general misery brought on by civil and foreign wars, the plague continued to take toll of life through much of his reign.

An official of the trading city of Palmyra in the east, Odenathus, given the title of *dux* by Gallienus, did organize an offensive against Persia, it seems. But soon he called himself king, gaining control of about the eastern third of the Empire. After his death his widow, Zenobia, continued to rule the area as queen. In the west, a general named Postumus both stabilized the Rhine frontier and defeated a pretender to the throne; but then he turned against Gallienus himself and seized control of a large chunk of the western Empire: Gaul, Britain, and Spain.

When Gallienus was assassinated (268) the Empire thus lay in three fragments. Gallienus' successor, Claudius, guided the war against the Goths to victory, earning the surname Gothicus, but died of the plague, which was still endemic, before he could restore the unity of the Empire (270).

Aurelian (270–275), of Danubian peasant stock, through heroic effort reunified the Empire and gained the title Restitutor Orbis. It is astonish-

This coin, an antoninianus (perhaps a double denarius), shows the progress of debasement; its silver content was quite low. The head and the legend are those of Aurelian.

ing how much action he packed into five short years of power. Twice he campaigned against the beautiful Zenobia, finally bringing her back captive to Rome (she was allowed to live out her life in comfort at Tivoli); twice or three times he repelled invasions across the Danube; he checked a threat within Italy again; and finally he recovered the western Gallic Empire for Rome. The wall he built around Rome, portions of which still stand, testifies to the dangers that threatened the capital itself. For the first time an emperor permanently abandoned an imperial province, Dacia. Aurelian hoped to reconquer Mesopotamia, but these plans were cut short by his assassination, followed by civil wars.

Absolutism: Political and Military Recovery Under Diocletian and Constantine (284–337)

Diocletian (284–305), a competent Illyrian, at long last managed to bring other generals under control and to establish lasting rule throughout the Empire. Though he was not a great military commander, he had a certain charisma, a strength of personality, that brought him to the top. Probably most citizens, high and low, realized that the near anarchy of the previous half-century simply could not go on if the Empire was to survive in any form, and it helped that there was somewhat less pressure on the frontiers for a time.

Diocletian held power and survived by making himself an absolutist, not only militarily, but also symbolically, through ceremony, court practice, and even dress. He was rather inaccessible except to trusted subordinates, whom he treated well, giving them great authority and honorific titles. His chief lieutenant, Maximian, was after a time made a partner and, under the title augustus, controlled much of the Empire. Each of the co-emperors had a second in command called a caesar; these men, Constantius Chlorus for Maximian and Galerius for Diocletian, also had separate courts and areas of command. Administratively the Empire was split in half: Diocletian and Galerius held the eastern half, while Maximian and Constantius held the west. Each of the tetrarchs had his own administrative center; none ruled from Rome. Diocletian's headquarters was at Nicomedia in Asia Minor; Galerius chose Sirmium in Pannonia; Maximian, Milan in northern Italy; and Constantius, Trèves in northeastern Gaul. The two praetorian prefects did everything but lead the armies, providing the money and supplies, controlling the bureaucracies, and supervising the administration of justice.

Diocletian reorganized the army, much enlarging it, perhaps from necessity; also of necessity, he used more men originating outside the Empire as soldiers. The cavalry contingents had grown and now comprised a much larger proportion of the military than in earlier ages. Frontiers were much strengthened; the legions, reduced in size, now were stationed farther back from the frontiers for defense in depth. The provinces were increased in number by a reduction in size. Only a few— the oldest, as well as Italy itself—were now ruled by senators. The reorganized provinces were grouped together in dioceses under thirteen vicars. The centralizing tendency continued even though the power at the top was divided among the tetrarchs. Thus local government units lost the functions of road building and recruiting for the army, perhaps gladly. Yet the larger army and the increased central functions—along with the four separate and expensive courts of the tetrarchy—required more money. A reorganized financial and tax structure met the needs.

Diocletian's tetrarchy seems to have been designed with three goals in mind: first, to make possible quicker response to threats across the frontiers; second, to prevent—or quickly eliminate—pretenders to the throne; and finally, to provide for an orderly succession. In the first two purposes the structure proved fairly successful. In the last—the perennial problem of the succession—the structure in the end failed.

Diocletian must have astonished the Roman world when he decided to retire, in 305, and forced Maximian to retire with him. The two caesars, Constantius and Galerius, as planned, became augusti. But instead of allowing each of them then to choose a caesar, Diocletian permitted Galerius, his trusted second in command, to choose both. Galerius left out Constantine the son of Constantius and Maxentius the son of Maximian. A short period saw the following changes: Constantius died and his troops hailed his son, Constantine, as augustus; Maxentius seized power, calling himself augustus, and Maximian came out of retirement to help him; a pretender arose in Egypt who of course called himself augustus, not caesar; and the two caesars appointed by Galerius, Maximinus and Licinius, named themselves augustus also. There were now no less than seven augusti and no caesars at all! At one point Diocletian came out of retirement and settled the competition by force of his personal authority, but soon after arms again prevailed. By 313 only two augusti remained: Constantine, in the west, and Licinius, now controlling the east. Galerius had died of disease in 311; the rest had been eliminated. Constantine defeated Licinius also in 324, and until his death in 337 controlled the whole Empire. The end of the tetrarchy did not mean an end to the division of authority in the Empire. Constantine created four praetorian prefectures, with each prefect exercising civil and judicial powers on delegation from the emperor.

In social and economic policy, Constantine (312–337) followed Diocletian and some of his predecessors. Like them he kept a tight rein on finance, effecting some reforms; he retained and extended restrictions on the careers of private persons, further restricting class mobility. However, in other ways Constantine was an innovator whose actions foreshadowed the future. His religion, of course, was a case in point. As early as 312 he was said to have seen a vision instructing him to use the

Christ-symbol, the Chi-Rho (☧), in the battle of the Milvian Bridge, just north of Rome, against Maxentius. He followed the victory with a declaration of tolerance. Though he retained the pagan trappings of tradition—he was still pontifex maximus—he gradually identified himself with Christianity and became the effective controller of church affairs, even intervening in doctrinal disputes.

In some of his political moves Constantine also set a new pattern. The powers of the praetorian prefects were trimmed, and some of their functions given to palace officials closer to the emperor. The new titles sound like those of the Middle Ages: "master," "count," "chamberlain." It was Constantine who first settled large numbers of the semibarbarian tribesmen, Sarmatians and Goths, in Roman territory—though on a smaller scale, of course, such settlements had been going on for centuries. And Constantine's new city, Constantinople, in the east on the site of ancient Byzantium, symbolized the coming demise of the west as well as the continuation of the eastern Empire, with the new capital its headquarters.

It is not difficult to find the reasons for Constantine's decision to find a new site for his second capital. Rome had not functioned as a true political and military capital for years; geographically it no longer suited. Moreover, in that city—now more like a museum than the center of the Empire—the past no longer served to instruct the present and make men wise for the future. As Constantine saw it, Rome's pagan past lay over everything like a web, obstructing, deadening. The emperor was never happy there, though for some years he built within the city, notably the basilica begun by Maxentius as well as various Christian churches, including the first St. Peter's. But the aristocracy and the urban crowd both disliked him, in part because of his religion. When he refused to carry out the time-honored ceremonies to Jupiter Optimus Maximus, it seemed to the Romans, most of them still loyal to old Rome, that he profaned and displayed unpatriotic disloyalty to the greatness of Rome past, and perhaps even endangered the city and the state. Constantinople was geographically better sited for rule and for defense, and it was also a place Constantine could mold into a capital of his liking, with his stamp—and of his building.

The Economy to the Time of Constantine

Unending civil struggles compounded by barbarian invasions and other wars, such as with the Persians, plus plague and a whole series of connected problems had produced a most serious effect on the Roman economy.

It is often not understood on what precarious foundations the ancient economy rested, how small dislocations might produce profoundly depressing effects. The class of the rich was always quite small. The great majority of persons, whether rural or urban, lived at the subsistence level. Most of their income went for food, most of the rest for rent. Any considerable drop in production for any cause, naturally producing higher prices for basic commodities, would immediately wipe out any extra buying power the ordinary person might have. All available money would have to go for food; there would be none left over to buy other necessities, let alone anything like luxuries. Thus, only a small percentage increase in food prices reacted on the rest of the economy. In antiquity, war often stifled agricultural production and forced up prices, accounting for the familiar pattern: war, famine, pestilence.

Businessmen and traders of all sorts also suffered in the often chaotic situations of the third century. Even earlier, trade had dropped off because of restrictions as well as a growing network of customs stations, which had expanded as a means of shoring up declining revenues. The rich were less affected than the poor, of course, by rises in food costs, since only a small percentage of their income went for basic foodstuffs. They were adversely affected financially, nonetheless, by other economic problems. Rich landowners often suffered along with the small holders, especially those with villas along the great military roads. Marching armies, often ill equipped, "requisitioned" food for their needs—and perhaps "liberated" a few other choice possessions at the same time. These requisitions were obligations on the state and technically legal (more or less), but in this age seldom paid. Rostovtzeff saw in the depredations of the soldiers deliberate class warfare, the lower-class soldiers intentionally preying on the rich. Probably that interpretation is wrong, but the effects were the same. Such ravaging of farms was especially prevalent in the provinces along the Danube, but it occurred in other places too. Those lucky enough to reside in provinces that were relatively unaffected did well, however. Africa, for example, declined little in its economy. In fact, higher prices for farm products may have actually allowed farmers there to do better for a time. Even in the affected provinces, the state kept certain basic activities going: the iron mines in Noricum, for instance, continued to work busily, for obvious reasons. That province was, however, less disturbed by military depredations than others in the Danube region.

The problem of abandonment of land intensified still further in this period. The passage of armies, friendly as well as unfriendly, partly accounts for the mounting seriousness of depopulation; repeated depredation would discourage anyone. Some land, long mistreated by overcropping without rest, manuring, or crop rotation, or by deforestation followed by erosion, lapsed into unproductiveness. Actual underpopulation may also have been a factor. The government, over two or three centuries, tried to deal with abandonment in several ways. Sometimes tax advantages were offered to those who put such land back in production, or individuals were given land not theirs if they farmed it. Landowners with contiguous holdings were occasionally forced to cultivate some of the deserted acreage. Decurions of nearby towns might be saddled with the burden of seeing to it that abandoned lands were worked.

The large farms, now more and more centered on the villas of the landowners, tended out of necessity to become more self-sufficient. This tendency, too, had affected rural life for a century or more. Even earlier, on the great slave-manned farms of the late Republic and early Empire, operations had begun to be diversified somewhat in order to make more efficient use of slaves, who had to be fed, clothed, and housed year-round. Now, however, in a development that would extend into medieval times, the great farms grew still more self-sufficient, not only in farming and local manufacturing, but also in self-protection. Large landowners sometimes managed to withdraw their lands from the jurisdiction of the local city-states that were the imperial administrative units. Such actions contributed to the economic and political debilitation of the urban centers. By the end of the third century many towns, especially in the northern provinces, had begun to move from the valleys to the hilltops in order to survive in a time of invasions and despoliation. Such fortified towns would be characteristic in the centuries to follow.

Accelerated Debasement of the Coinage

Coins provide our most conspicuous evidence for the financial distress of the Empire in the third century. Here, too, the first steps toward decline had been taken long before, when Nero first debased the silver and lightened both the silver denarii and the gold aurei. Some further debasement of the silver and lightening of the gold coins occurred even during the palmy days of the second century. At the beginning of the civil wars in 235 B.C. the denarius contained no more than half the silver it had had from the Second Punic War to Nero, and the aureus by now contained only fractionally more than half the gold. A new coin, the antoninianus, first issued by the Severi, from the beginning contained less silver in proportion to the denarius than its face value, which was apparently two denarii.

The emperors of the third century were forced to debase the money rapidly. By the time of Gallienus, a few years after the middle of the century, the antoninianus contained only about 5 percent of silver, and before the end of the century it had only a silver wash—extremely thin plating—on it. Often one must look carefully at surviving specimens with a magnifying glass to see the particles of silver still clinging, in protected places, to the base metal. Gresham's Law—the principle that bad money drives out good—certainly applies to the period. At the same

time, a loss of confidence in the whole monetary structure resulted in
runaway inflation and a return to barter, that is, payment in goods
instead of money, in areas all over the Empire. (Though of course in
many rural areas it is likely that barter had never ceased to be the chief
means of exchange, at least in the local markets.) This situation naturally compounded difficulties for traders, businessmen, and moneylenders as well as agents of the government itself.

Part of the reason for debasement of the coinage was a shortage of
silver and gold bullion, which may have been a problem even in the
high Empire; not enough existed any longer to make possible a volume
of currency equal to the money-supply demands of government and the
economy. We have little data, but the Spanish and other mines no longer
produced precious metals in the quantities of earlier centuries. Wars
and attendant disorders may also have reduced the output of the mines.

Sharp inflation followed from the practice of each short-lived ruler
to try to solve some of his financial problems by melting down old coins
and producing a larger number of new ones with the same face value but
less metal value. The inflation reflected the fact that people all over the
Empire refused to accept the money at its previous face value, in the
marketplace, at any rate—refusing an agent of the emperor accompanied by a squad of soldiers, or even refusing a soldier, required more
courage. In our own twentieth century, though the concept of fiat money
is accepted, its value drops when there is a lack of confidence in the
government or the economy. In antiquity the public would accept the
smaller bronze or copper coins as fiat money but insisted on intrinsic
value in the basic currency. Some of the evidence on relative values of
gold and silver in that age seems almost incomprehensible. Gold seems
to have been driven out of circulation. Yet the Price Edict of Diocletian
and other information indicates a price ratio of one to six for gold and
silver as compared to about one to twelve in the early Empire. Perhaps
the continuous attempt to overvalue the silver in the coins through
debasement was more successful than is sometimes thought. That is, the
"silver" coins circulated at a face value far above their intrinsic value,
despite constant change.

Economic Recovery

Heroic efforts made in the age of recovery under Diocletian and Constantine did much to restore the economy and the coinage; however, the
economy benefited more from internal peace and a restoration of the
frontiers than from any economic measures taken by the emperors.
Some serious wars continued to be fought, and in the years of Constantine's rise to power there was again internal civil conflict; yet nothing
like the chaos of the previous century returned. Breathing spells allowed economic revival between crises.

The absolutist character of the policies intended to stabilize the shattered Empire has already been pointed out. Diocletian attempted price and wage controls in his famous edict of 301, which seems to have been promulgated, however, only in the eastern half of the Empire. We may doubt that this attempt to put ceilings on prices and wages was very successful. Yet it may have had some effect, even if only to stem what we now term an "inflation psychology." Diocletian also reorganized the tax structure. A new assessment method was devised for lands and crops—again used particularly in the eastern part of the Empire—employing new land production units called *iuga*. The size of each *iugum* varied with the quality of the land and its use, whether it was planted in crops, vineyards, or orchards.

Diocletian introduced a new coinage system, based chiefly on gold coins weighing sixty to the Roman pound; there was also a new silver coin a little lighter than the denarius of the high Empire. The term *denarius* continued to be applied to the copper coins with a silver wash, of two or more sizes with face values of two and five denarii. To be sure, smaller bronze coins were minted also. Testimony that Diocletian could not find enough gold and silver to effect a return to a money economy is seen in the tax system: taxes could be paid in kind and apparently were indeed collected in goods rather than money in many sections of the Empire.

Since Diocletian also reorganized and enlarged the army, and since his political system, involving multiple courts under the two augusti and two caesars must have been considerably more expensive than before, there was continued pressure for higher imperial taxes and for required services of all kinds from the provincial citizens and towns. Some later legislation would seem to imply that Diocletian, in spite of his fairer tax system, went about the business of tax collection in the usual inexorable fashion: we hear of imprisonments, lashings, and tortures—which, of course, may have been common in earlier ages.

Constantine in general followed Diocletian's economic policies. He minted a gold coin called the solidus at seventy-two to the pound (as well as fractional gold) in sufficient quantity to make it the basis of the monetary system, as it was for centuries. Some bullion Constantine got from confiscated temple treasuries—one of the benefits of a Christian viewpoint? He issued silver coins rated at one twenty-fourth of the solidus. Constantine also came up with new taxes, imposing one on the nobility and another, collected only on special occasions, on most groups in the cities. Landowners, who paid taxes on their land, did not pay this latter tax, and there were some special exemptions: teachers, for example. But most others, including even prostitutes, paid. The state increasingly controlled directly many features of the economic sphere that had formerly been contracted out, including mining, collection of customs duties, construction of storage facilities, and actual manufacture as well as distribution of uniforms to the armies. Constantine's income was sufficient, as already implied, to permit him to continue the military and political changes begun by Diocletian, to build the city of Constantinople, and to put up numerous large churches and other structures in many places.

Society to the Time of Constantine

The rule of the military emperors during the middle of the third century caused some social changes and hastened others. The senatorial nobility, which had declined in prestige under the Severi, became even less influential. With important military commands no longer open to members of the Senate, they now governed only a few of the oldest provinces. Yet vestiges of the old power remained, and in the next century Constantine would find it useful to revive the order to a degree. Perhaps, like Augustus in an earlier age, he had either to revive and use the older aristocracy or to create a new one to help him administer the Empire.

The body of upper-level army officers during the third century became virtually a military nobility, increasing vastly in numbers and importance. Its members held the military commands that once were the preserve of the Senate. But the group was diffuse and hardly constituted an order in the old sense. Promotion from the ranks, at least the ranks of the centurions, possible even in the early Empire, was now common, and such men could reach higher office—even the throne itself, if fortune favored them.

Almost everywhere in this age of disorder, the local nobility, the class that furnished the decurions for the city-states that were still the component units of the Empire, suffered badly. Service in city offices and on these city councils once had brought great prestige, and if some expense was involved it was yet worthwhile because of the honor local office brought. But formerly voluntary contributions to towns or cities—indeed, the offices themselves—became obligatory, as did service as decurions. The imperial duties of these councillors grew and became most onerous: they collected taxes, furnished recruits for the armies (until Diocletian, although they could collect cash as a substitute in the case of Jews and some others), and performed other tasks. Members of the decurion class—the list of eligibles drawn up according to a property qualification varying from region to region—began to try to escape service in every possible way. Those in the higher service of the state, most private entrepreneurs who bid on state contracts, and certain professionals such as teachers and physicians were officially exempted. Some escaped by entering these ranks. Others moved away to areas where they might not be listed in the census, at least for a time. Laws and decrees attempted to deal with the situation. Under penalty for infraction, the decurions were forbidden to move from their home city-states. The rank, with its inherent obligations, was made hereditary. As a group, then, this class suffered heavily and diminished in numbers.

By contrast, the class of large rural landholders grew in importance and influence. The great landholders had once been mostly city inhabitants, absentee landowners. Now many removed themselves from the cities and established themselves as a rural nobility, what would become the class of manorial landlords of the Middle Ages.

What of the lower classes? The age of disorder ruined many traders, great and small, but in some places they continued as before. Such men were resilient; even in troubled areas they might serve imperial purposes by supplying the armies, or by purchasing spoils from the soldiers or furnishing them with personal supplies. With the return of peace under Diocletian their number would increase. Their activities in the late Empire were hampered by more and higher customs, collected by venal lower-level officials who looked out for themselves. And much of the old international trade doubtless was gone. Still, this group seems to have made a reasonable recovery with the return of order.

Many members of the lower classes found opportunity in the larger armies of this period. Even in the high Empire a large percentage of those who had enlisted in the auxiliary units came not from the lowest classes in the provinces, but from the middle group of the fairly well-to-do. In an age in which soldiers acquired more and more privileges, the tendency must have been accentuated. Perhaps youths of the lowest social classes now enlisted in the ethnic units, which served with the Roman armies as low-paid mercenaries. Such units, hired by Julius Caesar and perhaps some earlier generals, were increasingly employed by the emperors.

Many lower-class persons found their freedom restricted in various ways. Social mobility had been a characteristic of the early Empire, as the Christian New Testament indicates. Restrictions began to appear by the time of the Severi, and Diocletian and Constantine stiffened them: membership in the craft guilds, once voluntary, became obligatory. Men were "frozen" in their occupations and their children had to be trained in their fathers' crafts. Mobility was drastically reduced.

Much is heard of a new class, the half-free *coloni*, which, made up of tenants who worked the great farms all over the Empire, was not so new really. Tenancy had always existed, even in the early Republic, and when great farms became common in the middle to late Republic, tenancy was an alternative for the large landholders to slave-manned operations. Though no quantitative conclusions can be drawn it appears that, after a time of relative stability, considerable numbers of landlords had begun to supply their labor needs by turning increasingly to tenants and away from slaves from the second century onward. A possible reason was a decreased availability of relatively cheap slaves suitable for rough labor on the land. In the early period, such slaves had come in mainly as captives from the semicivilized areas that bounded the Empire on the east and north. Slaves were later kidnaped and sold—illegally—in the Roman markets. Slaves were of course also bred, but these were likely to be given at least a minimal education and trained for high-level positions; they were too valuable to be employed as farm laborers. Tenancy may also have been attractive because it required less capital investment; but then it may also have produced less profit than a slave-manned farm under good management. But, for whatever reasons, the use of tenants in place of slaves on the land gradually increased.

Another facet of tenant farming is frequently overlooked. The economic condition of tenants was often worse than that of slaves, who had to be kept healthy if they were to be profitable. Tenants had to look out for themselves. Nor were tenants always altogether free before the development of the *coloni*. Tenant farmers in all ages tend to get in debt, most commonly to the owner of the land. Once in debt, the tenant is no longer really free. Roman laws of debt, more severe than our own, required that a debt-ridden tenant work for his landlord until he paid the last denarius—which, often, was never. So grew the nucleus of the "new" class, the *coloni*. Freeholders in this uncertain age voluntarily bargained away their property in return for protection and a guarantee of specific rights in connection with the land, rights that were hereditary. We recognize the *coloni* immediately as the forerunners of medieval serfs.

The *coloni* did not, all at one time or in one century, become everywhere the dominant rural lower class. Moreover, aspects of this very complicated and various development have not been touched on: for example, the situation of the great imperial estates on which much of the development occurred. But these paragraphs do give some indication of the evolution of this important change in rural society.

Religion in a Time of Troubles

In retrospect we know that one of the more significant developments of the period of the middle and late Roman Empire was the rise of Christianity. Since it grew most rapidly as the Empire declined, in the third century and after, it has often been suggested, first by contemporary non-Christians, that Christianity contributed to the decline. If not overplayed, the point has some validity. Many Christians were comfortable as a part of Eternal Rome, but others felt themselves to be aliens in a world of false gods; their loyalty was to the church, not the Empire. Though not revolutionaries, many believed that God would bring an end to wicked Rome, and they were hardly distressed at the prospect.

The causes of imperial decline, however, were many, and Christianity seems to have played only a relatively minor role. Civil wars,

famine, plague, barbarian invasions—no complete list of the ills beset-
ting the Empire—had little to do with Christianity. Indeed, it may be
that these factors caused Christianity itself to flourish in an "age of
anxiety," as it has been called, rather than vice versa. The age brought
with it a wave of pessimism, of disillusionment with the Empire if not
the world itself, a felt need for a safe retreat for mind and spirit. The
trend is clearly seen in philosophy. Marcus Aurelius' *Meditations* ex-
press devotion to duty, but without optimism and without hope.
Plotinus, who in the third century advocated a system of philosophical
mysticism called Neoplatonism, saw man as a microcosm of all that is—
God or the One or the Good. For Plotinus, unification with "the Good"
of Plato, achieved—though rarely—through education, training, and
exercise of the will, was the highest human attainment. Nothing in the
physical world deserved such attention and effort.

The traditional religion changed too in the time of troubles. New
gods from the east, often combined syncretically with the older deities,
attained high status. In the early third century the emperor Elagabalus
united the sun god of Emesa, from whom he took his name, and all the
other major deities connected with the sun, into one cult. The same
Syrian god, Sol Invictus, had become the chief deity of the state—
though not exactly displacing Jupiter—by action of Aurelian and suc-
ceeding emperors of the latter half of the first century. Closely con-

Cult statuary of the Mithraic religion: Mithra killing the sacred bull, from
which he created the earth and all life. (*Alinari/Art Resource, New York*)

nected was Mithra, whose worship was most popular in the army. In this age Mithraism spread perhaps as rapidly as Christianity. The most appealing religions of the time abounded in mystery and mysticism.

As always in the pagan cults, the new deities could be worshiped along with the old; the cults were not exclusivistic. Devotees did indeed speak of Mithra as the "only god," but everyone understood that they meant only that all the gods were somehow comprehended in the conception of Mithra, and no one could be offended. Modern scholars often state that the efforts to combine similar gods or to unify pagan religions indicate the decline of paganism in the period. But the thesis that paganism was dying is difficult to demonstrate from contemporary evidence. The disordered age did cause a search for new gods and new ways of finding inner peace; several of the pagan cults seem, however, to have been well adapted to meet those needs.

The third century saw the instigation of great persecutions throughout the Empire aimed at wiping out Christianity, root and branch. Begun by Decius in mid-century and continued with varying intensity by most of the following emperors until just before the death of Galerius in 311, the campaigns harried, hounded, and sometimes slew Christians for their beliefs. Christian intolerance of pagan beliefs bred a virulent retaliatory hatred of Christianity. Christians were accused of cannibalism, especially of eating babies (through a distorted understanding of the Communion service); they were called atheists (as in a sense they were) and haters of mankind; they were labeled as skulking, hiding, and secretive; they were said to dishonor the emperor. Perhaps most important, they were blamed for all the evils that wracked the state. Tertullian, the Christian apologist of the second century, had noted even then how ready Romans were to shout "Christians to the lions!" when any disaster hit the state, from the flooding of the Tiber to earthquake or drought.

An antoninianus of the emperor Decius, the first ruler to persecute Christians throughout the whole Empire. He wears a radiate crown, symbol of the sun god.

In this time of troubles people found plenty of reasons to view with dark suspicion any group that might have displeased the gods and so brought down their wrath.

Thoughtful intellectuals by the late second century had begun to attack Christianity, though earlier such persons had given little attention to a cult they thought insignificant. Celsus in the second century and Porphyry in the third exemplify the pagan intellectuals who launched full-scale attempts to tear down the new religion by reason and ridicule, pointing out inconsistencies, contradictions, or impossibilities. Christian intellectuals answered in kind. Origen of Alexandria (ca. 185–254), in particular, not only replied; far more than Justin a century before, Origen provided a rational-philosophical basis for the Judeo-Christian faith. In any case, these attacks by pagan scholars and the responses of Origen and others little affected the growth of Christianity, which had slight appeal for intellectuals, though some were included in its ranks. For a long period, few from the upper classes converted. Enough educated members of the middle levels of society converted to provide leadership for some of the urban congregations; most Christians, however, were drawn from the lower classes. Some of the latter, indeed, were educated, but in a pragmatic, not an academic, sense. Most citizens paid little attention to the polemics of either side. Those who adopted the new religion did so because they accepted its relatively simple message of redemption from sin and salvation.

Celsus and Porphyry saw the evolving structure of the Christian church as a dangerous state within the state and leveled a charge of divided loyalty that would continue to plague the church in its relations with civil authorities for centuries, even after it became predominant in Europe. Neither of these learned opponents of the Christians sought their persecution, however. Nevertheless, a strong popular aversion to Christianity expressed itself in a demand for suppression as in the persecution in Lugdunum in the 170s, when an angry crowd might have wiped out all the local Christians had the provincial government not checked it.

The emperors of the high Empire, along with their officers and advisers, might indeed deplore what they considered the ignorance and obstinacy of the Christians, yet they did not seriously think them responsible for the natural or other disasters that befell the state, and they did not initiate any fierce, sweeping persecution. Many of the military emperors of the troubled third century, however, by no means aristocratic intellectuals, came of the same stock as the superstitious pagans who cried out for the blood of the Christians at Lugdunum. Some of those emperors may really have believed that that terrible age of disaster upon disaster that never seemed to end might reflect the wrath of the gods for some great affront—perhaps by the Christians. Such emperors might have felt duty-bound to free the state of so sacrilegious, blasphemous, and dangerous a group.

The persecutions did not succeed, of course, in eradicating the sect. The task was by then impossible: there were too many Christians, some of them in positions to protect the rest. And as the Christian historian Eusebius later wrote, the blood of the Christians was the seed of the church. At length came surcease of persecution and then the first Christian emperor, Constantine.

With official recognition, Christianity faced different problems. Already schisms had occurred and heresies had arisen; Tertullian himself had succumbed to one of these, Montanism. Gnosticism, in various forms, now often divided the Christian communities. Constantine attempted, at the Council of Nicaea in 325, to suppress the Arian heresy and so to settle one of the most difficult of numerous controversies over the nature of Christ, with only partial success. One of his own sons later became an Arian, in fact.

The history of both the growth of the church in structure and doctrine and the changes that came with the recognition of Christianity as the official state religion under Theodosius the Great toward the end of the fourth century—all this belongs more properly to the study of the Middle Ages than of Rome. The reign of Constantine essentially marks the end of the Roman period. The Christianized Greco-Roman culture that followed in the Middle Ages forms the core of Western civilization today.

14 Sequel: Heritage

Collapse of the Empire in the West

AFTER THE DEATH of Constantine the Great the Empire was for a time ruled by his three sons. The familiar pattern of the general who gained power and established a dynasty thus continued. A nephew, Julian, who ruled 360–363 after the death of the last son, was called the Apostate by the Christians because he attempted to restore a united and rather Neoplatonic religion that he named Hellenism. He also reduced the privileges of Christians, who, for example, were forbidden to hold professorships on the ground that they could not possibly understand and teach the traditional literature and culture. But the setback was temporary; under the general-become-emperor Theodosius (the Christians called him "the Great"), 379–395, Christianity became the official religion. Christians now often themselves became persecutors of pagans; they destroyed or made churches of temples; sometimes they destroyed synagogues as well. The growing influence of churchmen in the west is well illustrated by the power that Ambrose, bishop of Milan, exercised over Theodosius. Twice he excluded the emperor from the privileges of the church until he repented of acts that Ambrose disapproved of.

All during the fourth century barbarian tribes put constant pressure on the northern frontiers. In 378, at the fateful battle of Adrianople in Thrace, the heavy-armed cavalry of the Goths inflicted a disastrous defeat on the Roman legions, killing Valens, the emperor who led them. The Roman army was consequently reorganized over a long period, with greater dependence on heavy cavalry—a portent of the military structure of medieval feudalism. Goths now settled within the bounds of the Empire in large numbers, unassimilated and occasionally moving about, to the distress of the local population and the government, particularly in the west. Franks had earlier been allowed to settle west of the Rhine.

At the death of Theodosius the Empire was permanently divided between his two sons. Under Honorius in the west the legions were withdrawn from the province of Britain, which was then cast adrift, in order to defend Italy from a mixed group of invaders. Conducting the defense in these years—at times brilliantly—and in effect ruling the west was the general Stilicho, ironically himself of German descent, as were many of the soldiers by now. Honorius established his administrative capital at Ravenna, which was more easily defended than Rome or Milan (which had been a center of government in the west since Diocletian). Rome itself was taken and sacked during his reign by the Visigoths under Alaric in 410 but, fortunately, the city was not ravaged. Almost exactly eight hundred years had passed since Rome had last fallen, to the Gauls.

In this century much of the west was taken over by the invading or simply immigrating barbarians, who settled down and established kingdoms in the former provinces. In Britain the Picts, Scots, Angles, Saxons, and Jutes were soon in substantial occupation. The Vandals moved across Gaul into Spain, and finally into North Africa. They were besieging Carthage as Saint Augustine, bishop of Hippo, wrote the last of his *City of God*. Augustine's disintegrating universe surely influenced his theology. The Visigoths first occupied southern Gaul and then moved into Spain. From Africa, under Genseric, the Vandals descended on Rome by sea in 455 and the city was sacked again, this time thoroughly and brutally. The government had been neither passive nor altogether ineffective against the flood of invasions. The general Aëtius, under Valentinian III (who was assassinated just before the Vandals captured Rome), had achieved a spectacular victory against odds at Chalons in Gaul in 451 over the most terrifying invaders of all, the Huns, led by their fierce king, Attila.

Mosaic from Carthage, depicting a Vandal horseman. (*Reproduced by Courtesy of the Trustees of the British Museum, London*)

But the resources of the western Empire in money and especially men were no longer equal to the overwhelming task. Franks, Burgundians, and others occupied Gaul and the Ostrogoths northern Italy. In the view of many historians, the takeover of the western Empire by a German general, Odoacer, in 476 marked the end of the Roman Empire. That date serves as well as any, though Odoacer was Romanized and surely a more effective ruler than the last of the "Roman" emperors, the shadowy Romulus Augustulus, whom he deposed. Even Theodoric, the king of the Ostrogoths who supplanted Odoacer in Italy in 493 (with the approval of Zeno, emperor of the eastern Empire at the time) was hardly a barbarian; he had been exposed to Greco-Roman culture at Constantinople as a youth.

The eastern Empire yet held its ground; it would survive for another millennium, until Constantinople at last fell to the Turks in 1453. One of the eastern emperors, Justinian (527–565), the codifier of Roman law, made a valiant attempt to reconquer the west and for a time held Italy and large parts of North Africa and Spain. But the successor kingdoms of the Vandals, Visigoths, Franks, Ostrogoths, and others, continued, each adopting Roman ways and institutions in modified form. The concept of a great, unified state—a legacy of Eternal Rome—lived on, seen ideally now as embracing all Christendom. Charlemagne saw himself as the restorer of the Roman state in 800 when he took the old title, Emperor of the Romans; so did his successors in the Holy Roman Empire until Napoleon put an end to that particular conceit in 1806.

Assessing the Decline and Fall

In modern times Rome has interested all sorts of persons, not only historians. Poets, columnists, and politicians have been powerfully stirred by the crumbling of this great Empire. The most famous historical examination of the demise is that of Edward Gibbon in his renowned *Decline and Fall of the Roman Empire*. Though he took into account a number of factors, his basic conclusion was that the Empire's fall was a "triumph of Christianity and Barbarism." In the two centuries and more since Gibbon, many other factors have been suggested as the primary cause of the collapse. It has been laid to climatic change; to soil erosion or exhaustion, coupled with the rise of malaria in the choked mouths of rivers; to manpower shortage owing to plague and various other disasters; to a leveling process in education that diluted its quality; to a failure of nerve and a decline of patriotism; and, in the 1970s (by a scientist and a sociologist), to the decline in production of precious metals and to lead in the diet from water pipes and wine vessels (which in theory caused sterility, so that the population did not reproduce itself). New theories explaining the fall of Rome continue to be advanced; often the speculation relates to current problems that seem all but insolvable.

Readers of this volume will understand that the total problem of Rome's fall is very complex; no simple explanation exists, and many considerations must be taken into account. They will thus be able to discount the frequent, groundless predictions of impending doom that are inevitably based on a partial, biased, or even ignorant view of Roman history. But doomsday prophets notwithstanding, students of Roman history are also acutely aware that great states do indeed decline and fall.

The Roman Heritage

Every educated person is at least somewhat aware of the Roman legacy to the modern world. Aspects of the culture of the Near East and of Greece were passed on to later civilizations through Rome—indeed, one of the greatest contributions of the Romans was their role in transmitting the civilization of other parts of the ancient world. But Rome made original contributions as well, along with refinements of older achievements. The Latin language not only evolved into each of the Romance languages (Italian, French, Spanish, Portuguese, Romanian), but also provided at least half the vocabulary of English, the single most important modern tongue. Any survey of the great literature of the world would surely include some Latin selections. Roman law, surviving in the eastern Roman Empire, in the successor states in the west, and in the canon law of the Roman Catholic Church, has powerfully influenced legal systems in much of the modern world. Roman political ideas swayed not only Charlemagne and his successors in the Holy Roman Empire but many others as well: the founding fathers of the United States of America were profoundly influenced by the Roman political experience. Some of Rome's architectural and engineering know-how disappeared in the Middle Ages, but much continued, especially in the design and building of the great medieval churches, which developed from the Roman basilica. Until only the last few decades, most large public buildings erected in the United States (and elsewhere in the Western world) included Roman features. Christianity, though Near Eastern in origin, was much influenced, particularly in organizational structure and to some degree in outlook, by the Roman experience.

The world today—Europe, the Americas, and much of the rest—would be a very different place if the Mediterranean basin had been dominated not by Rome but by, say, the Carthaginians or one of the eastern peoples such as the Parthians or the Sassanid Persians or even Alexander the Great. But Alexander died young, before he could satiate his boundless ambition or firmly establish the empire he conquered, and the Carthaginians too long failed to see that the Romans were to be their indomitable foes. So by chance, good fortune, design, and resolve—all the kaleidoscopic elements Roman history comprises—it was the Romans who became our direct cultural ancestors. And so it is that every citizen of the United States encounters some form of Roman influence, some portion of our Roman heritage, with each passing day.

Select Bibliography

General Works

BALSDON, J. P. V. D. Romans and Aliens. Chapel Hill, 1979.

BROUGHTON, T. R. S. Edition of T. Mommsen. The Provinces of the Roman Empire. Chicago, 1968.

BRUNT, P. A. Italian Manpower, 225 B.C.–A.D. 14. Oxford, 1971.

COOK, S. A., et al. The Cambridge Ancient History. 1st ed., vols. vii–xii, Cambridge, 1928–1939. 2d ed., vols. iii–viii, 1982–1989.

FINLEY, M. I. Aspects of Antiquity. London, 1968.

GARZETTI, A. From Tiberius to the Antonines: A History of the Roman Empire, A.D. 14–192. London, 1974.

GRUEN, E. S. The Last Generation of the Roman Republic. Berkeley, 1974.

———. The Hellenistic World and the Coming of Rome. 2 vols. Berkeley, 1984.

JONES, A. H. M. The Later Roman Empire, 284–602: A Social, Economic, and Administrative Survey. 3 vols. Oxford, 1964.

MILLAR, F. The Emperor in the Roman World (31 B.C.–A.D. 337). Ithaca, 1977.

———, D. BERCIU, R. N. FRYE, G. KOSSACK, AND T. T. RICE. The Roman Empire and Its Neighbors. New York, 1967.

PETIT, P. Pax Romana. Berkeley, 1976.

ROSTOVTZEFF, M. I. Social and Economic History of the Roman Empire. 2 vols. Oxford, 1957.

SEAGER, R., ed. The Crisis of the Roman Republic. Cambridge, 1969.

SHERWIN-WHITE, A. N. The Roman Citizenship. 2d ed. Oxford, 1973.

SMITH, R. E. The Failure of the Roman Republic. Cambridge, 1955.

STARR, C. G. Civilization and the Caesars: The Intellectual Revolution in the Roman Empire. Ithaca, 1954.

STEVENSON, G. H. Roman Provincial Administration. New York, 1939.

SYME, R. The Roman Revolution. Oxford, 1939.

TALBERT, R. J. A. The Senate of Imperial Rome. Princeton, 1987.

Archaeology, Architecture, Construction

ASHBY, T. The Aqueducts of Ancient Rome. Oxford, 1935.

BLAKE, M. E. Ancient Roman Construction in Italy from the Prehistoric Period to Augustus. Washington, D.C., 1947.

———. Roman Construction in Italy from Tiberius Through the Flavians. Washington, D.C., 1959.

———, and D. T. BISHOP. Roman Construction in Italy from Nerva Through the Antonines. Philadelphia, 1973.

BOETHIUS, A. and J. B. WARD-PERKINS. Etruscan and Roman Architecture. Harmondsworth, Eng., 1970.

BRILLIANT, R. Pompeii A.D. 79: The Treasure of Rediscovery. New York, 1979.

BROWN, F. Roman Architecture. New York, 1961.

Deiss, J. *Herculaneum: Italy's Buried Treasure.* Rev. ed. New York, 1985.

Lanciani, R. *Ancient Rome in the Light of Recent Discoveries.* New York, 1895.

MacKendrick, P. L. *The Iberian Stones Speak: Archaeology in Spain and Portugal.* New York, 1969.

———. *The Mute Stones Speak: The Story of Archaeology in Italy.* New York, 1960.

———. *Roman France.* New York, 1972.

———. *Romans on the Rhine: Archaeology in Germany.* New York, 1970.

McKay, A. G. *Houses, Villas and Palaces in the Roman World.* Ithaca, 1975.

Richmond, I. A. *The City Walls of Imperial Rome.* Oxford, 1930.

Todd, M. *The Walls of Rome.* Totowa, N.J., 1978.

Von Hagen, V. W. *The Roads That Led to Rome.* New York, 1967.

Ward-Perkins, J., and A. Claridge. *Pompeii A.D. 79.* New York, 1978.

Wells, C. M. *The German Policy of Augustus: An Examination of the Archaeological Evidence.* Oxford, 1972.

Biography

Africa, T. W. *Rome of the Caesars.* New York, 1965.

Astin, A. E. *Cato the Censor.* Oxford, 1978.

———. *Scipio Aemilianus.* Oxford, 1967.

Balsdon, J. P. V. D. *Julius Caesar.* New York, 1967.

Barrett, A. A. *Caligula: The Corruption of Power.* New Haven, 1990.

Birley, A. *Marcus Aurelius: A Biography.* Rev. ed. New Haven, 1987.

———. *Septimius Severus: The African Emperor.* Rev. ed. New Haven, 1989.

Boren, H. C. *The Gracchi.* New York, 1969.

Bowersock, G. W. *Augustus and the Greek World.* Oxford, 1965.

Charlesworth, M. P. *Five Men: Character Studies from the Roman Empire.* Cambridge, Mass., 1936.

Gelzer, M. *Caesar: Politician and Statesman.* Cambridge, Mass., 1968.

Grant, M. *Cleopatra.* London, 1972.

———. *Julius Caesar.* New York, 1969.

———. *Nero, Emperor in Revolt.* New York, 1970.

———. *The Twelve Caesars.* New York, 1975.

Griffin, M. *Nero: The End of a Dynasty.* New Haven, 1985.

Hadas, M. *Sextus Pompey.* New York, 1930.

Henderson, B. W. *Five Roman Emperors.* Cambridge, 1927.

———. *Life and Principate of the Emperor Hadrian.* London, 1923.

Huzar, E. *Mark Antony: A Biography.* Minneapolis, 1978.

Jones, A. H. M. *Augustus.* London, 1970.

Keaveney, A. *Sulla: The Last Republican.* London, 1982.

Leach, J. *Pompey the Great.* London, 1978.

Levick, B. *Claudius.* New Haven, 1990.

MacMullen, R. *Constantine.* New York, 1969.

Momigliano, A. *Claudius.* 2d ed. Oxford, 1961.

Rawson, E. *Cicero: A Portrait.* London, 1975.

Reinhold, M. *Marcus Agrippa: A Biography.* New York, 1933.

Reiter, M. *Aemilius Paulus. Conqueror of Greece.* New York, 1988.

Seager, R. *Pompey: A Political Biography.* Berkeley, 1979.

————. *Tiberius.* Berkeley, 1972.

SMITH, R. E. *Cicero the Statesman.* Cambridge, 1966.

SPANN, P. O. *Quintus Sertorius and the Legacy of Sulla.* Fayetteville, Ark., 1987.

STOCKTON, D. *Cicero: A Political Biography.* London, 1971.

————. *The Gracchi.* Oxford, 1979.

VOLKMANN, H. *Cleopatra: A Study in Politics and Propaganda.* New York, 1958.

WARD, A. *Marcus Crassus and the Late Roman Republic.* Columbia, Mo., 1977.

WARMINGTON, B. H. *Nero: Reality and Legend.* London, 1969.

WILLIAMS, S. *Diocletian and the Roman Recovery.* London, 1985.

YAVETZ, Z. *Julius Caesar and His Public Image.* Ithaca, 1983.

The Decline

BROWN, P. *The World of Late Antiquity:* A.D. *150–750.* London, 1971.

DOWNEY, G. *The Late Roman Empire.* New York, 1969.

GRANT, M. *Fall of the Roman Empire: A Reappraisal.* New York, 1976.

HAYWOOD, R. M. *The Myth of Rome's Fall.* New York, 1958.

JONES, A. H. M. *The Decline of the Ancient World.* New York, 1966.

KATZ, S. *The Decline of Rome and the Rise of Medieval Europe.* Ithaca, 1955.

MacMULLEN, R. *Corruption and the Decline of Rome.* New Haven, 1988.

VOGT, J. *The Decline of Rome.* New York, 1967.

WALBANK, F. W. *The Decline of the Roman Empire in the West.* Rev. ed. Toronto, 1969.

Economic Policy, Numismatics, Crafts

BADIAN, E. *Roman Imperialism in the Late Republic.* Pretoria, 1967.

BROWN, D. *Roman Craftsmen and Their Techniques.* London, 1974.

BURFORD, A. *Craftsmen in Greek and Roman Society.* Ithaca, 1972.

CARSON, R. A. G. *Coins of the Roman Empire.* London, 1990.

CHILVER, G. E. F. *Cisalpine Gaul: Social and Economic History from 49* B.C. *to the Death of Trajan.* Oxford, 1941.

CRAWFORD, M. H. *Coinage of the Roman Republic.* 2 vols. Cambridge, 1974.

DUNCAN-JONES, R. *The Economy of the Roman Empire.* Cambridge, rev. ed., 1982.

————. *Structure and Scale in the Roman Economy.* Cambridge, 1990.

FINLEY, M. I. *The Ancient Economy.* Berkeley, 1973.

FRANK, T., ed. *An Economic Survey of Ancient Rome.* 6 vols. Baltimore, 1933–1940.

FRAYN, J. *Subsistence Farming in Roman Italy.* London, 1979.

GARNSEY, P. *Famine and Food Supply in the Greco-Roman World.* Cambridge, 1988.

————. K. HOPKINS and C. R. WHITTAKER, eds. *Trade in the Ancient Economy.* Berkeley, 1983.

HARL, K. *Civic Coins and Civic Politics in the Roman East* A.D. *180–275.* Berkeley, 1987.

HEICHELHEIM, F. *An Economic History of the Ancient World.* Leiden, 1959.

JONES, A. H. M. and P. A. BRUNT. *The Roman Economy: Studies in Ancient Economic and Administrative History.* Cambridge, 1972.

MATTINGLY, H. Roman Coins from the Earliest Times to the Fall of the Western Empire. 2d ed. London, 1960.
——, et al. Coins of the Roman Empire in the British Museum. 6 vols. London, 1923–1962.
——, et al. The Roman Imperial Coinage. 9 vols. London, 1923–1981.
MILLER, J. I. The Spice Trade of the Roman Empire 29 B.C.–A.D. 641. Oxford, 1969.
RICKMAN, G. The Corn Supply of Ancient Rome. Oxford, 1980.
SCHATZMAN, I. Senatorial Wealth and Roman Politics. Brussels, 1975.
SUTHERLAND, C. H. V. Roman Coins. London, 1974.
——. Roman History and Coinage 44 B.C.–A.D. 69. Oxford, 1987.
——. Coinage and Roman Imperial Policy 31 B.C.–68 A.D. London, 1958.
TOUTAIN, J. The Economic Life of the Ancient World. New York, 1951.
WHITE, K. D. Roman Farming. Ithaca, 1970.

The Etruscans

BANTI, L. Etruscan Cities and Their Culture. Berkeley, 1973.
BLOCH, R. The Etruscans. London, 1958.
HAMPTON, C. The Etruscan Survival. New York, 1970.
HARRIS, W. Rome in Etruria and Umbria. Oxford, 1971.
HUS, A. The Etruscans. New York, 1961.
MASSA, A. The World of the Etruscans. New York, 1973.
OGILVIE, R. Early Rome and the Etruscans. Atlantic Highlands, N.J., 1976.
PALLOTTINO, M. The Etruscans. Rev. ed. Bloomington, Ind., 1975.
RICHARDSON, E. The Etruscans: Their Art and Civilization. Chicago, 1964.

History, Literature, Drama

BREHAUT, E. Cato the Censor on Farming. New York, 1933.
BUTLER, J. H. The Theatre and Drama of Greece and Rome. San Francisco, 1972.
DOREY, T. A., ed. Latin Biography. New York, 1967.
——. Latin Historians. London, 1966.
DUDLEY, D. R., ed. Silver Latin I: Neronians and Flavians. London, 1972.
——. Silver Latin II: Empire and Aftermath. London, 1975.
DUFF, J. W. A Literary History of Rome from the Origins to the Close of the Golden Age. 3d ed. London, 1953.
——. A Literary History of Rome in the Silver Age, from Tiberius to Hadrian. London, 1927.
FRANK, T. Life and Literature in the Roman Republic. Berkeley, 1930.
GRANT, M. Roman Literature. Cambridge, 1954.
JONES, T. B. The Silver-Plated Age. Sandoval, N. Mex., 1962.
LAISTNER, M. L. W. The Greater Roman Historians. Berkeley, 1947.
MILLAR, F. A Study of Cassius Dio. Oxford, 1964.
PAUL, G. M. A Historical Commentary on Sallust's Bellum Jugurthinum. Liverpool, 1984.
SHERWIN-WHITE, A. N. The Letters of Pliny: A Historical and Social Commentary. Oxford, 1966.

SYME, R. *Sallust.* Berkeley, 1964.
———. *Tacitus.* Oxford, 1958.

The Military

ADCOCK, F. E. *The Roman Art of War Under the Republic.* Cambridge, 1960.
CAMPBELL, J. B. *The Emperor and the Roman Army, 31 B.C.–A.D. 235.* Oxford, 1984.
CARTER, J. *The Battle of Actium: The Rise and Triumph of Augustus Caesar.* New York, 1970.
CHEESMAN, G. L. *The Auxilia of the Roman Imperial Army.* Oxford, 1914.
FERRILL, A. *The Fall of the Roman Empire: The Military Explanation.* New York, 1986.
KEPPIE, L. *Colonisation and Veteran Settlement in Italy 47–14 B.C.* London, 1983.
———. *The Making of the Roman Army: From Republic to Empire.* Totowa, N.J., 1987.
LUTTWAK, E. N. *The Grand Strategy of the Roman Empire from the First Century A.D. to the Third.* Baltimore, 1976.
MANN, J. C. *Legionary Recruitment and Veteran Settlement During the Principate.* London, 1983.
SMITH, R. E. *Service in the Post-Marian Roman Army.* Manchester, 1958.
WATSON, G. R. *The Roman Soldier.* Ithaca, 1969.
WEBSTER, G. *The Roman Imperial Army.* New York, 1969.

Period Studies, Area Studies

BARFIELD, L. *Northern Italy Before the Romans.* New York, 1972.
BRAUER, G. *The Age of the Soldier Emperors: Imperial Rome, A.D. 244–284.* Park Ridge, N.J., 1975.
EARL, D. C. *The Age of Augustus.* New York, 1968.
HAMMOND, M. *The Augustan Principate.* Enl. ed. New York, 1961.
———. *The Antonine Monarchy.* Rome, 1959.
JONES, A. H. M. *The Cities of the Eastern Roman Provinces.* 2d ed. Oxford, 1971.
MACMULLEN, R. *The Roman Government's Response to Crisis (A.D. 235–337).* Leiden, 1976.
MAGIE, D. *Roman Rule in Asia Minor to the End of the Third Century After Christ.* 2 vols. Princeton, 1950.
MCKAY, A. D. *Ancient Campania.* Hamilton, Ont., 1972.
PALLOTTINO, M. *A History of Earliest Italy.* Ann Arbor, 1984.
ROWELL, H. T. *Rome in the Augustan Age.* Norman, Okla., 1962.
SCULLARD, H. H. *Roman Britain: Outpost of Empire.* London, 1979.
TRUMP, D. H. *Central and Southern Italy Before Rome.* New York, 1966.

Philosophy, Education, Rhetoric

ARNOLD, E. V. *Roman Stoicism.* London, 1911.
BONNER, S. *Education in Ancient Rome: From the Elder Cato to the Younger Pliny.* Berkeley, 1977.

CLARKE, M. L. *Higher Education in the Ancient World*. Albuquerque, 1971.
———. *Rhetoric at Rome: A Historical Survey*. London, 1953.
———. *The Roman Mind*. London, 1956.
FURLEY, D. J. "Lucretius the Epicurean," *Entretiens de la Fondation Hardt*, xxiv. 1978.
GWYNN, A. *Roman Education from Cicero to Quintilian*. Oxford, 1926.
KENNEDY, G. *The Art of Rhetoric in the Roman World 300 B.C.–A.D. 300*. Princeton, 1972.
MARROU, H. I. *A History of Education in Antiquity*. London, 1956.
RAWSON, E. *Intellectual Life in the Late Roman Republic*. Baltimore, 1985.
RIST, J. M., ed. *The Stoics*. Berkeley, 1978.
SANDBACH, F. *The Stoics*. London, 1975.

Religion

ALTHEIM, F. *History of Roman Religion*. New York, 1970.
CUMONT, F. *The Oriental Religions in Roman Paganism*. London, 1911.
DODD, C. H. *The Founder of Christianity*. New York, 1970.
DODDS, E. R. *Pagan and Christian in an Age of Anxiety*. Cambridge, 1965.
FOWLER, W. W. *The Religious Experience of the Roman People from the Earliest Times to the Age of Augustus*. London, 1911.
FOX, R. L. *Pagans and Christians*. New York, 1987.
FREND, W. H. C. *Martyrdom and Persecution in the Early Church*. Oxford, 1965.
———. *The Rise of Christianity*. London, 1984.
GRANT, F. C., ed. *Ancient Roman Religion*. New York, 1957.
GRANT, M. *The Jews in the Roman World*. New York, 1973.
GRANT, R. M. *Early Christianity and Society*. San Francisco, 1977.
HEYOB, S. *The Cult of Isis Among Women in the Graeco-Roman World*. Leiden, 1975.
LEON, H. J. *The Jews of Ancient Rome*. Philadelphia, 1960.
LEWIS, M. W. H. *The Official Priests of Rome Under the Julio-Claudians*. Rome, 1955.
LIEBESCHUETZ, J. *Continuity and Change in Roman Religion*. Oxford, 1979.
MACMULLEN, R. *Christianizing the Roman Empire*. New Haven, 1984.
———. *Paganism in the Roman Empire*. New Haven, 1981.
MARKUS, R. *Christianity in the Roman World*. London, 1975.
MEEKS, W. A. *The First Urban Christians: The Social World of the Apostle Paul*. New Haven, 1983.
MOMIGLIANO, A. *The Conflict Between Paganism and Christianity in the Fourth Century: Essays*. Oxford, 1963.
OGILVIE, R. M. *The Romans and Their Gods in the Age of Augustus*. New York, 1969.
ROSE, H. J. *Ancient Roman Religion*. New York, 1948.
SCULLARD, H. H. *Festivals and Ceremonies of the Roman Republic*. Ithaca, 1981.
SHERWIN-WHITE, A. N. *Roman Society and Roman Law in the New Testament*. Oxford, 1963.
TAYLOR, L. R. *The Divinity of the Roman Emperor*. Middletown, Conn., 1931.
THIESSEN, G. *Sociology of Early Palestinian Christianity*. Philadelphia, 1978.
WARDMAN, A. *Religion and Statecraft Among the Romans*. Baltimore, 1982.
WITT, R. *Isis in the Graeco-Roman World*. London, 1971.

Slaves and Freedmen

BRADLEY, K. R. *Slaves and Masters in the Roman Empire: A Study in Social Control.* Oxford, 1987.

———. *Slavery and Rebellion in the Roman World, 140–70 B.C.*

DUFF, A. M. *Freedmen in the Early Roman Empire.* Cambridge, 1958.

FINLEY, M. I. *Ancient Slavery and Modern Ideology.* New York. 1980.

HOPKINS, K. *Conquerors and Slaves: Sociological Studies in Roman History.* Cambridge, 1978.

TREGGIARI, S. *Roman Freedmen During the Late Republic.* Oxford, 1969.

WEAVER, P. R. C. *Familia Caesaris.* Cambridge, 1972.

WESTERMANN, W. L. *The Slave Systems and Greek and Roman Antiquity.* Philadelphia, 1955.

WIEDEMANN, T. *Greek and Roman Slavery.* Baltimore, 1981.

YAVETZ, Z. *Slaves and Slavery in Ancient Rome.* New Brunswick, N.J., 1988.

Society, Law

ALFOELDY, G. *The Social History of Rome.* Totowa, N.J., 1985.

ARNHEIM, M. T. W. *The Senatorial Aristocracy in the Later Roman Empire.* Oxford, 1972.

BALSDON, J. P. V. D. *Life and Leisure in Ancient Rome.* New York, 1969.

BRADLEY, K. R. *Discovering the Roman Family.* Oxford, 1991.

BRUNT, P. A. *Social Conflicts in the Roman Republic.* London, 1971.

CAMERON, A. *Circus Factions in the Roman Empire.* Oxford, 1976.

CARCOPINO, J. *Daily Life in Ancient Rome.* New Haven, 1940.

CASSON, L. *The Horizon Book of Daily Life in Ancient Rome.* New York, 1975

COWELL, F. R. *Everyday Life in Ancient Rome.* New York, 1961.

CROOK, J. A. *Law and Life of Rome.* Ithaca, 1967.

D'ARMS, J. H. *Romans on the Bay of Naples: A Social and Cultural History of the Villas and Their Owners from 150 B.C. to A.D. 400.* Cambridge, Mass., 1970.

DILKE, O. *The Ancient Romans: How They Lived and Worked.* London, 1975.

FRIEDLANDER, L. *Roman Life and Manners Under the Early Roman Empire.* 7th ed. 4 vols. New York, 1908–1913.

GARNSEY, P. *Social Status and Legal Privilege in the Roman Empire.* Oxford, 1970.

GELZER, M. *The Roman Nobility.* Oxford, 1969.

HANDS, A. R. *Charities and Social Aids in Greece and Rome.* Ithaca, 1968.

HARRIS, H. A. *Sport in Greece and Rome.* Ithaca, 1972.

HILL, H. *The Roman Middle Class in the Republican Period.* Oxford, 1952.

JOLOWICZ, H. F. *Historical Introduction to the Study of Roman Law.* 3d ed. Cambridge, 1972.

LINTOTT, A. W. *Violence in Republican Rome.* Oxford, 1968.

MACMULLEN, R. *Roman Social Relations 50 B.C. to A.D. 284.* New Haven, 1974.

MITCHELL, R. E. *Patricians and Plebeians: The Origin of the Roman State.* Ithaca, 1990.

SALLER, R. P. *Personal Patronage Under the Early Empire.* Cambridge, 1982

SCHULZ, F. *Classical Roman Law.* Oxford, 1951.

SHERWIN-WHITE, A. N. *Racial Prejudice in Imperial Rome.* Cambridge, 1967.

SYME, R. *The Augustan Aristocracy.* Oxford, 1986.

VEYNE, P., ed. A History of Private Life. Part I, The Roman Empire. Cambridge, Mass., 1987.

WALLACE-HADRILL, A., ed. Patronage in Ancient Roman Society. New York, 1989.

WATSON, A. The Law of the Ancient Romans. Dallas, 1970.

WHITE, K. D. Country Life in Classical Times. London, 1977.

WISEMAN, T. P. New Men in the Roman Senate, 139 B.C.–A.D. 14. London, 1971.

YAVETZ, Z. Plebs and Princeps. Oxford, 1969.

Women, Family

BALSDON, J. P. V. D. Roman Women: Their History and Habits. London, 1962.

CAMERON, A. and A. KUHRT, eds. Images of Women in Antiquity. London, 1983.

CANTARELLA, E. Pandora's Daughters: The Role and Status of Women in Greek and Roman Antiquity. Baltimore, 1987.

DIXON, S. The Roman Mother. London, 1990.

GARDNER, J. Women in Roman Law and Society. Bloomington, Ind., 1986.

HALLETT, J. Fathers and Daughters in Roman Society: Women and the Elite Family. Princeton, 1984.

HOLUM, K. Theodosian Empresses: Women and Imperial Dominion in Late Antiquity. Berkeley, 1982.

LEFKOWITZ, M. R. and M. B. FANT. Women's Life in Greece and Rome: A Source Book in Translation. Baltimore, 1982.

POMEROY, S. Goddesses, Whores, Wives, and Slaves: Women in Classical Antiquity. New York, 1975.

RAWSON, B., ed. The Family in Ancient Rome: New Perspectives. Ithaca, 1986.

TURTON, G. E. The Syrian Princesses: The Women Who Ruled Rome, A.D. 193–235. London, 1974.

WIEDEMANN, T. Adults and Children in the Roman Empire. New Haven, 1989.

Other Topics

CASSON, L. Travel in the Ancient World. London, 1974.

CORNELL, T. and J. MATTHEWS. Atlas of the Roman World. New York, 1982.

ECKSTEIN, A. Senate and General: Individual Decision-Making and Roman Foreign Relations, 264–194 B.C. Berkeley, 1987.

HAMMOND, M. The City in the Ancient World. Cambridge, Mass., 1972.

NASH, E. Pictorial Dictionary of Ancient Rome. 2d ed. 2 vols. New York, 1968.

NICOLET, C. Space, Geography, and Politics in the Early Roman Empire. Ann Arbor, 1988.

RAAFLAUB, K. and M. TOHER, eds. Between Republic and Empire. Berkeley, 1990.

SCARBOROUGH, J. Roman Medicine. London, 1969.

STAMBAUGH, J. E. The Ancient Roman City. Baltimore, 1988.

TODD, M. The Northern Barbarians 100–300 A.D. London, 1975.

WILSON, A. J. N. Emigration from Italy in the Republican Age of Rome. Oxford, 1971.

ZANKER, P. The Power of Images in the Age of Augustus. Ann Arbor, 1988.

Index